# A Treasure Chest of Quotations for All Occasions

# By the same authors ━━━━━━

**Herbert V. Prochnow**

Bank Credit
Dilemmas Facing the Nation
The Federal Reserve System
World Economic Problems and Policies
The New Speaker's Treasury of Wit and Wisdom

**Herbert V. Prochnow and
Roy A. Foulke**

Practical Bank Credit

**Herbert V. Prochnow and
Herbert V. Prochnow, Jr.**

The Changing World of Banking
The Toastmaster's Treasure Chest
A Dictionary of Wit, Wisdom and Satire
The Public Speaker's Treasure Chest
The Successful Toastmaster
A Treasury of Humorous Quotations

# A Treasure Chest of Quotations for All Occasions

Herbert V. Prochnow
and
Herbert V. Prochnow, Jr.

1817

**HARPER & ROW, PUBLISHERS,** New York
Cambridge, Philadelphia, San Francisco, London
Mexico City, São Paulo, Sydney

FIRST EDITION

*Designer: Jane Weinberger*

Library of Congress Cataloging in Publication Data

Prochnow, Herbert Victor, date
  A treasure chest of quotations for all occasions.

  1. Quotations, English. 2. Public speaking—Handbooks, manuals, etc. I. Prochnow, Herbert Victor, date
II. Title.
PN6081.P73 1983    082    82-48130
ISBN 0-06-015043-2

83 84 85 86 87 10 9 8 7 6 5 4 3 2 1

# Contents

# Preface

This book of more than 4,400 items is a practical and valuable reference for speakers, toastmasters, and those who preside at meetings. With it, we hope to bring them a wealth of helpful material to assure the successful discharge of their responsibilities. Many of these items will not only add zest to speeches and introductions but will also give sparkle and interest to conversation.

The book contains humorous stories, quips and witticisms, amusing definitions, inspiring quotations, anecdotes from famous lives, witty and wise proverbs, entertaining verses, toasts and quotations for many occasions, and the thoughtful comments of great leaders. Using items from this book, a speaker or presiding officer may effectively stress a point, add humor, or provide inspiration. There is genuine satisfaction in being able to use stories or quotations, humorous and serious, to illustrate a point convincingly and forcefully.

Because the many stories, epigrams, quotations, and illustrations may be suitable for use in different situations, this book is divided into chapters covering such major areas as education, business, government, family life, money, work, sports, the professions, success, health, and happiness. The first twelve chapters contain humorous items. Each chapter begins with a selection of entertaining stories and ends with a sampling of short quips and witticisms.

Chapters 13, 14, and 15 feature items of inspiration and wisdom and unusual biographical illustrations. Chapters 16, 17, and 18 offer entertaining verses, toasts, quotations for special occasions, and proverbs.

To help the reader find material relating to a particular subject, each item has been numbered and indexed. The comprehensive index in the back of the book assists the reader in quickly locating pertinent items.

The book should prove helpful not only to public speakers but also to the general reader who appreciates a humorous story or quip or an inspiring comment or illustration.

HERBERT V. PROCHNOW
HERBERT V. PROCHNOW, JR.

# Humor

# Youth and Age

### 1    *Smart Lad*

"Some plants," said the biology teacher, "have the prefix 'dog.' For instance, there is the dogwood, the dogviolet. Who can name another plant prefixed by 'dog'?"

"I can," shouted the little boy in the back row. "How about 'collie flower'?"

### 2    *Good Question*

Five-year-old to his grandfather: "Are you still growing?"

"Why do you ask, child?" inquired his grandpa.

"Well, the top of your head's coming through your hair!"

### 3    *Afraid*

The little boy started to cry after a large and friendly dog bounded up to him and licked his hands and face.

"What is it?" asked his mother. "Did he bite you?"

"No," sobbed the child, "but he tasted me!"

### 4    *Good Reason*

A three-year-old had been elected president of a local group of somewhat older boys. A father asked why the boys had elected such a young child.

"Well, Dad," the boy explained, "Billy couldn't be secretary because he can't read. We couldn't make him treasurer because he can't count. He's too little to throw anyone out, so we couldn't elect him sergeant-at-arms. And we knew he'd feel bad if we didn't elect him to something, so we made him president."

5    *Advice*

A professor who had taught for many years was counseling a young teacher. "You will discover," he said, "that in nearly every class there is a youngster eager to argue. Your first impulse will be to silence him. I advise you to think carefully. He may be the only one listening."

6    *Attention Please*

At her parents' dinner party, Susie found herself surrounded by grown-ups. Despite all her efforts, she could not get past the animated conversation of her elders.

Desperate, Susie pulled a whistle from a pocket and gave it a mighty blast. Struck dumb, all turned and stared at the little girl. Then sweetly, she asked, "Daddy, could you please pass me the potatoes?"

7    *Language*

Bobby was having much difficulty with his grammar. Finally one day he ran into the house and, throwing his books on the table, said to his mother: "I got it straight now. Hens set and lay, but people sit and lie."

8    *Next Question*

"Do you believe George Washington could have pitched a dollar across the Rappahannock River as he is said to have done?" quizzed the teacher.

"I suppose so," answered the student, "because our history book says he pitched his camp across the Delaware River when the British were chasing him."

9    *Odd Guy*

"Boss," said the dock foreman, "the men on the dock are a bit leery of that new freight handler you hired yesterday."

"How come?" the terminal manager replied. "He checked out well."

"Maybe he did," the dock foreman reported, "but this morning he tripped over a crate of iron castings and said, 'Oh, the perversity of inanimate objects!' "

10    *Right Decision*

A distinguished-looking fellow browsing in a toy store was entranced with a model train that whistled, belched smoke, delivered mail, and did practically everything that a real freight train does. He finally said, "I'll take it."

"A wonderful choice!" exclaimed the approving clerk. "I'm sure your grandson will love it."

"Why, you're absolutely right," said the old gentleman. "I'd better take two."

11    *Lucky*

John: "I'm glad you named me John."

Mother: "Why?"
John: "Because that's what all the kids at school call me."

### 12    *Do Not Open*

Sign on a boy's door: "Do not open this door or all the dark will leak out."

### 13    *He Will Sue*

A first-grader recently proved how practical schoolchildren can really be. He slipped in the hall of his school and skinned his knee. A teacher proffered psychological first aid with, "Remember, big boys don't cry, sonny."
The boy replied, "I'm not gonna cry—I'm gonna sue."

### 14    *Real Wool*

The little boy was visiting a farm for the first time in his life. He was taken out to see the lambs and finally built up enough courage to pat one. He was delighted. "Why," he cried, "they make them out of blankets!"

### 15    *Dramatic*

An English class was given the task of writing four lines of dramatic poetry. Selecting the verse of a bright boy, the teacher read:

> "A boy was walking down the track,
>     The train was coming fast;
> The boy stepped off the railroad track
>     To let the train go past."

"This verse is well done," said the teacher, "but it lacks drama. Try again, Johnny, and make it more dramatic." Whereupon, in a short time, Johnny produced the following verse:

> "A boy was walking down the track,
>     The train was coming fast;
> The train jumped off the railroad track
>     To let the boy go past."

### 16    *Ancestors*

"Dad, what are ancestors?"
"Well, my boy, I'm one of your ancestors. Your grandfather is another."
"Then, why do people brag about them?"

### 17    *Modern Youth*

"What's become of the locomotive and train of cars Santa brought you for Christmas?" Father asked of Junior.
"All smashed up," replied the boy. "We've been playing government ownership."

18 *Based on His Experience*

In church for the first time, the little boy watched, wide-eyed, as the choir, all in white surplices, filed in. With wonder in his voice he whispered, "Are all those people going to get their hair cut?"

19 *Two Rides*

An older gentleman went for an airplane ride. When he came down he said to the pilot, "Thanks for the two rides."

"Two rides?" asked the pilot. "You had only one."

"No, sir, two," replied the gentleman. "My first and my last."

20 *Five Signs of Growing Older*

1. When you look at the menu before you look at the waitress.
2. When you wait for a crowded escalator rather than walk up the empty stairs.
3. When an 8 looks like a 3 and a 3 like an 8.
4. When you would rather sit on the beach than go in the water.
5. When you leave a good party early because you don't want to feel bad the next day.

21 *Why Not?*

A reporter was interviewing a man who was believed to be the oldest resident in town.

"May I ask how old you are?" the newsman inquired.

"I just turned a hundred this week," the oldster proudly replied.

"Great! Do you suppose you'll see another hundred?" the reporter asked playfully.

"Well," said the man thoughtfully, "I'm stronger now than when I started the first one hundred!"

22 *Helpful*

A guest at a friend's home asked the children if they helped their mother around the house.

"Oh, yes. We do the dishes," replied the oldest. "I wash them."

"And I dry them," added the second child.

The youngest, eager to be recognized too, piped up, "I help too. I pick up all the broken ones."

23 *Fully Grown*

Overheard: "Children grow up so quickly. One day your car's gas gauge shows *Empty* and you realize they're teenagers."

24 *His Conclusion*

An Indian was observing his teenage daughter's party and was fascinated by the modern dances the youths were enjoying. Scratching his head, he said to his wife: "Well, if that doesn't bring rain, nothing will!"

### 25 *Up to Them*

Mother: "Today I want you to take your brother Eddie to the zoo."
Roy: "Not me. If they want him they'll have to come and get him."

### 26 *It Still Hurts*

Dentist: "Stop screaming! I haven't even touched your tooth. In fact, you're not even on the chair yet."
Boy: "I know, but you're standing on my foot!"

### 27 *Space*

The space business may be getting out of hand. The Browns, in the next block, have been saving up for a trip to see the world this summer. But last night their eleven-year-old suggested, "Aw, let's go somewhere else."—*Burton Hillis, Better Homes & Gardens*

### 28 *She Knew*

In a kindergarten class, flags were shown. "What flag is this?" asked the teacher.
"This is the flag of my country," answered a bright little tot.
"And what is the name of your country?" was the next question.
" 'Tis of thee," came the prompt reply.

### 29 *It Seems Obvious*

A small boy at the zoo asked why the giraffe had such a long neck.
"Well, you see," said the keeper gravely, "the giraffe's head is so far removed from his body that a long neck is absolutely necessary.

### 30 *Knew His Bible*

Small boy (who has been promised a visit to the zoo tomorrow): "I hope we have a better day for it than Noah had."

### 31 *The Lesson*

"Now, children," said the Sunday school teacher, "I have told you the story of Jonah and the whale. Willie, you may tell me what this story teaches us."
"Yes'm," said Willie, the bright-eyed son of the pastor; "it teaches that you can't keep a good man down."

### 32 *Nursery Rhymes*

Simple Simon met a pieman going to the fair. Said Simple Simon to the pieman, "Hello."

Mary had a little lamb, its fleece was white as snow; and everywhere that Mary went, she took a bus.

Little Jack Horner sat in a corner, eating a Christmas pie; he put in his thumb, and pulled out a plum, and said, "Aw, nuts, I thought this was apple."

Hickory, dickory, dock, the mouse ran up the clock; the clock struck one, the mouse ran down—I guess he couldn't take it.

Little Miss Muffet sat on a tuffet, eating of curds and whey; there came a great spider that sat down beside her, and said, "Is this seat taken?"

Little Boy Blue, come blow your horn, the sheep's in the meadow, the cow's in the corn; but where is the boy that looks after the sheep? Oh, he's across the street having a soda.

Mistress Mary, quite contrary, how does your garden grow? With cockleshells, and silver bells, and the rest haven't come up yet.—*Bonnie Blair*

### 33    *A Teenager's Definitions*

*Spouse:* A sort of spice.
*Parasite:* A person who lives in Paris.
*Brunette:* A young bear.
*Kodak:* The Bible of the Mohammedans.
*Mosaic law:* The law that requires us to set colored stones in certain floors.
*False doctrines:* Giving the wrong medicine to a patient.

### 34    *Pretty Old*

A child trying to guess another child's age said, "He must be pretty old. He blows his own nose."

### 35    *Give Him More Time*

Tourist: "Have you lived here all your life?"
Old Vermonter: "Not yet."

### 36    *No Complaint*

Two boys were walking down a street together. One was eating an apple.

The boy with no apple said to the one with the apple, "If I had an apple I would give it to you."

The boy with the apple said, "What are you kicking about—I've got it, haven't I?"

### 37    *It Looked That Way*

The small daughter watched her mother while she marked her ballot at the polls, then remarked, "You voted for the person you loved best, didn't you, Mother?"

"Gracious, child!" exclaimed the mother. "Why ask that?"
"Because you put a kiss by the name."

### 38     *Missed It*

Bill: "When were you born?"
Sam: "April second."
Bill: "That was a day too late."

### 39     *Any More Questions?*

A small boy, leading a donkey, passed by an army camp. A couple of soldiers wanted to have some fun with the lad.
"Why are you holding onto your brother so tight, sonny?" said one of them.
"So he won't join the army," the youngster replied.

### 40     *Different View*

"Did you see Mrs. Higgins's face light up when I told her she didn't look a day older than her daughter?"
"No. I was too busy watching the expression on her daughter's face."

### 41     *Different Problem*

An old gentleman, seeing a small boy having some trouble handling a very large apple, remarked, "Too much apple, isn't it, sonny?"
The small boy, his mouth full of apple, replied, "No sir, Mister, not enough boy!"

### 42     *Favorite Author*

"Who's your favorite author, Tommy?"
"My dad."
"What does he write?"
"Checks."

### 43     *Inflation Fighter*

Two old-timers were discussing a mutual friend. Said one, "Poor old John seems to be living in the past."
"And why not?" replied the other. "It's a lot cheaper."

### 44     *The Right Wish*

Little Johnny said excitedly, "I swallowed a wishbone yesterday."
Little Jimmy asked curiously, "What did you wish?"
"Wished I hadn't," Johnny answered.

45      *Also Today?*

> What are these,
> So withered, and so wild in their attire,
> That look not like the inhabitants o' the earth,
> And yet are on't?
>                 —*William Shakespeare, Macbeth*

46      *That's Not Fair*

Two boys met in the street. "What's that you've got in your buttonhole?" asked one.

"Why, that's a chrysanthemum," the other replied.

"It looks like a rose to me."

"You're wrong; it's a chrysanthemum."

"What is a chrysanthemum? Spell it."

"K-r-i-s— You're right; it is a rose!"

47      *Economics*

Most women are more economical than men give them credit for being. For instance, where is there a woman who will put more than thirty candles on her fortieth birthday cake?

48      *No Need to Worry*

At the age of twenty we don't care what the world thinks of us; at thirty we worry about what it thinks of us; at forty we discover that it isn't thinking of us at all.

49      *Went Direct*

"Mommy," said six-year-old Julie, "while you were away last night I looked for somebody to say my prayers to, but Nurse had gone away, and Auntie was talking on the phone, so I just said them to God."

50      *Professional*

"You say your son plays the piano like Paderewski?"

"Yes. He uses both hands."

51      *Thanksgiving*

"Now, children," said the teacher just before Thanksgiving, "tell me something you're thankful for."

"I'm thankful," said one small boy, "that I'm not a turkey."

52      *Can't Win*

If I'm noisy they spank me—and if I'm quiet they take my temperature.

53      *Getting Old*

Small girl: "I wonder how old Joan is?"
Small boy: "I bet she won't see four again."

54      *Vitamins*

Our little boy wants to know why vitamins are put in spinach and cod-liver oil instead of in pie and cake and candy.

55      *Age Requirement*

Dick: "Why have we never had a woman for President?"
Helen: "The President has to be over thirty-five years old."

56      *Playing It Safe*

Millie: "When he asked me how old I was, I couldn't remember whether I was thirty-four or thirty-five."
Tillie: "And what did you say?"
Millie: "Twenty-five."

57      *Seven Ages of Women*

The seven ages of women are: baby, infant, miss, young woman, young woman, young woman, and young woman.

58      *New Business*

An enterprising youngster in New York has started a new business. His business card reads as follows: "Mr. Harvey Hector, Jr. Person Escorter. Tots and kiddies took to school and returned, prompt in perfect condition—if received that way. Military discipline. Rates $1 a week. Refined conversashun. No extra charge for nose wiping. All I ask is a trial."

59      *That's Different*

Three Boy Scouts told the Scoutmaster they had done their "good deed" that day.
"Well, boys, what did you do?" asked the Scoutmaster.
"We helped an old lady across the street a little while ago," the boys chimed in unison.
"And did it take all three of you to do that?" asked the Scoutmaster suspiciously.
"Yes, it did," chorused the boys. Then the smallest one added, "She didn't want to go."

60      *Perplexed*

A kindly gentleman encountered a four-year-old standing on the street corner in deep perplexity.

"I want to run away," the tot confided.

"Oh," said the gentleman understandingly, "why don't you?"

"Well," said the youngster, "I'm not allowed to cross the street!"—*Earl Wilson*

### 61    *Time Moves Backward*

Henry: "How old are you?"
Ruth: "I'm just thirty."
Henry: "Thirty! Time marches backward."

### 62    *Based On Experience*

Johnny: "What is the difference between a hill and a pill?"
Tommy: "One is always hard to get down and the other is hard to get up!"

### 63    *Well Informed*

Larry: "Who had the largest family in America?"
Gary: "I don't know, who?"
Larry: "George Washington, because he was the father of his country."

### 64    *A Special Prize*

Distraught mother to a group of wild children at a birthday party: "There will be a special prize for the one who goes home first!"

### 65    *Is That Clear?*

After checking the license of the driver he'd stopped, the highway patrolman said, "It says here you're supposed to be wearing glasses."

"But officer, I have contacts."

"I don't care who you know, you're violating the law."

### 66    *Childhood*

> A little curly-headed, good-for-nothing,
> A mischief-making monkey from his birth
> —*Byron, Don Juan*

### 67    *Is That Fair?*

"How old are you, Ann?"

"Well, my father gives me ten dollars every birthday, and I have a hundred and seventy dollars!"

"How much does he owe you?"

### 68    *Life Story*

The evolution of a man's ambitions:
    To be a circus clown.
    To be like Dad.
    To be a fireman.

To do something noble.
To get wealthy.
To make ends meet.
To get an old-age pension.

### 69    *Glad to Be Older*

"I'm so glad that I finally turned eleven," exclaimed Julie on her birthday.
"Why?" asked her mother.
"Well, when a grown-up does something dumb, people usually say he's acting like a ten-year-old."

70      For the benefit of high school seniors, we think you should know the world is run by men who couldn't work an algebra problem.

71      Most of us never get too old to learn some new way of being stupid.

72      You can tell a person's real age by the pain he feels when he gets a new idea.

73      Bob Hope says: "I've found the secret of youth—I lie about my age."
—*Joey Adams*

74      Adolescence is the age at which children stop asking questions because they know all the answers.—*Jeanne Opalach*

75      *Screen door:* Something the kids get a bang out of.

76      How inimitably graceful children are in general—before they learn to dance.—*S. T. Coleridge*

77      There is little use to talk about your child to anyone; other people either have one or haven't.—*Don Herold*

78      After you lose your membership in it, the younger generation seems pretty bad.

79      Muttonchop sideburns are appearing on all ages—from young kids to old goats.

80      A small boy isn't happy unless he is doing one or more of three things: eating, getting dirty, or making noise.

81      It would be tough on the state of Kentucky if all those colonels should demand retirement pay.

82      There's one thing about being bald-headed—it's neat.

83      When asked if he knew what hay was, the young upstart said, "Sure, it's grass à la mowed!"

84 By the time we decide a television program is something the children should not see, we are too interested in it to turn it off.

85 Do you remember when a juvenile delinquent was a youngster who owed eight cents on an overdue library book?

86 *Old person:* One who can recall when a man wasn't called a reactionary when he said a good word for free enterprise.

87 *Middle age:* When you're willing to get up and give your seat to a lady —and can't.—*Sammy Kaye*

88 *Middle age:* Having a choice of two temptations and choosing the one that will get you home earlier.—*Dan Bennett*

89 *Middle age:* When you are sitting at home on Saturday night and the telephone rings and you hope it isn't for you.—*Ring Lardner*

90 "Special pains given to beginners" states a music teacher's ad. Few advertisements are that frank.

91 I'm saving that rocker for the day when I feel as old as I really am. —*Dwight D. Eisenhower*

92 If you want your children to turn out well, spend twice as much time with them, and half as much money.—*Abigail Van Buren*

93 Nowadays the voice crying in the wilderness is just a teenager with a radio.

94 Youth must be served—and cleaned up after, too.

95 Growing up is the period spent in learning that bad manners are tolerated only in grown-ups.

96 *Getting along in years:* When you know all the answers, but nobody asks you the questions.

97 The boy has grown up when he'd rather steal a kiss than second base.

98 You're young only once, but you shouldn't be immature indefinitely.

99 We like young people because they know all the answers.

100 The teacher asked the student to use the word *boycott* in a sentence. The student said, "The wind blew down my brother's neck and the boycott an awful cold."

101     By the time you have enough experience to be smart, your memory is shorter, your stamina is lower, and you are bald.

102     When I was young I used to think there were some big berries in the bottom of the box.

103     A statement isn't necessarily true just because it sounds reasonable—and that sounds reasonable too.

104     It's hard for the modern generation to understand Thoreau, who lived beside a pond but didn't own water skis or a snorkel.—*Bill Vaughan*

105     I'll never make the mistake of bein' seventy again!—*Casey Stengel*

106     Every youngster should be a why's guy.

107     It's a shame to waste a college education on a freshman who already knows everything.

108     Every small boy wonders why his father didn't go into the ice-cream business.

109     A man who has just switched to bifocals is never at a loss for conversation.

110     Life begins at forty, but so do lumbago, bad eyesight, arthritis, and the habit of telling the same story three times to the same listeners.

111     Middle age is when you would do anything to feel better except give up what's hurting you.

112     About the time the bedtime stories are televised, many youngsters are going out for the evening.

113     A towel is what a boy looks at to see if his face is clean after he has washed it.

114     Every now and then some big city shakes its finger at juvenile crime.

115     It's nice for children to have pets, until the pets start having children.

116     Life is just a symphony of snap, crackle, and pop. When you're young, it's cereal. When you're older, it's your joints.

117     Flaming youth generally cooks its own goose.

118     Nations that live by the sword perish by the pensions.

119     Nothing makes one grow old as fast as hardening of the heart.

120    It's surprising how many people our age are a lot older than we are.

121    The principal thing an inquisitive child learns is how little adults know.

122    We are not sure whether age comes with experience or experience with age.

123    You have to do your own growing up no matter how tall your grandpa was.

124    The young and old have all the answers. Those in between are stuck with the questions.

125    If you are looking for perpetual youth, you won't find it on a two-lane highway, but you may avoid old age.

126    Shouting to make your children obey is like using your horn to steer the car—and you get about the same results.—*Burton Hillis*

127    Many of the younger generation are alike in many disrespects.

128    In youth we run into difficulties; in old age difficulties run into us. —*Josh Billings*

129    A picture window will bring the outdoors into your living room, but a ten-year-old boy can bring a lot of it in with only two feet.

130    Once upon a time, a young man took the garage keys and came out with the lawn mower.

131    Watch out for schoolchildren—when they're walking, and when they're driving.

132    Time is a great healer, but it's no beauty specialist.

133    The child next door can't play the piano, and frankly, we wish he'd stop trying.

134    About the only thing children seem able to get along without these days is necessities.

135    Grandfather had a farm, his son has a garden, and his grandson has a can opener.

136    Nothing makes a woman feel older than meeting a bald-headed man who was two grades behind her in school.

137     A teenager is grown up when he thinks it is more important to pass an examination than to pass the car ahead.

138     The present generation needs a tabloid Bible.

139     Nothing is cuter than a little baby after the company is gone.

140     Some adults are willing to blame juvenile delinquency on everything but heredity.

141     Mealtime is when the youngsters continue eating but sit down.

142     You can live much longer if you quit everything that makes you want to live longer.

143     One of the hardest decisions in life is when to start middle age.

144     Another general aid to longevity is the fact that the good die young.

145     At the hour of birth, says one authority, human intelligence stands at the zero mark. Which proves that some adults weren't always as dumb as they are now.

146     This is the age when a child who is tied to his mother's apron strings isn't tied to his mother.

147     The best way to tell a woman's age is a mistake.

148     It's too bad that our ancestors didn't live long enough to realize how smart we are.

149     You're getting old when the gleam in your eye is from the sun hitting your bifocals.

150     One of the best things in the world to be is a boy; it requires no experience, but it needs some practice to be a good one.

151     One of the many things nobody ever tells you about middle age is that it's such a nice change from being young.—*Dorothy Canfield Fisher*

152     *Calendar:* Something that goes in one year and out the other.

153     Man was given five senses: touch, taste, sight, smell, and hearing. The successful man has two more: horse and common.

154     In youth the days are short and the years are long; in old age the years are short and the days long.—*Panin*

155     It is the malady of our age that the young are so busy teaching us that they have no time left to learn.—*Eric Hoffer*

156     Television has changed the American child from an irresistible force into an immovable object.—*Laurence J. Peter*

157     Old age is like everything else. To make a success of it, you've got to start young.—*Fred Astaire*

158     You know you're getting old when the candles cost more than the cake. —*Bob Hope*

159     Old age is like a plane flying through a storm. Once you're aboard, there's nothing you can do.—*Golda Meir*

160     You know you've reached middle age when your weightlifting consists merely of standing up.—*Bob Hope*

161     Middle age is that period in life when your idea of getting ahead is staying even.

162     An interesting rumor is that a London paper is about to make a feature of a whole page for grown-up readers.—*Punch*

163     Every little girl is in a hurry to grow up and wear the kind of shoes that just kill her mother.

164     As a man grows older and wiser, he talks less and says more.

165     Boy: Of all the wild beasts, the most difficult to manage.—*Plato*

166     The older one gets, the more reckless the new generation seems.

167     A youthful figure is what you get when you ask a woman her age.

168     A beautician says nothing is less attractive than an elderly woman with bleached or hennaed hair. Only the young dye good, it seems.

169     Beauty experts say a woman can look beautiful at forty-five but none of them ever get that old.

170     As soon as a man acquires fairly good sense, it is said that he is an old fogy.—*Ed Howe*

171     The best thing about getting old is that all those things you couldn't have when you were young you no longer want.—*L. S. McCandless*

172     *Disillusionment:* What takes place when a youngster asks his dad for help with his algebra.

173     Juvenile delinquency is when kids start acting like their fathers.

174     Age should think and youth should do.

175     Children are natural mimics; they act like their parents in spite of every attempt to teach them good manners.

176     *Genius:* Anyone under ten years of age.

177     When a man retires and time is no longer a matter of urgent importance, his colleagues generally present him with a watch.—*R. C. Sherriff*

178     An adolescent is one who, when not treated like an adult, acts like an infant.

179     If I'd known I was going to live so long, I'd have taken better care of myself.—*Leon Eldred*

180     A doctor says a baby doesn't know what's good for it. That goes for some pretty old ones, doc.—*Herbert V. Prochnow*

# Business, Industry, and the Professions

181    *Our Motto*

Boss: "Do you know what the motto of our firm is?"
New employee: "Sure, it's 'Push.' "
Boss: "What gave you that idea?"
New employee: "I saw it on the door when I came in."

182    *First Facts*

From "General Rules for the Observance of the Clerks of The First National Bank of Chicago," 1890: "Conversation during business hours, on matters not relating to the business of the Bank, will not be approved. . . . Loud talking . . . must be altogether avoided, on pain of dismissal."

183    *Wait Till Next Year*

Riding from the airport to the hotel in Washington, D.C., I noticed a beautiful government building that had the words "What Is Past Is Prologue" carved on the front of it in huge letters. I asked the cab driver what the phrase meant. Immediately he replied: "It's government talk for 'Wait until you see taxes next year!' "—*Dan Bennett*

184    *Truth-in-Advertising*

From the label on a box of prepared food recently purchased for a household pet—a bathtub-sized turtle: "Minimum Protein, 11.04%; Fat, 1.17%; Fiber 18.08%. Ingredients: Dried flies."

### 185    *Private Enterprise*

The famous Pony Express of the Old West was not operated by the federal government. It was a private enterprise.

### 186    *Seems Logical*

Annoyed diner: "You say you are the same waiter who took my order? Somehow I expected a much older man."

### 187    *Gobbledygook*

A Washington lawyer, instead of saying that two plus two make four, would say: "If by that particular arithmetical rule known as addition, we desired to arrive at the sum of two integers added to two integers, we should find—and I assert this boldly, and without fear of successful contradiction—we, I repeat, should find by the particular arithmetical formula before mentioned—and I hold myself perfectly responsible for the assertion that I am about to make—we should find that the sum of the two integers added to the two other integers would be four."—*Emily Lotney*

### 188    *Signs of the Times*

A few businesses really believe in their products. At a bakery, one sign reads, "You're the object of our confections." A produce market sign states, "Our watermelons are the best you ever seed." And "Our coffee urns its praise," claims a sign posted at one café.

### 189    *Of Course*

On a walking tour of New York's Lower East Side, Nelson Rockefeller, then Republican candidate for governor, stopped off in a delicatessen and bought a whole salami. "I charged him only the wholesale price," the shopowner proudly told the crowd. "For Rockefeller, he makes a discount," said one of the audience. —*Newsweek*

### 190    *Fast Thinking*

The young fellow had started on his new job. When the middle of the week came, he found himself short of money, so he called on the cashier. "Can I have a week's wages now?" he asked.

"But you've only been here three days," said the cashier.

"I know," replied the newcomer, "but if I can trust you for the first half of the week, surely you can trust me for the second half."

### 191    *Two Jobs*

The chief constable of a small Yorkshire town was also an expert veterinary surgeon. One night the telephone rang. The chief constable's wife answered it.

"Is Mr. Blank there?" inquired an agitated voice.

"Do you want my husband in his capacity as veterinary surgeon or as chief constable?" asked the woman.

"Both, madam," came the reply. "We can't get our bulldog to open his mouth —and there's a burglar in it!"

### 192    *No Deal*

Man: "Can I have a parrot for my son, please?"
Pet shop owner: "Sorry, sir, we don't swap."

### 193    *Employee Relations*

If it weren't for the pleasant surroundings, the considerate management, the fine salary, paid vacations, retirement fund, and profit-sharing plan, I'd quit this lousy job.

### 194    *Alarming*

Employer: "Why were you late this morning?"
Office boy: "On account of my alarm clock. Everyone in the house got up except me."
Employer: "Why was that?"
Office boy: "There are nine of us and the alarm clock was set for only eight."

### 195    *They Had Everything*

The diner ordered oysters. "Make sure they're neither too large nor too small, nor too salty nor too fat," he instructed.

The waiter raised his eyebrows and asked, "With or without pearls, sir?"

### 196    *He Understood*

The jokester was brought before the judge after being apprehended for going through a red light.

"I'll fine you ten dollars for your first offense, but next time, you'll go to jail. Understand?"

"Oh sure, your honor. It's just like a weather report; fine today, cooler tomorrow."

### 197    *Satisfied*

The Holeproof Sports Sock Company has thousands of letters on file from satisfied customers. The one they've chosen as the best came from a champion golfer who wrote, "Half an hour after I donned your socks, I got a hole in one."

### 198    *Order Please*

A meeting was getting badly out of hand. Spokesmen for various factions were talking simultaneously, with no one paying the slightest heed. Finally, the presiding officer whanged his gavel impressively. "Gentlemen," he pleaded. "Gentlemen! Please, let's keep this confusion orderly!"

### 199    *Strange License*

A Hartford, Connecticut, hearse has a license plate bearing the signet "U-2."

### 200    *Say That Again*

The utility company customer with a long-overdue bill claims to have received this rather unusual notice: "We would be delighted if you would pay your bill promptly. If not, you will probably be de-lighted."

### 201    *New Idea*

At last, someone has invented a solar clothes dryer—a length of rope and a handful of clothespins.

### 202    *Take Me Back!*

In days of old, when knights were bold, and sheet-iron trousers wore, they lived in peace, for then a crease would last ten years or more. In those old days they had the craze for cast-iron shirts, and wore 'em; and there was bliss enough in this—the laundry never tore 'em.

### 203    *The Businessman*

Sock him on the jawbone, put him on the pan, roll him in the gutter—he's a businessman. Pillory the sucker, poke him in the eye, jump upon his torso—he's a business guy.

Has he built a business to enormous heights? Brand him as a cheater, never mind his rights. Does he give employment, is the payroll big? Put the bum in irons, toss him in the brig! Does he pay in taxes what the law calls for? Why, the dirty reptile should be paying more! Blast him in the headlines, charge some crooked acts; let this be your slogan: "Anything but facts!" Has he made some money? Get his scalp today! Say, where does he think he's living, anyway?

Lives of rich men should remind us that if we make a lot of jack, always there'll be those behind us trying to knife us in the back.—*Stuart's Typo Graphic*

### 204    *Wrong Number*

Subscriber to operator: "Please give me Mr. Dillingburg's telephone number."
Operator: "Is the initial *B,* as in Bill?"
Subscriber: "No, it's *D,* as in pickle."

### 205    *His Debt*

"I feel that I owe a lot to my country.
"What, haven't you paid your income tax yet?"

### 206　*Last Laugh*

Peeved lecturer (who had told a story that failed to produce the expected outburst): "Well, I suppose you folks will laugh at that story next summer."

Voice from the audience: "No, sir; we laughed at it last summer."

### 207　*How Not to Write*

We beg to advise you, and wish to state, that yours has arrived of recent date. We have it before us, its contents noted; herewith enclosed are the prices quoted.

Attached you will find, as per your request, the sample you wanted. We would suggest that up to this moment your order we've lacked. We'd like it quite promptly, and that is a fact. We hope you will not delay it unduly, and we beg to remain yours very truly.

### 208　*Government Business*

There is far more danger in public monopoly than there is in private monopoly, for when the government goes into business it can always shift its losses to the taxpayers. If it goes into the power business, it can always pretend to sell cheap power, and then cover up its losses. The government never really goes into business, for it never makes ends meet, and that is the first requisite of successful business. It just mixes a little business and politics, and no one ever gets a chance to find out what is actually going on.—*Thomas Edison*

### 209　*Perfectly Clear*

On her way out of a cafeteria, a smartly dressed girl handed the cashier a slip of paper on which appeared the number 1004180. The cashier glanced at it, and let the girl pass without paying.

When the proprietor appeared, the cashier handed him the note. He studied the number, frowning, then demanded to know its meaning.

"You see," said the cashier, "it reads, 'I owe nothing for I ate nothing.' "

### 210　*Whose Profit?*

Plants grow better if the day is prolonged with artificial light. The plant that profits most is the electric light plant.

### 211　*No Rain*

An Indian was persuaded to attend a lecture. When it was all over, someone asked him what he thought of it. "Huh!" he grunted. "Big wind. Lotta dust. No rain."

### 212　*Modern Improvements Are Wonderful*

Instead of standing on the doorstep listening to a peddler, you just sit down in a chair and turn on the radio or television.

### 213 *Private Enterprise*

Then we have the story of the two ambitious little fleas who worked hard, saved their money, and finally went out and bought their own dog.

### 214 *Playing It Safe*

Foreman: "Did you write 'Fragile—This Side Up' on the carton before shipping it out?"

Newly hired clerk: "Why, yes, sir. And to make sure that everyone notices it, I carefully marked it on all sides of the box."

### 215 *The Right Person*

Salesman: "I would like to see someone with a little authority."

Clerk: "What can I do for you? I have as little authority as anyone else does."

### 216 *He Will Be in Trouble*

The ponderous judge interrupted the eloquent lawyer harshly: "All you say goes in one ear and out the other."

"What is to prevent it?" was the retort.

### 217 *An Explanation*

Customer: "But if it costs fifty dollars to make these watches, and you sell them for fifty dollars, where does your profit come in?"

Shopkeeper: "From repairing them."

### 218 *Thoughtful Service*

"I ordered a dozen oranges, but you only sent me ten."

"Part of our service, madam. Two were bad, so we saved you the trouble of throwing them away."

### 219 *Signatures*

I've studied names with tears and groans; sometimes I think the name is Jones —with sundry letters upside down. And then again I'd say it's Brown; perhaps it's Smith—it may be Duff. I give it up—I've toiled enough.

There ought to be some chloride cures for men with dizzy signatures. They make the angry passions rise; they bring hot water to the eyes; they waste the time of busy men by their gymnastics with the pen!

### 220 *Unusual Need*

Help must really be getting scarce. A recent notice in the post office said: "Man wanted for robbery."

### 221 *Was It Insured?*

The absentminded professor drove up to the door of his garage, looked inside, blinked, and then leaped back into his car and drove at breakneck speed to the police station. "Sergeant," he gasped, "my car's been stolen!"

### 222 *Shakespeare*

Let me have about me men that are fat, sleek-headed men, and such as sleep o' nights with Sanka coffee.

Yon Cassius has a lean and hungry look. Methinks he has not had his Wheaties this morn.

The quality of mercy is not strained: it falleth like the gentle rain from heaven upon the place beneath. Like gifts from Ye Olde Giftie Shoppe, it blesseth he who gives and he who takes.

### 223 *It Could Happen*

Man who mistakenly received a pay envelope without a check, to personnel department: "What happened? Did my deductions finally equal my salary?"

### 224 *He Was Prepared*

A young plumber was sent to a mansion in the best part of town to repair a gas leak.

The owner admitted him and said, "Please be careful of the floors."

"Oh, you don't need to worry about my slipping on them," replied the plumber. "I've got spikes on my boots."

### 225 *New Minister's Job*

"What do they do when they install a minister, Dad? Do they put him in a stall and feed him?"

"Oh, no, son, they hitch him to a church and expect him to pull it."—*George B. Gilbert*

### 226 *Beating It*

A man had to send an urgent telegram. Not wishing to spend more money than necessary, he filled out a telegraph blank in this manner:

"Bruises hurt erased afford erected analysis hurt too infectious dead." (Ten words)

The recipient at the other end, being kin, immediately understood the message: "Bruce is hurt. He raced a Ford. He wrecked it, and Alice is hurt too. In fact she's dead." (Nineteen words)

### 227 *Learned Quickly*

Genial general manager to new office boy: "Well, my lad, how are you getting on? Do you think you'll like the business?"

Boy: "Oh yes, sir, thank you."

General manager: "Well, don't forget the chief qualities we need in this office are brains and energy."

Boy: "Yes, sir; I have only been here two weeks, but I have found that out."

### 228 *Try One*

Restaurant ad: "Try our homemade pies. They are a real threat."

### 229 *Only One Answer*

"How can I show my appreciation?" said a woman client to Clarence Darrow, after he had won her legal case. "My dear madam," said the great lawyer, "ever since the Phoenicians invented money there has been only one answer to that question."

### 230 *Smart*

"But if you are selling these watches under cost price, where does your profit come in?"

"We make our profit out of repairing them."

### 231 *Frank*

Junk dealer: "All our cars are in first crash condition."

### 232 *Interesting Story*

During a fire in a certain Ohio town the editor of the local paper, being unable to locate the regular reporter, sent out the young society editor. The story of the fire appeared thusly:

"A brilliant fire was held yesterday afternoon at the residence of Mr. and Mrs. George Sopp on Crown Hill Avenue. A large number of people attended the function.

"Mrs. Sopp, who recently had her hair shingled, made a charming escape in an exceedingly handsome henna silk blouse, the pattern of which appeared on our woman's page last week.

"The firemen, who presented an attractive appearance, were suitably garbed in blue, the tunics being full cut.

"The weather was quite delightful for an affair of this kind, a strong wind blowing. It was rumored that the fire was on a larger scale than any previous affair of a similar kind for years. It is also rumored that it cost Mr. and Mrs. Sopp about $25,000."

### 233 *Don't Speak Too Long*

An executive who formerly delivered after-dinner speeches of considerable length, now expresses himself with commendable brevity. Asked to explain his reformation, he replied:

"It was a remark I overheard. During a pause in one of my speeches, I heard one man say to another, 'What follows Bamburger?' The other replied, 'Wednesday.' "

### 234    *Really Bad*

"How's business?"

"Terrible. Even the people who never pay have stopped buying."

### 235    *Pretty Dumb*

The old-fashioned blacksmith was rather dumb. When a horse was brought in to be shod, he didn't think of forty other things that ought to be done to it.

### 236    *That Got Attention*

He walked nervously up and down in the post office, trying to catch the eye of someone to whom he might state his requirements, but in vain.

Completely ignoring him, the clerks discussed the latest movie or examined the pattern of a smart sweater one of them was knitting.

At last he could stand it no longer. Dashing up to a window, he exclaimed to the clerk, "Miss, do you believe in the hereafter?"

"Of course I do," she replied.

"Well," said he, "I'm hereafter two twenty-cent stamps."

### 237    *Send Check*

A would-be customer wrote to a mail-order house as follows:

"Please send me one of the gasoline engines you show on page 87. If it's any good, I'll send you a check."

In time, he received this reply:

"Please send check. If it's any good, we'll send the engine."

### 238    *Art*

Son: "Daddy, what's an actor?"

Father: "An actor? Why, an actor, son, is a man who can walk to the side of a stage, peer into the wings filled with theatrical props, dirt and dust, and other actors, stagehands, old clothes, and a mess of claptrap, and say: 'What a lovely view there is from this window!' "

### 239    *How Else?*

A farmer planted a crop of flax and had a tablecloth made from the linen he produced. Sometime later he remarked to a guest at dinner, "I grew this tablecloth myself."

"Did you, really?" the lady remarked. "How do you ever manage to grow such things?"

"Promise you won't tell, madam?" he asked.

She promised.

"Well," he whispered solemnly, "I planted a napkin."

### 240   *Don't Worry*

An employee became ill and was rushed to the hospital. The next day his boss was among the first to visit him.

"Now John," he pleaded, "don't worry about a thing. Everyone at the office is going to pitch in and do your work—as soon as we're able to figure out just what it is you've been doing.

### 241   *No Heels Lost*

Tom: "Did you hear about the fire at the shoe factory?"

Tim: "No, what happened?"

Tom: "Well, two hundred soles were lost!"

### 242   *What Else?*

A lady checking over her grocery bill found this item: "One tom cat, eighty cents." Indignant, she called up her grocer and demanded an explanation.

"Oh, that's all right, Mrs. Jones," the grocer explained. "That's an abbreviation for tomato catsup."

### 243   *A Great Radio*

Two men were discussing the merits of their respective radios.

"Has yours good receptivity?" one asked.

"I'll say it has," said the other. "I was listening to a quartet the other night, and I didn't like the tenor, so I tuned him out and listened to the other three."

### 244   *Interesting Idea*

All publishers of periodicals receive curious letters from their readers, but the following written to the *Christian Science Monitor* stands out as the gem of the year:

"Dear Sir: When I subscribed a year ago you stated that if I was not satisfied at the end of the year I could have my money back. Well, I would like to have it back. On second thought, to save you trouble, you may apply it on my next year's subscription."

### 245   *Not Easy*

"Do you make life-size enlargements from snapshots?" asked the demure girl.

"Certainly, miss," said the photographer, "that's our specialty."

"Well," said the girl, "see what you can do with this picture of the Grand Canyon."

### 246   *Confused*

The treasurer, dictating a letter: "From the comparative size of the coal shipment and the bill, I should say you got them mixed up—you should have sent the coal by mail and the bill by freight."

### 247   *Smart Selling*

A storekeeper had for some time displayed in his window a card inscribed "Fishing Tickle."

A customer drew the proprietor's attention to the spelling. "Hasn't anyone told you of it before?" asked the patron.

"Oh, yes," the dealer said placidly, "many have mentioned it. But whenever they drop in to tell me, they always buy something."

### 248   *Be Careful*

Irate saleswoman to disagreeable customer: "Go easy, madam; the days when I used to insult customers are still fresh in my mind!"

### 249   *Punctuation*

Placement counselor: "Before I send you for the position, I want to remind you of the importance of punctuation."

Student typist: "Thank you. I promise you I'll always get to work on time."

### 250   *Little Difference*

A millionaire, as he climbed into his limousine, snarled at a newsboy, "No, I don't want to buy a paper!"

"Well, keep your shirt on, boss," the newsboy answered. "The only difference between you and me is that you are making your second million, while I'm still on my first."

### 251   *A Little Help Needed*

A telephone service girl received a call from an elderly lady: "My telephone cord," said the lady, "is too long. Would you please pull it back at your end?"

### 252   *Bank Trust Department*

Customer to bank trust officer: "If I make you guardian for my child, will I still need a baby-sitter?"

### 253   *Small Capital*

"When I began business on my own, I had absolutely nothing but my intelligence."

"That sure was a small beginning!"

### 254    *Courteous*

"Sorry I gave you the wrong number," said the telephone operator.

"Don't mention it," answered the man who was determined not to lose his temper. "I'm sure that the numbers you gave me three times were much better than the number I asked for, only it just happened I couldn't use them."

### 255    *Opposed*

Company director to board chairman: If any new ideas come up while I am out of the meeting for a brief telephone call, my vote is "No."

### 256    *Bank Teller's Window*

Customer: "Where will I find the department that explains how to kite checks?"

### 257    *Hard Question*

Two cowboys were talking. One said, "My name is Tex."

Second one: "You from Texas?"

The first one: "Nope, from Louisiana, but who wants to be called Louise?"

### 258    *Indignant*

A bakery customer complained about the pastry.

"I was making pastry before you were born," replied the indignant baker.

"Maybe so," said the customer, "but why sell it now?"

### 259    *Forever?*

Salesperson to customer searching for a Christmas gift: "This clock will run thirty days without winding."

Customer: "How long will it run if you wind it?"

### 260    *Being Helpful*

Sign in a restaurant: "If you want to put your ashes and cigarette butts in your cup and saucer, let the waitress know and she will serve you the coffee in an ashtray.

### 261    *Do Your Best*

Judge: "I sentence you to ninety-nine years on each of ten counts, or nine hundred and ninety years."

Prisoner: "Judge, that's going to be hard to do."

Judge: "Just do the best you can."

### 262    *Followed Orders*

The managing editor wheeled his chair around and pushed a button in the wall. The person summoned entered. "Here," said the editor, "are a number of directions from outsiders as to the best way to run a paper. See that they are all carried out." And the office boy, gathering them all into a large wastebasket, did so.

### 263    *He Didn't Mean to Intrude*

"I hope I don't protrude," said the foreigner learning English and joining a party uninvited.

### 264    *Not So Sure*

Professor Skinner invented a new hair restorer and sent sample bottles to various well-known people in the hope of securing testimonials.

"I don't know whether to publish this testimonial," he said to a friend.

"What does it say?" asked the friend.

"Well," answered the proud inventor, "it says, 'Before I used your hair restorer I had three bald spots; now I have only one.' "

### 265    *Trying to Be Helpful*

A woman missed her gloves as she was leaving the restaurant where she had dined with her husband. Asking him to wait, she hurried back to look for them, searching first on the table, then finally peering under it.

The waiter who had served them hurried up to her. "Pardon me, madam," he said, "but the gentleman is there by the door."

### 266    *Safe Bet*

A farmer had just made a purchase of a bushel of grass seed. "Is this seed guaranteed?" he asked.

"Guarantee the seed?" the merchant replied. "I should say so! If that seed doesn't grow, bring it back and we'll refund your money."

### 267    *Unreasonable*

Classified ad in the *Erie* (Pennsylvania), *Times:* "For rent: Four rooms, bath, laundry. Everything reasonable but the landlord."

### 268    *One Tip Lost*

A man entered a crowded restaurant and found a seat in the corner. A waitress handed him a menu and left to take care of other customers who were in a hurry.

After a long interval the waitress suddenly remembered the man in the corner and hurried over to take his order. He was gone, but propped up against his empty water glass was this sign, scrawled on a piece of notepaper: "Out to Lunch."

### 269    *Competitive*

Fu Ling, who had just opened a laundry on one corner, studied the signs on the business establishments on the other corners.

On the bakery was a sign reading: "We stay open all night." The restaurant sign read: "We never sleep."

The next morning over Fu Ling's laundry appeared a neat hand-printed sign: "Me wake too!"

### 270　*He Cut the Loss*

A storekeeper in a small Vermont town was greeted by a neighbor, who consoled him on the loss of some of his merchandise during a fire. "Did you lose much, Ephraim?" asked the friend.

"Not too much," came the laconic reply. "I'd just marked my stock down twenty-five percent."

### 271　*Exchanging Gifts*

In the crush of people exchanging gifts in a department store, a disgusted husband was heard to ask his wife, "Are you at least going to keep the baby?"

### 272　*Watch Out for Him*

Concerned uncle: "Now that you are through college, what are you going to do?"

Graduate: "I will study law and become a great attorney."

Uncle: "The legal profession is pretty crowded already, isn't it?"

Graduate: "I can't help that; I will study law, and those who are already in the profession will simply have to take their chances, that's all!"

### 273　*Clever Answer*

In one of Dallas's large hotels there is a man who takes hats at the door to the dining room but who never gives checks in return.

A traveling salesman became interested in him and asked one of the men in charge how the checkroom attendant managed to keep track of so many hats.

"Why, he's been doing it for years," said the man, "and prides himself on never making a mistake."

As the salesman was leaving, the attendant passed him his hat. "How do you know this hat is mine?" he asked.

"I don't know it, sir," admitted the hat man.

"Then why do you give it to me?"

" 'Cause you gave it to me, sir."

### 274　*The Line Is Busy*

The Indian brave was waiting to send a message by smoke signals. Behind, in the distance, a huge forest fire was sending up billows of smoke.

The Indian chief came up and asked impatiently, "Haven't you sent my message yet?"

The young brave pointed to the distant fire and said, "Sorry, the line is busy."

### 275    *Sleeps Well*

A speaker at the Executives Club of Chicago asked Jack Hanley, the head of Monsanto, a company beset by all kinds of pressures from employees and demands from government, how it was possible for a chief executive of a company like that to sleep with all this turmoil going on.

"It's easy," he said. "I sleep like a baby. Every two hours I wake up and cry."

### 276    *No Problem Too Small*

In offices and plants we have this problem of the experts intimidating the nonexperts. In one plant there was a sign that said, "No problem is too small to baffle our experts."

### 277    *The Difference*

Waiter: "Steak or hamburger?"
Diner: "What's the difference?"
Waiter: "One day."

### 278    *Understandable*

The shoe salesman had almost emptied the shelves of their stock for a hard-to-please customer. As she still couldn't decide, he pulled up a stool, sat down, and sighed: "Do you mind if I rest a minute, lady? Your feet are killing me."

### 279    *Attorney Gives an Orange Away*

Burdett Root, Bridgeport attorney, gives an orange away:

"I hereby give and convey to you, all and singular, my estate and interest, right, title, claim, and advantages of and in this orange, together with all its rind, juice, and pulp, and pips, and all rights and advantages therein, with full power to bite, cut, suck, and otherwise to eat the same or give the same away with or without the rind, pulp, juice or pips, anything hereinbefore or hereafter or in any other means of whatever nature or kind whatsoever to the contrary in any wise notwithstanding."

### 280    *Status*

If status can be achieved by adopting a high-sounding name, near the top should be the scavenger service that hung on one of its garbage trucks: "Used Vitamin Convoy Service."

### 281    *That Makes It Clear*

A shopper in a downtown department store happened to see a clerk standing behind the complaint desk. The clerk caught her attention because she just smiled at everyone who spoke to her and kept her voice pleasant and low, despite the rudeness of irate customers.

The observant shopper was astounded at the way the clerk managed to remain so calm until she noticed the woman's earrings. One bore the inscription "In" and the other, "Out."

282     One of these days a smart manufacturer will produce a good portable automobile.

283     Trying to understand modern art is like trying to follow the plot in a bowl of alphabet soup.

284     Don't worry if Washington takes the shirt off your back—they've got a bureau of some kind to keep it in.

285     Who can remember when people were killed by fireworks instead of automobiles on the Fourth of July?

286     Many are smart enough to rise to the occasion, but few are smart enough to sit down.

287     The Supreme Court's rule—Blessed are those who pray, but not on school time.

288     Business without profit is not business any more than a pickle is a candy.—*Charles F. Abbott*

289     There's one consolation about both life and taxes. When you're through with one, you're through with the other.

290     In a nation with private enterprise, a profit is not without honor in the country.

291     The smoothest thing about a used car is the salesman.

292     Button shoes are said to be coming back. The manufacturers hope for a national hook-up.

293     The United States is a country of quiet majorities and loud minorities.

294     Our laundry has just sent back some buttons with no shirt on them.

295     *Modern technology:* An American company announces an invention; the Russians claim they made the same discovery twenty years earlier; the Japanese start exporting it.

296     We heard recently of a big businessman who had to stop going to baseball games. He just couldn't stand hearing the umpire call a strike.

297    We didn't all come over on the same ship, but we're all in the same boat.—*Bernard Baruch*

298    What this country needs is a car that will go no faster than its driver can think.

299    We need more watchdogs at the United States Treasury and fewer bloodhounds at the Internal Revenue Service.

300    *A good day:* When the wheels of your shopping cart all go in the same direction.

301    When you pay your taxes, you understand the shear-the-wealth idea.

302    Surveys would probably show more deaf people engaged in writing popular songs than in any other occupation.

303    What this country needs is a good one-dollar cigar with ashes to match the rug.

304    Nothing can be so deceptive as statistics, except figures.

305    A toastmaster at a dinner is the person who gets up to tell you the best part of the evening is over.

306    A man may be a twenty-ton truck in the office and only a two-wheel trailer at home.

307    The ideal combination in traffic is to have the horse sense of the driver equal the horsepower of the car.

308    Nothing makes a motorist enjoy the scenery more than seeing a motorcycle policeman just behind him.

309    No wonder the grocery bill is high, when you see all those nylons, cosmetics, and drugs your wife bought at the supermarket.

310    No matter what happens in business, someone always says he knew it would.

311    Civilization has spread until television and jet bombers can be heard almost everywhere.

312    When better business predictions are made, economists won't make them.

313    Many of us have trouble seeing where our business ends and the other person's begins.

314     *Moron:* a person who proofreads the Xerox copy against the original.

315     *In conclusion:* The phrase that wakes up the audience.

316     *Shut up:* The generic term for "the meeting will now come to order."

317     It's a good thing we don't pay taxes on what we think we're worth.

318     The government does not require a person to understand the income tax forms before he pays the tax.

319     The trouble is that there are so many traffic laws and such a limited supply of respect.

320     Whenever your ship comes in, the government is ready to dock it.

321     A taxpayer is a person who doesn't have to take a civil service examination to work for the government.

322     If we do not revise the tax laws, we may have the problem of reviving the taxpayer.

323     Law enforcement week seems to be the principal week of each year.

324     On tax reduction, it may be said that never did so many wait so anxiously for so little so long.

325     How can the critics call this country lawless when we have more laws than any other country.

326     An appeal is when you ask one court to show its contempt for another court.—*Finley Peter Dunne*

327     Most laws seem reasonable till silly cops try to enforce them against nice people like us.

328     When an irresistible force meets an immovable object, there's usually a lawyer who will take the case.

329     Business economy:A reduction in the other fellow's salary.

330     Farmacy: A veterinarian's dispensary.

331     The ancient Hebrews had a goat on which all the sins were placed, so the holding company idea isn't new.

332     A Pennsylvania town advertised for a drugstore. It seems the regular restaurant had closed down.

333     Why don't efficiency experts go into business for themselves and make fortunes?

334     The successful farmer can't be lazy. It takes energy to fill in the blanks for the various government reports.

335     Young boy finding salesman at the front door: "Hey, Mom, it's a live commercial."

336     The Post Office says thousands of letters are mailed every year without addresses—but not from the Internal Revenue Service.

337     America is a country where they lock up juries and let the defendants out.

338     When all the world acquires an education, how are you going to pick a jury?

339     A barking dog may never bite, but he's no help to public relations.

340     Why can't some of these "yes" men be bank officers?

341     A large corporation has a machine for testing the strength of cartons. Apparently the Post Office can't be relied upon to do it anymore.

342     If the Department of Agriculture really wants to help us, they could teach us how to pick out a ripe cantaloupe.

343     What this country needs is a soap that won't do anything for you but get the dirt off.

344     Suggested advertising slogans: "Good to the last drop" for Nookwood pottery and also Arden elevators; "The Hams What Am" for any amateur theatrical group.

345     An ice-cream store advocates preparedness with this sign: "Take home a brick. You may have company."

346     If they continue to increase the size of trucks, trains will have to approach crossings cautiously.

347     Competition is the life of trade, but it may be the death of profit.

348     Gossip is one form of crime for which the law provides no punishment.

349     Some say the biggest advance in the area of communications in the United States isn't television—it's the coffee break.

350    When we see those big, flashing electric signs, we think how wonderful they must look to the person who can't read.

351    If we can only keep out foreign goods, the foreigners won't earn enough dollars to buy our farm products.

352    You never realize how many parts a car has until it hits the end of a big truck.

353    An efficient employee is one who keeps on his toes but never steps on the other fellow's.

354    Business is always improving for the beauty-parlor operator.

355    Business never comes back unless you go after it.

356    A good executive not only knows how to take advice, but also how to reject it.

357    A small town today is where the runways aren't long enough for a four-engine plane.

358    A go-getter who becomes his own boss is apt to wind up a nervous wreck.

359    Vanity may be bad, but it keeps the looking-glass industry going.

360    Remember the old days when you threatened to move if the landlord didn't do something?

361    There are enough automobiles now so every man, woman and child could ride at the same time, but that wouldn't be any fun without pedestrians crossing the streets.—*Herbert V. Prochnow*

362    Journalists were never intended to be the cheerleaders of a society, the conductors of applause, the sycophants. Tragically, that is their assigned role in authoritarian societies, but not here—not yet.—*Chet Huntley*

363    The oilcan is mightier than the sword.—*Everett Dirksen*

364    I won't buy a magazine that will publish what I write.—*Goodman Ace*

365    Caution is the eldest child of wisdom.—*Victor Hugo*

366    Our national flower is the concrete cloverleaf.—*Lewis Mumford*

367    What garlic is to salad, insanity is to art.—*Augustus Saint-Gaudens*

368    *Executive:* An ulcer with authority.—*Fred Allen*

369     *Public relations counselor:* A press agent with a manicure.—*Alan Gordon*

370     A committee is a cul-de-sac to which ideas are lured and then quietly strangled.—*John A. Lincoln*

371     You can tell the ideals of a nation by its advertisements.—*Norman Douglas*

372     Most of us never recognize opportunity until it goes to work in our competitor's business.

373     It must be tough to be a traffic cop—and have to stay mad all the time.

374     What would the suspenders business amount to without the law of gravity?

375     Statistics are like alienists—they will testify for either side. *F. H. La-Guardia*

376     *Statistician:* A man who can go directly from an unwarranted assumption to a preconceived conclusion.

377     According to the latest magazines in doctors' waiting rooms, Wilbur Wright has made his first flight.

378     *Mailing list:* A sucker list.

379     If a man can make a better mousetrap than his neighbor, though he build his house in the woods, the other mousetrap makers will beat a path to his door—and try to steal it.

380     Those rambling one-story ranch houses have become so widely accepted that today there are more twelve-year-old boys in this country who have flown in airplanes than have slid down banisters.—*Bill Vaughan*

381     There is no such thing as "soft sell" and "hard sell." There is only "smart sell" and "stupid sell."—*Charles Brower*

382     *Parking lot:* A place where you pay to leave your car while dents are put in the fenders.—*Herbert V. Prochnow*

383     *Receivership:* When business is conducted as usual during legal arguments.

384     Before the development of modern transportation and communication, half the world didn't know how the other half lived. Today, in our enlightened age, half the world doesn't care.

385 Samson had the right idea about advertising. He took two columns and brought down the house.

386 A farmer is always going to be rich next year.—*Philemon*

387 The life of a bill collector is not so unpleasant. Almost everybody asks him to call again.

388 A shoe manufacturer says that banana skins make the best slippers.

389 American enterprise is the art of making toeless shoes a fashion instead of a calamity.

390 *Abstract art:* A product of the untalented, sold by the unprincipled to the utterly bewildered.—*Al Capp*

391 *Xerox:* A trademark for a photocopying device that can make rapid reproductions of human error, perfectly.—*Merle L. Meacham*

392 When a company says, "Our coffee is good to the last drop," you wonder what is wrong with the last drop.

393 Sign in optometrist's window: "If you don't see what you want, you've come to the right place."

394 We have often wondered whether a rock musician gets more money than a riveter for making noise.

395 A deaf and dumb man runs a phonograph and record store, which is a case of the right man in the right place.

396 In our civilization man comes first, then the machine. Next, the ambulance.

397 The corner drugstore is one of the few places where you can still get home cooking.

398 What would have happened to this country if the elder Henry Ford had gone in for the mass production of saxophones or banjos?

399 If you make a better mousetrap, people who need money for various purposes will beat a path to your door.

400 A scientist says a butterfly eats practically nothing. He apparently never took one out to dinner.

401 Some waiters should visit a zoo and watch the turtles zip by.

# III

# Education, Wisdom, Ignorance, and Knowledge

### 402 *Humor in Language*

If one is a tooth and a whole set are teeth, then why shouldn't booth in the plural be beeth? If the plural of man is always called men, why shouldn't the plural of pan be called pen? You may find a lone mouse or a whole nest of mice, but more than one house is most surely not hice. A cow in the plural is properly kine, but a bow if repeated is never called bine. Then one may be that and two would be those, yet hat in the plural would never be hose. We speak of a brother and also of brethren, but though we say mother, we never say methren. The masculine pronouns are he, his, and him, but imagine a feminine she, shis, and shim! So English, I fancy you all will agree, is the funniest language you ever did see.

### 403 *Geography*

Teacher: "Johnny, where is Brazil?"
Johnny (stalling): "Where do you think it is?"
Teacher: "I don't think. I know."
Johnny: "I don't think I know, either."

### 404 *Modern Education*

An editor came upon a bit of juvenile homework that intrigued him. On a sheet of notepaper he observed the letters "e-g-a-k-s-h-i-o-n."
"What," he asked, "is that supposed to spell?"
"Oh," said the child confidently, "that spells 'education.'"

### 405 *The Old Days*

Two schoolteachers were talking.

"Remember when students brought their teachers apples?" one asked.

"Instead of driving them bananas," said the other.

### 406    *Say That Again*

Overheard near the subway at Harvard Square, Cambridge, Massachusetts: "How's your motivational pattern today?"

### 407    *Creative Writing*

Danny hated to write themes. So when his teacher told the class to write a 300-word theme about family pets, Danny came up with this masterpiece:

"My family got a kat. It went out. Ma said to me to go git that kat. I went out on the frunt porsh and hollered here kitty, kitty, kitty, kitty, kitty, kitty, kitty, kitty . . ."

### 408    *Mystery*

A librarian recently commented that a certain patron got more out of mystery novels than any other patron.

"How's that?" she was asked.

"She begins reading in the middle," the librarian explained, "so she not only wonders how it will come out, but also how it began."

### 409    *Advice*

"Well, son," wrote a fond mother to her soldier boy, "I hope you have been punctual in rising every morning so that you haven't kept the regiment waiting for breakfast."

### 410    *Modern Youth*

The kindergarten teacher had spoken at length about cheerfulness and the abundance of frowns.

"What do you think we need most of all in this room?" she finally asked. "What do we need every day?"

Young Timmy loudly volunteered, "Television."

### 411    *Really Needed*

The principal of one of those ultra-modern high schools whose nonteaching staff already included dentists, a psychologist, and a business manager was shocked to hear a member of the faculty suggesting they add a handwriting expert.

"Handwriting analysis?" he snapped. "That's ridiculous!"

"Who said anything about analyzing?" the teacher said wearily. "We just need someone who can read it!"

### 412    *Inside Him*

The class was having a composition lesson. The teacher said, "Do not imitate what others have written. Simply be yourself and write what is in you."

Following this advice, Bobby wrote: "I am not imitating others. I am writing about what is in me. In me there are my stomach, liver, two apples, one piece of pie, a lemon drop, and my lunch."

### 413   *Of Course*

A lawyer named Strange was asked by a friend what he would like to have inscribed on his tombstone. "Just put, 'Here lies an honest lawyer,' " he said.

"But," said the friend, "that doesn't tell who it is."

"Certainly it does," the lawyer argued. "Passersby will say, 'That's Strange.' "

### 414   *Helpful*

A gypsy family had just departed from near the vicar's home and had left a dead donkey partly covered. The vicar wrote to the council about the donkey. They responded, rather facetiously, saying it was the vicar's duty to bury the dead.

The vicar replied that he knew that, but had thought he should let the relatives know first.

### 415   *Awful*

A mother pigeon and her young son were getting ready to migrate to Florida. The baby was afraid he couldn't make it.

"Don't worry," Mamma Pigeon said. "I'll tie one end of a piece of string around my leg and the other end to your neck. If you tire, I'll help you along."

Junior Pigeon began to wail. "But," he protested, "I don't want to be pigeon-towed!"

### 416   *Better*

"How are your children doing at school?" a woman asked her friend.

"Better," replied the friend. "But I still go to PTA meetings under an assumed name.

### 417   *The Mule*

"The mule," wrote a schoolboy, "is a hardier bird than a goose or a turkey, and different. He wears his wings on the side of his head. He has two legs to walk with, two more to kick with, and is usually backward about going forward."

### 418   *Proud*

Teacher: "Why haven't you brought your report card back yet, Johnny?"

Johnny: "Because you gave me an A in something and they're still mailing it to relatives."

419    *Good Reason*

A teacher was asked why she preferred teaching in an elementary school.
"Well," she explained, "I love children of all ages, but at the grade school, I'm always sure of finding a parking space."

420    *Distracted*

The absentminded professor paused a moment to chat with one of his students and then asked, "Which way was I going when I stopped to talk with you?"
"That way," the student said, pointing.
"Good," murmured the man of letters. "Then I've already had my lunch."

421    *Naturally*

When a Texas school class was told that the next day they would learn to draw, eighteen youngsters showed up with pistols.

422    *Intelligence*

The peak years of mental activity are undoubtedly between the ages of six and eighteen. At six we know all the questions. At eighteen we know all the answers.

423    *Not That Kind*

Man to friend: "What do you have if you have fifty rabbits all in a row and they all back up one step?"
Friend: "I don't know. Tell me."
Man: "A receding hare-line!"

424    *Emergency*

A ninth-grader "floored" telephone folks recently with this portion of an essay entered in a contest. "The telephone is very necessary in cases of emergency," the youngster wrote. "For example, if your house is on fire, you can use the telephone to call the insurance company."

425    *Wrong Identity*

In the supermarket a man was pushing a cart that contained a screaming baby. The gentleman kept repeating such admonitions as "Don't get excited, Albert," "Don't scream, Albert," "Don't yell, Albert," "Keep calm, Albert."
A woman standing next to him said, "You certainly are to be commended for trying to soothe your son Albert."
The man looked at her and then said soberly, "Lady, I'm Albert."

426    *A Survey*

An education survey polled freshmen entering colleges as to what careers they hoped to follow. Here are some of the choices the students wrote: "Busness,

Buseness, Finnace, Holesaid Salisman, Denestry, Physist, Technection, Airnotics, Treacher, Stewardes, Secteral, and Engenering." One was "Undesided," while another was "Undecieded."

### 427 *Talking Dog*

Claiming the dog could talk, a man entered himself and Fido in a talent show. On stage, the man asked the dog, "What is all over a tree?" "Bark, bark!" Fido answered. The audience began to boo.

"What is found on top of the house?"

"Roof, roof!" The audience began throwing garbage on the stage.

In desperation, the man asked, "Who was the greatest baseball player?"

"Ruth, Ruth!" the dog replied.

The two were thrown off the stage. Backstage, Fido turned to his master with a bewildered look and inquired, "DiMaggio?"

### 428 *His Answer*

Teacher: "Can you name the principal river in Egypt?"

John: "It's the Nile!"

Teacher: "Splendid, John. Now can you name some of the small tributaries?"

John (thinking hard): "The juveniles?"

### 429 *Learning?*

Some interesting facts that students reported learning in school:

Appomattox is the person you are against.

The artichoke was an ancient instrument of torture.

The cold at the North Pole is so great that the towns are not inhabited there.

Often when people are drowned, you can revive them by punching in their sides, but not too hard. This is called resurrection.

Heresy is where a child looks like his father.

The Mediterranean and the Red Sea are connected by the sewage canal.

Hallucination is an eye trouble such as corrosions of the illusions.

A goblet is a male turkey.

A microscope is used to see things that are smaller than a naked eye.

### 430 *Extra Duty*

We all know that librarians have to take care of checking books in and out and shelving them, but librarians must also be prepared to provide information. These are just a few of the questions librarians have been asked by people who sincerely wanted to know: What do unicorns eat? Do camels have to be licensed in India? When did people start twiddling their thumbs? And is it legal to keep an octopus in a private house?

### 431    *Howlers*

Comic blunders by schoolchildren have been collected by H. Cecil Hunt and published under the title *Hen-Picked Howlers.* Some examples, as published by *The Lookout* of Cincinnati, are given here:

An epistle is the wife of an apostle.

Chivalry is the attitude of a man to a strange woman.

Louis XVI was gelatined.

Catarrh is a musical instrument, especially in Spain.

Philosophy means being able to explain why you are happy when you are poor.

When letters are in sloping type, they are in hysterics.

The Tropic of Cancer is a rare and dangerous disease.

An antidote is a funny story you have heard before.

Doctors say that fatal diseases are the worst.

Ali Baba means being somewhere else when the crime was committed.

A symposium is something like a symphony, only not as bad.

Contralto is a low kind of music that is sung only by ladies.—*Sunshine Magazine*

### 432    *So That's It*

A teacher asked a seven-year-old girl what a bridegroom was.

"Please, teacher," was the reply, "it's a thing they have at every wedding."

### 433    *Good Teaching*

The first-grader who sent in his letter to the *Washington Post*'s "favorite teacher" essay contest readily admitted liking "Miss Davis."

In fact, he scrawled: "I wish she was smart enough to teach second grade too next year."

### 434    *Similarities*

"Daddy, what is a millennium?"

Father: "It's the same as a centennial, except it has a lot more legs."

### 435    *Being a Sergeant*

Not long ago some patrolmen took an examination for promotion to sergeant. One of the examining officials maintains the following were some of the responses to the questionnaires.

*Question:* What would you do in case of a race riot? *Answer:* Get the number of both cars.

*Question:* What is sabotage? *Answer:* Breaking the laws of the Sabbath.

*Question:* Name an act that would constitute reckless driving. *Answer:* Driving without regard to the Presbyterians on the street.

*Question:* To what extent may an officer use force in effecting an arrest? *Answer:* Use good common sense, and if not capable, summon help.

### 436 *Give 'Em Credit*

The following are reported to be answers in grade-school examinations:

Because of the good roads in Rome, Christianity traveled faster than ever before.

Trial by ordeal is when you walk and your feet hurt.

Angles are unseen things which have wings and fly around helping the poor.

The Greeks were lazy people because they worshiped idles.

### 437 *Still Available*

Remember those old-time dime novels? Don't you wish they were still around? They are, they are. Only now they sell for $10.98.

### 438 *Right*

"Now, then, Tommy Brown," said the teacher, "I want to give you a little problem. Suppose there were five children and their mother had only four potatoes to share among them. She wanted to give each child an equal share. How would she do it?"

"Mash the potatoes," the boy replied.

### 439 *He Ought to Know*

Professor: "Here you see the skull of a chimpanzee, a very rare specimen. There are only two in the country—one is in the National Museum and I have the other."

### 440 *Machines*

The teacher was discussing the wonders of modern science, and in particular various kinds of machines. Asking the nine-year-olds to name the most wonderful machines they had ever seen, she got all the stock answers—airplanes, televisions, robots, etc.—until one thoughtful little girl answered, "A hen!"

"Why, Maudie," said the teacher, "whatever makes you think a hen is a wonderful machine?"

"Well," said Maudie, "do you know anything else that will take all our leavings and turn them into fresh eggs?"—*Leonard G. Vine, Rotarian*

### 441 *Next Question*

Teacher: "Use the word 'tackle' in a sentence."

Student: "A tack'll make you sore if you sit on it."

### 442 *That's What It Says*

Little Jerry was diligently reading his animal book. Suddenly he exclaimed, "Mother, how do rabbits bark?"

His mother looked up in surprise. "Rabbits don't bark, dear."

"That's funny!" said Jerry. "Here in this story it says that rabbits eat cabbage and bark."

443    *A Spoonerism*

It's a grammatical invention, named after the man who first used it—William Archibald Spooner—an intentional twist of words or phrases such as "I remember your name perfectly, but I can't think of your face." Can you think of a good one?

444    *That's What He Heard*

The teacher asked the second-graders if they knew the last line to "The Star-Spangled Banner." Tommy raised his hand and answered, "And the home of the brave. Play ball!"

445    *Four-Day Week*

Teacher: "Does anyone know who invented the four-day week?"
Student: "Robinson Crusoe."
Teacher: "Why do you say that?"
Student: "Because he had all his work done by Friday."

446    *How's That?*

The sign on the university bulletin board read, "Shoes are required to eat in the cafeteria."
Below was scribbled, "Socks may eat wherever they wish."

447    *Difficult*

He had never had such a tough time in his life. First he got angina pectoris, followed by arteriosclerosis. Just as he got through with that, he got pneumonia, and then pulmonary phthisis and tuberculosis. He recovered just in time to get appendicitis, to say nothing of pyorrhea. All in all, he never knew how he survived, for it was the hardest spelling test he had ever experienced.

448    *Good Question*

A farmer visited his son's college. Watching students in a chemistry class, he was told they were looking for a universal solvent.
"What's that?" asked the farmer.
"A liquid that will dissolve anything," he was told.
"That's a great idea," agreed the farmer, "but when you find it, what kind of container will you keep it in?"

449    *Correct*

Teacher: "What happened in the year 1809?"
Johnny: "Lincoln was born."
Teacher: "Correct. Now what happened in 1812?"
Johnny (counting on his fingers): "Lincoln had his third birthday."

### 450    *Snakes!*

A Girl Scout camper wrote in a letter to home: "Mother, there are snakes all over my tent and on my bed." When her counselor asked why she wrote such a thing when it was not true, she replied, "Because I don't know how to spell caterpillar."

### 451    *Qualified*

Employer: "For this job, we need someone who is responsible."

Applicant: "That's me. On my last job, whenever anything went wrong, they always said I was responsible."

### 452    *He Was Right*

Applicants for jobs on a state dam project had to take a written examination. The first question was "What does hydrodynamics mean?"

One applicant hesitated a moment, then wrote slowly, "It means I don't get the job."

### 453    *Unbelievable*

With obvious reluctance a small boy handed his report card to his father, who studied the card, then signed it. The boy glanced at the signature, then asked, "Why did you sign with an X instead of your name?"

"Because," his father said, "with these grades, I don't think your teacher would believe you had a father who could read or write."

### 454    *Answers Teachers Get*

*Question:* "What are glaciers?" *Answer:* "Guys that fix windows when they're broken."

*Question:* "Why does a dog hang out its tongue when running?" *Answer:* "To balance its tail, of course."

*Question:* "What is a peninsula?" *Answer:* "A black and white bird that lives on icebergs."

### 455    *Not So Dumb*

A visitor at an asylum saw one of the inmates pushing a wheelbarrow upside down.

"That's not the way to push that thing," the visitor exclaimed. "You've got it upside down."

"Oh, have I?" answered the lunatic. "I used to push it the other way, but then they put bricks in it."

### 456    *Next Question*

The teacher was explaining to her fourth-graders why heat makes objects expand whereas cold makes them contract. Asking one of her pupils to give an example, young Tommy piped up, "In the summertime, the days are long, but in the winter, they're short."

### 457   *More Education Coming*

A young man, having just received his degree from the university, rushed out saying, "Here I am, world; I have a B.A."

The world replied: "Sit down, son, and I'll teach you the rest of the alphabet."

### 458   *He Knew Him*

Tommy did not seem to understand subtraction, so the teacher tried to make it plain with the following example:

"Now, suppose Billy had fifty cents," said the teacher.

"Yes'm," said Tommy.

"And you asked him for twenty-five."

"Yes'm."

"How much do you think Billy would have then?"

"Fifty cents," said Tommy with a discouraged look.

### 459   *Alphabet*

"Willie," the teacher asked the new pupil, "do you know your alphabet?"

"Yes, miss," answered Willie.

"Well, then," continued the teacher, "what letter comes after A?"

"All the rest of them."

### 460   *Unfortunate*

Mother: "My child certainly has a lot of original ideas, doesn't he?"

Teacher: "Oh, yes, but it is unfortunate they are in spelling."

### 461   *Logical Conclusion*

Teacher: "Johnny, what is the meaning of the word 'furlough'?"

Johnny: "Mule."

Teacher: "How do you explain that, Johnny?"

Johnny: "Well, I saw in the paper the picture of a soldier riding on a mule, and underneath the picture it said, 'Going home on his furlough.' "

### 462   *Hurry*

The teacher said she wanted all the little boys and girls to be very, very still —so still that they could hear a pin drop. Very soon all were silent and motionless. Suddenly an excited little voice cried out, "Now, teacher, now's your chance —let 'er drop!"

### 463   *Why Not*

The parent-teacher group was involved in a serious discussion about possible after-school activities for the students. Among the many suggestions made were playgrounds, youth huts, bicycle trails, canteens, and even a student center with a paid supervisor.

Finally, a practical, gray-haired grandmother quietly asked, "Couldn't they go home?"

### 464 *Endangered*

After receiving a rather poor report card, the boy asked his teacher if she would reconsider his grades, adding, "At home I'm already on the list of endangered species."

### 465 *No-Fault Insurance*

An insurance investigator for auto claims indicates that he spends most of his time investigating collisions between cars, each of which was on its own side of the road, each of which had honked its horn at the other driver, and each of which was practically standing still at the time of impact.

### 466 *Agreeable*

"What's the shape of the earth?" the teacher asked Willie.

"Round."

"How do you know it's round?"

"All right, it's square. I don't want to start an argument."

### 467 *Not Fair*

Two little boys who had been naughty all day were told by the teacher that they must stay after school and write their names five hundred times. One of them began to watch the other unhappily. "Why aren't you writing, Tommy?" asked the teacher. Tommy burst into tears. "It ain't fair!" he sobbed. "His name's Lee and mine's Schluttermeyer!"

### 468 *Pennsylvania Dutch*

The pie is all but the cake is yet.

Go look the window out and see who comes the yard in.

When I was in town today, I bought myself poor.

### 469 *Interesting Language*

"What's the difference between a begonia and a double begonia?" asked one of the Quiz Kids.

And the other answered: "Well, a begonia is a kind of sausage, and sausage and battery is a crime, and monkeys crime trees, and trees a crowd, and roosters crow and make a noise, and a noise is a feature of your face just like eyes, and the opposite of eyes is nays, and a horse nays when it has a colt, and a colt is a very serious thing because it might develop into double begonia."—*Glenmore Jigger*

470    *A Short Dozen*

Two men were unloading a freight car of Florida fruit when they came across a broken box of grapefruit. Noticing the size, Pat exclaimed: "Mike, them's sure mighty fine or'nges. Do ye see the size of 'em?"

Mike took one look. "Begorra," he said, " 'twouldn't take very many of 'em to make a dozen!"

471    *That Explains It*

Teacher: "When I was your age I could answer any question in arithmetic."
Tommy: "Yes, miss, but you had a different teacher."

472    *Diet Would Help*

Teacher: "George, give me a sentence that includes the word 'fascinate.' "
Pupil, after deep thought: "My father has a vest with nine buttons, but he can only fascinate."

473    *Pretty Smart*

An elderly lady was visiting an asylum. Approaching one of the inmates, she strove to be congenial. "Have you," inquired the lady, "any idea of the time?"

The inmate smiled. "Certainly, madam," he replied. "Just one moment, please." He took a large ruler from his pocket and held it in the sunlight. Then he marked out the shadow that was cast, and made some rapid calculations. He fiddled with a compass and a plumb line, and then he turned triumphantly to the woman.

"Madam," he announced proudly, "it is exactly fourteen minutes after two o'clock."

"That's fine," the woman cried. "That was marvelous. But tell me—how do you do it?"

The inmate looked down modestly. "Oh," he returned, "it's just something that I have studied. I tell it by the sun."

"Wonderful!" exclaimed the lady. "But tell me something else. What do you do when it rains and the sun doesn't come out?"

"Oh," he shrugged, "I've got something for that, too."

"What's that?" urged the woman, showing new interest.

The inmate smiled. "Well," he answered proudly, "in that case I simply look at my watch!"—*Mark Hellinger, New York American*

474    *Sorry He Asked*

Lecturer: "Now, is there anyone here who would like to ask a question?"
Member of the audience: "Yeah, what time is it?"

### 475 *Pardon Me*

Nature lover, gazing at a giantic tree: "Oh, mammoth oak, if you could talk, what would you tell me?"

Gardener, nearby: "S'cuse me, ma'am, but he would most likely say, 'If you please, ma'am, I am not an oak; I am a spruce.' "

### 476 *They Weren't Farmers*

Three sailors were spending their leave in the country. Two of them got into a heated argument over what kind of animal a heifer was.

"It's a sort of pig," said one.

"Not on your life," replied the other. "It's a kind of sheep."

Finally they called in the third.

"Bill," said the first sailor, "what's a heifer—is it a pig or a sheep?"

Bill scratched his head. "To tell you the truth, shipmates," he said, "I don't know much about poultry."

### 477 *Head of the Class*

Teacher: "Use 'vicious' in a sentence."

Bright boy: "Best vicious for a merry Christmas and a happy New Year."

Teacher: "Don't you know the King's English?"

Bright boy: "Sure, and so is the Queen."

### 478 *Not in the Dictionary*

Here are some definitions not attributed to Webster:

*Archives:* Where Noah kept his bees.

*Athletics:* The excuse for institutions of higher learning.

*Bacteria:* Back of a cafeteria.

*Compliments:* Falsehoods in full dress.

*Darwin:* The man who made a monkey out of Adam.

*Etc.:* The sign used to make people think you know more than you do.

*Pedestrian:* A man who has two cars, a wife, and a son.

*Social tact:* Making people feel at home when you wish they were.

### 479 *More Fun Then*

The father of an eleven-year-old looked at his pride and joy, who was watching television with a bored expression.

"When I was your age," the father remarked, "I walked miles in blizzards, milked seven cows early each morning, and rode a horse to school instead of riding a comfortable bus. What do you think of that?"

The child looked up at his father and said, "Gee, I wish we could have that kind of fun now."

480    *Suit Yourself*

Bobby had handed in his composition with a long list of dots and dashes at the bottom of the sheet.

"What is the meaning of these marks?" asked the puzzled teacher.

"Those marks?" replied Bobby. "They are punctuation marks; you can put them in to suit yourself."

481    *Say That Again, Please*

The teacher was giving a lesson in natural history when suddenly she noticed that one of the boys was not listening.

"Johnny," she exclaimed, "what is the use of the reindeer?"

"Please, teacher, to make the flowers in the garden grow," said the happy little fellow with a blush.

482    *So They Said*

Said one eye to the other: "Just between us, there's something that smells."

Said one ear to the other: "Fancy meeting you on this block!"

Said the big rose to the little rose: "Hiya, bud."

Said the ceiling to the wall: "Hold me up, I'm plastered."

Said the dentist to the patient: "The Yanks are coming."

Said one stocking to another: "So long, I gotta run."

Said the salmon as he took the hook: "I'll get canned for this."

Said the cub to the north wind: "Don't blow so hard, I'm a little bear."

—*Robin Round-Table*

483    *As the Crow Flies*

Counsel for the prosecution was examining the witness. "Exactly how far is it between the two towns?" he asked.

"About five miles as the cry flows," replied the witness.

"You mean," corrected the attorney, "as the flow cried."

The judge leaned forward helpfully. "No," said he, "he means as the fly crows."

484    *Not Satisfied*

When the teacher of a progressive school was getting tired of endless discussion, she said: "Children, we've had enough talk. Let us now have some snappy arithmetic drill. How much is nine times nine?"

"Sixty-two," shouted an eager beaver.

"You are wrong, Alfred. Nine times nine is eighty-one."

"Let's put it to a vote," insisted the lad.

### 485 *Learned Them Good*

A poor student said to his English teacher at the end of the year: "Thanks! You was a good teacher, and you've learned us good!"

### 486 *It Must Be a Boid*

When some small-city slum children were taken on a field trip, little Tony, clinging to his teacher, shouted:

"Hey, teach—look at that boid!"

"Tony, that isn't a boid. It's a bird."

"Gee, but it choips just like a boid."

### 487 *He Is Learning*

When a first-grade pupil was asked what he had learned the first day in school, he said: "First of all, I learned that my name isn't Precious—it's Henry."

### 488 *Yes*

Question: "Are Santa's helpers subordinate clauses?"

### 489 *Any Other Choices?*

A student who had just completed a series of multiple-choice tests was asked by the teacher whether it pays to be honest. He promptly wanted to know what the five choices were.

### 490 *The Real Question*

Teacher: "Is a hen 'setting' or 'sitting'?"

Farmboy: "That doesn't interest me. When I hear a hen cackle, I want to know whether she's 'laying' or 'lying.'"

### 491 *A Child's Essay on Cats*

"Cats and people are funny animals. Cats have four paws, but only one ma. People have forefathers, but only one mother.

"Cats carry tails, and a lot of people carry tales, too.

"All cats have fur coats. Some people have fur coats, and the ones who don't, say catty things about the ones who do."

And then the teacher said, "Thus fur and no further."

### 492 *Waste of Time*

"I'm not going to school anymore," announced the youngster. "It's a complete waste of time. I can't read and I can't write, and they won't let me talk."

### 493 *He Had Experience*

Teacher: "What do you consider the greatest achievement of the ancient Romans?"

Student: "Speaking Latin."

494     *Dangerous "Animal"*

A first-grade teacher was telling her pupils about different wild animals. In order to test what they had learned, she asked, "Now, who can tell me the name of an animal that has horns and is very dangerous for us to get near?"

Little Bobby piped out enthusiastically, "I know, teacher—it's a truck!"

495     *English as Spoken*

"What does this expression 'Sez you' mean?" asked the British judge.

The clerk of the court replied: "My lord, it appears that this is a slang expression of American origin which has gained regrettable currency in the language of our people through the insidious agency of the cinema, and is, as I am led to understand, employed to indicate a state of dubiety in the mind of the speaker as to the veracity or credibility of a statement made to him."

"Oh yeah?" said the judge.

496     *Chopin to Liszt?*

Said Chopin, "It is easy to tell that the singer was English—he didn't sound his *h*'s when he sang."

Said Liszt, "That shows how little you know about music—the scale doesn't run above *G.*"

497     *A New Book*

Latin student to bookseller: "I want a copy of *Caesar's Garlic Wars.*"

498     *Great Poet Discovered*

Professor: "Did you write this poem without any outside help?"
Student: "I did."
Professor: "To think I would be lucky enough to have Lord Byron in my class!"

499     *Not Happy*

I didn't mind the waiters laughing at my French, but I didn't like it when they spoke better English than I.

500     *Good Reason*

"I'm glad I'm not a Frenchman.
"Why?"
"Because I can't speak French."

501     *Did It Alone*

Teacher: "Did your father help you with this example?"
Student: "No, I got it wrong myself."

### 502    *The Professors' Cars*

A father who visited his son at college asked him what he wanted for his birthday. The son replied that he wanted a new car. His father, looking at the college parking lot, said, "Look at all those ancient jalopies. Your present car is in much better shape than any of them."

The college student replied, "Those old cars don't belong to the students. They belong to the professors."

### 503    *No Excuse*

Traffic cop: "You're going the wrong way on a one-way street, sir, and you don't have your lights on."

Confused motorist: "I'm sorry, Officer. I'm a professor at the college nearby."

Traffic cop: "Ignorance is no excuse."

### 504    *Just Average*

Visitor: "You must have an unusually bright class. Whenever you asked a question—no matter how difficult—every student raised his hand."

Teacher: "They're just average students. Confidentially, the explanation for their hand-raising is that whenever we have a visitor, all students raise their hands. Those who know the answer raise the right hand; those who don't know the answer raise the left hand."

### 505    *All Bad*

Teacher to student: "Your work isn't half bad." Before the student could thank him for the compliment, the teacher added: "It's not half bad. It's all bad."

### 506    *Not I*

"Who wrote *Macbeth*?" the teacher asked.

"Honest, teacher—I didn't do it."

"You are fresh. Bring your father to school."

The father came and said, "My boy is not a liar. If he says he didn't do it, I believe him."

### 507    *Not Sure*

Another first-termer told his teacher that he wasn't quite sure whether his real name was Shoddup or Johnny Don't—the two names his parents called him.

### 508    *On the Dotted Line?*

Teacher: "Jimmy, where was the Declaration of Independence signed?"

Jimmy: "At the bottom, I guess."

509    *Young Critic*

Johnny: "My two-year-old brother tore up my composition."
Teacher: "What? Can he read already?"

510    *Don Quixote*

"Why are there so many different Spanish words for 'donkey'?"
"That's not surprising. Even their greatest book is called 'Donkey Jote.' "

511    *Appreciates Intelligence*

Professor, when asked why he talks to himself: "Because I like to talk to an intelligent person and I like to hear an intelligent person answer."

512    *A Funny Thing Happened*

Historians claim they have discovered a speech that Christopher Columbus made at the first Columbus Day dinner after his discovery of the New World. It began: "A funny thing happened to me on the way to India."

513    *He Didn't Cheat*

Parent: "Why do you think my son isn't good enough to remain in school?"
Principal: "Because your son has been flunking every subject."
Parent: "I still think he's a good boy. He may be flunking, but at least it shows he isn't cheating."

514    *Unfair Question*

The superintendent of a school in a neighboring town was unexpectedly called upon to address a group of youngsters in the schoolroom. To gain time, he asked, "Well, what shall I speak about?"

A young one in the front row, who had committed to memory a number of declamations, held up his hand, and in a shrill voice asked, "What do you know?"

515    *Important Question*

The professor was delivering the last lecture of the term. "The examination papers are in the hands of the printer," he concluded. "Now, are there any questions you would like answered?"

Silence prevailed for a moment. Then a voice piped up, "Who's the printer?"

516    *Unusual Counting*

When the teacher asked a first-grader to count from six up, the child promptly answered, "Six, seven, eight, nine, ten, jack, queen, king."

### 517 *Welcome Back*

Telegram received on opening of school after the summer vacation: TO ALL TEACHERS: HALLELUJAH! WE'RE GLAD YOU ARE BACK. HURRAH! It was signed by the mothers.

### 518 *Ambitious Youth*

The teacher asked his pupils to write an essay telling what they would do if they had a million dollars.

Every pupil except Willie began writing. Willie sat idle. When the teacher collected the papers, Willie handed in a blank sheet.

"How is this, Willie?" asked the teacher. "Is this your essay? All the other pupils have filled two sheets or more while you have done nothing!"

"Well," replied Willie, "that's what I'd do if I had a million dollars!"

### 519 *O Say Can You See*

One morning a recent arrival from Ireland was visiting an American school in company with a recent arrival from Spain. Their mission was to enroll their children. Each, in turn, was surprised to hear the students greet them with a song —which, to the former, sounded like "O'Shea can you see?" and to the latter "José can you see?"

### 520 *New Language*

Teacher: "What is the meaning of the word 'cubic'?"
Bright boy: "Cubic is the language in Cuba."

### 521 *That Explains It*

Anxious teacher: "Jimmy, you look very pale this morning. Are you ill?"
Jimmy: "No ma'am, but my mother washed my face for me this morning."

### 522 *Aging Slowly*

Teacher: "How old would a person be now if he was born in 1903?"
Student: "Man or woman?"
Teacher: "Why do you ask that?"
Student: "Because ten years ago when my brother graduated from high school he was seventeen and his girlfriend was sixteen. Now he's twenty-seven and she says she's twenty-one."

### 523 *Misprints*

The school paper carried a coupon with the following note: "Please sin and return." The error was corrected to read, "Please sing and return." Another reporter wrote: "The subject was cussed from various angles." The latter was a correction of the original report that the subject was "cursed." And one other report said that the "Glue Club did not sing so well."

### 524  *Could Be*

Jackie: "My teacher says I would stand a lot better in my class if I had more spunk. What is spunk?"

Ronnie: "I'm not sure, but I think it's the past participle of spank."

### 525  *Of Course*

The first grade was learning the letters of the alphabet. "What comes after T?" the teacher asked.

Nettie quickly answered, "V."

### 526  *Indecisive*

Dear Frank: I must explain that I was only joking when I wrote that I didn't mean what I said about reconsidering my decision not to change my mind. I really mean this.

### 527  *One Answer*

Teacher: "George, what is the third letter of the alphabet?"

George: "I don't know."

Teacher: "Of course you do. What do you do with your eyes?"

George: "Mom says I squint."

### 528  *Taxis or Taxes?*

When the teacher asked her class what caused the Revolutionary War, Jimmy volunteered the information that it "had something to do with automobiles."

"Oh, no, Jimmy!" protested the teacher. "That was in the days before the automobile."

"Well," retorted Jimmy, "they said it was on account of unjust taxis."

### 529  *After-Dinner Speaker*

Said Daniel, entering the lions' den: "Well, whoever does the after-dinner speaking, it won't be me!"

### 530  *Correct*

Teacher: "Have you ever heard of Julius Caesar?"

Pupil: "Yes, sir."

Teacher: "What do you think he would be doing now, if he were alive?"

Pupil: "Drawing an old-age pension."

### 531    *Unheard Of*

Jones: "Look at that bunch of cows."
Smith: "Not bunch—herd!"
Jones: "Heard what?"
Smith: "Herd of cows."
Jones: "Sure, I've heard of cows."
Smith: "I mean—a cow herd!"
Jones: "What do I care if a cow heard? I didn't say anything I shouldn't have."

### 532    *Good Question*

The children in Miss Jones's kindergarten class were thoroughly enjoying their field trip to the neighborhood fire department. The firefighters were also enjoying the youngsters' questions. One little boy asked, "But how do you get back up the pole?"

### 533    *Next Question*

Asked to paraphrase the sentence, "He was bent on seeing her," the pupil responded, "The sight of her doubled him up."

### 534    *He Was Lucky*

The teacher was instructing the class in physics. She was saying, "Sir Isaac Newton was sitting on the ground looking at a tree. An apple fell on his head, and from that he discovered gravity. Just think, children, isn't that wonderful?"

A small boy in the back row replied, "Yes'm, and if he had been setting in school looking at his books he wouldn't have discovered nothing."

### 535    *His Mistake*

It was Sunday morning in the men's class in a church. "Will you please tell me," said a member to the teacher, "how far in actual miles Dan is from Beersheba? All my life I have heard the familiar phrase 'from Dan to Beersheba,' but I have never known the distance."

Another member inquired, "Do I understand that Dan and Beersheba are names of places?"

"Yes," replied the teacher.

"That is one on me," continued the man. "I always thought they were husband and wife, like Sodom and Gomorrah."

### 536    *Right Answer*

Kenny could sense his teacher's displeasure as he struggled at fractions. "Suppose," she said, with a heavy sigh, "your family of eight has only one pie."

"There would be seven pieces," answered Kenny, " 'cause Mom would say she didn't want any."

537 *Heard in School*

A gladiator is something that keeps a room warm.
An easel is a small but vicious rodent.
In some countries people are put to death by elocution.
A saint is a dead clergyman.

538 *In No Hurry*

"All the little boys and girls who want to go to Heaven," said the Sunday school teacher, "please stand up."
All rose but Johnny.
"And doesn't this little boy want to go to Heaven?"
"N-not yet."

539 *Are You Sure?*

A teacher asked her students to compose sentences containing the word "beans."
The usual bright boy produced "My father grows beans," and the usual bright girl was ready with "My mother cooks beans."
Then a little one made this effort: "We are all human beans."

540 *The Quick and the Dead*

"What little boy can tell us the meaning of the expression 'The quick and the dead'?" asked the Sunday school teacher.
"Please, ma'am," Willie said, "the quick are the ones that get out of the way of automobiles, and the dead are the ones that don't."

541 *Stop—Go Hi Hi!*

Traffic rules are said to be the same in any language, but here's what a visitor to Japan copied from a printed document for English-speaking tourists who drive their own cars there:
1. At the rise of the hand of the policeman stop rapidly. Do not pass him by or otherwise disrespect him.
2. If pedestrian obstacle your path, tootle horn melodiously. If he continues to obstacle, tootle horn vigorously and utter vocal warning such as hi, hi.
3. If wandering horse by roadside obstacle your path, beware that he do not take fright as you pass him. Go soothingly by, or stop by roadside till he pass away.
4. If road mope obstacle your path refrain from pass on hill or round curves. Follow patiently till road arrive at straight level stretch. Then tootle horn melodiously and step on, passing at left and waving hand courteously to honorable road mope in passing.

5. Beware of greasy corner where lurks skid demon. Cease step on, approach slowly, round cautiously, resume step on gradually.

### 542    *Don't Quote Me*

After making a public address, the bishop said to the young reporter who was covering the event: "When you do your write-up, I would appreciate it if you didn't mention the anecdotes I related. I may want to use them in other speeches."

The newsman obliged by inserting this line in his article: "The bishop told several stories which cannot be repeated here."

### 543    *Boners*

Here is a choice collection of typographical boners.

The absence of the letter b in a word made these lines outrageous: "A man was arrested yesterday on the charge of having eaten a bus driver for demanding more than his fare." Another missing b accounted for this preposterous item: "An employee in the service of the government was accused of having stolen a small ox from the mails."

The society editor wrote concerning a bride: "Her feet were encased in shoes that might be taken for fairy boots." But what appeared was this: "Her feet were encased in shoes that might be taken for fairy boats."

Which recalls another: "Miss Blank will present a program of Easter music; Mrs. Bobbs will beat (Should have read, "be at.") the organ."

### 544    *It Sounded That Way*

"I hear you got expelled from school for calling the dean a fish."

"I didn't call him a fish. I just said, 'That's our dean,' real fast."

### 545    *Like Sap in a Tree*

Energy in a nation is like sap in a tree; it rises from the bottom up; it does not come from the top down. . . . When I was a schoolmaster, I used to say that the trouble about the college sophomore was that the sap of manhood was rising in him, but hadn't reached his head.—*Woodrow Wilson*

### 546    *Not So Dumb*

One of the greatest marksmen of the FBI was passing through a small town, and everywhere he saw evidence of amazing shooting. On trees, on walls, on fences, and on barns were numberless bull's-eyes with the bullet holes in the exact center. He asked to meet the one responsible for this great marksmanship.

The man turned out to be the village simpleton.

"This is the most wonderful marksmanship I have ever seen," exclaimed the FBI man. "How in the world do you do it?"

"Easy as pie," replied the simpleton. "I shoot first and draw the circles afterward."

### 547 *Practical Use*

The teacher was having trouble getting her students to learn decimals until she pointed out that they were necessary to figure out baseball batting averages.

### 548 *Good Choice*

"Suppose you found yourself on a desert island, Bob," said the teacher, "and could have only one book. Which book would you prefer?"

After thinking a moment, Bob replied, *"Boat Building for Amateurs."*

### 549 *Absentminded*

An absentminded professor went into a barber shop, and on being told to take off his hat, replied, "Certainly—I didn't know there were ladies present."

### 550 *Wait Until Dad Speaks*

Voice over telephone: "Tommy Hagan won't be in school today."
Teacher: "Who is this speaking, please?"
Voice: "This is my father speaking."

### 551 *A Good Course*

Daughter: "Dad, I'd like to take Domestic Silence."
Father: "Please do. It's about time we had a little peace and quiet at home."

### 552 *Not So Fast*

"Do you think it's right to punish folks for things they haven't done?" asked Johnny of his teacher.
"Of course not!" replied the teacher.
"Well, I haven't done my arithmetic."

### 553 *Education*

There's not much future in learning. The more you study, the more you know. The more you know, the more you forget. The more you forget, the less you know. The less you know, the less you forget. The less you forget, the more you know.

### 554 *He Named One*

Teacher: "What is a comet, Johnny?"
Johnny: "A star with a tail."
Teacher: "That's right. Can you name one?"
Johnny: "Mickey Mouse."

### 555    *Fast Thinking*

A small boy was told by his teacher to form a sentence using the words "defeat," "defense," and "detail." After thinking awhile, the boy handed this in: "De feat of de cat went over de fence before de tail."

### 556    *He Won't Pass*

Professor (endeavoring to impress on class the definition of the word *cynic*): "Young man, what would you call a man who pretends to know everything?"
Senior: "A professor!"

### 557    *But Good for You*

Teacher: "Tommy, what is nutritious food?"
Tommy: "Aw, it's something to eat that's filling but ain't got no taste to it."

### 558    *Easy Question*

Teacher: "Henry, analyze this sentence: 'It was getting to be milking time.' What mood?"
Henry: "The cow."

### 559    *Of Course*

Jimmy: "If you crossed an elephant with a fish, what would you get?"
Timmy: "Swimming trunks."

### 560    *Right*

Teacher: "Name two pronouns."
Susie: "Who? Me?"

### 561    *Nothing*

Fred: "Give me an example of nothing."
Ed: "That's easy—a bladeless knife with no handle."

### 562    *Strange*

The little boy at the zoo stared at the stork for a long time, then turned to his father and said, "Gee, Dad, he doesn't recognize me."

### 563    *Ain't Nobody Going*

The teacher asked the little girl if she was going to the birthday party. "No, I ain't going," was the reply.
The teacher corrected the child: "You must not say, 'I ain't going'; you must say, 'I am not going.' " And to impress the point she added: "I am not going. He is not going. We are not going. You are not going. They are not going. Now, dear, can you say all that?"

The little girl nodded and smiled brightly. "Sure!" she replied. "They ain't nobody going."

### 564   *Just a Suggestion*

Professor: "Every time I breathe, someone passes into eternity."
Friend: "Try cloves."

### 565   *The Difference*

*American novel:* A story in which two people want each other from the beginning but don't get each other until the end of the book.
*French novel:* A story in which the two people get together right at the beginning, but from then until the end of the book they don't want each other anymore.
*Russian novel:* A story in which the two people don't want each other or get each other—and for 800 pages brood about it.—*Erich Maria Remarque*

### 566   *Look, Mom*

Little Willie, exhibiting his skill in riding a new bicycle, came down the street in front of his house. "Look, Mom," he cried, folding his arms, "no hands!"
Again he came into view, this time coasting with his feet off the pedals. "Look, Mom," he shouted, "no feet!"
Half an hour passed, and Willie again put in his appearance. This time, somewhat subdued, he gurgled, "Look, Mom, no front tooth."

### 567   *Of Course*

Teacher: "What are your parents' names?"
Johnny: "Papa and Mamma."

### 568   *Misinformed*

A grade-school student was having trouble with punctuation.
"Never mind, sonny," said the visiting school board president, consolingly. "It's foolish to bother about commas; they don't amount to much, anyway."
"Elizabeth Ann," said the teacher, "please write this sentence on the board: 'The president of the board says the teacher is misinformed.' Now," she continued, "put a comma after 'board' and another after 'teacher.' "

### 569   *Correct Total*

A sugar planter in Hawaii took a friend from Oregon to the edge of a volcano. "That crater is 70,004 years old," he explained to the friend.
"How do you get the exact age?" asked the newcomer. "I can understand the seventy thousand, but where do you get the four?"
"Well," said the planter, "the volcano was seventy thousand years old when I arrived, and I've been here four years."

### 570    *One Explanation*

An American engineer returned recently from a mission to the Soviet Union. The Russians, he reported, were fascinated by the Americans' use of the expression "O.K."

"But what is this 'Okie-Dokie'?" one Russian asked him.

Before he could answer, another Russian interrupted with, "Don't be a dope. It's the feminine of 'O.K.' "

### 571    *Logical Answer*

Alice: "Alex, do you know why they are not going to make telephone poles any longer?"

Alex: "Of course I do—because they are long enough."

### 572    *One Explanation*

Small boy, scowling over report card, to his dad: "Naturally I seem stupid to my teacher; she's a college graduate."

### 573    *Amazing Intellect!*

Here is an assortment of answers from high school test papers:

It was raining cats and dogs, and there were poodles in the road.

Diphtheria and smallpox are prevented by intersection.

Moses died before he reached Canada, but he saw it from a mountain.

Filet Mignon is an opera written by Puccini.

### 574    *It Seems That Way*

Teacher: "What is the longest word in the English language?"

Student: "The one following the statement, 'And now a word from our sponsor.' "

### 575    *Penny Wise*

Economy is too late at the bottom of the purse.—*Seneca*

### 576    *Another Reason*

The teacher was trying to impress upon her class the advantages of peace and disarmament. "How many of you object to war?" she asked.

Up went several hands. "Jimmy, tell us why you object to war."

" 'Cause wars make history," replied Jimmy soberly.

### 577    *Common Ground*

A group of professional men had gathered in the lobby of a hotel where a banquet was being given, and they proceeded to make themselves known to each other.

"My name is Rodale," said one, extending his hand. "I'm a painter, work in watercolors chiefly."

"I'm happy to know you," replied the other. "I'm an artist, too. I work in bronze."

"Now, isn't that a coincidence?" chimed in a third. "I happen to be a sculptor. I work in marble."

Then a quiet little fellow, bespectacled and with a short beard, extended his hand. "Glad to make the acquaintance of you gentlemen," he said, "for I have a common interest with you. I work in ivory. I'm a college professor."

## 578   *Looking Ahead*

After a junior high school class toured the White House, the teacher asked the students to write their impressions of the visit. One boy wrote: "I was especially glad to have this opportunity to visit my future home."

## 579   *He Knew the Answer*

Teacher: "Now, Willie, if James gave you a dog, and David gave you a dog, how many would you have?"

Willie: "Four."

Teacher: "Now, Willie, think hard. Are you sure you'd have four dogs if James gave you one and David gave you one?"

Willie: "Yep. You see, I already got two dogs."

## 580   *His Impression*

A teacher had told her class of youngsters that Milton, the poet, was blind. The next day she asked if any of them remembered what Milton's great affliction was.

"Yes'm," replied one little fellow, seriously. "He was a poet."

## 581   *Valuable Information*

Sign at a railroad crossing: "The average time it takes a train to pass this crossing is fourteen seconds—whether your car is on it or not."

## 582   *Correct?*

Teacher: "Annie, give the formula for water."

Annie: "Yes, sir. *HIJKLMNO.*"

Teacher: "Whatever are you driving at? Do you think you're in kindergarten?"

Annie: "No sir. Yesterday you said it was 'H to O.' "

## 583   *Not His Name*

"Does this package belong to you? The name is blurred."

"Can't be mine. Mine's McGinty."

### 584 *Pretty Smart*

The teacher was giving a mental drill. "Bobby, which month has twenty-eight days?"

Bobby had forgotten. But after a moment he came up with the answer: "They all have."

### 585 *English as She Is Taught*

Many years ago (1905) Caroline B. LeRow was the editor of a book, *English as She Is Taught*. Mark Twain wrote the introduction. The book contained the actual answers to questions asked in the public schools. It is obvious when one reads the answers which follow that the problems of education have been with us for a long time.

#### The Meaning of Words

*Aristocracy:* To be stuck up.
*Burglarize:* To make burglars.
*Capillary:* A little caterpiller.
*Emissary:* A foreign missionary.
*Equestrian:* One who walks on foot.
*Erudition:* State of being erude.
*Interloper:* One who runs away to get married.
*Miscellaneous:* All mixed up.
*Parasite:* A kind of umbrella
*Plagiarist:* A writer of plays.
*Prism:* A prim precise person.
*Publican:* A man who does his prayers in public.
*Technology:* according to the text.
*Technology:* something which teaches you to be very tecknical in your remarks.
*Tenacious:* Ten acres of land.
A great many people alienate from their country to this.
She is related to me by animosity.
She dresses very auspicious.
He had a chronic disease—something the matter with the chrone.
We should never commiserate a person even if we dislike them.
The officer is to be tried for dissertation of his office.
He was exhilarated to a better place.
You should fascinate the vine to the wall.
The marriage was illegible.
I liquidate you from all blame.
The strawberry crop was magnanimous.
This examination makes me feel very nauceous.

You will see how pecuniary he is when I tell you he is going to marry for money.

The earth perennially revolves round the sun.

She was very quick at repertoire.

People become full of retisense when they are silent.

The men employed by the Gas Company go round and speculate the meter.

The birds subsidize in the summer for the most part on fruits.

The telescope is very transparent because you can see through it.

They had a strawberry vestibule.

The earth makes a vicissitude around the sun once a year.

### 586     *Grammatical*

Capital is used at beginning of parigraf.

Every sentence and name of God must begin with a caterpillar. (You mean capital letter?)

An Exclamation Point is what causes supprise.

Grammer is how to talk good.

Grammar gives us the languish.

Grammar is to tell us the parts of speeth.

A common noun is small things.

A proper noun is peoples names.

A pronoun is a word when we cant get a noun.

A pronoun is a word which is just as good as a noun.

The two kinds of Pronouns is I and O.

The horses run *fastly.* This is an adverb.

The comparative degree expresses that one thing is up higher than another and the Supulative is the highest of all.

All sentences are either simple or confound.

Rhythm is a horse trotting on a road.

### 587     *Mathematical*

A straight line is any distance between two places.

Parallel lines are lines that can never meet until they run together.

A Horace uncle line is a line that isn't crooked.

A circle is a round straight line with a hole in the middle.

Things that are equal to each other are equal to anything else.

To find the number of square feet in a room, you multiply the room by the number of the feet. The product is the result.

### 588     *Geographical*
####     (American)

The three natural divisions of America are Europe, Ashea, and Africa.

America is divided into the Passiffic slope and the mississippi valey.

The climit of America is very worm.

The Rocking Mountains are the graitest in America.

The great lakes of America are Siperior, Ontarria and Hurryon, Michigan.

The United States is quite a small country compared with some other countries, but is about as industrious.

The manufactured products of the United States is fish and agriculture and imports.

New York is bounded by Montreal.

Philadelphia is the capitol of New York and it is in the south West Part.

The Rocky Mountains are on the western side of Philadelphia.

The Alaginnies are mountains in Philadelfia.

The Arondack Mountains are north of Canada.

The Yosemity Valley is the highest mountain in the world.

The Mississippi River runs soulth and empies into Mexico.

Mason and Dixon's line is the Equater.

Canada is south of New York.

California is the capitol of San Francisco.

### (European)

In Austria the principal occupation is gathering Austrich feathers.

The principal industries of Germany are manufacturing, agriculture, and the cultivation of the intellect.

Russia in the time of Peter the Great was a very cold country and its inhabitants lived in Siberia.

Portugal is separated from Spain by the Mediteranian Sea.

The two most famous volcanoes of Europe are Sodom and Gomorrah.

Ireland is called the Emigrant Isle because it is so beautiful and green.

The imports of a country are the things that are paid for. The exports are the things that are not.

Pine apples grow on pine trees.

Climate lasts all the time and weather only a few days.

589    *Historical*
### (American)

Christopher Columbus was called the Father of his Country.

Queen Isabella of Spain sold her watch and chain and other millinery so that Columbus could discover America.

The Puritans found an insane asylum in the wilds of America.

They were called Puritans because they were more quiet than the Episcopalians.

William Penn discovered Philadelphia and laid out its streets.

Benedict Arnold was greatly regretted by the Americans as well as by the English.

George Washington was born in 1492.

Gen. Washington is famous for the Washington Monument.

Washington wrote the Declareation of Independence in 1492.

### (English)

The Habeas Corpus Act said that a body whether alive or dead could be produced in court.

Chivalry is a fight on horseback between two horsemen in an open field.

The Middle Ages come in between antiquity and posterity.

Henry Eight was famous for being a great widower having lost several wives.

### (Roman)

Julius Caesar was quite a military man on the whole.

Julius Caesar is noted for his famous telegram despatch I came I saw I conquered.

### 590    *Intellectual*

Longfellow has indeed told the tale of Evangeline fully well.

Edgar Allan Poe was a very curdling writer.

Webster is noted for his getting up the dictionary. He also wrote other things besides this.

Ben Jonson survived Shakespeare in some respects.

Chaucer was the father of English pottery.

Milton had a very intellectual mind.

Tennyson is a very populus poet.

### 591    *Philosophical*

Sun melts ice by the law of cohesion of atoms.

The reason a body falls when not supported is that there is not enough air under it to keep it up and so it has to fall or the specific gravity is not great enough to hold it up.

### 592    *Physiological*

When food is swallowed it passes through the windpipe and stops at the right side and some of it goes to make blood.

In the stomach starch is changed to cane-sugar and cane-sugar to sugar-cane.

We all have a very important elementary cannal.

The heart manufactures the blood and the liver keeps it going.

When the heart beats it stirs up the blood and that digests the food.

The work of the heart is to repair the different organs in about half a minute.

The optic nerve is the principal nerve used in digestion.

Nerves always give us the toothache.

The bones need constant oiling. This oil is called cartilege and runs from all the glands in the body.

The eyes are set in two sockets in a bone which turns up at the end and then becomes the nose.

The blood flows through the alimentery canal into the abdominal canopy.

The blood is putrefied in the lungs by inspired air.

The cow has a pulse as well as anybody else.

All animals that have feet are called quadrupeds.

### 593 *Political*

The world would be in a state of cosmos if it had no system of government.

The Constitution of the United States is that part of the book at the end which nobody reads.

The three departments in the general government are the White House, Custom House and United Treasury.

The three departments of the government is the President rules the world, the governor rules the state, the mayor rules the city.

There are two political divisions in the United States the democrats and republican.

### 594 *Oratorical*

Elocution is opening the mouth wide open.

Vigorous breathing gives you wind in the lungs.

Emphasis is putting more distress on one word than another.

### 595 *Exam Time*

More boners are pulled on school exams than there are jokes on television. A few standouts follow:

William Tell invented the telephone.

In mathematics, Persia gave us the dismal system.

Chemistry is the study of how a thing that is busted gets together under certain situations, and how them that's together gets separated.

A circle is a round line with no kinks in it, joined up so as not to show where it began.

To keep milk from turning sour, keep it in the cow.

Universal suffrage was when the whole world suffered.

Savages are people who don't know what wrong is until missionaries show them.

An antique is something no one would be seen with if there were more of them, but which everyone wants when no one has any.—*Chatham Blanketeer, Elkin, North Carolina.*

### 596 *Logical*

The teacher was trying to explain the meaning of the word "sufficient."

"Now," she said brightly, "suppose there was a cat here and I gave him a saucerful of milk, which the cat drank. Then I gave him another saucerful and he drank that also. But when I gave him a third, he would drink only half of it. We can say that the cat had sufficient. Now, Billy, what does 'sufficient' mean?"

The youngster pondered for a moment, then replied: "Sufficient means a cat full of milk."

### 597     *Banana vs. Sausage*

A Japanese boy learning English is credited with the following thesis on the banana:

"The banana are great fruit. He are constructed in the same architectural style as sausage, different being skin of sausage are habitually consumed, while it is not advisable to eat wrappings of banana.

"The banana are held aloft while consuming, sausage are usually left in reclining position. Sausage depend for creation on human-being or stuffing machine, while banana are pristine product of honorable Mother Nature.

"In case of sausage, both conclusions are attached to other sausage; banana, on other hands, are attached one end to stem and opposite termination entirely loose. Finally, banana are strictly of vegetable kingdom, while affiliation of sausage often undecided."

### 598     *Why Fire Engines Are Red*

Here's a string of reasoning, illogical, but how are you going to get around it?

$2 \times 2$ is 4.

$3 \times 4$ is 12.

Twelve is a ruler.

Queen Mary was a ruler.

Queen Mary is a ship.

A ship sails the sea.

The sea has fish.

A fish has fins.

The Russians beat the Finns.

The Russians are red.

Fire engines are always rushin'.

Hence, fire engines are red.

### 599     *Malapropisms*

The king wore a robe trimmed with vermin.

The watchwords of the French Revolution were Liberty, Equality, Maternity.

A quorum is a place to keep fish in.

A vegetarian is a horse doctor.

Socrates died from an overdose of wedlock.

### 600 Coming or Going?

An absentminded professor went through a revolving door and said, "Bless me! I can't remember whether I was going in or coming out."

### 601 Shakespeare Must Have Known!

There weren't any automobiles in those days, but Shakespeare certainly must have known what was coming, judging by these lines from his plays:

Horns to make one mad.—Merry Wives of Windsor, III, 5

O, how the wheel becomes it.—Hamlet, IV, 5

Whence is that knocking?—Macbeth, II, 2

The battery once again.—Henry V, III, 3

A horse! A horse! My kingdom for a horse!—Richard III, V, 4

### 602 Easy

The father was very curious when he observed that Junior was working quite diligently on his homework, so he inquired as to what the child was studying.

The boy replied that he was preparing a report on the condition of the world, to which his father asked, "Isn't that a pretty tough assignment for a third-grader?"

"Oh, no, Dad," said the youth, "there are four of us in the class working on it."

### 603 Mangled Expressions

You could have knocked me down with a fender.

He's a ragged individualist.

Home wasn't built in a day.

Up at the crank of dawn.

Words of one cylinder.

The fly in the oatmeal.—Goodman Ace

### 604 Modern Math

Teacher: "Tell me, Johnny, what is half of eight?"

Johnny: "Which way do you mean?"

Teacher: "What do you mean by 'which way'?"

Johnny: "Well, on top or sideways?"

Teacher: "What possible difference could it make?"

Johnny: "See, the top half is 'zero' but sideways, it's 'three.' "

### 605 Seems Unreasonable

Teacher: "How much is six and four?"

Pupil: "That's about eleven, ain't it?"

Teacher: "Six and four are ten."

Pupil: "But six and four can't be ten—five and five are ten.

606 *Smart*

Man on the street: "Hey there, you've got that ladder upside down."
Man on ladder: "I know. I put it that way so I would be nearer the bottom if I should happen to fall from the top.

607 *Good at History*

Teacher: "Billy, what did Paul Revere say at the end of his ride?"
Billy: "Whoa, whoa."

608 *A Good Combination*

"So your son is in college? How is he making it?
"He isn't! I'm making it, and he's spending it."

609 *He Didn't Pass*

The pastor was testing the knowledge of the junior class at Sunday school. "What," he asked, "are the sins of omission?"
After a few moments of silence, one of the youngsters timidly answered: "They're the sins we should've committed but didn't."

610     "I may say without boasting" is always the beginning of a boastful remark.

611     Every time we get down to brass tacks, the points are sticking up.

612     I've over-educated myself in all the things I shouldn't have known at all.—*Noel Coward*

613     An et cetera and a vice versa, make any sentence sound much worsa.
—*Herbert V. Prochnow*

614     A tactful person never blows his knows or his nos.

615     Patience is something you admire about the driver behind you and don't understand in the one ahead.

616     If the world keeps on having trouble, Americans will find out where all those foreign countries are located.

617     I always learn more by listening than talking, but it isn't as much fun.

618     America is the only country left where we teach languages so that no pupil can speak them.—*John Erskine*

619     It's what you learn after you know it all that counts.—*John Wooden*

620     We have met some persons who never drank at the fountain of education; they just gargled.

621    The main thing you learn from radio and television is that the country is full of sopranos and rock bands.

622    If you can't run things your way, you can always say a little later, "I told you so."

623    Some people know more when you try to tell them something than when you ask them something.

624    He who laughs last must be pretty stupid or he wouldn't wait that long.

625    The only man who really needs a tailcoat is a man with a hole in his trousers.

626    The fellow who keeps tooting his own horn has everyone dodging to keep out of his way.

627    Nothing beats a cold shower before breakfast except no cold shower before breakfast.

628    *Free verse:* The triumph of mind over meter.

629    Everything is relative: If a monkey had fallen from the tree in place of an apple, Newton would have discovered the origin of species instead of the law of gravity.

630    If you aren't too conceited, people will give you credit for knowing more than you do.

631    *Patience:* The willingness to listen to the other person tell you his troubles before you tell him yours.

632    He is the kind of person who believes he can save time by stopping his watch.

633    When a little bird whispers some gossip in your ear, be sure it isn't a cuckoo bird.

634    The horsepower of our cars is increasing about 10 percent faster each year than the horse sense of our drivers.

635    Among the things we don't understand is how a mosquito can get along without any sleep.

636    If the bravest are the tenderest, the cow that provided our dinner was a coward.

637    A citizen wants to know where the population of this country is the most dense. That's an easy one—from the neck up.

638     The way to win an argument is to stay out of it.

639     I do not believe in the collective wisdom of individual ignorance.—
*Thomas Carlyle*

640     Of the six senses, the most important is common sense.

641     They say a mosquito can fly ten miles. But it isn't the distance he flies that bothers us. It's what he does when he stops.

642     A stop sign can't talk, but it's not as dumb as the guy who pays no attention to it.

643     We like a man who comes right out and says what he thinks—when he agrees with us.

644     What you don't know won't hurt you, but it will amuse a lot of people.

645     There are two sides to every question that we're not especially interested in.

646     Many an argument is sound—merely sound.

647     The fewer the facts, the better the argument.

648     America has more than 100 million motor-vehicle missiles, some of them not very well guided.

649     It is always dullest just before the yawn.

650     Those without a college education have one advantage. They aren't filled with gloom when the football team loses.

651     A college star proved a washout in pro baseball. Four years an athlete on the campus and nothing to show for it but an education.

652     The person who says the art of conversation is dead never waited outside a phone booth for someone to finish talking.

653     "Only a fool is certain about anything," declares a college professor. Are you certain about this, doctor?

654     Remember, no locomotive whistles at a railroad crossing to keep up its courage.

655     Being bald has its good points. If you have no hair on your head, there is no temptation to part it in the middle.

656     A 100 percent optimist is a man who believes the thinning out of his hair is only temporary.

657     A bee expert says a bee has from 4,900 to 13,800 eyes. If that's true, then why does it so often sit down in the wrong place?

658     Experience is the one perpetual best-seller—everybody is continually buying it.

659     Learn to say kind things—nobody ever resents them.

660     Rear lights for pedestrians are sometimes advocated. But this would make it too easy for motorists.

661     A motorist complains that you sometimes have to get into the middle of an intersection to see the signpost. Lots of drivers get into the middle of the signpost before they see the intersection.

662     A Texas inventor thinks he will soon be able to run an automobile on water alone. Meanwhile, it wouldn't be such a bad scheme if the drivers tried out the idea on themselves.

663     Nothing pleases an ignorant person so much as giving advice.

664     Motto for users of the Harvard Classics—"Know thy shelf."

665     *Flaw:* What a Harvard graduate thinks you walk on in a house.

666     A shallow thinker never leaves a deep impression.

667     The person with a mind that is too open gets a lot of worthless ideas dumped into it.

668     If you rest your chin in your hands when you think, it will keep your mouth shut so you won't disturb yourself.

669     Opinion is the substitute we use for thought.

670     It takes brains to know whether a knock at the door is opportunity or education.

671     There are five senses, but still some people don't seem to have any.

672     Before you criticize a person for letting the grass grow under his feet, you ought to find out if his power mower is out of order.

673     With haircuts at their present price, two heads are not better than one.

674     A prehistoric skeleton has been found, its legs wrapped around its neck. This would seem to indicate that the compact car is older than we had supposed.

675     If you don't do your own thinking, you may do someone else's work.

676     Some people think they are generous because they give away free advice.

677     Canon Barnes said the men who by superior mental power ought to mold the thought of their time are ignored. We felt just like this when our first manuscript was sent back to us.

678     Most of us know how to say nothing—few of us know when.

679     We all admire the wisdom of people who ask us for advice.

680     A newspaper carried the notice that John Doe was a "defective" on the police force. This was a typographical error. It should have said, "John Doe is a detective on the police farce."

681     Two heads may be better than one, but they can certainly confuse a driver if they are both in the back seat.

682     Experience is knowing all the things you shouldn't do.

683     Nothing gives a man indigestion like eating his own words.

684     The person who gives everyone a piece of his mind ends up with a vacuum.—*Herbert V. Prochnow, Jr.*

685     After you hear two eyewitnesses to an automobile accident, you're not so sure about history.

686     A wise man is certain of few things—a fool of everything.

687     Protect the birds. The dove brings peace and the stork brings tax exemptions.

688     Sometimes you can make a very effective statement by holding your tongue.

689     Unfortunately, a person who tells all he knows doesn't stop there.

690     *Cynic:* A person who knows everything and believes nothing.

691     The trouble with most of us is that we would rather be ruined with praise than saved by criticism.

692     *Expert:* A person who can take something you already knew and make it sound confusing.

693     No one is exempt from talking nonsense; the misfortune is to do it solemnly.

694     A skeptic is a fellow who won't take know for an answer.

695     "It is I," said he, for he had bought a book called *Thirty Days to Perfect Grammar.*

696     Education is the method by which an ignorant man is given confidence in himself.

697     Someday an enterprising statistician will figure the time lost in figuring statistics.

698     A person is never too old to learn, and that's probably why so many of us keep putting it off.

699     The man who goes through life looking for something soft will find it between his ears.

700     The fellow who says there is nothing new in the world might try thinking.

701     When father gets the bill, he knows that higher education certainly is.

702     A youngster's low math grade nowadays may be due to a weak battery in his pocket calculator.

703     The United States has a very large corn crop this year, as we have observed on TV.

704     If lawyers are disbarred and clergymen defrocked, doesn't it follow that electricians can be delighted, musicians denoted, cowboys deranged, models deposed, tree surgeons debarked and dry cleaners depressed?—*Bloomer (Wisconsin) Advance*

705     Traffic violators should be sentenced to thirty days as pedestrians.

706     If you want a person to repeat something, tell him it is in the strictest confidence.

707     Children who can't read are hard to manage because they can't mind their Ps and Qs if they don't know their ABCs.

708     It takes two kinds of people to make the world—poets to write about the glories of autumn, and the rest of us to rake them.

709     If ignorance is bliss, what's the sense of giving intelligence tests?

710     To me the charm of an encyclopedia is that it knows—and I needn't. —*Francis Yeats-Brown*

711     We sort of like the moron who said when his feet get hot he turns the hose on them.

712     Sometime during the course of every day one ought to make at least a few sensible remarks.

713     A woman drives an automobile as well as a man, except when she's in the back seat.

714     A prejudiced person is anyone who is too stubborn to admit I'm right.

715     A person's mind may be broad but have no depth.

716     "Man has twelve billion brain cells," says an anatomist. And if he get in an especially tight corner he will use a dozen or so of them as a last resort.

717     Asked by his teacher what he would say if he cut down a cherry tree, a student cried: "Timberrrrrrr!"

718     Free speech is a great blessing—until the other fellow begins talking too much.

719     The weaker the argument, the stronger the words.

720     It often shows a very fine command of language to say nothing.

721     Great minds discuss ideas; average minds discuss events; small minds discuss people.

722     Overheard: "We don't want nothing else but the English language spoke in this country, and don't you forget it!"

723     An astronomer says there is "practically" no limit to space. That's the way we like our astronomers—conservative.

724     In 1870 it took eight days to cross the United States by train.

725     Always hold your head up, but be careful to keep your nose at a friendly level.

726     *Censor:* One who knows more than he thinks you ought to know.

727     If you know you don't know much, you are smarter than most people.

728     A committee meeting is a long and tortuous route to an obvious conclusion.

729     *Definition of a bore:* Here today and here tomorrow.

730     To feel themselves in the presence of true greatness many men find it necessary only to be alone.—*Tom Masson*

731     An idea isn't responsible for the people who believe in it.—*Don Marquis*

732     A man is usually conservative on the subject with which he is best acquainted.

733     The little boy's definition of a professor: Someone who goes to college and never gets out.

734     No one gains by listening only to the things he believes.

735     We're never quite sure of the economy of saving on education and spending more for jail wardens.

736     A college senior is educated if he can ask for his roommate's suit in a way that makes it seem like an honor to let him wear it.

737     Sometimes a book on child psychology can be more helpful as a paddle.

738     *Education:* One of the few things a person is willing to pay for and not get.—*William Lowe Bryan*

739     Time marches on. Back in Barnum's day there was only one sucker born each minute.

740     It is reported that students in one university voted their approval of the Ten Commandments. Now let's tackle some other problem.

741     It is said that the sister states are Miss Ouri, Mary Land, Allie Bama, Ida Ho, Callie Fornia, Della Ware, Louisa Ana, Minnie Sota, and Flora Da.

742     There's no fool like an old fool—because it's the experience that always counts.

743     *Expert:* A man who has stopped thinking.—*Frank Lloyd Wright*

744     You can lead a boy to college, but you can't make him think.—*Elbert Hubbard*

745     A conceited person is one who believes that what he doesn't know isn't knowledge.

746     It's all right to have an open mind if you know what to let in.

747     If as much time were spent polishing brains as polishing fingernails, the world would have more polish.

748    After hearing five different ways of pronouncing Solzhenitsyn, we finally decided to pronounce it Solzhenitsyn.

749    A low-brow tells what he thinks. A high-brow tells what others think.

750    A man may have an open mind with nothing taking advantage of the opening.

751    An intelligent person is one who understands the obvious.

752    It's good to be with someone who doesn't know anything and keeps it to himself.

753    It doesn't pay to tell your son that most great men have forgotten all they knew about algebra.

754    Johnny, doing homework: "Dad, is water works all one word, or do you spell it with a hydrant?"

755    Small boy, explaining to police why he was running away from home: "Today is report card day."

756    *Precocious child:* The one who took his nose apart to see what made it run.

757    A chip on the shoulder always indicates that there is wood higher up.

758    Usually the first screw to get loose in a person's head is the one that controls the tongue.

759    It has been said that the only thing we learn from history is that we do not learn.—*Chief Justice Earl Warren*

760    *Zoo:* A place devised for animals to study the habits of human beings.
—*Oliver Herford*

761    Anything parents haven't learned from experience they can now learn from their children.

762    *Et cetera:* A word that makes people think you know more than you do.

763    The highest tuition in the world is for the school of experience.

764    Confidence is the feeling you sometimes have before you fully understand a situation.

765    Man cannot live by incompetence alone.—*Laurence J. Peter*

766     One good thing about a college education is that it helps you to worry more intelligently about things all over the world.

767     Never lend books, for no one ever returns them; the only books I have in my library are books that other folks have lent me.—*Anatole France*

768     Mr. (Irvin) Cobb took me into his library and showed me his books, of which he has a complete set.—*Ring Lardner*

769     A university is what a college becomes when the faculty loses interest in students.—*John Ciardi*

770     There is only one rule for being a good talker: learn to listen.—*Christopher Morley*

771     If someone did not have the courage to be stupid now and then, the world would be a terribly dull place.

772     The Romans would never have found time to conquer the world if they had been obliged first to learn Latin.—*Heinrich Heine*

773     Never learn to do anything. If you don't learn, you will always find someone else to do it for you.—*Mark Twain*

774     Illiteracy is bad, but it's not as bad as being able to read all the daily news.

775     The student in the middle of the class has the best chance for success. He is not smart enough to be a professor and he's too smart to have to work.

776     The American housewife is going to have to go to school longer to be as smart as some of the gadgets she now gets for her home.

777     A great many people mistake opinions for thoughts.—*Herbert V. Prochnow, Jr.*

778     All of us ought to swap problems because we all know exactly how to solve the other person's problem. *Herbert V. Prochnow, Jr.*

779     Many men shine in life—some inside their heads and others on top of their heads.

780     Wise words are sometimes spoken in jest, but many more foolish ones are spoken in earnest.

781     In a lifetime most people decide whether they are going to be wise or otherwise.

782     The less a person knows, the more he wants to tell it.

783     No one is ignorant until someone finds it out.

784     The high school is the place where the band practices.—*Robert M. Hutchins*

785     Research is something that tells you a mule has two ears.—*Albert D. Lasker*

786     What is history but a fable agreed upon?—*Napoleon*

787     *Repartee:* The snappy comeback a person thinks of on the way home.

788     A wise man thinks all he says; a fool says all he thinks.

789     If ignorance is bliss, why aren't there more happy people?

790     *Genius:* The ability to turn off the cold and hot water faucets at the same time.

791     *Rhetoric:* A long speech with words of many syllables.

792     *Ponder:* To arrive at a stupid conclusion slowly.

793     *Possibly:* Three syllables that mean either yes or no.

794     *Plagiarists:* All the makers of dictionaries.—*Voltaire*

795     One reason so many poets are poor is that there are so many poor poets.

796     There's one thing to be said for ignorance—it sure causes a lot of interesting arguments.

797     A wise man isn't as certain of anything as a fool is of everything.

798     Historians tell us about the past and economists about the future. Only the present is confusing.

799     A narrow mind and wide mouth usually go together.

800     Genius is an infinite capacity for picking brains.

801     Few families are so well off that they don't know it when Junior is in college.

802     The only thing to do with good advice is to pass it on. It is never of any use to oneself.—*Oscar Wilde*

803     *Consult:* To seek another's approval of a course already decided on.—*Ambrose Bierce*

804     A brilliant conversationalist is one who is adept in the art of using meaningless words to say a lot about nothing.

805     Honestly, now, which is more offensive: trying to talk when one's mouth is full, or when one's head is empty?

806     We must stand up to be seen, speak up to be heard, shut up to be appreciated.

807     Sometime a Ph.D. candidate will write a thesis on the average life of an undented fender on a Sunday afternoon.—*Herbert V. Prochnow*

808     Talking comes by nature; silence by wisdom.

809     No one has yet been able to perform the feat of keeping the mouth and the mind open at the same time.

810     When you know the right answers, no one asks you the right questions.

811     Always listen to the opinion of others; it probably won't do you any good, but it will them.

812     If you don't learn anything from your mistakes, there's no sense in making them.

813     *Mason-Dixon Line:* The division between "you all" and "youse guys."

814     *Collective noun:* A garbage can.

815     *Innocent bystander:* A person who was not smart enough to get out of the way.

816     *Caterpillar:* A fishing worm with a raccoon coat.

817     Abraham Lincoln wouldn't have had such a tough time getting an education if he'd lived in these times. His height would entitle him to a basketball scholarship.

818     Columbus was wrong—the world is flat.

819     First, man learns to talk. After many years, he learns to keep still.

820     The best advice—don't give it.

821     Learn from the mistakes of others. You can't live long enough to make them all yourself.

822     We might all be successful if we followed the advice we give the other fellow.

823     Lincoln once walked nine miles to borrow a book. Now they close the libraries on his birthday.

824     Algebra is now taught in the third grade and spelling in college.

825     The age of chivalry is not dead—yet. If a teenage girl drops her book, a teenage boy will kick it over to her.

826     Be obscure clearly.—*E. B. White*

827     Slang is the language that takes off its coat, spits on its hands, and goes to work.—*Carl Sandburg*

828     Writing free verse is like playing tennis with the net down.—*Robert Frost*

829     *TV:* Chewing gum for the eyes.—*Frank Lloyd Wright*

830     "Reeling and Writhing, of course, to begin with," the Mock Turtle replied, "and the different branches of Arithmetic—Ambition, Distraction, Uglification, and Derision."—*Lewis Carroll, Alice's Adventures in Wonderland*

831     I am, at heart, a tiresome nag complacently positive that there is no human problem which could not be solved if people would simply do as I advise. —*Gore Vidal*

832     Teacher to class: "There were ten men in a boat and it tipped over; nine men got their hair wet, but the other man didn't get his hair wet. Can one of you tell me why?"
Class clown: "Because the other man was bald."

833     You save unnecessary conversation if you remember people aren't going to take your advice unless you're a doctor or a lawyer, and charge them for it.

834     One is never too old to learn something foolish.

835     I would rather have my ignorance than another man's knowledge, because I have got so much more of it.—*Mark Twain*

836     Whatever some people can't understand, they make fun of, which gives them unlimited opportunities.

837     To the small part of ignorance that we arrange and classify we give the name "knowledge."

838     It always pays to smile in the morning, because later in the day you may not feel like it.

839     An ignorant person likes nothing better than to give advice.

840     It is a far, far better thing to have a firm anchor in nonsense than to put out on the troubled seas of thought.—*John Kenneth Galbraith*

841     Student musing: "What is so rare as an A in June?"

842     When we studied geography back in the eighth grade, the world was flat only at the poles.

843     Many of the so-called open minds should be closed for repairs.

844     The less of it they have, the more willing people are to speak their mind.

845     There's a difference between a philosophy and a bumper sticker.—*Charles M. Schulz*

846     If the nation's economists were laid end to end, they would point in all directions.—*Arthur H. Motley*

847     If harsh criticism is needed to improve the American novel, it is hard to understand why it isn't perfect now.

848     A prejudice is a vagrant opinion without visible means of support.—*Ambrose Bierce*

849     *Child:* A creature that stands halfway between an adult and a television set.

850     On a crowded highway we often wonder how much pigiron there is in our own automobile.

851     I had always assumed that cliché was a suburb of Paris, until I discovered it to be a street in Oxford.—*Philip Guedalla*

852     The fellow who is always happy may be too dumb to complain.

853     The more one thinks about Latin, the easier it is to see why the Roman Empire fell.—*Lord Derby*

854     *Genius:* A person who always happens to be ahead of his time but behind in his rent.

855     Most ideas have a hard time getting into a man's head if they have to squeeze in between his prejudices.

856     He is so stupid that during a recent power blackout, he was stuck on an escalator for four hours.

857     Nobuddy kin talk as interestin' as th' feller that's not hampered by facts or information.—*Kin (Frank McKinney) Hubbard*

858     No one can explain why nature makes the head swell when the mind stops growing.

859     Hanging is too good for a man who makes puns; he should be drawn and quoted.—*Fred Allen*

860     Ignorance is a voluntary condition of bliss.

861     You can always spot a well-informed man. His views are the same as yours.

862     *Erudition:* Dust shaken out of a book into an empty skull.—*Ambrose Bierce*

863     No one finds fault with his own intelligence.

864     The brain is a wonderful thing. It never stops functioning from the time you're born until the moment you stand up to make a speech.

865     How can you expect our youngsters to get an education in college if they can't find a place to park their cars?

866     *Philosophy:* Unintelligible answers to insoluble problems.—*Henry Adams*

867     Economists report that a college education adds many thousands of dollars to a man's lifetime income—which he then spends sending his son to college.—*Bill Vaughan*

868     A little learning is a dangerous thing, but a lot of ignorance is just as bad.—*Bob Edwards*

869     He who has burned his mouth blows his soup.—*German proverb*

870     If a man is right, he can't be too radical; if he is wrong, he can't be too conservative.—*Josh Billings*

# Hope, Honesty, Faith, and Ambition

### 871  *Heaven*

A Roman Catholic priest whose parish is in a slum in Liverpool, England, spent three days in a beautiful home with spacious grounds in Beverly Hills, California. As he took leave of his host he said, "It's perfectly beautiful here. I don't know how you are going to appreciate heaven!"—*Robert J. McCracken*

### 872  *His Wishes*

The pastor, looking over the unusually large Easter congregation, announced: "Dear brethren, I realize that I shall not see many of you again until next Easter, so permit me to take this opportunity to wish you all a very merry Christmas and a most prosperous New Year!"

### 873  *Wisdom*

Several farmers were passing a rainy day at the feed and supply store, arguing the merits of various religions. The eldest said nothing, but just listened. Finally, he was asked, "Well, what do you think, grandpa?"

"I'm thinking there are three ways from here to get to the big grain elevator. When you get there, they're not going to ask which way you came. They'll just want to know how good is your grain."

### 874  *Generous*

A church needed new choir robes, so one Sunday the pastor asked all members who would contribute $5 to the robe fund to please stand. Then the alert organist began a lively rendition of "The Star-Spangled Banner," with astounding results.

### 875 *Certainly*

Little Sammy, age four, had an appendectomy and was obliged to take his meals intravenously for a while. The nurse explained the situation to him, and started to administer the glucose.

"Wait a minute," Sammy said. "Aren't you going to say grace?"

### 876 *Expecting Too Much*

A young woman boarded a crowded bus. A tired little man got up and gave her his seat. There was a moment of silence. "I beg your pardon?" said the tired man.

"I didn't say anything," replied the young woman.

"I'm sorry," said the man. "I thought you said 'Thank you.'"

### 877 *He Was Sorry*

Chided by his Sunday school teacher for misbehaving on the playground, six-year-old Peter was told to stand by the fence in punishment. Obediently, he went, but soon the teacher saw him playing as if nothing had happened.

"I thought I told you to stand by the fence," she said reprovingly.

"I did," Peter answered, "but I told Jesus I was sorry, and he said, 'Okay, Pete, you can go play ball now.'"—*Sister Mary Gilbert*

### 878 *Naturally*

"I wonder why people say 'Amen' and not 'Awomen'?" Bobby questioned. His little friend replied, "Because they sing hymns and not hers, silly."

### 879 *Qualifications*

What are the qualifications of a good church pastor? Here's one version: "Must have small family, if any, and be able to furnish a horse and come to church unassisted. Must not be afraid to work, have no hobbies, have a good clear head, a warm, loving heart—and big feet."—*Advertisement in the Methodist Recorder, Pittsburgh, Pennsylvania, 1903*

### 880 *Some Problems*

A new Sunday school teacher had to iron out some problems with the Lord's Prayer. One child had to be corrected after repeating, "Howard be thy name." Another youngster prayed, "Lead us not into Penn Station." Still another surprised the teacher with, "Our Father, who are in Heaven, how'd you know my name?"

### 881 *Too Young*

A little child in church for the first time watched the ushers pass the offering plates. When they neared his pew, the youngster piped up so that everyone could hear, "Don't pay for me, Daddy. I'm under five."

### 882 *Letter to Santa*

Dear Santa: Please give till it hurts. Thanks. Tom.

### 883 *Advice*

"Tell me how to get on in life," said the kettle.
"Take panes," said the window.
"Never be led," said the pencil.
"Do a driving business," said the hammer.
"Aspire to great things," said the nutmeg grater.
"Make light of everything," said the fire.
"Make much of small things," said the microscope.
"Never do anything offhand," said the glove.
"Reflect," said the mirror.
"Do the work you are suited for," said the chimney.
"Be sharp," said the knife.
"Find a good thing and stick to it," said the glue.
"Try to make a good impression," said the sealing wax.
And that's why the kettle sings as she works, and works as she sings.

### 884 *The Tie That Binds*

Some will say that a gent's cravat should only be seen, not heard. But I want a tie that will make men cry, and render their vision blurred.

I yearn, I long, for a tie so strong it will take two men to tie it. If such there be, just show it to me—whatever the price, I'll buy it!

Give me a tie—a wild, wild tie—one with a barrel of sins! A tie that will blaze in a hectic haze, down where the vest begins.—*Sandy Lake Breeze*

### 885 *Too Personal*

The editor of a weekly midwestern paper found himself short of material, so he had his composer set up the Ten Commandments, which were run without editorial comment.

After the paper was published, he received a letter, as follows: "Cancel my subscription; you're getting personal."

### 886 *Looking Ahead*

A teenager who was soon to be confirmed asked her mother if she could send confirmation cards to some of her friends, who were also to be confirmed.

"Confirmation cards? What are they?" her mother asked.

"Oh, they just say something like 'Congratulations on your confirmation and best wishes for after life!' "

### 887 *He Knows Them*

A little girl was asked: "When you pray at night, do you tell God the bad things you did that day?"

"No," was the soft reply. "He already knows them."

### 888 *Seems Better*

An Indian petitioned the judge of an Arizona court to change his name.

"What is your name now?" asked the judge.

"Chief Screeching Train Whistle," said the Indian.

"And what do you wish your name to be?"

The Indian folded his arms majestically, and grunted, "Chief Toots."

### 889 *Her Prayers Came First*

A little girl was to undergo an operation. As the surgeon was about to place her on the operating table, he said, "Before we can make you well we must put you to sleep."

The little girl smiled and said, "Oh, if you are going to put me to sleep I must say my prayers first." She prayed, "Now I lay me down to sleep . . ."

The surgeon said later that he prayed that night for the first time in thirty years.

### 890 *Needed Help*

A four-year-old was spending a night away from home. At bedtime she knelt at her hostess's knee to say her prayers, expecting the usual prompting. Finding the hostess unable to help her, she continued thus: "Please, God, excuse me. I can't remember my prayer and I'm staying with a lady who doesn't know any."

### 891 *Life and Death*

Two boys were deep in a discussion of life and death. "It's this way," explained one. "If you live right on the day before you die, all will be forgiven."

"Yes," said the other, "but how do you know when you're going to die?"

The first patted his friend's shoulder. "That's it—you don't."—*Earl A. Holmes*

### 892 *The Security*

Dean Swift, preaching a charity sermon, promised, "I shall be brief. My text: 'He that giveth unto the poor lendeth unto the Lord.' Brethren, you have heard the terms of the loan. If you are satisfied with the security, put down your cash."

### 893 *Look Inside*

Some folks in looks take so much pride, they don't think much of what's inside. Well, as for me, I know my face can ne'er be made a thing of grace. And so I rather think I'll see how I can fix the inside o' me so folks'll say, "He looks like sin, but ain't he beautiful within!"

### 894 *To Worship God*

When Henry Ward Beecher was minister at Plymouth church, Brooklyn, his brother agreed to fill the pulpit one Sunday. The house was packed, but when it was noticed that the regular minister would not preach, a number arose to leave.

"Father Tom," as the other Beecher was known, announced: "All who came to worship Henry Ward Beecher this morning may depart at this time. The rest will stay to worship God." The exodus ceased.—*Christian Science Monitor*

### 895 *Not for Him*

A convention speaker once remarked: "There are three things I have never wanted to be: the front pew in a church, the sixth verse of a hymn, and the last speaker on a convention program."

### 896 *Seemed Appropriate*

The new chaplain wanted very much to entertain as well as instruct his men, and so, on one occasion, he arranged for an illustrated lecture on Bible scenes and incidents.

One seaman was detailed to play appropriate music between pictures. The first of these represented Adam and Eve in the Garden of Eden. The sailor cudgeled his brain and ran through his lists, but could think of no music exactly appropriate to the picture.

"Please play up!" whispered the chaplain.

Then an inspiration came to the seaman, and to the consternation of the chaplain and to the delight of the audience, he played, "There's Only One Girl in This World for Me!"

### 897 *Passed*

The editor of the local newspaper queried the new applicant for the job of rewrite man. "Well," said the editor, "are you good?"

"Sure," was the reply.

"All right, then fix this, and cut it short," instructed the editor, handing him a list of the Ten Commandments.

The applicant gave it a glance and seemed a little nonplussed. But then he stepped over to the desk, quickly marked the copy, and handed it to the surprised

editor, who studied the paper for only a moment before saying, "You're hired!"
The rewrite on the paper was, "Don't."

### 898    *No Stranger*

The following quatrain was written by a fourteen-year-old boy, and quoted in
the *Steubenville* (Ohio) *Register:*

> Each time I pass a church,
> I stop to make a visit,
> So that when I'm carried in
> Our Lord won't say, "Who is it?"

### 899    *Please Tell Us*

Sign on a chaplain's desk: "If you have troubles, tell me about them. If you
don't, tell us how you do it."

### 900    *Dad Came First*

Young Harold was late for Sunday school, and the minister asked the cause.
"I was going fishing, but Father wouldn't let me," announced the lad.
"That's the right kind of a father to have," replied the reverend gentleman.
"Did he explain the reason he would not let you go?"
"Yes, sir. He said there wasn't bait enough for two."

### 901    *No Ambition*

The Scot is frequently the goat when jokes are on tap, but not always.
In an English political oration: "I was born an Englishman, I have lived an
Englishman, I hope I shall die an Englishman."
From the back of the hall, in an unmistakable burr, came the question, "Mon,
hae ye no ambeetion?"

### 902    *On a Bus*

A man gave a woman a seat. She fainted. On recovering, she thanked him.
Then he fainted.

### 903    *A Difficult Question*

Dennis the Menace once said, "How can you be lost if you don't care where
you are?"

### 904    *Not Advisable*

A man who survived the Johnstown Flood made a speech on the subject every
time he had an opportunity. Eventually he died and went to Heaven. Saint Peter
said, "On your first day the schedule is light. There is tea at four o'clock, and

all those who arrived today will be welcomed. You may stand and merely say thank you or at the most say a few words."

The man replied, "I should like to speak on the subject 'How I Survived the Johnstown Flood.'"

Saint Peter said, "Are you sure you want to do that? You know that Noah will be in the audience."

905     An evangelist denounces betting as a "means of getting money for nothing." Worse, it frequently is a means of getting nothing for your money.

906     Our idea of a hypocrite is the man who carefully folds his *New York Times* around his tabloid before starting home.

907     The lamb and the lion will lie down together when the lamb hasn't anything the lion wants.

908     Sometimes you fear the world is headed for destruction, and then you read the ads in confession magazines, and don't care if it is.

909     You never know how much a man can't remember till he is called as a witness.

910     No one has improved on the definition of a reformer as a person who insists on his conscience being your guide.

911     Nothing goes to sleep as easily as one's conscience.

912     The Supreme Court has handed down the Eleventh Commandment: "Thou shalt not, in thy classrooms, read the first ten."—*Fletcher Knebel*

913     The church collection plates run a hard race with the golf courses and filling stations on Sunday.

914     A man gets thirty days for stealing sixty cents worth of groceries. Americans have their faults, but they do hate a piker.

915     It isn't the style of the Bible that makes it unpopular with the moderns, but the fact that it cramps their style.

916     The problem with some church congregations is the number of souls compared with the number of heels.

917     A crook is a person who was out for what he could get and in for what he got.

918     We think the Gideons should leave a Bible at each hotel reservation desk.

919     A balanced person isn't one who talks out of both sides of his mouth.

920     The fellow with a chip on his shoulder may wind up with a scrap on his hands.

921     The effort to keep straight may be either a moral struggle or a diet.

922     You aren't much of a sinner if you can correct your mistakes with an eraser.

923     Conscience is that still small voice that makes you feel still smaller.

924     If you can't be thankful for what you have received, be thankful for what you didn't get but deserved.

925     All the things I really like to do are either immoral, illegal or fattening. —*Alexander Woollcott*

926     Conscience is the voice that says you shouldn't have done something after you did it.

927     When great nations arm to the teeth, they aren't necessarily wisdom teeth.

928     There's a lot to be said for the fellow who doesn't say it himself.

929     A gentleman sometimes works under pretty tough handicaps in the world.

930     The way of the transgressor is crowded because there are so many of them.

931     When you're in trouble and your knees knock, kneel on them.

932     What makes resisting temptation difficult for many people, is that they don't want to discourage it completely.—*Franklin P. Jones*

933     Before you call yourself peace-loving, tell us how you act when the umpire calls a close one against your home team.

934     We suppose the reason there is so much crime is that there are so many crooks.

935     As Confucius say: Taking line of least resistance often makes men and rivers crooked.

936     You don't get rid of your temper when you lose it.

937     It is reported that about 25,000 Bibles are stolen annually from hotel rooms. How does the recording angel enter the act of stealing a Bible?

938     A quarter isn't as good as a dollar, but it goes to church quite often.

939    If you think you're important, remember that many persons famous a century ago have weeds growing on their graves today.

940    Honesty may be the best policy because it has so little competition.

941    It doesn't do any good to have the right and the intelligence to speak unless you also have the courage.

942    Most of our modern plays must be sin to be appreciated.

943    When you forget a wrong, you surely confuse the fellow who did it.

944    It is a striking coincidence that the word "American" ends in "I can."

945    The thing that makes temptation difficult is when you can't find any.

946    The saying that "the good die young" probably originated because we meet so few of them as adults.

947    Nothing raises false hopes in a human being like one good cantaloupe.

948    With the present campaigns against litter on the highways, we ought also to keep litter out of our literature.

949    Ancient biblical nations had a goat on which all sins were placed, so the United Nations isn't a new idea.

950    A crooked person fears a Senate Committee that comes baring gifts.

951    A statesman is a person who takes his ears from the ground and listens to the still small voice.

952    Notice on a church bulletin board: "Don't keep the faith—spread it around."

953    Some people always tell the truth, but tilt it their way.

954    Nothing makes temptation so easy to resist as being broke.

955    Women are to blame for most of the lying men do. They insist on asking questions!

956    Money can't buy you happiness—unless you spend it on somebody else.

957    A sermon is always better if you listen like a Christian rather than a critic.

958    The noun "honesty" now is usually preceded by "old-fashioned."

959     When some people break a promise, they give you one that is just as good.

960     The more you stretch the truth, the easier it is to see through it.

961     This would be a better world if people ran as fast at the church bell as they do at the fire bell.

962     No person holds his own in a battle of tongues.

963     No one ever gets paid for being disagreeable, except a traffic cop, a head waiter, and a theater ticket agent.

964     Few people have good enough sight to see their own faults.

965     He who takes but never gives may last for years but never lives.

966     An optimist is anyone who reaches for the car keys in his pocket when an after-dinner speaker says, "In conclusion . . ."

967     Some people expect a receipt when they pay a compliment to someone else.

968     It's a little difficult to reconcile the religious creed of some people with their greed.

969     Reputation is a large bubble that bursts when you try to blow it up yourself.

970     Hope is the feeling that you will succeed tomorrow in what you failed at today.

971     We are never sure whether contentment is largely a matter of intelligence or laziness.

972     Don't be so cocky. Every Eskimo's sitting on top of the world, too.

973     Most of us spend the first six days of each week sowing wild oats, then we go to church on Sunday and pray for a crop failure.—*Fred Allen*

974     We are all on a spaceship and that spaceship is Earth. Four billion passengers—and no skippers.—*Wernher von Braun*

975     We are confronted with insurmountable opportunities.—*Pogo*

976     Try not to become a man of success but rather try to become a man of value.—*Albert Einstein*

977     A Christian is a man who feels repentance on a Sunday for what he did on Saturday and is going to do on Monday.—*Thomas R. Ybarra*

978     With people of only moderate ability modesty is mere honesty; but with those who possess great talent it is hypocrisy.—*Arthur Schopenhauer*

979     I feel it is time that I also pay tribute to my four writers, Matthew, Mark, Luke, and John.—*Bishop Fulton J. Sheen*

980     Telling lies is a fault in a boy, an art in a lover, an accomplishment in a bachelor, and second nature in a married woman.—*Helen Rowland*

981     I just want to lobby for God.—*Billy Graham*

982     The most difficult secret for a man to keep is his own opinion of himself. —*Marcel Pagnol*

983     A fly sat on the chariot wheel and said, "What a dust I raise."—*Jean de La Fontaine*

984     *Ambition:* An overmastering desire to be vilified by enemies while living and made ridiculous by friends when dead.—*Ambrose Bierce*

985     One of the nicest things about telling the truth is that you don't have to remember what you said.

986     The world is equally shocked at hearing Christianity criticized and seeing it practiced.—*D. Elton Trueblood*

987     The tiniest dewdrop hanging from a grass blade in the morning is big enough to reflect the sunshine and the blue of the sky.

988     Another human weakness is the nice man's belief that wrong isn't wrong if done by a nice man like him.

989     When opportunity knocks nowadays, you find that your door has to be unlocked, the chain removed, and the alarm system disconnected.

990     Maybe what this country needs is more and better mouthtraps.

991     A polite man today is one who offers a lady a seat when he gets off the bus.

992     Before you get hot about somebody else's faults, take time to count ten —of your own.

993     Honesty is still the best policy, but some people are satisfied with less than the best.

994    When it comes to doing for others, some people will stop at nothing. That's the problem.

995    Everybody has the opportunity to grow up and not be President if he doesn't want to.

996    Read your Bible. A chapter a day keeps Satan away!

997    *Classical music:* The kind that we keep hoping will turn into a tune. —*Abe Martin*

998    The human race has improved everything except the human race.— *Adlai Stevenson*

999    What is moral is what you feel good after.—*Ernest Hemingway*

1000    Women can never expect to be man's equal until they can sport a large bald spot on top of their heads and still think they are handsome.

1001    You don't judge a person's generosity by the amount of advice he gives away.

1002    The world would be better off if people paid as much attention to their consciences as they do to their neighbor's opinions.

1003    When a woman stops in front of a shop window, she may merely have stopped to reflect.

1004    An honest man today, Diogenes, is one who doesn't lie about his golf score, the fish he caught, or his income tax.

1005    If you can't give me your word of honor, will you give me your promise?—*Samuel Goldwyn*

1006    It is easier to love humanity as a whole than to love one's neighbor.— *Eric Hoffer*

1007    A cynic is just a man who found out when he was about ten that there wasn't any Santa Claus, and he's still upset.—*James Gould Cozzens*

1008    Dignity is the capacity to hold back on the tongue what never should have been on the mind in the first place.

1009    It is more blessed to give than to receive—and it is often deductible.

1010    There is nothing so well known as that we should not expect something for nothing—but we all do and call it Hope.—*E. W. Howe*

1011    We use religion like a bus—we ride on it only while it is going our way.

1012    We are an idealistic people and we'll make any sacrifice for a cause that won't hurt business.

1013    If he does really think that there is no distinction between vice and virtue, when he leaves our houses let us count our spoons.—*Samuel Johnson*

1014    An exaggeration is a truth that has lost its temper.—*Kahlil Gibran*

1015    He that lives on hope has but a slender diet.

1016    If you wish to be original, be yourself; no two people are alike.

1017    Next to getting a free meal, the prospect of getting into a convention picture will bring out the largest number of people.

1018    Some people go to church for the same reason that they buy insurance.

1019    *Crank:* A man with a new idea until it succeeds.—*Mark Twain*

1020    The closest to perfection a person ever comes is when he fills out a job application form.—*Stanley J. Randall*

1021    He who refuses praise the first time that it is offered does so because he would hear it a second time.—*Duc de La Rochefoucauld*

1022    An optimist is a driver who thinks that empty space at the curb won't have a hydrant beside it.—*Changing Times*

1023    *Pessimist:* One who, when he has the choice of two evils, chooses both. —*Oscar Wilde*

1024    The many revised editions of the Bible in recent years probably are efforts to find an easy way to enter Heaven.

1025    An idealist is one who, on noticing that a rose smells better than a cabbage, concludes that it will also make better soup.—*H. L. Mencken*

1026    I am an idealist. I don't know where I'm going but I'm on my way. —*Carl Sandburg*

1027    America has few great cathedrals, but you should see some of our motels.—*Herbert V. Prochnow*

1028    Ambition is but avarice on stilts and masked.—*Walter Savage Landor*

1029    Justice is what we get when the decision is in our favor.

1030     If man is only a little lower than the angels, it makes you wonder a little about the angels.

1031     Modesty is the only sure bait when you angle for praise.—*Lord Chesterfield*

1032     Vanity is so secure in the heart of man that everyone wants to be admired: even I who write this, and you who read this.—*Blaise Pascal*

1033     Be virtuous and you will be eccentric.—*Mark Twain*

1034
                    Tell the truth
                    But tell it slant.
                    —*Emily Dickinson*

1035     Popularity? It's glory's small change.—*Victor Hugo*

1036     How much better this world would be if we would let Opportunity do all the knocking.

1037     A telescope will magnify a star a thousand times, but a good press agent can do even better.—*Fred Allen*

1038     Snobbery is the pride of those who are not sure of their position.—*Berton Braley*

# Life, Enthusiasm, Experience, and Love

### 1039    *Of Course Not*

During a community drive to round up unlicensed dogs, a policeman whistled an automobile to the curb. When its driver asked why he had been stopped, the officer pointed to the dog on the seat beside him. "Does your dog have a license?" he asked.

"Oh, no," the driver answered quickly. "He doesn't need one. I do all the driving myself."

### 1040    *It's Easy*

An old-timer in the Everglades was warning a new work party about alligators. "They're fast and tricky," he said, "but one thing—it's easy to tell when one's nearby."

"How do you tell?" a new man asked nervously.

"Nothing to it, son," said the old-timer smoothly. "Say you and one of these other boys is standing around talking. And all at once you notice you're talking to yourself. Son, you just located your first 'gator."

### 1041    *Saves Time*

The mathematics professor and his fiancée were out strolling in a park when she picked a daisy and, looking sweetly at him, began to pull off the petals, saying, "He loves me, he loves me not . . ."

"You are giving yourself a lot of unnecessary trouble," said the professor. "You should count up the petals, and if the total is an even number, the answer will be in the negative; if an uneven number, in the affirmative."

### 1042 *The Evidence*

"How do you know this man was drunk?" the judge asked the police officer.

"Well, Your Honor," responded the officer, "when I came up to him he had just dropped a penny in the mailbox and was looking up at the clock and I heard him say, 'Man, I've lost eleven pounds.' "

### 1043 *Considerate*

The old inmate greeted his new cell partner with the question "How long you in for?"

"Twenty-five years," the new prisoner replied.

"Then you take the bed nearest the door," said the old-timer. "You'll be getting out first."

### 1044 *Excuse*

Two men, fishing on a Sunday morning, were feeling a bit guilty.

One said to the other, "I suppose we should have gone to church."

"Heck," said the other, "I couldn't have gone to church anyway. My wife's sick in bed."

### 1045 *Life's Rewards*

"Remember, sugar, when we were first married? I was just a salesman and you were just a housewife. Now, forty years later, I've just retired as president of the company and you're the grandmother of eight."

### 1046 *He Will Learn*

My wife-to-be had a relative in Little Rock, Arkansas, who was a well-known attorney. His reputation was so good he felt he could take a chance on inviting me to speak to a service club in Little Rock on my trip to Camden, Arkansas, to be married. As a young man, I had done some research on highly speculative and fraudulent securities and how people lost money on them. So I told this attorney, "I shall speak on the subject of 'How to Keep from Getting Rich.' " When he introduced me at the luncheon he said, "This young man will speak to us today on the subject of 'How to Keep from Getting Rich.' I should tell you that he is on his way to Camden to be married next Saturday. After that, he will learn a great deal more about his subject."—*Herbert V. Prochnow*

### 1047 *Pretty Silly*

Mary had a little watch; she swallowed it—it's gone. Now, everywhere that Mary walks—time marches on!

### 1048 *Did He?*

Have you heard this one? Said Romeo: "Sweetheart of mine, I'm burning up with love for you!" Said Juliet: "Don't make a fuel of yourself."

1049   *Physical and Mental Peaks*

The average person is said to reach the peak of his strength at the age of thirty. The peak of his knowledge apparently comes in the teens.

1050   *Are You Ready to Order*

Sign in a restaurant in northern Michigan: "Mary had a little lamb—what will you have?"

1051   *Giving the Blessing*

The graduation banquet was about to begin when the master of ceremonies was informed that the invited clergyman would not be able to attend. He quickly asked the main speaker to give the blessing. The speaker nodded, rose, bowed his head, and, in all sincerity, said, "There being no clergyman present, let us thank God."

1052   *Wrigley Theme Song*

When you gum to the end of a perfect day.

1053   *Perhaps*

The young woman looked carefully at her boyfriend as he examined the check following their dinner at an exclusive restaurant.

"You don't look well," she said. "Is it something I ate?"

1054   *No Hero*

"It was grand of you to dive from that height, fully clothed, to effect such a magnificent rescue," exclaimed the onlooker, patting the hero.

"That's all very well," replied the hero, "but what I want to know is, who pushed me in?"

1055   *News Item*

"Long-legged sheep in the Himalayas can run forty miles an hour." Only that kind could follow Mary now.

1056   *No Extra Parts*

Joe saw the train, but couldn't stop, so they dragged his flivver to a shop. It only took a week or two to make his lizzie good as new. But though they hunted high and low, they found no extra parts for Joe.

1057   *Sorry to Trouble You*

Once upon a time there were two morons. One of them called the other on the telephone at three o'clock in the morning.

"Hello, is this University one one one one?"

After a while came the answer. "Nope, this is University eleven eleven."

"Well, then, sorry to bother you at this time of night."
"Oh, that's all right; I had to get up to answer the telephone anyway."

1058    *Story in* **China Mail** *Newspaper—Hong Kong*

"You remember Jim Barrington?"
"Yes, what's his name?"
"How should I know?"

1059    *Different Strokes*

At a country club a man was overheard saying to his wife, "You'll drive me out of my mind, dear."

"That would be a putt, dear," his wife responded.

1060    *Jingle Bells*

> Jingle bells, jingle bells,
> Jingle all the way.
> The family runs up great big bills
> That Dad will have to pay.
> —*Herbert V. Prochnow*

1061    *O Come*

> O come all ye faithful,
> To Gimbels, Field's, and Macy's.
> Buy everything you possibly can,
> On your credit card or lay-awake plan.
> —*Herbert V. Prochnow*

1062    *Hark*

> Hark the newspaper ads do sing,
> Make the old cash registers ring,
> Clear the shelves and buy like wild,
> God and easy credit reconciled.
> —*Herbert V. Prochnow*

1063    *How Quiet*

> Oh little town of Bethlehem,
> How quiet dear Daddy lies.
> He's thinking of tomorrow
> And what he will have to borrow.
> —*Herbert V. Prochnow*

### 1064 *The True Christmas Carol*

> Silent night, holy night,
> That's the way it ought to be,
> A manger, a Mother and Child,
> Holy infant, so tender and mild.
> —*Herbert V. Prochnow*

### 1065 *Justice*

An elderly man of convivial habits, but also bookish, was hailed before the bar of justice in a small country town.

"Ye're charged with bein' intoxicated and disorderly," snapped the magistrate. "Have ye anything to say why sentence should not be pronounced?"

"Man's inhumanity to man makes countless thousands mourn," began the prisoner, in a flight of oratory. "I am not so debased as Poe, so profligate as Byron, so ungrateful as Keats, so intemperate as Burns, so timid as Tennyson, so vulgar as Shakespeare, so—"

"That'll do, that'll do," interrupted the magistrate. "Seven days. And, officer, take down that list of names he mentioned and round 'em up. I think they're as bad as he is."

### 1066 *Not Social*

Mrs. Asker: "Is Mrs. Smith an active member of the Ladies' Aid Society?"

Mrs. Gabby: "My goodness, no! She never has a word to say. She just sits and sews all the time!"

### 1067 *All of Us Are*

Two fellows met. One was wearing the initials IATK. The other said, "My friend, I never saw a button like that. What kind of a lodge or organization is it?"

"It's an organization I belong to. The initials mean, 'I am thoroughly confused.' "

### 1068 *Preventing an Accident*

The judge was questioning a driver who had just been brought in by a traffic officer.

"Young man," he said, "I understand you were driving sixty miles an hour when the officer caught you.

"Your Honor," replied the driver, "that's not true; I wasn't even going twenty miles. As a matter of fact I wasn't even going ten miles. I was—

The judge interrupted: "I'm going to hurry and fine you twenty dollars before you back into something."

1069 *Unbelievable*

An inebriate was watching a man enter a revolving door. As the door swung around, a pretty girl stepped out. "Unbelievable," he muttered.

1070 *Confidential Information*

During a convention of atomic scientists at Las Vegas, one of the professors spent his free time at the gambling tables. Two colleagues were discussing their friend's weakness.

"Hotchkiss gambles as if there were no tomorrow," said one.

"Perhaps," commented the other, "he knows something!"

1071 *Beauty*

Beauty is indeed a good gift of God; but that the good may not think it a great good, God dispenses it even to the wicked.—*Saint Augustine*

1072 *Love*

A philosopher defined the difference between life and love: "Life is just one fool thing after another; love is just two fool things after each other."

1073 *Greed*

Teacher: "What type of person lives longest?"

Student: "A rich relative."

1074 *A Mess*

When the Creator gave out brains, I thought he said trains—and I missed mine!

When he gave out good looks, I thought he said books—and I didn't want any.

When he said noses, I thought he said roses—and I ordered a big red one.

Boy! Am I a mess!

1075 *Good Reason*

A man stood on the street corner waiting to cross while the traffic streamed by, swift and continuous. After a long wait, the man became impatient, but he dared not risk going out into the traffic. He spied another pedestrian on the other side of the street and called to him, "Hey, I say, how did you get over there?"

The other man cupped his hands about his mouth and shouted, "I was born over here."

1076 *Time to Walk*

A husband and his wife were watching television when the screen suddenly went black. They could not understand why, until the mystery was solved by their dog. He came up to them with the electric outlet plug in his mouth, dropped it in front of them, and remarked, "Isn't it time for our evening walk?"

### 1077    *Comforting*

"It may help you," Mark Twain once said to an obviously nervous guest of honor at a dinner, "if you keep one thing in mind. Just remember that they don't expect much!"

### 1078    *The Secret*

A psychologist says that any girl can marry any man she wants if she repeats very often to him these magic words: "You are so wonderful."

### 1079    *The Difference*

She: "I'm so glad we're engaged."
He: "But you knew all the time that I loved you, didn't you?"
She: "Yes, dear, I knew it, but you didn't."

### 1080    *A Lovers' Quarrel*

George: "Why don't Jack and Laura make up?"
Kate: "They'd like to, but unfortunately they can't remember what they quarreled about."

### 1081    *No Guitars*

Saint Peter to new arrival from rock group: "I'm sorry, you'll have to be satisfied with the harp. We don't have electric guitars here."

### 1082    *That's Different*

Be early if you are the bird, there's lots of wisdom in it, but if you chance to be the worm, you'd better wait a minute.

### 1083    *Surprise*

Of all the sad surprises, there's nothing to compare with treading in the darkness on a step that isn't there!

### 1084    *Simple*

He: "How old are you?"
She: "Just turned twenty-four."
He: "Ah, I see; that's forty-two."

### 1085    *Strange*

Men are queer animals. They have always known that one horse can run faster than another, and yet they will squander millions of dollars to see that simple fact demonstrated over and over.

1086    *The Way It Sounded*

"What's the name of this number the rock band is playing?"
"I don't know, but it sounds like 'Revenge on the Public.' "

1087    *His Trouble*

Suburban resident: "It's simply grand to wake up in the morning and hear the leaves whispering outside your window."
City feller: "It's all right to hear the leaves whisper, but I never could stand to hear the grass mown."

1088    *According to the Bard*

'Tis beauty that doth oft make women proud; 'tis virtue that doth make them most admired; 'tis modesty that makes them seem divine.—*William Shakespeare*

1089    *Lincoln Looked Ahead*

The novice was not enjoying his first trip through the air, and his more experienced companion regarded him with amusement.
"I say, what's on your mind?" he demanded.
"I was just thinking about Abraham Lincoln," the novice replied.
"Abraham Lincoln?"
"Yes, I was thinking how truthfully he spoke when he said a man's legs ought to be just long enough to reach the ground."

1090    *That Will Be Extra*

Waitress: "How will you have your eggs cooked, sir?"
Customer: "Does it make any difference in the price?"
Waitress: "No."
Customer: "Then I'll have them cooked with ham."

1091    *Blew His Top*

Did you hear about the French horn player whose toupee fell into his instrument? He spent the evening blowing his top.

1092    *Too True*

The toastmaster commented in a few appropriated words.

1093    *And Traffic Cops*

Sign on a truck: "This truck stops for all crossroads, railroads, blondes, and brunettes; for redheads it will back up 50 feet."

1094    *Just Learning*

The young lady pulled up to the curb and smiled sweetly when the policeman told her sternly that she had been doing seventy-five.
"Isn't that marvelous!" she exclaimed. "And I'm just learning to drive!"

#### 1095 *Only in the Deep South*

"Where does a sheep get his hair cut?"
"At the baa baa shop."

#### 1096 *Please Repeat That*

I want to put in a person-to-person call to Mike Zanda—Zanda! No—Z *a-b-c-d-e-f-g-h-i-j-k-l-m-n-o-p-q-r-s-t-u-v-w-x-y-Z*—like in Zilch.

#### 1097 *Had to Be Careful*

"Soup, sir?"
"No, please. I just had my suit cleaned."

#### 1098 *Things We Can Learn*

Here are a few things you can learn from your dog:
    To love children.
    To keep your place.
    To size up an enemy.
    To drink plenty of water.
    To be a dependable friend.
    To express pleasure when treated well.
    To guard faithfully the interests of those who care for and protect you.
    To be faithful unto death.

#### 1099 *Tell the Pope*

It often happens that I wake at night and begin to think about a serious problem and decide I must tell the Pope about it. Then I wake up completely and remember that I am the Pope.—*Pope John XXIII*

#### 1100 *Take a Chance*

In a Pacific coast town a junk shop near a railroad crossing displayed this sign: "Go ahead; take a chance. We'll buy the car."

#### 1101 *Which One Are You?*

A person who—
    Says what he believes
    Believes what he says,
    Says what he does not believe,
    Does not say what he believes.

#### 1102 *What Happens*

Old bankers never die, they just lose interest.
Old brick layers never die, they just throw in the trowel.

Old golfers never die, they just putter away.
Old gardeners never die, they just spade away.
Old volcanoes never die, they just blow their tops.
Old quarterbacks never die, they just pass away.
Old cows never die, they just kick the bucket.
Old farmers never die, they just go to seed.
Old scuba divers never die, they just get their depth certificates.

1103    The girl who thinks no man is good enough for her may be right—and then again, she also may be left.

1104    When the world laughs at you, laugh back; it's just as funny as you are.

1105    Always try to drive so that your license will expire before you do.

1106    It is a serious drought when washing your car won't produce rain.

1107    Since we don't always know on which side our bread is buttered, we play safe by eating both sides.

1108    One good thing about a one-way street is that you can get bumped only in the rear.

1109    The bad thing about a popular song is that it makes a lot of people think they can sing.

1110    When you talk to a person about himself, he is never bored.

1111    Some people walk through life like a seal balancing a ball on his nose.

1112    Memory is what makes you try to remember what you forgot.

1113    *Steering committee:* Three people trying to park a car.

1114    *Ginger ale:* A drink that tastes the way your foot feels when it's asleep.

1115    *Impatience:* Waiting in a hurry.

1116    *Oboe:* An American tramp (an Englishman's definition).

1117    *Hole:* Nothing at all, but you can break your neck in it.—*Austin O'Malley*

1118    Lovemaking hasn't changed. Three thousand years ago Greek maidens would listen to a lyre all evening.

1119    *Hors d'oeuvre:* A ham sandwich cut into forty pieces.—*Jack Benny*

1120    News Item: "The fire was put out before the fire department could do much damage."

1121    *Appetizers:* Those little bits you eat until you lose your appetite.

1122    Tomorrow is the day that comes just when we have figured out today's problems.

1123    *Guitar:* A hillbilly harp.

1124    It's strange how you can hear a rattle in your car but not in your head.

1125    Life is a constant struggle to keep up appearances and keep down expenses.

1126    Don't be conceited. Just because you're sitting in the front seat doesn't mean you're driving the car.

1127    When a person's first love is himself, he never finds a good successor.

1128    Some people spend more time looking into the mirror than into the heart.

1129    It's hard to believe the Darwinian theory that only the fit have survived.

1130    Nothing carries gossip faster than a sour grapevine.

1131    The green light is the signal for the man behind you to blow his horn.

1132    All things come to he who crosses the street against the red light.

1133    Then there was the moron who went to a secondhand store to get one for his watch.

1134    It's easy the night before to get up early the next morning.

1135    From time to time the Secretary of Commerce and the Secretary of the Treasury announce that business is excellent, which indicates each understands the duties of his office.—*Herbert V. Prochnow*

1136    If a conservative doesn't understand something, he opposes it; whereas, if a liberal doesn't understand something, he supports it.

1137    *Martyr:* A person who sacrifices himself to the unavoidable.

1138    A yawn is silence with the mouth open.

1139    If other people are going to talk, conversation becomes impossible.—
*James McNeill Whistler*

1140    Flattery is the best cure for a stiff neck, because it will turn most heads.

1141    Gossip still runs down more people than automobiles.

1142    The house by the side of the road isn't a house—it's a trailer.

1143    When the average person stands up to speak, his mind sits down.

1144    Absence makes the heart go wander.

1145    No one is so hard to answer as a fellow who keeps his mouth shut.

1146    The person who looks down on his neighbors usually lives on a bluff.

1147    All the world loves a lover and loves to snicker at his love letters in
court.

1148    We should forgive our enemies, but only after they have been hanged
first.—*Heinrich Heine*

1149    It's too bad Nature can't learn by looking at the pictures on flower seed
packages.

1150    My lady, be wary of Cupid, and list to the lines of this verse. To let
a fool kiss you is stupid, to let a kiss fool you is worse.

1151    We ought to be able to fiqure out something for the people to do Sunday
afternoons besides piling into their cars and heading for collisions and hospitals.
—*Herbert V. Prochnow*

1152    Rubbing elbows teaches you a great deal about another person you
didn't know, and so does rubbing fenders.

1153    Love makes the world go round, but so does too much red pepper in
the chili.

1154    We certainly have a bumper crop on the highways.

1155    We can't remember ever getting any good news out of an envelope with
a window in it.

1156    Everyone has fun at the fat man's expanse.

1157    Some people who laugh out loud at the family album look in the mirror
and never crack a smile.

1158    Don't tell your friends anything you don't want your enemies to know.

1159    A woman may sometimes know less than a man but she generally understands more.

1160    The simplest things are often the hardest to grasp—like soap in a bath.

1161    The excuses we think up for ourselves never seem so good when someone else uses them.

1162    There is a difference between being out of breath and being out of wind.

1163    Some people have eyes but see not, ears and hear not, but never tongues and talk not.

1164    The person who says you can't mix liquor and driving must not read the traffic accident lists.

1165    Some folks who think they are busy are just confused.

1166    You wouldn't worry about what people think of you if you knew how seldom they do.

1167    Evening is that period of the day when people do the craziest things to keep from going to bed.

1168    What a big gap there is between advice and help.

1169    Dr. Samuel Johnson once said that of all noises he found music the least disagreeable.

1170    A newspaper is an object used by tired men to avoid seeing a woman standing in a bus.

1171    Some people are so prejudiced they will not listen to both sides of an argument.

1172    Heard in a crowded bus: "Step to the rear. The backs of our buses go your way too."

1173    *Glutton:* A person who takes the piece of pastry you wanted.

1174    One can put more feeling into one good yawn than into many, many words.

1175    The trouble with Father Time is he doesn't make any round trips.

1176    The apple is well known in history, but the grapefruit stays in the public eye.

1177    We come and we cry, and this is life; we yawn and we depart, and this is death!—*Ausone de Chancel*

1178    A pinch of probably is worth a pound of perhaps.—*James Thurber*

1179    During last summer's heat wave, a church in the Midwest put this on the bulletin board: "You think it's hot here?"—*T. Harry Thompson*

1180    Love makes a man think almost as much of a girl as he does of himself.

1181    A lot of nice fat turkeys would strut less if they could see into the future.

1182    Know thyself? If I knew myself, I'd run away.—*Johann Wolfgang von Goethe*

1183    He is so unlucky that he runs into accidents which started out to happen to somebody else.—*Don Marquis*

1184    Everything seems to be evened up in this life. The fellow with less hair to comb always has more face to wash.

1185    In the good old days the pedestrian had the right of way.

1186    Temper is one of the few things that improves when you don't use it.

1187    Before you put your tongue in high gear, be sure your brain is turning over.

1188    The English may not like music, but they absolutely love the noise it makes.—*Sir Thomas Beecham*

1189    A great many people are like buttons—always popping off at the wrong time.

1190    You may not be too wise, but if you keep your mouth shut you can fool a lot of people.

1191    The years teach much which the days never know.—*Ralph Waldo Emerson*

1192    Her hair was mouse brown, with a tendency to scamper.—*Ellery Queen*

1193    An obstinate person does not hold an opinion—it holds him.

1194    I conceived at least one great love in my life, of which I was always the object.—*Albert Camus*

1195 If living conditions don't stop improving in this country, we're going to run out of humble beginnings for our great men.—*Russell P. Askue*

1196 Some persons want the benefit of doubt when there isn't any.

1197 *Elevator operator:* One who never hears the end of a good story.

1198 Don't expect too much of another person, because he is about like you and me.

1199 A backseat driver never runs out of gas.

1200 As long as the American people park their own cars they will never lose the art of walking.

1201 When the fellow in the audience nods, he may be agreeing with you or sleeping.

1202 When you see some modern art, you realize things are not as bad as they are painted.

1203 All of us are born equal, but it's what we are equal to that's important.

1204 We knew a careful motorist who speeded through intersections to get out of the way of reckless drivers.

1205 The kind of vegetables we enjoy are those the cow eats before we eat the cow.

1206 Three highway menaces are drinking, thumbing, and spooning—or hic, hike, and hug.

1207 As man becomes more civilized, he makes his locks stronger and stronger and his defenses bigger and bigger.

1208 Racehorses eat very little before a race. The customers don't eat afterwards.

1209 A bore is a man who, when you ask him how he is, tells you.—*Bert Leston Taylor*

1210 If you think trifles won't be noticed, just let a catsup bottle drip on your white flannel trousers at a picnic.

1211 With all these missiles, it may only be a question of time until some of us leave this little globe entirely.

1212     The purpose of traffic lights for pedestrians is to be sure a few of the species survive.

1213     It is better to wait for the green light than for the ambulance.

1214     An optimist cherishes vain hopes and a pessimist nurses vain regrets. A normal person does both.

1215     The first thing that strikes a foreigner in the United States will probably be a car at a street crossing.

1216     Perpetual motion is the noise outside a hotel window at night.

1217     Some motorists think signs at railroad crossings are only for the locomotive engineer.

1218     Some people are quieter than others even when they have less to be quiet about.

1219     It's annoying to talk to someone who insists on talking to you.

1220     No one is more disappointed than the person who gets what he has coming to him.

1221     If most of us practiced what we preach, it would certainly keep us busy.

1222     Famous last words: "Is that thing you're wearing a hat?"

1223     A secret is either not worth keeping or too good to keep.

1224     Experience is what you get after the opportunity to use it is gone.

1225     Most speeding is done by people who are not going anywhere in particular.

1226     Being told things for your own good seldom does you any.

1227     Prejudice is an unwillingness to be confused with facts.

1228     A person who is reckless in crossing busy streets may be known either as "a jaywalker" or "the deceased."

1229     The only fool bigger than the person who knows it all is the person who argues with him.

1230     Some visitors keep you from being lonely when you wish you were.

1231     A reckless driver is one who passes you when you are going 75 miles an hour.

1232    He said he would die if she didn't marry him and, sure enough, he did
—seventy-five years later.

1233    A person isn't necessarily orderly if he has a place for everything but
always puts it somewhere else.

1234    Most people believe everything they think and most of what they hear.

1235    *Man:* The only animal with brains enough to find a cure for the diseases
caused by his own folly.

1236    If we could really see ourselves as others see us, we wouldn't believe it.

1237    Punctuality is the art of guessing how late the other fellow is going to be.

1238    You may be able to read someone like a book, but you can't shut him
up as easily.

1239    Considering what's taking place outside, you wonder why these prison-
ers keep breaking out of prisons.

1240    Instead of putting others in their place, try putting yourself in their
place occasionally.

1241    We like the man who calls a spade a spade, especially after he stumbles
over one in a dark basement.

1242    *Tact:* Looking around to be sure no one is related to the person about
whom you are going to gossip.

1243    Some persons find that there is nothing quite as useful as a good elastic
code of morals.

1244    It's easy to be beautiful, if you listen to the TV commercials.

1245    Some men and women have a keen sense of humor. The more you
humor them the better they like it.

1246    It's easy to pick out the best people because they'll help you do it.

1247    The biggest stumbling block a man may have is the one under his
hat.

1248    We've never noticed that a woman's intuition is any better than a man's
when she is deciding which way to turn in traffic.

1249    Not all antiques are highly prized. There are the old virtues.

1250    Too often a grade crossing is the meeting place of headlights and light
heads.

1251 An alarm clock is all right if a person likes that sort of "ting."

1252 Some men are born great, some achieve greatness, and others thrust greatness upon themselves.

1253 Mammals are classified thus: man and the lower animals. Man does the classifying.

1254 A chip on the shoulder finally gets to be a very heavy load.

1255 *Reckless driving:* A person with a hammer and some nails working on a freshly painted living-room wall.

1256 What may be the perfect accident has been achieved in Santiago, Chile, where a concert soprano fell from a hotel window onto a dentist.

1257 When a newspaper headline said, "Half of the City Council are Crooks," the City Council demanded a retraction. The next day the headline said, "Half of the City Council are not Crooks."

1258 *Playing by note:* To learn to play the piano by note instead of by ear. Twelve payments on the note and the piano is yours to learn to play.

1259 All things come to he who waits, but most of us aren't sure what we're waiting for.

1260 *Farsighted:* A term used to describe a man who wouldn't take a chance on an auto raffle because he didn't have a garage; or the fellow who buys two lawn mowers—one for the neighbors to use.

1261 A beautiful blonde in an office may not be able to add, but she can certainly distract.

1262 The best way to save face is to keep the lower part of it closed.

1263 One of the more irritating aspects about living in a trailer is that there's no place to put anything except where it belongs.

1264 There are a lot of people who never forget a kind deed—if they did it.

1265 A great deal of what we see depends on what we are looking for.

1266 The pessimist doubts that man's descent from the monkey has started yet.

1267 That's an optical illusion about the world growing smaller. It's merely that the new artillery has a longer range.

1268    One reason there is so much humor in the world is that there are so many people who take themselves seriously.

1269    The only time people dislike gossip is when you gossip about them.—*Will Rogers*

1270    Every time Uncle Sam spends one dollar, he takes in 90 cents. With a tax cut he hopes, based on experience, to spend it faster, take in less and balance the budget. Is that clear?—*Herbert V. Prochnow*

1271    The most welcome guest is the one who knows when to go home.

1272    Gossip is something that goes in the ear and comes out the mouth greatly enlarged.

1273    Comedians say people don't like new jokes, but how would they know?

1274    Half the people in this country are somewhat crazy, but it's hard to tell which half.

1275    The person who tells you all his troubles at least keeps your mind off yours.

1276    Truth crushed to earth will rise, because it will not lie.

1277    Some people know how to live everyone's life but their own.

1278    All that could be said for an earthquake in the Middle East is that it would be redundant.

1279    When some drivers put out a hand, you know they expect to do something.

1280    The person who is wrapped up in himself is generally overdressed.

1281    No two of us are alike—and boy, is that a break.

1282    A person who loses his head usually is the last one to miss it.

1283    You can get some firsthand knowledge from a secondhand car.

1284    A half truth is generally the worst half.

1285    Uneasy lies the head that ignores a telephone call at 2 A.M.

1286    Only two groups of people fall for flattery—men and women.

1287    It's difficult to look spick if you have too much span.

1288    A traffic cop is a person who is mad even when he wins the race with you.

1289    The fellow who tries to be the whole show will soon lose his audience.

1290    If you have never seen a total eclipse, just watch the groom at a wedding.—*Herbert V. Prochnow*

1291    There is nothing so annoying as to have two people go right on talking when you're interrupting.

1292    Puppy love is one of the few things that can reconcile a boy to washing his ears.

1293    No two people are alike, and they're both glad of it.

1294    *Patience:* The ability to stand at the screen door while your guest holds it open for a half hour and lets in the flies.

1295    By the time your feet get warm in bed in the wintertime, you have probably overslept.

1296    When a person says he will meet you halfway, he generally thinks he is on the dividing line.

1297    On television they don't always seem to know the difference between a beautiful singer and one who can sing beautifully.

1298    If you think before you speak, the other fellow gets in his joke first.—*Ed Howe*

1299    When you think of how much went into developing television, you wonder why so little comes out of it.

1300    A pedestrian is a person with three good tires.

1301    An educator finds girls lead boys—and a marry chase it is.

1302    When a woman really loves a man, he can make her do anything she wants to do.

1303    The teenager sent his girlfriend her first orchid with this note: "With all my love and most of my allowance."

1304    *Pitiful figure:* A truck driver with an inferiority complex.

1305    *Compliment:* The applause that refreshes.—*John W. Wierlein*

1306    A small boy is a pain in the neck when he is around, and a pain in the heart when he is not.

1307 A hick town is one where there is no place to go that you shouldn't.

1308 *Pseudonym:* A nym that is not your real nym.

1309 *Gossip:* Letting the chat out of the bag.

1310 In certain parts of the world people pray in the street. In this country they're called pedestrians.

1311 Foolishness always results when the tongue outraces the brain.

1312 The ability to speak several languages is an asset, but to be able to hold your tongue in one language is priceless.

1313 *Busybody:* A person with an interferiority complex.—*Calgary (Canada) Herald*

1314 *Cat:* A pygmy lion who loves mice, hates dogs, and patronizes human beings.—*Oliver Herford*

1315 To the pedestrian the beauty of the one-way street is that he always knows which way he's going to get knocked down.

1316 Courtship is the period during which the girl decides whether or not she can do any better.

1317 'Tis love that makes the world go round with that worried expression.

1318 A man never knows how careful he can be until he gets a new car or wears white shoes.

1319 The woman who looks back now doesn't turn into a pillar of salt, but into a telephone pole.

1320 When a woman speaks of a permanent wave, she means a temporary permanent wave.

1321 One thing you must say about the modern woman—she isn't effeminate.

1322 Does any woman have enough clothes so she doesn't ask, "What will I wear?"

1323 We'll contribute to a statue for the fellow who finds out how to keep a frying pan handle cool.

1324 If you spill ink on the rug, all you have to do is listen after the family sees it.

1325    The annual beauty bill for women runs into billions, which shows women are running into big figures to avoid them.

1326    No woman will wear what another woman wears, except a mink coat.

1327    *Flatterer:* One who says things to your face that he wouldn't say behind your back.—*G. Millington*

1328    People usually get what's coming to them—unless it's mailed.

1329    All things come to the other person if you sit down and wait.

1330    *Careful driver:* One who looks in both directions when he passes a red light.—*Ralph Marterie*

1331    *Edible:* Good to eat, and wholesome to digest; as a worm to a toad, a toad to a snake, a snake to a pig, a pig to a man, and a man to a worm.—*Ambrose Bierce*

1332    If we could see ourselves as others see us, we probably wouldn't take a second look.—*Herbert V. Prochnow*

1333    Shakespeare on daylight saving: The times are out of joint, O cursed spite: one place your watch is wrong; another, right.

1334    Automobiles are almost foolproof, but the fool has to stay awake at the wheel.

1335    An alarm clock in front of a speaker is a good thing, except that it wakes up the audience.

1336    If all the people who sleep through after-dinner speeches were laid end to end, they would be more comfortable.

1337    You may be a fine upstanding person, but that means nothing on a slippery sidewalk.

1338    We sometimes get a hotel room so quiet we can hear the piledriver working in the lot next door.

1339    If, as a psychologist tells us, there is no such thing as pain, what is it some people give us?

1340    An optimist can always see the bright side of the other fellow's misfortune.

1341    A person who boasts of having an open mind often mistakes a vacancy for an opening.

1342    Gossip is like an old joke—there's always somebody around who hasn't heard it yet.

1343    He who carries a tale makes a monkey of himself.

1344    The suburbs were discovered quite by accident one day in the early 1940s by a Welcome Wagon lady who was lost.—*Erma Bombeck*

1345    Natives who beat drums to beat off evil spirits are objects of scorn to smart American motorists who blow horns to break up traffic jams.

1346    It's love, it's love that makes the world go round.—*French song*

1347    You don't have to explain something you haven't said.—*Calvin Coolidge*

1348    We always love those who admire us, and we do not always love those whom we admire.—*La Rochefoucauld*

1349    Nothing improves the average person's driving habits like the sight of a motorcycle cop parked along the highway.

1350    The driver is safer when the roads are dry; the roads are safer when the driver is dry.

1351    We never heard of a mob rushing madly across town to do a needed kindness.

1352    Some people are never pious until they find themselves in trouble.

1353    There is no wholly satisfactory substitute for brains, but silence does pretty well.—*Herbert V. Prochnow*

1354    An onion a day keeps everyone away.

1355    Some people like everything about Russia but the idea of living there.

1356    Pride goes before destruction, especially when it goes 60 miles an hour on a slippery road.

1357    Wit is cultured insolence.—*Aristotle*

1358    When a young man in love asks for advice, he is no longer in love.

1359    A man can be happy with any woman as long as he does not love her. —*Oscar Wilde*

1360    There are three classes of men in the United States—the intellectual, the handsome, and the majority.

1361     You have had too much to drink if you feel sophisticated and can't pronounce it.

1362     *Woman's shoe:* An example of the lesser containing the greater.

1363     An automobile is as sober as the driver.

1364     *Haircut:* What you have when all is said and done.

1365     There's always an easy solution to every human problem—neat, plausible and wrong.—*H. L. Mencken*

1366     It pays to stand up for your rights, but not in the middle of a busy intersection.

1367     Most of the time I don't have much fun. The rest of the time I don't have any fun at all.—*Woody Allen*

1368     Competition is so keen that only the big crimes get on the front page now.

1369     A speeding tourist crashed through a billboard. Probably wanted to see the scenery.

1370     Sometimes we wish General Sherman could come back long enough to describe the present situation.

1371     Another great drawback to success is that by the time you are rich enough to sleep late, you're so old you wake up early every morning.

1372     When the pretty coed was asked what could be worse than a man without a country, she replied, "A country without a man."

1373     It is better to decline the bait than to struggle on the hook.

1374     When you have to keep your back to the wall and your ear to the ground, your shoulder to the wheel and your nose to the grindstone, your head level and both feet on the ground—you're not a contortionist; you're just like the rest of us.

1375     He was so tall that I was not sure he had a face.—*Mark Twain*

1376     They tell me he fell in love with a pair of blue eyes—then he made the mistake of marrying the whole girl.—*Joey Adams*

1377     A kiss is a pleasant reminder that two heads are better than one.

# Families, Home, and Relatives

### 1378 *Perfect*

You can say this for these ready mixes—the next generation isn't going to have any trouble making pies exactly like mother used to make—*Earl Wilson*

### 1379 *The Telephone Did It*

"My teenage daughter gave us a time last night," a weary office worker said. "She started to run away from home. Luckily she never got beyond the front door."

"What happened?" a concerned colleague asked.

"The telephone rang," the father replied.

### 1380 *Easy*

Young Bobby had gone to his first junior high school dance. When he got home his mother asked him what he thought of it.

"Aw, it was okay," he replied.

"Did you dance any?" she persisted.

"Aw, no," Bobby responded. "But I could have 'cause it's easy. All you have to do is turn around and keep wiping your feet!"

### 1381 *America*

A Russian who had fled from the Soviet Union had been living with his wife in America for some time. One day he came home with a proud look on his face and announced, "Today we finally got the right to be American citizens."

"Wonderful," beamed his wife as she tied an apron around him. "And now wash the dishes."

### 1382   *Rover Expects It*

Wife to husband at restaurant: "I promised Rover we'd bring him home a doggie bag, so order something he likes."

### 1383   *Good Reason*

Three men were in the hospital waiting room when the nurse came from the maternity ward. She said to the first man, "Congratulations, you're the father of twins."

"Wonderful," he exclaimed. "Isn't that a coincidence? I'm a member of the Minnesota Twins baseball team."

Later the nurse returned and said to the second man, "Congratulations, you are the father of triplets."

"Wow," the new father said, "another coincidence. I work for the 3M Company."

The third man said, "Please excuse me nurse while I get an aspirin. I work for 7-Up."

### 1384   *A Father*

A father is a thing that is forced to endure childbirth without an anesthetic.

A father is a thing that growls when it feels good and laughs when scared half to death.

Fathers are what give daughters away to other men who aren't nearly good enough, so they can have grandchildren who are smarter than anybody's.—*Paul Harvey*

### 1385   *She Wanted the Horse*

Said Mrs. Paul Revere: "I don't care who you say is coming. It's my night to use the horse!"

### 1386   *Frank*

Her father asked his prospective son-in-law if he could support a family, and we have to admire the young man's answer: "No, sir, I was only planning to support your daughter. The rest of you will have to take care of yourselves."

### 1387   *Turn About*

A woman waiting at the door ready to go to the store had her arms full of coats and four little children at her side.

Her husband, coming down the stairs asked why she was standing there. She replied, handing him the coats, "This time you put the children's coats on and I'll go honk the horn."

### 1388   *Dad Needs One*

Mamma: "Robert's teacher says he ought to have an encyclopedia."
Papa: "Let him walk to school like I did."

1389    *Playing Ball with God*

A five-year-old surprised his father one day by saying, "I guess I'll go outdoors and play ball with God."

"How do you play ball with God?" asked the father.

"Oh, it's not hard at all. I just throw the ball up and God throws it back down to me."

1390    *Treating*

Bobby came to school with a bag of candy and passed the candy proudly around to his school chums. He even treated his teacher. "What is the occasion for all this?" the teacher asked kindly. "Is it your birthday?"

"No," he said, "I became a brother last night."

1391    *It Helped*

A father was telling a friend how he finally cured his seventeen-year-old son of habitually being late to school: "I bought him a car," he explained.

"But how did that help?"

"Well," replied the father, "he has to get going an hour earlier to find a place in the school parking lot."

1392    *Progress*

It used to be that Papa dealt out a stern code of discipline to Junior. Then the electric razor took away his razor strap, furnaces took away the woodshed, and tax worries took away his hair—and consequently the hairbrush. So to the degree kids are running wild today it may be because their fathers ran out of weapons.

1393    *He Knew Granny*

Johnny praying in a loud voice before his birthday: "Dear God, I pray that I will get a new bicycle for my birthday."

His brother: "What are you shouting for? God isn't deaf."

Johnny: "I know, I know, but Granny is."

1394    *All He Had*

She was sixteen, he was seventeen, and the parents were opposed to their wedding. But they couldn't prevent it without making a scene, so they agreed to it. When the officiating clergyman asked the bridegroom to repeat after him, "With all my worldly goods I thee endow," his father nudged his wife and whispered, "There goes his motor scooter."

1395    *Good Method*

"I got two free ice cream cones again," proudly announced Peter to his mother.

"How did you do that?" she asked distrustfully. "I hope you didn't steal them."

"How can you think such a thing?" replied Peter. "I simply took one cone in my right hand, the other in my left hand, and said to the checker, 'Would you please get my money out of my pocket . . . but be careful not to hurt my little pet toad.' "

## 1396  *Be Careful*

The wife wanted to do some shopping during the day, so at breakfast she asked her husband for $20.

"Money, money, money!" he shouted. "Every day of the week you want more money. If you ask me, I think you need brains more than you need money."

"Perhaps so," his wife agreed, "but I asked you for what I thought you had the most of."

## 1397  *Not Fair*

The bride of only a few months was at the airport to meet her husband. They were waiting for his luggage when he pointed out a good-looking stewardess from the plane, Miss Tracy.

"How do you happen to know her name?" the young wife asked.

He explained that it was listed, together with the names of the pilot and co-pilot, on the door of the cockpit.

The wife's next question was a classic which he could not answer. "Dear," she asked, "what was the pilot's name?"

## 1398  *A Good Reason*

A lady says that she is always sorry when Christmas is over because she knows that after her family has hung up their stockings on Christmas Eve, it will be a whole year before any one of them will hang up anything again.

## 1399  *Baby-Sitter*

Grandma was baby-sitting with the three-year-old and the five-year-old when she fell asleep on the davenport. The five-year-old tugged at her arm. "Wake up, Grandma," he said. "We're not baby-sitting you. You're baby-sitting us—and we want to go to bed."

## 1400  *Don't Blame Him*

Four-year-old Johnny was visiting his grandmother in San Francisco when an earthquake struck. Johnny was in the yard playing, and his alarmed grandmother ran to the door screaming, "Johnny!"

"I didn't do it, Grandma. I didn't do it!" the boy protested.

### 1401  *Wrong Kind*

"I baked a sponge cake for you, darling," said the bride, "but it didn't turn out right. I think the grocer gave me the wrong kind of sponges."

### 1402  *Father's Answer*

Son: "What does 'procrastinate' mean?"
Dad: "I'll tell you later."

### 1403  *Good Idea*

Mark: "Dad, can you sign your name without looking?"
Dad: "Yes, I think so."
Mark: "Good! Please close your eyes and sign my report card."

### 1404  *Smart Dad*

"I guess my father must have been a pretty mischievous boy," said one youngster.
"Why?" inquired the other.
"Because he knows exactly what questions to ask when he wants to know what I've been doing."

### 1405  *He Remembered*

"You think so much of your old golf game that you don't even remember when we were married," complained the wife.
"Of course I do, honey," the husband reassured her. "It was the day after I sank that forty-foot putt."

### 1406  *Changed His Will*

Granddad bought a small, almost unnoticeable hearing aid and was so pleased he returned to the office to express his satisfaction.
"I imagine your relatives are very happy, too," said the salesman.
"Oh, they don't know I have it," chuckled the elderly man. "And am I having fun. In the past two weeks I've changed my will three times."

### 1407  *Is That Nice?*

Mrs. Jones: "That's a lovely coat you're wearing."
Mrs. Smith: "Oh, thank you. My husband gave it to me for my fortieth birthday."
Mrs. Jones: "It certainly wears well, doesn't it?"

### 1408  *His Fault*

"Peter," a mother asked her small son, "why are you making faces at the bulldog?"
"Well," the child defended himself, "he started it."

1409    *Not Easy*

Gary: "Getting money from my dad is like taking candy from a baby."
Mary: "Really?"
Gary: "Yes, he sure puts up a terrific yell."

1410    *It Works*

Woman to her neighbor: "I have the most marvelous recipe for meat loaf—all I have to do is mention it to my husband and he says, 'Let's eat out.' "

1411    *He Understood*

Johnny gazed at his one-day-old brother who was yelling at the top of his voice. "Did he come from Heaven?" Johnny asked his mother.
"Yes, dear," she replied.
"Well," Johnny mused, "I can see why they put him out."

1412    *Funny People*

A young boy stayed at a friend's house for supper. When he came home, his mother asked him if he'd enjoyed himself.
"They're funny," he said. "They didn't even have napkins. They just gave us some pieces of cloth."

1413    *Hidden*

Mrs. Apple: "How do you keep your children out of the cookie jar?"
Mrs. Orange: "I lock the pantry door and hide the key under the soap dish in the bathroom."

1414    *He Was First*

The little boy came home crying to his mother that the neighbor had hit him. "Did you hit him back?" she asked.
"No," replied the youngster, "I hit him first."

1415    *Looking Ahead*

Teenage girl to a saleslady: "I'm really crazy about this outfit, but can I exchange it for something else if my mother happens to like it?"

1416    *Tact*

"William, you've forgotten my birthday again," sobbed the disappointed wife.
"Darling," soothed the husband, "how can you expect me to remember your birthday when you don't ever look a day older?"

1417    *Daddy or Me*

It was very nice of Santa Claus to bring that lovely train, but just the same, I don't believe I'll ask for one again; 'cause he forgot to make it clear, or we never looked to see, who the train was for, that Santa left—for Daddy or for me!

### 1418 *The Walker*

Father bought a little car, he feeds it gasoline; and everywhere that father goes, he walks—his son's sixteen.

### 1419 *That Makes It Clear*

She was talking about her various relatives. "Yes," she said, "my sister and me ain't no more alike than if we wasn't us; and she's just as different as me, in the other way!"

### 1420 *Forgotten Quotations*

Mrs. Isaac Newton: "Another apple just fell off the tree, dear. Why don't you come out and look at it—maybe you'll make another discovery."

### 1421 *Odd Years*

Mrs. Smith: "How long have you been married?"
Mrs. Jones: "Thirty odd years."
Mrs. Smith: "Why have they been odd?"
Mrs. Jones: "Just wait till you see my husband."

### 1422 *Afraid to Marry*

A young colleague admitted to Theodor Fontane that he could not make up his mind to get married because he was afraid of women.

"But that's just why you should marry," advised Fontane. "A married man only has to be afraid of one woman; an unmarried man has to be afraid of all of them!"

### 1423 *It Looked That Way*

Bob: "I think my mother wants to get rid of me."
Don: "Why do you say that?"
Bob: "Well, this morning she wrapped my lunch in a road map."

### 1424 *Substitute*

Little Mary insisted that she be allowed to serve the tea when her mother was entertaining one afternoon. Mother, with crossed fingers, consented. However, she became annoyed by the long delay and asked, "Why did you take so long, child?"

"I couldn't find the tea strainer," answered Mary.

"Then how did you strain it so well?"

"I used the fly swatter."

### 1425  *Economical*

"Our daughter and son-in-law thought of a foolproof method of saving money on food," a woman told her good friend. "They purchased one of those economy cars—and began driving to our house for dinner."

### 1426  *Different*

Seven-year-old William had been taught that Sunday is not a day of play, but one to be set aside for church and kindred matters. Naturally his mother was surprised one Sunday morning to find him sailing his toy boat in the bathtub.

"William! Don't you know better than to sail boats on Sunday when you should be dressing for Sunday school?"

"Don't get excited, Mother," replied William calmly. "This isn't a pleasure trip. This is a missionary boat going to Africa."

### 1427  *Looking Ahead*

Uncle: "And what are you going to be when you grow up, Freddy?"

Freddy: "I'm going to be a philanthropist; they always have such a lot of money."

### 1428  *A Good Bad Reason*

"It's time for all good boys to be in bed," said Mother to Billy.

"But Mother," said Billy, "don't you remember that I wasn't good today?"

### 1429  *Had a Problem*

A father returned home from work one day and found his small daughter sitting on the front porch steps, looking very unhappy. "What's wrong, honey?" he asked.

"Just between me and you," the child replied, "I can't get along with your wife."

### 1430  *We Doubt It*

Little boy: "I et four eggs for breakfast this morning."

Big sister: "You mean ate."

Little boy: "Maybe you're right. Maybe I et eight eggs for breakfast this morning."

### 1431  *Is That Fair?*

Pop: "I'm just conceited enough to think that our son gets his intelligence from me."

Mom: "Well, he must. I've still got mine."

### 1432    *Rush Order*

"Dear Sandy Klaus: I wanna put in a new order quick as I jest found all the things which I ast you for under the spare room bed."

### 1433    *In December*

The most important question of the month: "What size bedroom slipper does Dad wear?"

### 1434    *Fast Thinking*

Father: "Did I hear the clock strike three when you came home last night?"
Son: "Yes, Dad. It was going to strike eleven, but I stopped it so it wouldn't wake you up."

### 1435    *It Isn't Fair*

Life isn't fair to us men. When we are born, our mothers get all the compliments and the flowers. When we are married, our brides get the presents and the publicity. When we die, our widows get the insurance and the winters in Florida.
—*Viking Vacuum*

### 1436    *Doing His Best*

"What are you doing in the pantry, Willie?" his mother asked sternly.
"Fighting temptation, Mother," Willie replied meekly.

### 1437    *Tactful Question*

"Mother," asked little Johnny one day when a number of guests were present at dinner, "is the dessert not good for me or is there enough to go around?"

### 1438    *May Not Be Adequate*

A college freshman was expounding on her idea of the perfect mate. "The man I marry," she said, "must shine among company, be musical, tell jokes, sing, dance, and stay at home."
Her boyfriend replied, "What you want is a television set."

### 1439    *Getting Even*

Irate mother: "If you don't behave I'll call a policeman and tell him about you."
Naughty boy: "And if you do, I'll tell him we've got a dog and no license."

### 1440    *Marriage*

"The rapidly increasing divorce rate," remarked the wit, "indicates we are indeed becoming the land of the free."
"Yes," replied his practical friend, "but the continuing marriage rate suggests this is still the home of the brave."

### 1441    Gift Wrap

The father watching his daughter select a very expensive wedding gown: "I don't mind giving you away, but must I gift-wrap you, too?"

### 1442    Her Loss

A woman asked a butcher, "Have you a fifteen-pound roast?" The butcher wrestled the roast out of the refrigerator and laid it on the counter. The woman looked at it, sighed happily, and turned to leave.

The butcher, eager to make a sale said, "It is U.S. prime. Doesn't it suit you?"

"Oh, I didn't want to buy it," the woman said. "I've just lost fifteen pounds and wanted to see what so much meat looks like."

### 1443    Tough Question

Dad: "That boy will be the death of me!"

Mom: "What's wrong now?"

Dad: "He wants to know what would happen if he mixed a bottle of ink eradicator with a bottle of ink!"

### 1444    Be Careful

Uncle: "You boys today want too much money. Do you know what I was getting when I married your aunt?"

Nephew: "Nope, and I bet you didn't either."

### 1445    In Trouble

The Newlyweds were giving their first Christmas dinner. Since her husband was a novice at carving, Mrs. Newlywed insisted that he study that section in her new cookbook lest he display his ignorance before the guests.

At the proper time the turkey was placed before the inexperienced host, who was plainly at a loss to know how to proceed.

"Go on, dear, carve it!" whispered the loyal young wife. "You know exactly how to do it from the directions in the book."

"Of course, I do," came back the troubled answer, "but I can't find any of the dotted lines!"

### 1446    Modern Youth

A little girl about five received a box of crayons for Christmas and made a great many pictures.

"What is this one?" her mother asked.

"That's the Baby Jesus in the manger."

A little to one side were three vertical lines—the wise men perhaps, or the shepherds. The mother inquired what they were.

"Mary and Joseph are going out for the night," the child explained, "and that's the sitters coming in."—*Capper's Weekly*

### 1447    *No Promises*

A New York mother took her five-year-old son to Gimbels to say "Hello" to Santa Claus, who, in turn, asked, "What would you like for Christmas, sonny?"

"A bicycle, a football, and a pair of skates," the youngster replied promptly.

"I'll certainly try to see that you get them," said Santa.

Later, mother and son visited Macy's and stopped to see Santa there. Again the same question and the same answer, but Santa asked, "And are you going to be a good boy?"

The boy turned to his mother and said, "Let's go back to Gimbels; I didn't have to make any promises there."

### 1448    *Hopeless*

"Papa?"

"Well, my son?"

"Is there a Christian flea?"

"What on earth put that idea into your head?"

"The preacher read it today from the Bible: 'The wicked flee, when no man pursueth.' "

"Why, Tommy, that means that wicked men flee."

"Oh! Is there a wicked woman flea, too?"

"No, no; it means that the wicked flee—run away."

"Why do they run?"

"Who?"

"The wicked fleas."

"No, no. Don't you see? The wicked man runs away when no man is after him."

"Oh, then is there a woman after him?"

"Tommy—go to bed!"

### 1449    *Helpful*

At the breakfast table, Johnny told his father, "A Boy Scout is supposed to do a good deed every day. I've already done mine today."

"Fine, Johnny," said the proud father; "what is it you've done so bright and early?"

"Well, you know how big and fat Jake Brender is," Johnny said. "Well, when I saw him he was winded and puffing a lot, and I was sure he was going to miss the bus and be late for work at the airplane plant. So I set Tige on him. He made it!"

### 1450    *A Priceless Book*

Little Timmy had bought Grandma a Bible for Christmas and wanted to write a suitable inscription on the flyleaf. He racked his brain for something to write, until he remembered that his father, an author, had a stack of books that he presented to his friends, and each one had the same inscription. So Tommy decided to copy it.

Imagine Grandma's surprise on Christmas morning when she opened her gift, and found a Bible neatly inscribed as follows: "To Grandma, with the best wishes of the author."

### 1451 *Of Course*

"And would you love me as much if my father lost all his money?"

"Has he?"

"Why, no."

"Of course I would, darling."

### 1452 *Naturally*

Mrs. Jones went into a photographer's studio and asked him to enlarge a picture of her late husband. She gave him explicit instructions and concluded by saying, "And for heaven's sake, take off that awful-looking hat."

The photographer said: "I think I can do that. What color hair did he have and what side did he part it on?"

Mrs. Jones thought for a moment, then smiled and said: "I can't remember, but when you take off the hat you can see for yourself."

### 1453 *Bad Both Ways*

Dobb: "What's that piece of cord tied around your finger for?"

Botham: "My wife put it there to remind me to mail her letter."

"And did you mail it?"

"No. She forgot to give it to me!"

### 1454 *Good Reason*

Mrs. Muggins: "It's raining, and Mrs. Goodrich wants to go home. I have no umbrella to lend her except my new one. Can I let her have yours?"

Mr. Muggins: "Hardly! The only umbrella I have has her husband's name on the handle."

### 1455 *Well Said*

Little boy with hiccoughs addressing his mother: "Look, Ma, I'm percolating."

### 1456 *The Truth*

Grandmother was escorting two little girls around the zoo. While they were looking at the stork, she told them how it was instrumental in bringing them to their mother.

The children looked at each other with sly glances, and one whispered to the other: "Don't you think we ought to tell Grandma the truth?"

### 1457 *Experienced*

One of the ladies was describing the wedding she had just attended:

"And then, just as Frank and the widow started up the aisle to the altar, every light in the church went out."

"And what did the couple do then?" someone questioned.

"Kept on going. The widow knew the way."

### 1458 *Worried*

Mother, to her small son who was standing near a raspberry bush: "You seem to be worrying."

Son: "Have raspberries any legs?"

Mother: "No."

Son: "Then I think I just swallowed a caterpillar."

### 1459 *Perfect Agreement*

Mother: "Hush! You two children are always quarreling. Why can't you agree once in a while?"

Georgia: "We do agree, Mama. Edith wants the biggest apple and so do I."

### 1460 *Looking Ahead*

The newly married pair quarreled. The wife in a passion finally declared, "I'm going home to Mother!"

The husband maintained his calm in the face of this calamity, and took out his pocketbook. "Here," he said, counting out some bills, "is the money for your plane fare."

The wife took it and counted it. Then she said scornfully, "But that isn't enough for a return ticket."

### 1461 *The Postage Stamp*

There was a little postage stamp, no bigger than your thumb, but still it stuck right on the job until its work was done. They licked it and pounded it till it would make you sick! But the more it took the licking, why, the tighter it would stick.

Let's be like that postage stamp, in playing life's big game, and stick to what we know is right, and we can't miss our aim.

### 1462 *A Triangle*

A young actor leaped into fame, but remained his own most ardent fan. He came home one night to find his wife weeping. She told him the eternal triangle was going to break up their happy home.

"Nonsense!" exclaimed the young star. "I'm world famous today, and yet I've never so much as looked at another woman. How can you say there's a triangle?"

"But there is a triangle!" sobbed the wife. "You see, both you and I are in love with you!"

### 1463    *Hard to Believe*

Mother: "Well, Mollie, what are little girls made of?"

Mollie: "Sugar and spice and all that's nice."

Mother: "And what are little boys made of?"

Mollie: "Snips and snails and puppy dogs' tails. I told Bobby that yesterday, and he could hardly believe it."

### 1464    *Of Course*

The little girl in the zoological park tossed bits of a bun to the stork, which gobbled them greedily and bobbed its head toward her for more.

"What kind of a bird is it, Mamma?" the child asked.

The mother read the placard, and answered that it was a stork.

"Oh!" the little girl cried, as her eyes rounded. "Of course, it recognized me!"

### 1465    *Expecting Too Much*

Father: "Peter, how do you like school?"

Peter: "I like school okay, but not the teacher."

Father: "Don't like the teacher? Why not, son?"

Peter: "Because she told me to sit in the front seat for the present, and then she didn't give me the present!"

### 1466    *He Was Careful*

Mother: "It is rude to whisper, Humphrey."

Humphrey (aged five): "Well, I was saying what a funny nose that man's got. It would have been much ruder if I'd said it aloud."

### 1467    *Be Careful*

A young husband did not like hash. His wife acquired a French cookbook, which gave recipes for using leftovers. The next evening she had one of the fancy mixtures in a covered dish on the table. The husband raised the cover and began to serve himself.

The wife looked on questioningly and asked, "Why don't you ask the blessing first, dear?"

The husband replied, "I don't believe there is anything here that hasn't already been blessed."

### 1468    *Economical*

"Jimmy, isn't it rather extravagant to eat both butter and jam on your bread at the same time?"

"Oh, no, Mother. It's economy. You see, the same piece of bread does for both."

### 1469 *Hard Question*

The explorer, bowing low, approached the savage chief. "I come to you," he began ceremoniously, "from beyond the sunset, from the Great White King—"

"Tell me," interrupted the chief, "why don't you guys do something about the lousy radio programs you send over here?"

### 1470 *Taking Turns*

Mother: "Did you remember to pray for everybody, dear?"

Daughter: "Well, Mommy, I prayed for you, but Jack prayed for Daddy. He's looking after him just now."

### 1471 *Bragging*

Three small boys were bragging about their fathers. The first boy said, "My dad writes a few short lines on a paper, calls it a poem, and gets ten dollars for it."

"My dad," spoke up the second, "makes some dots on a piece of paper, calls it a song, and gets twenty-five dollars for it."

"That's nothing," declared the third boy. "My father writes a sermon on a sheet of paper, gets up in the pulpit and reads it, and it takes four men to collect the money!"

### 1472 *Try Anyway*

Johnny was stuck with his arithmetic lesson. "Grandpa," he pleaded, "could you help me with this?"

"I could, my boy," replied his grandfather, "but it wouldn't be right, would it?"

"I don't suppose it would," was Johnny's reply, "but take a shot at it anyway, Grandpa."

### 1473 *Expensive*

"You don't mean to say it cost you seven thousand dollars to have your family tree looked up?"

"No. Two thousand dollars to have it looked up and five thousand dollars to have it hushed up."

### 1474 *Worried*

Small bridesmaid (loudly, in the middle of the ceremony): "Mommy, are we all getting married?"

### 1475    A Comparison

As the orchestra on the radio struck up a new rock tune, the daughter exclaimed, "Did you ever hear anything so stunning?"

"No," replied her father. "The nearest thing to it I ever heard was when a truck loaded with empty milk cans had a collision with a truck loaded with live ducks."

### 1476    It Was His Fault

Betty: "Mother, Robert broke a window."
Mother: "My, my! How did he do it?"
Betty: "I threw a rock at him and he dodged."

### 1477    Simple

She was sick, and her husband, who was fixing her a cup of tea, called out that he couldn't find the tea.

"I don't know what could be easier to find," she answered. "It's right in front on the pantry shelf in a cocoa tin marked 'Matches.'"

### 1478    Son, Be Careful

You wear his socks, and borrow his ties—or anything else that may be your size. And when you finish, they're tossed on the floor—now do you wonder why father gets sore?

### 1479    Both Pairs the Same

Dad: "You brought me the wrong boots, son. Can't you see that one of them is black and the other brown?"
Son: "Yes, Dad, but your other pair is just the same."

### 1480    The June Groom

Do you weary of society notes about June brides? Believing in a square deal, we present this news item:

"Mr. Hiram Norcross became the bridegroom of Miss Emily Lewis in a pretty ceremony today. He was attended by Mr. Schultz as best man. As the groom came in he was the cynosure of all eyes.

"He was charmingly clad in a going-away three-piece suit, consisting of coat, vest, and pants. A story was current among the guests to the effect that the coat was the same one worn by his father and grandfather on their wedding days, but he shyly evaded questions on this sentimental touch.

"The severe simplicity of the groom's pants was relieved by the right pants leg being artistically caught up by a hose supporter, revealing a glimpse of brown holeproof sock above the genuine leather shoe.

"Blue galluses gracefully curved over each shoulder were attached to the pants fore and aft, while a loosely knotted blue tie rode under his left ear above a starched collar with a delicate saw-edging. This gave the effect of studied carelessness which marks supreme artistry in male attire.

"Mr. Schultz's costume was essentially like the groom's and as the two approached the altar a hush of awed admiration enveloped the gathered throng.

"The presence of the bride was also observed by many."

### 1481  *Confused*

Told to put her right hand on her heart, a kindergartener put her hand behind her back. When the teacher asked the child why she did that, she replied: "Every time I go to see my Grandma Jones, she always pats me on the back and says to me, 'Bless your little heart.' "

### 1482  *Say That Again!*

The following notice appeared in a small-town paper: "On next Wednesday evening the Ladies' Aid Society will hold a rummage sale. Good chance to get rid of anything not worth keeping but too good to throw away. Ladies, bring your husbands."

### 1483  *Repetition*

The alert boy of the household very much wanted a watch for Christmas. The family had the custom of repeating Scripture memory verses at the breakfast table, and by way of keeping them all reminded, he made frequent use of the verse: "What I say unto you I say unto all: watch."

### 1484  *Certainly*

"Yes, I'm a cosmopolitan. My father was Irish, my mother Italian. I was born in a Swedish boat off Barcelona, and a man named McTavish is my dentist."

"What's McTavish to do with it?"

"Why, that makes me of Scottish extraction."

### 1485  *Natural Conclusion*

Tommy had been going to kindergarten for several months. He was walking down the street one day with his mother when they passed another small boy. Tommy said, "Hello, Johnny!"

When they had gone, his mother asked Tommy what the other boy's last name was.

"It's Johnny Sitdown," replied Tommy. "That's what the teacher calls him."

### 1486  *Logical*

We heard a fellow say the other day that baseball players ought to make good husbands, because they're always in a hurry to get home.

1487    *Statistical Expert*

Mother wanted to spend Saturday afternoon shopping, and father—a statistician—reluctantly agreed to abandon his golf and spend the afternoon with the three small, energetic children.

When mother returned, father handed her this:

Dried tears—9 times

Tied shoes—13 times

Served water—18 times

Toy balloons purchased—3 for each child

Average life of balloon—exactly 12 seconds

Cautioned children not to cross street—21 times

Children insisted on crossing street—21 times

Number of Saturdays father will do this again—0

1488    *How He Learns?*

Son: "Pop, what's the capital of Uruguay?"

Father: "I don't know, son."

Son: "Where was Washington born?"

Father: "I don't know."

Son: "What's a polygon."

Father: "I don't know."

Mother: "Don't bother your father!"

Father: "Let him ask questions. How else is he going to learn?"

1489    *He Might Complain*

The woman motorist touring Europe posed for a souvenir snapshot before the fallen pillars of a historic ruin in Greece.

"Don't get the car in the picture," she said, "or my husband will swear I ran into the place!"

1490    *It's Different Now*

Remember when your mother used to say, "Go to your room"? This was a terrible penalty. Now when a mother says the same thing, a kid goes to his room. There he's got an air conditioner, a TV set, an intercom, a shortwave radio—he's better off than he was in the first place.—*Sam Levenson*

1491    *What He Learns*

There's nothing like a wedding to make a fellow learn—at first he thinks she's his'n, but later learns he's her'n!

1492    *His Orders*

Mr. Peterson was preparing to go to market and his wife told him to get a head of cabbage.

"What size?" he asked.

"Oh, about the size of your head," she told him.

On the way, Peterson met a friend who was a gardener. "Just go over to my garden and take any head of cabbage you want," the friend offered generously.

Later, another friend asked the gardener, "What kind of idiot did you have walking in your garden? When I went by, he was trying his hat on one head of cabbage after another."

## 1493  *Modesty*

Mrs. Smith was vigorously powdering her face before going out. "Why do you go to all that trouble?" asked Mr. Smith, who was patiently waiting.

"Modesty, my dear," replied Mrs. Smith.

"Modesty?"

"Yes—I've no desire to shine in public."

## 1494  *Knows His Geography*

Johnny had finished a difficult geography lesson. On his way home he witnessed a serious accident. He came running into the house and exclaimed, "Jack Williams fell out of his car and nearly broke his peninsula."

"What in the world do you mean, Johnny?" asked his mother.

"Peninsula—he fell out and almost broke his peninsula: a long neck stretching out to see."

## 1495  *Definite Complaint*

Susan was seven, and she didn't want to take her music lesson. "Why, Susan," said her mother, "don't you like music?"

"No!" exclaimed Susan. "I hate those little black things sitting on the white fence!"

## 1496  *Miracle*

Wife to husband: "Isn't it wonderful? My check stubs come out exactly even this month! One for each check."

## 1497  *Looking for a Diet Menu*

A small boy asked his mother: "Do you know what makes the Tower of Pisa lean?"

And she said: "No—if I did, I would take some."

## 1498  *At Home*

Wife to husband: "According to my figures, the Old Reliable Bank has made a mistake of $3,221.50 in their favor."

1499 *Great Shopping Spree*

Wife to husband (after a big shopping afternoon): "And to think it isn't going to cost us a cent. The bank has started returning our checks."

1500 *Love*

Oh, yes, each man spoils the one he loves, and gratifies her wishes—the rich man showers her with gifts, while the poor man does the dishes!

1501 *No Faults in Her Children*

Mother: "Mrs. X can never see any faults in her children."
Father: "Mothers never can."
Mother: "What a silly thing to say! I am sure I could see faults in our children —if they had any."

1502 *Treating Parents with Awe*

Psychologists say the modern child treats his parents with awe. It's always: "Aw, why can't I have the car?" or "Aw, why can't I have a bigger allowance?"

1503 *His Program*

Boy: "When I get to high school I will go in for baseball, handball, and football."
Father: "Is that all you'll take up in high school?"
Boy: "Yes, Pop—I don't care for basketball."

1504 *Surprised*

Mother: "Were you surprised when they nominated you for president of the club?"
Daughter: "I'll say I was. My acceptance speech nearly fell out of my hand."

1505 *Great Impression*

Problem child: "Dad, you must have made a marvelous impression on my teacher last month."
Dad: "Is that so?"
Problem child: "Yes, she wants to see you again tomorrow."

1506 *Dad Is Stuck*

"But Dad, it wouldn't be cricket if I helped you with my homework."

1507 *Not Certain*

"Now, Billy, what are you going to give your dear little brother for Christmas?"
"Don't know," replied Billy. "Last year I gave him the measles."

### 1508    Unfair

Wife (to husband holding canceled checks): "You mean the bank saves all the checks I write and sends them to you? What an underhanded thing to do!"

### 1509    A Logical Thought

Junior was having his first ride in an elevator. He squeezed his father's hand nervously as they went up floor after floor in the skyscraper. Finally he asked in an awed whisper, "Daddy, does God know we're coming up?"

### 1510    Howling Accompaniment

The ten-year-old had just started taking trumpet lessons, and every time he practiced, his dog yowled. Annoyed, the boy complained, "You'd think there'd be one song he doesn't know!"

### 1511    He Should Know Better

Mother: "John, it's positively shameful the way Junior talks. I just heard him say, 'I ain't went nowhere.' "
Father: "I should say it is a shame! Why, he has traveled twice as much as most boys his age!"

### 1512    No Picnic

A woman who got on the bus with ten children was asked by the conductor if they were all her own, or was it a picnic? "They're all mine," she sighed. "And believe me, it's no picnic!"

### 1513    Quintuplets

Joe: "The stork's getting lazy."
Sam: "Getting lazy?"
Joe: "Well, he's bringing them five at a time now."

### 1514    It's Cleaner

Mother: "Oh, Mary, why do you wipe your mouth with the back of your hand?"
Mary: " 'Cause it's so much cleaner than the front."

### 1515    Prepared

Mother (briefing son before a party): "Be sure to thank Mrs. Jones for having you, and tell her you are sorry that you were so naughty!"

### 1516    She Knew What She Liked

The four-year-old was asked how she liked her Thanksgiving dinner.
"I didn't like the turkey much, but I sure loved the bread it ate."

### 1517 *Minor Detail*

Bride-to-be: "Mother, this wedding must be absolutely perfect. We mustn't overlook the most insignificant detail."

Mother: "Don't worry—he'll show up!"

### 1518 *Today Is Tomorrow*

Joyce: "Dad, is today Wednesday?"

Dad: "No, today is Thursday."

Joyce: "But you said yesterday that today is Wednesday."

Dad: "Well, today was Wednesday yesterday. Yesterday Thursday was tomorrow today. When today is tomorrow, today will be yesterday. Today is today, now. Now do you understand?"

### 1519 *Good Reason*

Little Eddie was almost through his nightly prayer. "Bless my dad, bless my mommy, bless Aunt Jenny." Then he added fervently, "And please make St. Louis the capital of Missouri. Amen."

"Why, Eddie!" exclaimed his mother. "Why on earth did you say such a thing."

"Because," explained Eddie, "I put that on my examination paper today."

### 1520 *Which Talk*

Mother: "How was your talk this morning in the public-speaking class?"

Son: "Which one do you mean? The one I was going to give, the one I did give, or the one I delivered so brilliantly to myself on the way home in the bus?"

### 1521 *Observant Boy*

Small boy: "Mommy, you're beautiful even when you yawn!"

### 1522 *Don't Try Peas*

Mom: "Son, why are you eating with your knife?"

Son: "My fork leaks."

### 1523 *Don't Cry*

Little Tommy, crying lustily, came out of a room in which his father was doing some amateur carpentering.

"Why, Tommy, what's the matter?" his mother asked.

"D-d-daddy hit his finger with the hammer," sobbed Tommy.

"Well, you needn't cry about anything like that," comforted his mother. "Why didn't you laugh?"

"I did!" sobbed Tommy.

### 1524 *Safe*

After many exciting days in preparation for their vacation trip, the Smiths had at last caught the plane. Now, while they were sitting quietly, they began to wonder if they had forgotten anything. Suddenly Mrs. Smith shrieked, "Oh, Harry, I forgot to turn off the electric iron!"

"Don't worry, dear," he replied, "nothing will burn. I just remembered that I forgot to turn off the shower."

### 1525 *Similar Situation*

Policeman: "Why didn't you report the robbery right away? Didn't you suspect something when you came home and discovered all the drawers opened and the contents scattered about?"

Woman: "No, I didn't suspect a thing. I just thought my husband had been looking for a clean shirt."

### 1526 *No Easy Answer*

The young lad had been told to eat well so he'd grow up tall.

"Are you going to grow any bigger, Daddy?" asked the youngster.

"Why, no, son," said the father.

"You mean," said the amazed son, "that you're not going to grow any more the rest of your life?"

"That's right," replied Father.

"Well," the lad said, "then why do you keep on eating?"

### 1527 *The Answer?*

The mother plopped her four-year-old daughter on a chair and told her to stay there because she had been naughty. The little girl sat there awhile in silence and then exclaimed, "I'll bet if Daddy had known you were going to act this way, he wouldn't have married you!"

### 1528 *Full Day*

Housewife, having finally tucked small boy into bed after an unusually trying day: "Well, I've worked today from son-up to son-down!"

### 1529 *Oh Boy!*

A young mother had trouble with a small son who locked himself in the bathroom, then either could not or would not open the door.

Finally, she called the fire department and explained the predicament. When the fireman who showed up was told it was a little boy, he called out, "You come out of there, little girl!"

Promptly the door flew open, and an indignant boy marched out. The fireman grinned. "Works nearly every time," he said.

1530    *Ask Dad*

Daughter: "Tell me, what do you think makes a marriage successful?"
Mother: "I think you'd better ask your father. After all, he made a more successful marriage than I did."

1531    *Applies to All of Us*

Jones: "How do you spend your income?"
Johnson: "About thirty percent for shelter, thirty percent for clothing, forty percent for food, and twenty percent for amusement."
Jones: "But that adds up to a hundred and twenty percent!"
Johnson: "Don't I know it!"

1532    *A Secret?*

The fortuneteller at a tearoom in Texas told a real-estate dealer's wife that her second husband would be handsome and clever.
"What's that?" the husband demanded when the wife told him about it. "Do you mean to say you were married once before and never told me about it?"

1533    *Halfway*

Brother (after quarrel): "Sis, I'll meet you halfway."
Sister: "How?"
Brother: "I'll admit I'm wrong, if you'll admit I'm right."

1534    *Be Careful*

A budget-minded bride had been preparing hamburger in as many different ways as she knew how. On the twelfth straight night, as she served chopped meat, her husband surveyed it and sighed: "How now, ground cow?"

1535    *Didn't Do Nothing*

Little Steve sometimes used bad language. One day Steve got an invitation to a birthday party. As he left the house, his mother's final caution was, "Stephen, I've asked Mrs. Wilson to send you home the minute you use a bad word."
Twenty minutes later Steve was back home. His mother was angry. Steve was sent to bed. His attempts at explanation were ignored. A little later, however, his mother went upstairs to see how Steve was doing. Sitting at his bedside, she inquired, "Tell me truthfully, Steve, just why Mrs. Wilson sent you home. What did you do?"
Little Steve, humiliated, but still wrathful, replied, "Do? I didn't do nothing! That party ain't till tomorrow!"

### 1536    *Don't Disturb*

At the side of the road a woman looked helplessly at a flat tire.

A passerby stopped to help her. After the tire was changed the woman said, "Please let the jack down easy. My husband is sleeping in the back seat."

### 1537    *The Real Question*

Young husband: "You must economize! Think of the future—if I were to die, where would you be?"

Young wife: "I'd be here all right, the question is—where would you be?"

### 1538    *A Mystery*

One of the great mysteries of family life is where parents learn about all the things they later tell their children not to do.

### 1539    *As She Heard It*

A youngster who had listened to too many TV commercials started singing, "Sing a song of six-packs."

### 1540    *Not Appreciated*

The son in college was applying pressure for more money from home. "I cannot understand why you call yourself a kind father," he wrote his dad, "when you haven't sent me a check for three weeks. What kind of kindness do you call that?"

"That's unremitting kindness," wrote the father in his next letter as he enclosed a check.

### 1541    *School Daze*

What they think when little Johnny starts to school for the first time:

His mother: My little darling is almost grown up!

His father: I hope he makes fullback.

His sister: Now I've got to walk to school with him and can't go with the other kids.

The neighbors: Thank goodness! Now we can have peace for a few hours a day.

His dog: Yoo-o-ow!!!

### 1542    *Progress*

"I am Red Eagle," said the Indian to the paleface visiting the reservation. "This is my son Fighting Bird. And here," he added, "is my grandson Boeing 747."—*The Fabricator, Detroit, Michigan*

### 1543    *Any More Questions?*

A young man was trying to impress some people he'd just met at a party.

"My family's ancestry is quite old and dates back to the days of King Henry the Eighth of England," he boasted, and turning to an elderly woman seated next to him, asked, "How old is your family, dear?"

"Well," she replied with a reserved smile, "I can't really say because all of our family records were lost in the Flood."

## 1544  Smart Child

A young mother tiptoed into her daughter's room one night during a rather noisy electrical storm, just to make sure the child was not frightened.

The sleepy little girl, awakened by the noise outside, asked her mother, "Is Daddy still working on the TV?"

## 1545  Only Six More

Mother: "How much do you charge for taking pictures of children?"
Photographer: "Twenty dollars a dozen."
Mother: "Oh, I guess I'll have to wait awhile, I only have six children now."

## 1546  Never Heard of It

An Eskimo mother was sitting in the igloo reading from a storybook to her small son. "Little Jack Horner," she read, "sat in a corner."

"Mother," asked the boy, "what's a corner?"

## 1547  Helpful

"Could I have a day off, sir, to help my wife with the spring cleaning?"
"No, I'm afraid not—"
"Thank you, sir. I knew I could rely on you."

## 1548  Really Needed Help

Little girl to policeman: "Please, sir, will you take my little brother home? He's lost."
Policeman: "Why can't you take him home?"
Girl: "Because I'm lost too."

## 1549  An Idea?

"Why is father singing to the baby so much tonight?"
"He is trying to sing him to sleep."
"Well, if I was baby, I'd pretend I was asleep."

## 1550  Lucky

John was out with the boys one evening and before he realized it the morning of the next day had dawned. He hesitated to call home but finally hit upon an idea.

He rang his house. When his wife answered the phone he shouted, "Don't pay the ransom, honey, I escaped!"

1551    Small boy's definition of Father's Day: "It's just like Mother's Day only you don't spend so much."

1552    No cowboy hero was ever faster on the draw than a grandmother pulling baby pictures out of her purse.

1553    Wrinkles are hereditary. Parents get them from their children.—*Doris Day*

1554    I sometimes try to argue with my wife, but every time I do, words flail me.

1555    There's nothing like a dish towel for wiping that contented look off a married man's face.

1556    *Opera:* Where women who are bored at home take their husbands to be bored.

1557    After all the discussions about peace, statistics show the usual number of couples were married last year.

1558    A baby will make love stronger, days shorter, nights longer, bankroll smaller, home happier, clothes shabbier, the past forgotten, and the future worth living for.

1559    Unmarried men commit most of our crimes but are not told about them so often.

1560    An allowance is what you pay your children to live with you.

1561    The latest description of a bigamist is a man who makes the same mistake twice.

1562    "Better Boys—Better Men" is the fitting slogan that has been given Boy Scout Week. Also, it can be turned around.

1563    A bride of eighteen faces the task of cooking 50,000 meals, but not if she has a can opener.

1564    One of the excuses alleged by a Chicago attorney for a client up for robbery was "inherited glandular maladjustments." Something wrong with the fellow's glandparents?

1565    A court says a man has the right to get drunk in his own home. Thus is the sanctity of the home preserved.

1566    All a married man expects his wife to be is a sweetheart, a valet, an audience, and a nurse.

1567    As an incentive to industry, enterprise, and thrift, there isn't anything that can beat twins.

1568    A pedestrian is a car owner with a wife and two daughters.

1569    A burglar in London takes nothing but wedding presents. A little discrimination could establish this fellow as a benefactor of mankind.

1570    *Grandparent:* Something so simple a child can operate it.

1571    The supreme example of vanity is a parent trying year after year to make his child just what he is.

1572    Overheard: "My wife loves to buy anything marked down. Today she came home from the store with two dresses and an escalator."

1573    A wife is a person who is expected to buy without money and sew on buttons before they have even become loose.

1574    Many women have always been firm believers in recycling, only they call it by a different name—garage sales.

1575    By the time he whispers, "We were made for each other," she's already planning alterations.

1576    The modern hitching post is the third finger of a girl's left hand.

1577    If you think women are better qualified than men to pick the best candidates, look at who they marry.

1578    If a husband has troubles, he should tell his wife, and if he hasn't he should tell the world how he does it.

1579    A family is a unit composed not only of children, but of men, women, an occasional animal, and the common cold.—*Ogden Nash*

1580    Probably no man ever got so much conversation out of a surgical operation as Adam did.

1581    One thing about drive-in movies: you know where the wife's shoes are when you start for home.

1582    If men acted after marriage as they do during courtship, there would be fewer divorces—and more bankruptcies.—*Frances Rodman*

1583    In a supermarket the other day, I heard a wife remark philosophically to her husband: "Look at it this way, dear—the more it costs, the more green stamps we get!"

1584    Many a boy at sixteen can't believe that someday he will be as dumb as his dad.

1585    Appearances are often deceiving. A woman's thumb may have a man under it.

1586    A psychologist says if a child is naughty, you should switch his attention. How's that?

1587    The husband who brags about being the boss at home probably doesn't tell the truth otherwise either.

1588    If your wife laughs at your jokes, you either know some good jokes or you have a loving wife.

1589    The average husband works hard all year to buy conveniences for his home and then spends his summer at a shack on the lake with no conveniences.

1590    Even back in Grandpa's time there was something to make you sleep. They called it work.

1591    Many a spoiled child is the kind of youngster his mother tells him not to play with.

1592    A bride today has so many showers that all her friends get soaked— some several times.

1593    When a woman marries now, she gets a husband and unskilled domestic help.

1594    No husband ever has a private income—for long.

1595    Give your wife enough rope and she will put up another clothesline in the bathroom.

1596    There are a lot of forty-hour-a-week fathers with seventy-hour-a-week wives—and vice versa.

1597    One thing about mischievous youngsters is that they get their parents home from the party early.

1598    If all men are alike, why do women find it so hard to pick one?

1599 It may be bad manners to go down the street between your wife and the shop windows, but it isn't so dumb.

1600 No woman is married to the same man long, because he isn't the same man long.

1601 The laziest man in the world is the fellow who asks his wife to read a "Do It Yourself" book to him.

1602 Before criticizing your wife's faults, remember that they may have prevented her from getting a better husband.

1603 An optimist is a person who thinks you can take a nice leisurely drive with the family on Sunday afternoon.

1604 A boy's best friend is his father, and if he gets up early and stays up late he may get to see him.

1605 You are born in a hospital, marry in a church, die in a car—what do you need a home for?

1606 A wedding shower is the beginning of a long reign.

1607 Every girl should remember in seeking a model husband that there are two models: sport and working.

1608 Marriage is a good thing. A man who is raising a family isn't raising what Sherman said war was.

1609 Dumbbells will get color in a girl's face, and color in a girl's face will get dumbbells.

1610 The small hat will be in style again this summer, but not the small hat your wife had last summer.

1611 Not all family checkbooks have a happy ending.

1612 No intelligence test known matches matrimony—or driving a car on Sunday afternoon.

1613 Just because a woman says she hasn't a thing to wear doesn't mean her husband can find a spare hook in the closet.

1614 When a wife says she wishes she had gone in for a career instead of marriage, she may not wish it any more than her husband does.

1615 If a husband will just be patient he can train his wife in ten years to do the things she would like to do.

1616    One way to dampen love at first sight is to price a few houses and apartments.

1617    Time flits when you pay the youngster who baby-sits.

1618    Nothing makes a good wife like a good husband.

1619    If the son shines, the parent beams.

1620    If your wife doesn't treat you as she should, be thankful.

1621    If a married couple wants peaceful coexistence, all one of them has to say in an argument is "Yes, my dear."

1622    Youngsters brighten up a home, especially by leaving the lights on everywhere.

1623    A smart husband is one who doesn't have to be told to bring home a little applesauce with the bacon.

1624    Before marriage he spoons around, and later he forks over.

1625    The family you come from isn't as important as the family you're going to have.—*Ring Lardner*

1626    The person who drives the car never knows where the family spent its vacation.

1627    Marriage is the only life sentence that can be commuted for bad behavior.

1628    When divorces become so cheap that poor people can afford them, the last social distinction will be gone.

1629    There are two times when a man doesn't understand a woman—before marriage and after marriage.

1630    A close relative may be a skinflint and yet be the skinflint you love to touch.

1631    No smart pickpocket wastes his time on a married man.

1632    If Mother and Father will hold their noses to the grindstone, their children's may turn up.

1633    No perfume holds a husband like the aroma of a pot of hot coffee.

1634    When a husband acts like a mule, his wife frequently becomes a nag.

1635    The man who goes around finding out who is boss in his home might be happier if he didn't know.

1636    When I was a boy of fourteen, my father was so ignorant I could hardly stand to have the old man around. But when I got to be twenty-one, I was astonished at how much he had learned in seven years.—*Mark Twain*

1637    How much it costs to get married depends on how long you live.

1638    A successful marriage requires falling in love many times—with the same person.

1639    Perhaps nobody becomes more competent in hitting a moving target than a mother spoon-feeding a baby.

1640    There's this to be said for those who have loved and lost—they don't have to attend P.T.A. meetings!

1641    When parental control is remote control, you have juvenile delinquency.

1642    Marriage vows might also include the phrase "until debt do us part."

1643    The only males who boss the household are under three years of age.

1644    The husband who apologizes always has the last word in an argument with his wife.

1645    A model husband is one who, when his wife is away, washes the dishes every day—both of them.

1646    This is a free country, and every man can do just as his wife pleases.

1647    The stork is one thing that gives the poor as good a break as the rich.

1648    The really smart housewife knows exactly what to do with leftovers—throw them out.

1649    Behind every successful man in this world is a woman who couldn't be more surprised.

1650    The person who makes an ashtray out of the living-room rug is not necessarily a magician.

1651    Let's not be hard on relatives. They had no choice in the matter either.

1652    To win friends you must always act surprised when people tell you what you already know.

1653    A baby smiles, cries, and puts his foot in his mouth. So does an adult.

1654    Never tell your wife something is as plain as the nose on her face.

1655    A girl doesn't believe a man who says he is unworthy of her until after they're married.

1656    A poetic husband may long for the wings of a dove, but he will settle for a couple of drumsticks at dinner.

1657    What is home without a mother? The answer is "Modern."

1658    Here's a way to punish your children: take them away from their grandparents.

1659    About the only thing we have left that actually discriminates in favor of the plain people is the stork.

1660    Every married woman gets a man's wages, sooner or later.

1661    Double jeopardy is when a husband with a two-pants suit discovers both pairs need to be replaced.

1662    The bride thinks of three things when she walks into the church—aisle, altar, hymn.

1663    Clothes may make the man, but his wife's may break him.

1664    What the modern home needs most is a family.

1665    The parent who used to say his fifteen-year-old son was ten so he could travel half-fare now says he is sixteen so he can drive the car.

1666    Today's housewife enjoys cooking—especially when it's done by the chef at one of the better restaurants.

1667    "Charity begins at home and generally gets no further" is an old saying of Confucius which I just wrote.

1668    Modern education has changed the commandment to read, "Parents, obey your children."

1669    Life is becoming more complex. Ten years ago a man couldn't understand his wife. Now he can't understand his wife, color television, or jet propulsion.

1670    *Discretion:* When you are sure you are right, and then ask your wife.

1671    Parents don't bring up children anymore; they finance them.

1672    *Overworked:* To be busy continually. Example—a can opener in most families.

1673    A great many prominent family trees were started by grafting.

1674    Many foreigners are seeking homes in America. So are many Americans.

1675    Marriage is the alliance of two people, one of whom never remembers birthdays and the other never forgets them.—*Ogden Nash*

1676    My views on birth control are somewhat distorted by the fact that I was seventh of nine children.—*Robert F. Kennedy*

1677    An archaeologist is the best husband any woman can have: the older she gets, the more interested he is in her.—*Agatha Christie*

1678    A man in love is incomplete until he has married. Then he's finished. —*Zsa Zsa Gabor*

1679    Valentine's Day is approaching, a time to recall that your wife still likes candy and flowers. Show her you remember, by speaking of them occasionally. —*Earl Wilson*

1680    People who've had a hanging in the family don't like to talk about a rope.—*Calvin Coolidge*

1681    A woman wrote of her husband, "He's the sort of man who always hits the nail right on the thumb."

1682    I don't have to look up my family tree, because I know that I'm the sap.—*Fred Allen*

1683    You've been around a long time if you can remember when a pie was set on the windowsill to cool, not to thaw.

1684    In marriage, one quarrels over whether the bedroom window should be open or shut, not about the destiny of the race or the future of mankind.

1685    Being a husband is just like any other job; it's much easier if you like your boss.

1686    We used to say "What's cooking?" when we came home from work. Now it's "What's thawing?"

1687    There is only one pretty child in the world, and every mother has it. —*English proverb*

1688    *Kitchenette:* A narrow aisle that runs between a gas stove and a can of tomatoes.—*Bob Burns*

1689    *Infant Prodigy:* A small child with highly imaginative parents.—*R. H. Creese*

1690    God could not be everywhere, so therefore he made mothers.—*Hebrew proverb*

1691    Marry, or marry not—you will always regret it.

1692    *Marriage:* An armed alliance against the outside world.—*G. K. Chesterton*

1693    *Marriage:* A deal in which a man gives away half his groceries in order to get the other half cooked.—*John Gwynne*

1694    A good housewife now is one who thaws out the meals all by herself.

1695    Before marriage he talks and she listens. After marriage she talks and he listens. Later they both talk and the neighbors listen.

1696    There may still be something to be said for the old days when some child welfare work was done in the woodshed.

1697    A marriage can last a long time if two people are determined to see how long they can stand each other with neither one giving up.

1698    When I was a young man I vowed never to marry until I found the ideal woman. Well, I found her—but, alas, she was waiting for the ideal man.—*Robert Schuman, French Foreign Minister*

1699    A perfect example of minority rule is a baby in the house.

1700    Dogs may be excellent companions for children—but not substitutes for parents.

1701    The man who boasts that he owes everything to his wife should pay her and stop talking about it.

1702    I can't tell you if genius is hereditary, because heaven has granted me no offspring.—*James McNeill Whistler*

1703    *Husband:* A person who expects his wife to be perfect and to understand why he isn't.

1704    *Housewife:* One who buys the cold cuts and potato salad herself.

1705 A wise husband will buy his wife such fine china that she won't trust him to wash the dishes.

1706 If you are losing an argument with your wife, try a kiss.

1707 You may not realize it when it happens, but a kick in the teeth may be the best thing in the world for you.—*Walt Disney*

1708 When your wife promises to meet you at six o'clock, her promise may carry a lot of wait. (Also vice versa!)

1709 A father is a person who spends several thousand dollars on his daughter's wedding, then reads in the paper that he gave the bride away.

1710 The man who remembers what he learned at his mother's knee was probably bent over it at the time.

1711 *Home:* Where we are treated best and grumble most.

1712 We can fly jet airplanes, broadcast color television, and make atomic power, but we're not so sure about how to bring up children.—*Herbert V. Prochnow*

1713 Any man who thinks he's more intelligent than his wife is married to a really smart woman.

1714 No self-made man ever did such a good job that some woman didn't want to make a few alterations. *Kin (Frank McKinney) Hubbard*

1715 You never hear of anyone giving the groom a shower. They figure he's all washed up anyway.

1716 A bachelor never quite gets over the idea that he is a thing of beauty and a boy forever.

1717 Many a husband, knowing nothing about music, learns he can produce real harmony in the home by playing second fiddle.

1718 A pedestrian is a man whose son is home from college.

1719 Among the things that grow by leaps and bounds are the children in the apartment above you.

1720 A husband's last words are always, "Okay, buy it."

1721 A woman who has never seen her husband fishing doesn't know what a patient man she has married.—*Ed Howe*

1722    Heredity is something people believe in if they have a bright child.

1723    The happy family is but an earlier heaven.— *Sir John Bowring*

1724    Don't you sometimes marvel at how little our parents knew of child psychology and how wonderful we are?

1725    *Marriage:* One business that usually has a silent partner.

1726    Marriage is a good thing. If it weren't for marriage, husbands and wives would have to quarrel with strangers.

1727    Sign in a beauty shop window: "Don't whistle at the girl leaving here, she may be your grandmother."

# Money, Inflation, Property, and Wealth

### 1728    *A Little Gift*

Did you hear about the Texan whose son wanted a chemistry set for his birthday? His dad bought him E. I. duPont.

### 1729    *Money*

About money, former Mayor Edward Kelly of Chicago expressed the universal feeling more pithily and brightly than all the Latin epigrams and Persian wisecracks to be found in the books of quotations. It was some years ago, according to Edward Dean Sullivan, that Mr. Kelly, addressing the South Park Board, of which he was president, said: "Money is a strange commodity and a baffling subject. Time and again it has been proved a non-essential to happiness. It doesn't buy life, affect law, assure the respect of other men or win a place for its possessor in thinking society. I am referring, of course, to Confederate money."—*Gilbert Seldes, in the Saturday Evening Post*

### 1730    *Useful Gift*

Clerk to customer: "So you are looking for a gift for the man who has everything? Why not get him this calendar, which will remind him when the payments are due?"

### 1731    *Occupant*

A charitable organization that made a mass mailing addressed "Occupant" received a check for $500. It was signed "Occupant."

### 1732    *Fourth-Grade Students Define Inflation*

"Inflation is the stuff you put in your attic and in the walls. It keeps you warm in the winter and cool in the summer."

"Inflation is when prices go higher than they really are, like cookies are 99 cents then it goes up to $1.20."

"The creeping form of inflation is especially poignant."

"Inflation means that the prices will get higher. Example: 50 cents in February, $1 in July, $1.50 in August, $2 in December."

"I think inflation means that prices of things will go up. For instance, last year you could buy a hamster for $1—now $2.50."

"I think it means that prices are going higher. Like when you blow up a balloon it gets bigger and bigger."—*From the Tulsa (Oklahoma) World*

### 1733    *Spending It All*

A couple bought an expensive motor home and traveled from state to state leisurely seeing the sights.

They wrote their friend a letter that began: "Having such a great time, we decided to retire and enjoy spending our children's inheritance."

### 1734    *Logical*

Young boy explaining why he wasn't putting money in his piggy bank: "It turns kids into misers and parents into bank robbers."

### 1735    *Worth More*

A lady went into an art gallery and asked to see a still-life. Eventually she chose one representing a bouquet of flowers, a plate of ham, and a roll.

"How much?" she inquired.

"One hundred dollars. It's very cheap."

"But I saw one just like it the other day for seventy-five dollars."

"It must have been of inferior quality," insisted the dealer.

"Indeed, it was even better. There was a lot more ham on the plate."

### 1736    *Paid in Full*

Two partners agreed that when one of them died, the other would bury him with his half of the partnership's money. And when the first partner eventually did die, his partner buried him—with a check for the exact amount.

### 1737    *What Happened to Thank You*

The grandmother took little Linda on a Christmas shopping trip. After watching her grandmother buy gifts all morning, Linda was taken for her visit to Santa Claus.

She made her requests politely, and as she started to leave, the jolly gentleman handed her a large candy cane.

"What do you say?" prompted the grandmother.

Little Linda smiled brightly and announced, "Charge it!"

### 1738 *Inflation*

An astronaut assigned to a twenty-year orbital flight around our solar system phoned his stockbroker before blasting off and told him to invest a thousand dollars for him.

Twenty years later his spaceship returned. As soon as he could get to a phone, he called his broker.

"Glad to hear you got back safely."

"Thanks, how'd my stock do?"

"Great. You made three million dollars."

The astronaut was excited. "Oh boy, I'm set for life. I can retire, buy a new house, car, my own airplane . . ."

The long-distance operator interrupted: "Your three minutes are up. Please deposit another million dollars."

### 1739 *A Riddle and Answer*

There's a five-letter word troubling all of the earth: Not "enemy," "study," or "dying," or "birth." But springtime or autumn, in dark days or sunny, a five-letter word—a real problem—is "money."

### 1740 *It Works*

Son: "Dad, why do you carry that rabbit's foot in your pocket on top of your money?"

Father: "Because every time your mother puts her hand in there, she thinks it's a mouse!"

### 1741 *Unreasonable*

Wife to husband: "You keep saying money isn't worth much these days, but then you make a fuss when I spend some!"

### 1742 *Prepared*

Shortly after the latest price increase on heating oil, a fuel company received a telephone call from the mother superior of a convent.

"How much," the nun asked, "has the price of oil gone up?"

Desiring to break the news gently, the sales official asked, "Are you sitting down, sister?"

Replied the nun, "I'm kneeling."

### 1743    *Now He Knows*

A soldier who lost his rifle was lectured by his captain and told he would have to pay for it. "Sir," gulped the soldier, "suppose I lost a tank? Surely I wouldn't have to pay for that."

"Yes, you would, too, if it took you the rest of your army life."

"Man," said the soldier, "now I know why a captain goes down with his ship."

### 1744    *Research*

A small boy came hurriedly down the street and stopped in front of a stranger. "Have you lost a dollar bill?" the boy asked.

"Yes, yes, I believe I have!" said the man, feeling his pockets. "Have you found one?"

"Oh, no. I just wanted to find out how many have been lost today. Yours makes fifty-five."

### 1745    *Thinking Big*

A father told his son to think in bigger terms when he saw the boy's sign: TURTLE FOR SALE—ONE CENT. The next day the boy changed his sign to read: TURTLE FOR SALE—$10,000. Later the father asked the boy if he'd managed to sell his $10,000 turtle. "I sure did," the little boy responded, "but I had to trade it for a pair of five-thousand-dollar goldfish."

### 1746    *Rising Prices*

Every morning at his office building entrance, the executive gave the sidewalk vendor a dime but never took the pencils offered.

One day after making his usual donation, he felt a light tap on his shoulder. "I'm sorry, sir," the vendor said, "but pencils are now twenty cents."

### 1747    *Higher Bid*

A man was having a good time at a party when he suddenly discovered his wallet was missing. He jumped up on a table and shouted to the crowd, "My wallet is missing. It's got over five hundred dollars in it. I'll give fifty dollars to anyone who finds it and returns it."

A voice from the other side of the room shouted, "I'll give seventy-five dollars!"

### 1748    *That's It*

We like the showgirl, newly married, who was asked her husband's occupation. Her simple answer: "Rich."

### 1749 *No Hoeing*

A tourist stopped to talk with a farmer. "I see you raise hogs almost exclusively around here," he said. "Do they pay better than corn and potatoes?"

"Well, no," drawled the farmer, "but hogs don't need hoeing."

### 1750 *By Accident*

A man was dining in an expensive restaurant. The waiter came over and inquired, "How did you find your steak, sir?"

"Purely by accident. I moved the potatoes and the peas, and there it was."

### 1751 *An Important First*

The first bathtub to be used in the United States was made of wood. The mahogany tub, lined with sheet metal, was first installed and used in 1842, in a home in Cincinnati, Ohio.

### 1752 *No Credit*

There is a bit of good, sound philosophy in the following sign observed in a Chinese laundry:

> You want credit.
> Me no give.
> You get sore.
> You want credit.
> Me give.
> You no pay.
> Me get sore.
> Better you get sore.

### 1753 *Say "Yes"*

Would you work for a cent a day, and double your wage each day? Say "Yes" if someone should offer you a month's contract, because you would receive for your thirty-first day's work a check for over $10 million.

### 1754 *A Confidence Scheme*

The three elements in a confidence scheme are: (1) "This opportunity affords you a great deal for little." (2) "Don't tell anyone; keep it to yourself." (3) "Sign now; this opportunity will never come again."

### 1755 *In Addition*

"The amount you see on the tag, ma'am," stated the salesman to the woman who was looking at a washing machine, "covers city, state, and federal taxes. The price is additional."

1756   *Give Him Time*

"Have you forgotten that five dollars I lent you six weeks ago?"
"Not yet; give me time!"

1757   *It Works*

This collection letter is said to have worked wonders:
"Dear sir: Please send us the name of a good lawyer in your city. We may have to sue you."

1758   *New Idea*

Mrs. Hopemore walked busily into the bank and told the cashier, "I want to open an account with your bank."

The cashier asked courteously, "Do you want a savings account or a checking account?"

"Neither," Mrs. Hopemore replied. "I want a charge account, like I have at the department store."

1759   *A Real Problem*

Mrs. Smith: "I wonder why we never manage to save anything."
Mr. Smith: "It's the neighbors, dear. They're always doing something we can't afford."

1760   *Sold*

A Texas frontiersman came into camp riding an old mule.
"How much for the mule?" asked a bystander.
"Just a hundred dollars," answered the rider.
"I'll give you five dollars," said the bystander.
The rider stopped short, as if in amazement, and then slowly dismounted. "Stranger," he said, "I ain't going to let a little matter of ninety-five dollars stand between me and a mule trade. The mule's your'n."

1761   *Timely Reply*

Ed: "Don't you ever try to do anything on time?"
Ted: "How do you think I bought my car?"

1762   *Wanted More*

A Spaniard, an American, and a Scotchman were discussing what they would do if they awoke one morning to discover that they were millionaires.

The Spaniard said he would build a bull ring.

The American said he would go to Monte Carlo and have a good time.

The Scotchman said he would go to sleep again to see if he could make another million.

1763 *One View*

An examination included the following question: "If a man buys an article for $12.25 and sells it for $9.75, does he gain or lose by the transaction?"

One answer: "He gains on the cents but loses on the dollars."

1764 *Helpful*

The package arrived from the counterfeiter. But when the crook opened it, he found he had spent his good money for a batch of $18 bills instead of the $20 bills he had ordered. Since complaints were frowned upon by his supplier, he decided to try passing them off on some unsuspecting hill folk deep in the heart of the Ozarks. At a crossroads general store, he presented one of the bills and asked for change.

"Sure thing," said the storekeeper. "Howdya want it—two nines or three sixes?"

1765 *By the Pair*

The customer was a would-be comic. "How much are your twenty-dollar shoes?" he asked the salesman.

The salesman quickly replied, "Ten dollars a foot."

1766 *Conscientious*

Jones: "I don't see why you haggle so about the price with the tailor; you'll never pay him, anyhow."

Jakes: "But I'm conscientious; I don't want the poor fellow to lose more than necessary."

1767 *The Test*

"When I look at this congregation," the minister told the audience, "I ask myself, 'Where are the poor?'

"But then, when I look at the collection, I say to myself, 'Where are the rich?' "

1768 *Sharing the Wealth in Verse*

Let us turn bottoms up and drink to the health of those who advocate sharing the wealth. A dandy good scheme, a boon to the nation, and I'm tooth and nail for it—with this reservation:

That I be allowed to pick a "sharee" like Mellon or Morgan or Ford or John D. But if I'm expected to cast in my lot, and share with a guy who has less than I've got, the whole scheme is the bunkum—there's nothing in it, so put in the record that I'm dead agin' it.—*Ashton Hill*

### 1769 *Correction*

The rich uncle wrote to his nephew: "I am sending you the $10 you requested, but must call your attention to a spelling error in your last letter—10 is written with one naught, not two."

### 1770 *Certainly*

"Yes," said the farmer, "when a feller has got to know the botanical name of what he raises, and the entomological name of the bugs that eat it up, and the pharmaceutical name of what he sprays on it—things is bound to cost more."

### 1771 *He Had Him*

A man of Scottish descent was attracting much attention in the hotel lobby with tales of his great accomplishments.

"Well, now," said an Englishman at last, "suppose you tell us something you cannot do, and I will undertake to do it."

"Thank ye," replied the Scot. "I canna pay me bill here."

### 1772 *A Modest Request*

Bank customer to loan officer: "I just need enough to tide me over until I can figure out where to get some money."

### 1773 *Needs Help*

Spendthrift to bank teller: "In the future, if my account becomes overdrawn, don't give me any money until I deposit more."

### 1774 *No Favorites*

Bank cashier to new teller: "When cashing checks you must not play favorites with your friends. Do not give them more money than their checks call for."

### 1775 *Hopeful*

Prospective bank customer to cashier: "I'd like to open an account with someone who has money."

### 1776 *Good Question*

Bank customer to trust officer: "How much would the tax be if I leave it all to the government?"

### 1777 *She Still Does Not Listen*

Two men are cleaning the bank's quarters during the night. One says to the other: "Twenty years on this job, and my wife still won't listen to me on money matters."

1778 *At the Bank Teller's Window*

Teller to customer: "This check will have to be made out for a specific amount, not just for 'oodles.' "

1779 *It Isn't Everything*

Money isn't everything, and don't let anybody tell you it is. There are other things, such as stocks, bonds, letters of credit, travelers' checks, and drafts.

1780 *A New Rule*

"Do you know any rule for estimating the cost of living?"
"Yes. Take your income and add twenty percent."

1781 *Fast Deal*

A Newfoundlander was attending a funeral. He was standing next to a friend of his from Ontario. When the casket was about to be lowered, the gentleman from Ontario leaned over and placed a twenty-dollar bill on the casket.
The Newfoundlander said, "What did you do that for?"
He said, "I have owed him that twenty dollars for a long time, and I have to pay up before he goes so I'll have a clear conscience."
The Newfoundlander thought about that and said, "You know, I think I owed him twenty dollars too, for a long time." And with that he hurriedly made out a check for $40, laid it on the casket, and took the $20 bill.—*H. Neil Windsor*

1782 *A Stroke of Luck*

The editor of the country weekly went home smiling radiantly. "Have you had some good luck?" his wife questioned.
"Luck! I should say so. Mr. Tracey, who hasn't paid his subscription for five years, came in and stopped his paper."

1783 *Bad Mistake*

"Two mistakes here, waiter—one in your favor, one in mine."
"In your favor, sir? Where?"

1784 *Queer*

"It's funny that you should be so tall. Your brother is short, isn't he?"
He (absently): "Yes, usually."

1785 *Corner It*

The eminent financier was discoursing.
"The true secret of success," he said, "is to find out what the people want."
"And the next thing," someone suggested, "is to give it to them."
The financier shook his head contemptuously and said, "No—to corner it."

### 1786 *Safe*

An Ohio woman states that for eighteen years she has been hiding her spare dollar bills in the family Bible, and her husband has never found one of them yet.

### 1787 *Making Money*

A man and his wife found a gas bill on the footpath when they were out for an evening stroll. The man picked it up and looked it over carefully. "I'm going to pay this bill, Maggie," he said.

"What do you want to do that for; it isn't your bill."

"I know it isn't," he replied, "but there's a discount on it, and I might as well have it as anybody else."

### 1788 *Not New*

There was an old woman who lived in a shoe—so this shortage of houses is nothing new.

### 1789 *Smart Bird*

A woman purchased a mynah bird at an auction following some high-spirited bidding.

"I assume this bird can talk," she said to the auctioneer.

"Talk!" exclaimed the man. "Who do you think has been bidding against you for the past fifteen minutes?"

### 1790 *Helpful*

Sign in a French gift shop: "Never mind your French. We speak good broken English."

### 1791 *Cheaper Rates*

Little Jimmy was through with his nightly prayer and asked me what prayers were. I told him they were little messages to God. Quickly he said, "Oh, yes! And we send them at night to get the cheaper rates."

### 1792 *Honesty*

One of two women riding on a bus suddenly realized she hadn't paid her fare. "I'll go right up and pay it," she declared.

"Why bother?" her friend replied. "You got away with it."

"I've found that honesty always pays," the other said virtuously, and went up front to pay the driver.

"See, I told you honesty always pays!" she said when she returned. "I handed the driver a quarter and he gave me change for fifty cents."

1793     *Naturally*

Customer to banker: "Naturally I'm going to be overdrawn if you start adding up my checks to the penny!"

1794     *The Answer Is No*

Customer to banker: "My check came back marked 'No Funds.' Is the bank failing?"

1795     *Doubtful*

Customer to stockbroker: "Have you a stock that will go up enough in time to let me build a new summer cottage?"

1796     *Be Careful, Timmy*

Uncle John was going away and wanted to be generous with his little nephew. So he gave Timmy a five-dollar bill and said, "Now, Timmy, be careful with that money. Remember that saying 'A fool and his money are soon parted.' "

"Yes, Uncle John, but thank you for parting with it, just the same."

1797     *How to Solve the Problem*

Jack Sprat could eat no fat, his wife could eat no lean, but now they eat what they can get, and lick the platter clean.—*Grit*

1798     *Too True!*

We all can save a little dough if we will only try. The problem is to find something that a "little" dough will buy.

1799     *The Tip Is Extra*

Customer: "I'd like a four-dollar dinner, please."
Waiter: "Yes, sir. On white or rye, sir?"

1800     *Time to Complain*

Sam got a dollar too much in his pay envelope one week, but did not say anything. The next week the paymaster discovered the error and deducted a dollar.

"Say," Sam said, "I'm a dollar short."

"Well," said the paymaster, "you didn't complain last week when you were a dollar over."

"Yes, but a guy can overlook one mistake. But when it happens twice, it's time to complain."

### 1801    *Give Him Credit*

A man had barely paid off the mortgage on his house when he mortgaged it again to buy a new car. Having the car, he sought out a banker to try to get a mortgage on the car to build a garage.

"If I do make the loan," the banker said, "how will you get the money to buy gas for the car?"

"It seems to me," the man replied with dignity, "a fellow who owns his own home, car, and garage should be able to get credit for gas."

### 1802    *Restraint Is Costly*

Customer: "This hat costs far too much. It doesn't have even one small feather."

Salesman: "Madam, this is the cost of restraint in fashionable attire."

### 1803    *He Sighs for $5*

There was a trunk and suitcase store in New Haven, Connecticut, which had a pile of trunks and traveling bags on the front sidewalk. The big trunk on the bottom had a sign on it: "This size for $15." Above it was a smaller trunk: "This size for $10." On top was a traveling bag: "This size for $5."

A vagabond paused and looked longingly at the signs. "So do I," he said at last.

### 1804    *Common Ailment*

Two men were discussing a mutual acquaintance. "Nice fellow," said one, "but have you noticed how he always lets his friends pick up the dinner bill?"

"Yes," replied the other. "He has a terrible impediment in his reach."

### 1805    *Fair Exchange*

Motorist: "Some of you pedestrians walk along just as if you owned the streets."

Pedestrian: "And some of you motorists drive around just as if you owned the car."

### 1806    *Debt*

If you owe $100 you're a piker; if you owe $50,000 you're a businessman; if you owe $50 million you're a corporation, and if you owe $1 trillion you're the government.

### 1807    *Come and Get It*

In a country newspaper appeared the following advertisement: "The man who picked up my wallet on Main Street was recognized. He is requested to return it."

In the next issue the reply was published: "The recognized man who picked up the wallet requests the loser to call and get it."

## 1808    *A Bargain*

"See this stickpin? Well, it once belonged to a millionaire."

"What millionaire?"

"Woolworth."

## 1809    *Don't Worry*

A diner walked boldly up to the cashier in an expensive restaurant and said he had no money to pay for his meal. The cashier was cordial. "That's okay," he told the diner. "Just write your name on the wall and pay the next time you are here."

The diner protested that he'd be embarrassed to have his name publicly exposed.

"Don't worry about that," the cashier said. "Your coat will be covering it."

## 1810    *Still Cleaning Up*

Here it is the middle of January and we're still cleaning up from Christmas. Last week we cleaned out our checking account; this week we cleaned out our savings account.

## 1811    *Inflation*

A young boy sat gazing into space. His father said, "Penny for your thoughts, son."

"Well, to be honest, Dad," said the boy, "I was thinking of a quarter."

## 1812    *Simple Solution*

A quick-witted native of Ireland applied for a position as patrolman on the Dublin police force.

"Suppose, Pat," interrogated the man in charge, "suppose you saw a crowd congregated at a certain point on your beat, how would you disperse it quickly and with the least trouble?"

"I'd pass the hat!"

## 1813    *Simply Stated*

An economist spoke on the "whys" and "wherefores" of our economic system. His speech ran about an hour and covered the subject well. The chairman summed it up this way:

"Ladies and gentlemen, what our speaker has been telling you is that, if your outgo exceeds your income, then your upkeep will be your downfall."

### 1814 *Good Explanation*

Neighbor: "You have a nice collection of books, but it seems to me you ought to have more shelves."

Second neighbor: "Yes, I know, but no one ever lends me any shelves."

### 1815 *No Sale*

Salesman: "This hair tonic is so powerful that it will grow hair on a golf ball."

Customer: "That's fine, but who wants hair on a golf ball?"

### 1816 *Unusual Business*

First boy: "My! Look at that guy's car! I bet he's got plenty of money."

Second boy: "Yes, and I know how he got it. He makes jewelry for Indians! My granny says that he's got a big Injun-erring business."

### 1817 *Many of Us Do*

"Say, Phil, what do you do with your old clothes?"

"I just take them off at night and put them on again next morning."

### 1818 *Easy Money*

"How do you become a millionaire in the stock market?"

"You start with two million."

### 1819 *Thrifty*

It is reported that there is one daily patron of a restaurant in Charleston, South Carolina, who always drinks his coffee black. But he has an arrangement with the management whereby at the end of each month he gets a quart of cream free, to take home.

1820    The burning question is often whether a family should eat or buy something else on the installment plan.

1821    It's rough to watch a boy arrive in a $10,000 sports car to take your daughter to a $15 rock concert while you are making payments on an old Chevy.

1822    The safest way to double your money is to fold it over once and put it in your pocket.—*Elbert Hubbard*

1823    Why do you have to pay $2 to park your car so you will not be fined $5 while spending 50 cents for a cup of coffee?

1824    A gentleman farmer is one who has more hay in the bank than in the barn.

1825    If you want to see a short summer, borrow some money due in the fall.

1826    Here's a simple way to identify the owner of a car. He's the one who, after you pull the door shut, always opens it again and slams it harder.

1827    *Revolving credit plan:* Every time you turn around you have to make a payment.

1828    Nowadays a miniature backyard is one so tiny that it's no disgrace to be caught cutting it with a hand mower.

1829    Optimist: "There are still a few things you can get for a dollar—like nickels, dimes, and quarters."

1830    Inflation is a state of affairs when you never had it so good or parted with it so fast.

1831    You can't take it with you, but that's not the worst. The frustrating part is it mostly goes first.

1832    When the tip is hid 'neath the edge of the plate, the waitress knows it's not all that great.

1833    Every time history repeats itself, the prices go up.

1834    Americans who are fond of boasting in terms of biggest, tallest, and most can hail our national debt as being far the largest in the world.

1835    An attic is where you store junk you'd throw away if you didn't have one.

1836    A good many young writers make the mistake of enclosing a self-addressed stamped envelope, big enough for the manuscript to come back in. This is too much of a temptation to the editor.—*Ring Lardner*

1837    Write out of love; write out of instinct; write out of reason. But always for money.—*Louis Untermeyer*

1838    The modern child hearing the Cinderella story asks whether it's straight income or a capital gain when a pumpkin turns into a golden coach.

1839    In today's supermarkets, the shopping carts easily attain speeds of more than $55 per hour.

1840    It has reached a point where taxes are a form of capital punishment.

1841    You are a careful buyer if you have made the merchandise outlast the payments.

1842    It's no longer a sin to be rich—it's a miracle.

1843    A modern American believes there is a pot of credit cards at the end of the rainbow.

1844    It is reported that the people of Glasgow, Scotland, recently raised their streetcar fares so they could save more money walking.

1845    Today's version of a true patriot is the man who is sincerely sorry that he has but one income to give to his country.

1846    Some who are not paid what they are worth ought to be glad.

1847    The rich man gives small tips because he doesn't want anyone to know he's rich, and the poor man gives large tips because he doesn't want anybody to know he's poor.

1848    Misers aren't much fun to live with, but they do make wonderful ancestors.

1849    Anybody could get rich if he could guess the exact moment at which a piece of junk becomes an antique.

1850    *Extravagance:* The way the other fellow spends his money.—*T. Harry Thompson*

1851    Wanting less is sometimes greater riches than having more.

1852    It is a rather pleasant experience to be alone in a bank at night.—*Willie Sutton, Bank Robber*

1853    The main reason that people drive more now than they once did is because it's cheaper to drive than to park.

1854    What becomes of furniture that is too old even for poor folks and not yet old enough for rich folks?

1855    We are told to live within our income. Nothing doing! We may be poor, but not that poor.

1856    The way to a man's pocketbook is through his hobby.

1857    In another hundred years civilization will have reached all peoples except those that have no resources worth stealing.

1858    Civilization is just a slow process of creating more needs to supply.

1859    If you lend a friend $5 and you never see him again, it's worth it.

1860    There, little luxury, don't you cry—you'll be a necessity by and by.

1861    We have come to the conclusion that it's not money but theories about it that are the root of all evil.

1862    Until "easy payments" came along, the four-card flush was the hardest known thing to complete.

1863    The man who first called it the "easy" payment plan was mighty careless with his adjectives.

1864    Someday the Gideons, who see to it that there's a Bible in each hotel guestroom, are going to fix it so that the person who sets the hotel rates has one, too.

1865    The same person who doesn't believe in miracles will buy a sweepstakes ticket in the hope of winning.

1866    One reason we are a great nation is because we have been unable to exhaust our resources in spite of our best efforts.

1867    Some banjo players get $50 an hour. That's pretty easy picking.

1868    An ideal sign for a pawnbroker would be: "See me at your earliest inconvenience."

1869    An advertisement says that the secret of poise is money in the bank. At least it's the secret of balance.

1870    A plumber was recently given a fortune by one of his customers. We seem to remember having paid one or two bills like that.

1871    "Is your skin an annoyance?" asks an ad. Well, no; we are glad to have something we can occupy without paying rent.

1872    Headline: "Prices Soar"—and so are we.

1873    Prices seem to think there is plenty of room at the top.

1874    *Credit-card holder:* Member of the debt set.

1875    The poorest hour is just before the pawn.

1876    *Standpatter:* One who is getting his under the present system.

1877    One trouble is that nations are off not only the gold standard but also the golden rule standard.

1878    Some people find a shortage of cash annoying, and some don't buy on the installment plan.

1879    A gentleman today is a man who holds the door open so his wife can carry in $50 worth of groceries in two small sacks.

1880    A bargain is something you can't use but which is so cheap you can't afford not to buy it.

1881    Traffic would have been pretty bad in the good old days if everyone could have bought a horse and buggy for a dollar down and a dollar a week.

1882    In the old days, before inflation, you could be down to your last $10 bill and have enough to pay for at least three meals.

1883    One mystery is how men with white-collar jobs can afford to have them laundered.

1884    If the Secretary of the Treasury has insomnia, it's probably from counting sheep by the billions.

1885    There are many things money can't buy, including what it used to.

1886    Nothing makes the family budget look sicker than high living.

1887    It's the size of the down payment and not the total cost that counts nowadays.

1888    So far it has cost the United States many hundreds of billions of dollars in debt to make history.

1889    Dollars and sense go together.

1890    Countdown on the money in your pocketbook—fifty-forty-thirty-twenty-ten-zero—and there she goes until next payday.

1891    You never realize the things you can do without until the installment payments come along.

1892    Many of us are like the letter B—in debt when there is no need for it.

1893    Scientists say the earth may last one billion years, but no one has figured out what the installment debt will be then.

1894    With installment payments we don't need a five-day week as much as a six-week month.

1895    What the world seems to want from us is handouts across the sea.

1896    The only international language seems to be the one in which money talks.

1897    If some company will make a horn for pedestrians that just sneers, it will make a fortune.

1898    Many a meeting that opens at 8 P.M. sharp closes at 10 P.M. dull.

1899    What most of us want is less to do with more time and more pay to do it.

1900    Nowadays when people speak of the higher things of life, they refer to the cost of living.

1901    A dollar earned is a nickel saved.

1902    When a check comes back marked "no account," it also applies to the person who wrote it.

1903    If you work hard and save, someday you will have enough to divide with those who don't.

1904    No collision injures an automobile like a trade-in.

1905    You can keep up with the Joneses, but don't try to pass them on a hill.

1906    Sometimes a man can't sleep because he bought too much on the lay-awake plan.

1907    It's the mink in the closet and not the wolf at the door that gets you into trouble.

1908    It's not only the cost and the upkeep of a car that worry you, but also the possible turnover.

1909    It's strange you never hear of a beetle, fly, or weevil that threatens to destroy the spinach or artichoke crops.—*Herbert V. Prochnow*.

1910    "My, how dimes have changed," said the fellow who paid $3 for a dime novel.

1911    The nice thing about life is that one extravagance always suggests another.

1912    Paper money may be covered with germs, but these days we don't hold on to any long enough to catch anything.

1913    There are things more urgent than money—for instance, your bills.

1914    In the United States you can start out carrying bricks and wind up behind a big desk, if you don't mind earning less.

1915    Famous last words: "No woman is going to tell me what to do."

1916    In its present weakened condition, the buck is liable to stop just about anywhere.

1917    "What is so rare as a day in June?" asked Lowell. Well, we would say it was a day when the deficit in the federal budget didn't increase.—*Herbert V. Prochnow*

1918    When the meek inherit the earth, they will also inherit a good many installment payments from those who were not so meek.

1919    If you get something for nothing, someone else gets nothing for something.

1920    Some men keep up with the Joneses by wearing last year's suit and driving this year's car on next year's salary.

1921    Prosperous times are those in which all of us have more installment payments than we can afford.

1922    The family that keeps up with the Joneses doesn't always keep up with the bill collector.

1923    Another thing the installment buyer pays is the salary of the installment collector.

1924    To have national prosperity we must spend, but to have individual prosperity we must save—which clears up everything.

1925    With most of us money talks, and it usually talks about more money.

1926    One book that always has a sad ending is a checkbook.

1927    Guests at a nightclub were held up and robbed of all their money and valuables. The club management took the loss philosophically, realizing that these are days of keen commercial competition.

1928    If only philanthropists would give it back to the same people they took it from.

1929    When a man makes an anonymous donation, he simply hopes that people will find out about it without his telling them.

1930    The world is full of willing people. Some are willing to save money, and others are willing to let them.

1931    About the time the family is pretty well satisfied with what we have, the Joneses buy something else.

1932    Of course the country is prosperous. We have more money and it buys less.

1933    We tried to pay our income taxes with a smile, but the collector wanted cash.

1934    *Homeowner:* A person who is always on his way to a hardware store. —*Herbert V. Prochnow, Jr.*

1935    A rich uncle is liked by everyone because of his purseonality.

1936    A budget is a system for worrying at regular intervals.

1937    You get paid for what you know and pay for what you don't know.

1938    The high cost of living is no joke—nor, for that matter, is the average joke.

1939    An itch for public office often settles in the palms.

1940    The fellow with one suit always knows where his wallet is.

1941    *Rich person:* One who is never afraid to ask a shopkeeper to show him something cheaper.

1942    A dime goes a long way these days; you can carry one for several weeks before you can find anything that it will buy.

1943    In these high-priced restaurants they ought to have one table at which you could starve at reasonable prices.

1944    A good many families with installments due every month probably enjoy hearing bankers worry about tight money.

1945    It's possible to own too much. A man with one watch knows what time it is; a man with two watches is never quite sure.—*Lee Segall*

1946    A lot of time could be saved if salary checks were sent by the employer directly to the installment people.

1947    In the Far East a man shakes hands with himself when he meets a creditor. Over here he shakes hands with himself when he doesn't.

1948    This is a free country, and a good many people who are getting some of it that way will have to pay later.

1949    No dime ever looks so big as the one you didn't get back from the telephone box.

1950    If you burn the candle at both ends, you may be able to make both ends meet.

1951    Money doesn't always bring happiness. People with $10 million are no happier than people with $9 million.—*Hobart Brown*

1952    No man would like to get some easy money more than a poor man—except a rich man.

1953    Many Americans wish they were as rich as the foreigners think they are.

1954    The dew is pretty heavy nowadays, especially on the car, the house, and the television.

1955    In the old days a spender went broke spending his own money and not other people's money.

1956    Good business management is a matter of keeping the overhead underfoot.

1957    Sometimes it appears man did descend from a fish, because so many men still can't keep their heads above water.

1958    We have no prejudice against a $2 bill, as it will buy a dollar's worth of goods.

1959    The life of a paper dollar is only seven or eight months, and yet we never had one die in our hands.

1960    We not only want sound money, but we want a dollar that can talk above a whisper.

1961    When you try to get something for nothing, you can't complain about the quality.

1962    Two can live as cheaply as one. In fact, they have to.

1963    A woman buys something because everyone has it or because no one has it.

1964    The one crop that is harvested green here and in other countries is the American traveler.

1965    Your income is the amount of money you spend more than.

1966    A luxury is something that becomes a necessity if your neighbor has it.

1967    Only one fellow in ten thousand understands the currency question, and we meet him every day.—*Kin (Frank McKinney) Hubbard*

1968    A luxury is something that becomes a necessity if you can buy it on the installment plan.

1969    A man may pass the buck and still be a tightwad.

1970    The rich man and his daughter are soon parted.

1971    Consumer credit is over hundreds of billions, and there are moments around the first of the month when that amount seems conservative to some consumers.

1972    You have to be pretty well off not to be ashamed to ask the clerk for something cheaper.

1973    The only thing I like about rich people is their money.—*Lady Astor*

1974    The fellow who puts on the dog may be putting off his creditors.

1975    Every good idea must have a beginning. Maybe all of us could start living within our incomes on Monday and Friday.

1976    When you get something for nothing, you are probably paying the highest price possible for it.

1977    How to get rich: Earn a little more than you spend—and keep doing it.

1978    More money is now spent amusing children than was spent on the education of their parents.

1979    The only redeeming feature of a pawnshop is the ticket.

1980    Meeting your bills isn't as hard as dodging them.

1981    With inflation you don't hear so much about counterfeiters wasting time on $10 and $20 bills.

1982    Remember the old days when families thought they ought to earn the money before they spent it?

1983    If we had to count 100 cents before we spent a dollar, we might have more sense about handling our money.

1984    If you want to be reminded of Christmas all year, buy your Christmas gifts on the monthly payment plan.

1985    You have reached the pinnacle of success as soon as you become uninterested in money, compliments, or publicity.—*Dr. O. A. Battista*

1986    For many of us the high cost of living is largely due to the cost of our high living.

1987    Nowadays we spend so much on luxuries we can't afford the necessities.

1988    Man's lifespan may eventually be increased to 100 years, which will greatly help the installment business.

1989    Despite the increase in the cost of living, the demand for it continues.

1990    Inflation is also what you don't have when your tire blows out.

1991    Destiny may shape our ends, but it doesn't help us make ends meet.

1992    It is better to have old secondhand diamonds than none at all.—*Mark Twain*

1993    All prices seem to have been quite stable in the last five years—except the prices of the things you have to buy.

1994    The price of eggs is moving up. Someone—not the hen—is laying for the consumer.

1995    It's always easy to be generous with the other fellow's cash.

1996    There are times when the dollar has not had much resemblance to money.

1997    As the man said, "If you will lend me twenty dollars, I'll be everlastingly indebted to you."

1998    Little things count, and three of them give you a large tax exemption.

1999    If you want to learn to tell fortunes, you need to read Dun and Bradstreet.

2000    Money is what you wouldn't need if other people weren't so crazy about it.

2001     One thing about some of our poor housing is that when the roof leaks, the tenant can go out and get in his automobile.

2002     The taxpayer stayed up all night to figure out what happened to last year's income and it finally dawned on him.

2003     It's always better to spend less money than you haven't earned.

2004     The first-of-the-month bills fall like due drops.

2005     If all the automobiles that aren't paid for were placed end to end, you wouldn't have any traffic congestion.

2006     We didn't know how old consumer credit was until we saw the book *Custer's Last Charge*.

2007     If Columbus came back today he would find that the world is flat.

2008     It's only a short distance from a lay-away plan to a lay-awake plan.

2009     All we know about how the other half lives is that it's probably beyond their income.

2010     A nickel goes a long way now. You can carry it around for days without finding a thing to buy.

2011     Poverty is not a disgrace, but name anything else in its favor.

2012     When a politician says "Consumer outlook better," you should read it backwards.

2013     Every cloud has a silver lining, and even an old blue suit has its shiny side.

2014     We are living in a land of plenty—everything we want costs plenty.

2015     An income is what you can't live without or within.

2016     Why do people spend money they haven't earned to buy things they don't need in order to impress people they don't like?

2017     Money is called legal tender, but when you don't have it, it's tough.

2018     A good architect can make an old house look a lot better by just discussing the cost of a new one.

2019     Prosperity provides enough credit to live beyond your means.

2020     Animals can't be related to man. They don't keep on grabbing for more when they have enough.

2021    At twenty he thinks he can save the world; at thirty he begins to wish he could save part of his salary.

2022    In the old days history was made for a tenth of what it costs today.

2023    Always borrow from a pessimist—he never expects it back anyhow.

2024    There are some men who spend half their lives borrowing money and the other half not paying it back.

2025    *Hard times:* A season during which it is very difficult to borrow money to buy things you don't need.

2026    Some people say we have more gold than is good for us. Still, if we have to be afflicted with something, we probably would like gold as well as anything.

2027    We live expensively to impress people who live expensively to impress us.

2028    If we had no faith in one another, all of us would have to live within our incomes.

2029    Buying what you do not need is an easy road to needing what you cannot buy.

2030    No one who sees many ministers trying to live on their salaries can fail to believe in miracles.

2031    You can't help loving life in this world of change—if you have enough of it.

2032    Most automobiles are paid for as they are used, but sometimes not so speedily.

2033    We know one family that has no washing machine, no television, no mink coat—just money in the bank.

2034    Give most people credit for anything and they will take it.

2035    The dollar doesn't do as much for us as it did, because we don't do as much for a dollar as we did.

2036    Among other things we're paying for on the installment plan are two world wars.

2037    The reason some people can't get ahead is that they borrow $20 to pay back the $10 they owe.

2038    No man talks economy like the one who accompanies his wife on a shopping trip.

2039    In America you can easily recognize the poor: They're the ones who drive and wash their own cars.

2040    In these changing times we suppose there is some comfort in a public debt that is permanent.

2041    An executive is a man who is able to have everything he needs charged.

2042    Some people believe you needn't live by principle if you have enough principal.

2043    The expert who says your house should not cost more than twice your annual income must work for a tent and awning company.

2044    A tough winter now and then is relished by the fuel man.

2045    An installment collector is a person who doesn't put off until tomorrow what should be dun today.

2046    Whenever a strike is settled, the consumer knows who will have to do the settling.

2047    *On the rocks:* A person who is either bankrupt or working in jail. The difference is inconsequential.

2048    *Jack:* A thing that lifts a car and also keeps it going.

2049    With the Gulf of Aqaba, the Middle East not only has the oil but also the troubled waters.

2050    A lot of animals would be wearing their fur coats next winter if it weren't for the installment plan.

2051    A fool and his money may soon be parted, but not a fool and his car.

2052    With the price of wool where it is, counting sheep must keep a farmer from sleeping.

2053    The genius who invents a self-parking car will make a fortune.

2054    *Diamond:* A woman's idea of a stepping stone to success.

2055    When you hear a man say that poverty is a great thing for one's character, the chances are you're listening to a millionaire.

2056    The average person's idea of comfortable circumstances is having enough money to be scared to death of a share-the-wealth program.

2057    You can tour the world now on the installment plan, but don't fall down on the payments in the middle of the Atlantic.

2058    A banker says marriage promotes thrift. Demands it, he means.

2059    A dollar doesn't go as far as it did, but its acceleration is much better developed.

2060    With inflation, progress is an exchange of something less expensive for something more expensive.

2061    A few people try to get something for nothing, but the others pay $10 down and $10 a month for the rest of their lives.

2062    A middle-class family is one that lives in public as the rich do by living in private as the poor do.

2063    It's comforting to think we are all getting richer by charging each other more.

2064    The fellow who doesn't believe in saving says wealth is wrong.

2065    Few of us care to be such misers that we are willing to live within our income.

2066    With all those credit cards now, everyone has a fat pocketbook.

2067    Nothing makes your car run better than finding out how much cash you need to buy a new one.

2068    In a few years the average family will make $20,000 a year, and the way we are spending, they had better.

2069    A fool and his money soon go partying.

2070    With postage at present rates, you wonder whether most letters are worth it.

2071    The person who has a secondhand car knows how hard it is to drive a bargain.

2072    Money talks, but dollar for dollar its voice keeps getting weaker and weaker.

2073    Financing has sure become scientific down through the ages. Do you realize that a money order would have saved the prodigal son the trouble of coming home?—*Arthur "Bugs" Baer*

2074    *Insurance:* A guarantee that, no matter how many necessities a person had to forego all through life, death was something to which he could look forward.—*Fred Allen*

2075    *Lottery:* A tax on fools.—*Henry Fielding*

2076    *Money:* A good thing to have. It frees you from doing things you dislike. Since I dislike doing nearly everything, money is handy.—*Groucho Marx*

2077    Today's outrageously high prices make us do without many necessities in order to be able to buy our customary luxuries.

2078    *Gambling:* The sure way of getting nothing for something.—*Wilson Mizner*

2079    A billion here, a billion there . . . after a while that begins to be real money.—*Everett Dirksen*

2080    Benjamin Franklin may have discovered electricity—but it was the man who invented the meter who made the money.—*Earl Wilson*

2081    We all live in a state of ambitious poverty.—*Juvenal*

2082    If you can count your money, you don't have a billion dollars.—*J. Paul Getty*

2083    It would be nice to have all the money you spent foolishly just to enjoy spending it foolishly again.

2084    The Treasury says the dollar bill only lasts a few months. That's another good laugh.

2085    The purpose of drive-in banks is to make it possible for cars to meet their real owners.

2086    Income tax song: "Everything I Have Is Yours."

2087    One of our troubles today is that too many adults, and not enough children, believe in Santa Claus.

2088    *Aristocracy:* Rectitude, platitude, high-hatitude.—*Margot Asquith*

2089    Benjamin Franklin had an axiom: "A penny saved is a penny earned." But that was before the sales tax was invented.

2090    Some people get what they want because they have the takenique.

2091    *Auctioneer:* The man who proclaims with a hammer that he has picked a pocket with his tongue.—*Ambrose Bierce*

2092    Inflation is when you pay $50 for a watch and $60 to have it repaired.

2093    Most of us are so busy trying to get what we don't have that we can't enjoy what we do have.

2094    The person who spends what his friends think he makes is probably in debt.

2095    Money used to talk, but now it goes without saying.

2096    I had announced earlier this year that if successful I would not consider campaign contributions as a substitute for experience in appointing ambassadors. Ever since I made that statement, I have not received one single cent from my father.—*John F. Kennedy*

2097    The entire essence of America is the hope to first make money—then make money with money—then make lots of money with lots of money.—*Paul Erdman*

2098    The world at large does not judge us by who we are and what we know; it judges us by what we have.—*Dr. Joyce Brothers*

2099    Nowadays people can be divided into three classes—the Haves, the Have-Nots, and the Have-Not-Paid-for-What-They-Haves.—*Earl Wilson*

2100    According to a collector, some people pay when due, some overdue, and some never do. How do you do?

2101    Nothing gets you in debt faster than trying to keep up with people who are already there.

2102    A banker is a person who is willing to make a loan if you present sufficient evidence to show you don't need it.—*Herbert V. Prochnow*

2103    Money swore an oath that nobody that did not love it should ever have it.—*Irish proverb*

2104    A budget is what you stay within if you go without.

2105    *Abscond:* To "move" in a mysterious way, commonly with the property of another.—*Ambrose Bierce*

2106    We understand that in Russia the children are forbidden to believe in Santa Claus. In this country the politicians encourage even the grown-ups to believe in him.—*Herbert V. Prochnow*

2107    We have noticed that people who complain about their income taxes can be divided into two classes—men and women.

2108    *Spinach:* An expensive source of sand.

2109    *Inflation:* Being broke with a lot of money in your pocket.

2110    *Psychiatrist:* A person who deals with people who have the same problems we all have, but have more money.

2111    Nowadays the earth revolves on our taxes.

2112    Among the things that money can't buy are what it used to.

2113    Two heads aren't better than one with the present price of haircuts.

2114    There is one thing about life: whether you are rich or poor, it's always good to have plenty of money in the bank.

2115    Income is an amount of money that no matter how large it is, you spend more than.

2116    Inflation is the one form of taxation that can be imposed without legislation.—*Milton Friedman*

2117    Buck passing is not new, but they never passed faster than they do now.

2118    The secret of financial success is to spend what you have left after saving, instead of saving what is left after spending.

2119    *Luxury:* Something you don't need and can't do without.

2120    Never before has the American dollar had such good-byeing power.

2121    There's no justice nohow! If you make out your income tax correctly, you go to the poorhouse; if you don't, you go to jail.

2122    A depression is a period when people do without things their parents never had.

2123    Every family has a choice of keeping up with the neighbors or with the creditors.

2124    The huge national debt they will inherit should keep our children from one indulgence—ancestor worship.

2125    I don't like money, actually, but it quiets my nerves.— *Joe Louis*

2126    Optimism is the ability to speak of the shiny, new red automobile as "my" car, in the face of the ten payments still to be made.

2127    Unless America has financial sense this could be the national debt to end national debts.

2128    Many of us would be delighted to pay as we go, if we could only catch up from paying as we've gone.

2129    When it is a question of money, everybody is of the same religion.— *Voltaire*

2130    The child who knows the value of a dollar will usually wind up asking for two.

2131    Many nations are having a hard time meeting the installments on their machine guns and tanks.

2132    *Prosperity:* A period when you spend money you don't have.

2133    *Optimist:* A person who thinks he can get by with saying "thanks" to the headwaiter.

2134    We're not sure how the nations can finance another war unless they can get a trade-in allowance on the last one.

2135    *Inflation:* A condition in economics during which money talks but never seems to have enough cents to say something worthwhile.

2136    A man who pays $2,000 for a used car will find it doesn't pay to drive a bargain.

2137    Money is what you'd get on beautifully without if only other people weren't so crazy about it.—*Margaret Case Harriman*

2138    As a general rule, nobody has money who ought to have it.—*Benjamin Disraeli*

2139    The only thing that hurts more than paying an income tax is not having to pay an income tax.—*Lord Thomas R. Duwar*

2140    I never write "metropolis" for seven cents because I can get the same price for "city." I never write "policeman" because I can get the same money for "cop."—*Mark Twain*

2141     They say the Russians give all they make above a bare living to the government. They call it communism. A cynic says it's the same here, only we call it taxes.

2142     Just think how many poor people were denied a horse and buggy in the olden days because nobody had thought of this convenient dollar-down idea.

2143     The world seldom asks how a man acquired his property. The only question is: Has he got it?

2144     You may not be any happier when you save money and pay your bills than you were when you couldn't pay the rent. But we imagine the landlord is.

2145     Santa Claus doesn't come down through the chimney anymore but through a large hole in your pocketbook.

2146     Wealth is something that is wrong if the other person has it.

2147     Everything is subject to gravity except the tax rate.

2148     Junk food isn't so expensive if you pay for it with junk money.

2149     A luxury looks ordinary by the time you get where you can afford it.

2150     One thing about easy money is that it's about as easy to spend as it is to make.

2151     Whoever said there's no use crying over spilled milk said it back in the days when milk was less expensive.

2152     The man who knows exactly what he would do if he had a million dollars doesn't have it.

2153     The things that come to those who wait are probably not worth waiting for.

2154     Faith is not dead when many people believe a bull market lasts forever.

2155     There can't be much peace in the world when one half thinks of Red China as an outlaw and the other half as a possible customer.

2156     The most civilized people are those who pay the highest prices for beads.

# Success, Fame, Hardship, and Failure

### 2157    *Don't Let Him Get Away*

A policeman was talking to the chief of police over the telephone: "A man has been robbed down here, and I've got one of them!"

"Which one have you?" the chief asked.

"The man who was robbed," the policeman replied.

### 2158    *Foresight*

A reporter just back from Cape Canaveral remarked at the National Press Club bar that he had made an interesting discovery among the electronic brains and Buck Rogers–like equipment of the Florida missile base. It was an ancient Chinese abacus, encased in a glass wall cabinet. On the cabinet were these instructions: "Break Glass in Case of Emergency."

### 2159    *Time Flies*

A jewelry store friend across the street says he hopes to introduce a new watch which will do an hour in fifty minutes. It is designed for modern living, and especially for youngsters with music lessons to practice.

### 2160    *Too Slow*

A clothing store received this letter from a customer who had ordered a maternity dress.

"Dear Sir: Please cancel the order for a size 44 dress, which I placed last week. My delivery was faster than yours. Sincerely, R.S."

2161 *Real Problem*

A policeman called to a drunk who was driving the wrong way on a one-way street.

"Can't you see the arrows?" he asked.

"Arrows?" the drunk slurred back. "I can't even see the Indians."

2162 *Not Easy*

As the young newlyweds window-shopped at the local furniture store, the wife remarked, "I just don't see how they can make such beautiful furniture from all of those crinkly little walnuts."

2163 *They Never Win*

The Jungle Animal Olympics had concluded, and a dejected cheetah was sitting on the sidelines, for he hadn't won a single prize.

"I can understand why we lost the other events," he said to another cheetah, "but I thought since we are supposed to be so fast that we'd surely win the races. Imagine, we were outrun by an elephant!"

"Well, that's the way it goes," his friend replied philosophically. "Cheetahs never win."

2164 *Thoughtful*

A man went up to a hot-dog stand and ordered a hot dog from the bottom of the pile. "No problem," said the vendor, "but how come?"

"I'm always for the underdog," the man explained.

2165 *Fair*

As an exasperated candidate was being heckled, he exclaimed, "There seem to be a great many fools here tonight. I wonder if it would be advisable to hear them one at a time?"

"That's fair enough," shouted one listener. "Finish your speech."

2166 *Too Much Pizza*

Waitress: "How would you like your pizza sliced—six or eight pieces?"

Customer: "Six, please—I couldn't possibly eat eight!"

2167 *She Thought of It*

One winter morning, a man heard his wife trying unsuccessfully to start her car. He went outside and asked, "Did you try choking it?"

"No, but I felt like it," she replied, gritting her teeth.

2168 *A Slight Error*

Rancher: "Say, young man, you're a brave one to come down in a parachute in this here 60-mile-an-hour gale!"

Man: "But, mister, I didn't come down in a parachute. I went up in a pup tent!"

### 2169 *Dates of Great Tragedies*

The saxophone was invented in 1846. World War I began in 1914. Jazz started in 1915. Radio crooning broke loose in 1926. The Wall Street crash was in 1929.

### 2170 *Twinkle! Twinkle!*

Twinkle, twinkle, little star, how I wonder where you are! Up above you seem to shine, but according to Einstein you are not where you pretend; you are just around the bend. And your sweet, seductive ray has been leading us astray all these years. Oh, little star, ain't you 'shamed of what you are?—*Boy's Life*

### 2171 *Last Guy Wins*

Two veteran soldiers were bragging about their respective outfits when they were in active service.

"When we presented arms," said one, "all you could hear was slap, slap, slap, click."

"Pretty fair," replied the other. "With us it was slap, slap, click, jingle."

"Jingle? What was that?"

"Our medals."

### 2172 *Dense Crowd*

The candidate, known for his anti-agriculture stand, flashed a bright smile at the audience in the packed hall. "I'm truly delighted to see this dense crowd gathered tonight to support my candidacy!"

"Don't be too delighted," shouted one of the grim-faced farmers. "We ain't that dense!"

### 2173 *Struck Out*

One of the briefer musical criticisms appeared in a local paper: "An amateur string quartet played Brahms last night. Brahms lost."

### 2174 *Squawk Right Out*

I hate to be a kicker. I always long for peace. But the wheel that does the squeaking is the one that gets the grease. It's nice to be a peaceful soul, and not too hard to please, but the dog that's always scratching is the one that has the fleas.

The art of soft-soap spreading is the thing that palls and stales, but the guy who wields the hammer is the one who drives the nails.

Let us not put notions that are harmful in your head, but the baby that keeps yelling is the baby that gets fed.—*Moore's Monthly*

2175   *Wrong Grease*

Shorty: "How did you get so tall?"
Giant: "I rubbed grease on my head."
Shorty: "I rubbed grease on my head, too, but I didn't get any taller.
Giant: "What kind of grease did you use?"
Shorty: "Crisco."
Giant: "No wonder. That's shortening!"

2176   *Forgot His Glasses*

A workman had climbed a step ladder and was perched precariously on the rim of the City Hall clock. He was cleaning the huge dial when a passerby stopped to watch. "What's wrong?" the passerby asked. "Is there something wrong with the clock?"

"It's fine," replied the workman. "I'm just nearsighted."

2177   *Any Light Bulbs*

"Have you," asked the shopper, "any four-volt, two-watt bulbs?"
"For what?"
"No, two."
"Two, what?"
"Yes."
"No."

2178   *Not Bad*

Politician: "What did you think of my speech on the agricultural problem?"
Farmer: "Not bad, but a good day's rain would probably have helped more."

2179   *Wrong Choice*

The restaurant customer, after studying the menu, said, "I'll have some Simoni Vermatelli."
The waiter replied, "I'm sorry, sir, but that's the proprietor's name."

2180   *Played It Safe*

To celebrate his birthday, Old Jud was taken for a plane ride over the little town where he'd spent all his life. When he was back on the ground, a friend asked him, "Were you scared?"
"No-o-o," was the hesitant answer, "but I never did put my full weight down."

2181   *Try Again*

A thoughtful-looking gentleman came to the circus. He stood for a long time, studying a camel. At length, he stooped, picked up a straw, and placed it on the camel's back—nothing happened. "Wrong straw," the man said with a shrug, then turned and walked away.

### 2182   *No Escape*

A first-grader's mother put a bowl of hot soup in front of him. He halted his first spoonful in midair and examined it with a frown.

"What's the matter?" she asked.

"Alphabet soup," he snorted. "Can't you let a guy forget school even for a minute?"

### 2183   *Maybe*

A customer, after browsing for about ten minutes in the popular music section, stepped up to the counter and—evidently attempting to impress the clerk with his appreciation of the finer things in music—asked, "You got something, maybe, by Joehand Batch?"

### 2184   *Be Calm*

At the end of a driving lesson, the instructor sighed as he studied his nervous pupil clutching the steering wheel.

"We still have a few minutes left," he said. "Shall I show you how to fill out the accident forms?"

### 2185   *The Importance of Little Things*

If you think you cannot do very much, and that the little you can do is of no value, think of these things:

A tea kettle singing on a stove was the beginning of the steam engine.

A shirt waving on the clothesline was the beginning of a balloon, the forerunner of the Graf Zeppelin.

A spider web strung across a garden path suggested the suspension bridge.

A lantern swinging in a tower was the beginning of a pendulum.

An apple falling from a tree led to the discovery of the law of gravity.

### 2186   *Experiments*

A man rocked a boat to see if it would tip. It did.

A laborer stepped on a nail to see if it would go through his shoe. It did.

A man looked into a gun to see if it was loaded. It was.

A helper smelled escaping gas and lighted a match to find the leak. He found it.

### 2187   *Couldn't Fool Him*

"I've been running boats on this river so long I know where every sandbar is located," boasted the steamboat pilot.

Just then, the boat struck a submerged snag with a loud crunch.

"There!" said the pilot triumphantly. "There's one of them now!"

### 2188   *Your Troubles*

If you talk about your troubles, and tell them o'er and o'er, the world will think you like 'em, and proceed to give you more.

### 2189   *He Tin Whistle Now*

I bought a wooden whistle, and it wooden whistle. I bought a steel whistle, and it steel wooden whistle. And I bought a lead whistle, and the steel wooden lead me whistle. I bought a tin whistle. Now I tin whistle all the time.

### 2190   *Not Interested*

"Lend you money to build a boat that runs on steam? See here, Fulton, do I look crazy?"

"A machine to pull seeds out of cotton! Don't make me laugh, Whitney; I've got a chapped lip! Me put up dough for that? Be yourself, Eli, be yourself!"

"Talk over a wire? Why, you poor nut, of course I won't put up any cash for stock in a thing like that. You might find some prospects in that building over there, though. That's the insane asylum."

"Buy stock in a gasoline gig? Mr. Ford, I want you to take note of that cop over there while I'm telling you no, no, *no!*"

### 2191   *Smart Parrot*

A man bought himself a parrot and to induce him to talk kept repeating, "Hello, hello," to the bird.

Finally, the parrot opened one sleepy eye and commented, "What's the matter? Line busy?"

### 2192   *He Had Proof*

Minister to Church Elder: "I heard you went to the ball game last Sunday instead of to church."

"That's not true!" the Elder protested, "and what's more I still have one of the fish to prove it!"

### 2193   *Worth Trying*

Smile, and the world smiles with you. Kick, and you kick alone. For a cheerful grin will let you in where the kicker is not known.

### 2194   *Good Advice*

As you ramble on through life, whatever be your goal, keep your eye upon the doughnut, and not upon the hole.

### 2195  *Bad Mistake*

Aunt: "I'm sorry, Jack, that you don't like your gift. Remember, I asked you whether you preferred a large check or a small one."

Jack: "But I didn't know you were talking about neckties!"

### 2196  *Went Around It*

Lincoln is reported to have said: "Some men are like the stump the old farmer had in his field—too hard to uproot, too knotty to split, and too wet and soggy to burn." His neighbors asked him what he did about it. "Well, now, boys," he answered, "I just plowed around it." That is a good thing to do with the obstacles that we encounter.—*Thomas H. Warner, Church Management*

### 2197  *The Mayor Had Some Answers*

Before a doctor receives his medical degree in a Central American country, he is required to serve a number of months in a community not having a doctor.

A young doctor, who is a member of the faculty of a university in that country, recently told me of an experience he had in the little community to which he was sent. He suggested to the mayor that the people be instructed not to dirty the streets. "But," said the mayor, "a horse dirties the streets, and surely you would not argue that a horse is more important and has more rights than a man."

The doctor also suggested that the mayor have someone go around and pick up the garbage. "But," said the mayor again, "why should I ask someone to go around and pick up what someone else has already thrown away because he doesn't want it?"

With great patience and perseverance, these young doctors are gradually changing such viewpoints and are improving conditions in the backward communities.—*Herbert V. Prochnow*

### 2198  *He Will Pass*

"Who are the three greatest sailors in British history?" asked an admiral who was conducting an examination for the navy.

The candidate: "I didn't catch your name when I entered the room, sir, but the other two are Nelson and Drake."

### 2199  *Successful*

"How did you make out on your first job?"

"I was a complete success. The boss said I was absolutely superfluous."

### 2200  *Why?*

Exasperated housewife: "Why didn't Noah swat those two flies when he had the chance?"

### 2201  *Mistake*

"Why do you look so unhappy, pal?"

"I called on my girl last night and her mother said: 'Young man, what are your intentions regarding my daughter?' Just then my girl called from upstairs, 'Mamma, that isn't the one.'"

### 2202  *Useful Testimony*

An 865-year jail sentence imposed by a Bangkok court on an embezzler has been cut to 576 years because his testimony "proved useful."—*News item, Financial Times (London)*

### 2203  *His Opinion*

"What do you think of the violinist?" George Bernard Shaw was once asked by his hostess at a music party.

"He reminds me of Paderewski," replied Shaw.

"But Paderewski is not a violinist."

"Neither is this gentleman."

### 2204  *Gave Up*

Drug clerk: "Did you kill any moths with those moth balls I sold you the other day?"

Customer: "No, I tried for five hours, but I couldn't hit one."

### 2205  *Doing the Best He Can*

A diner walked into a crowded restaurant during the holiday season. Catching the waiter's eye, he said, "You know it's been ten years since I came here."

"Well, it's not my fault," snapped the harried waiter. "I'm working as fast as I can."

### 2206  *A Real Pane*

A speaker was called upon to substitute for another speaker who was delayed in a snowstorm. The speaker began by explaining the meaning of a substitute. "If you break a window," he said, "and then place a cardboard there instead, that is a substitute."

After the address, a woman, who had listened intently, shook hands with him, and wishing to compliment him, said, "You were no substitute—you were a real pane!"

### 2207  *Great Invention*

"Did you hear about the fellow who invented a device for looking through walls?"

"No, what does he call it?"

"A window."

2208 *The Problem*

One trouble in this country is the number of people who are trying to get something for nothing. Another trouble is the high percentage that succeed.

2209 *Perfection*

Of all major team sports, baseball alone acknowledges perfect games in its record book. Only ten had been pitched in the history of the major leagues until 25-year-old righthander Len Barker of the Cleveland Indians set down 27 consecutive Toronto Blue Jay batters on a drizzly night in Cleveland Stadium. It was the first no-hit, no-walk, no-error, no-nothing game in the major leagues since "Catfish" Hunter, then of the Oakland A's, beat the Minnesota Twins on May 8, 1968. After his perfectly pitched game, Barker's 92-year-old grandmother, Mrs. Tokie Lockhart, living near Ona, West Virginia, said, "I'm very proud of him. I hope he does better next time."—*Good Reading Magazine*

2210 *That's Different*

Phil May, the Australian artist, once down on his luck, took a job as a waiter in a very low-class restaurant. An acquaintance came into the place and was aghast when he discovered the artist as a waiter.

"Man!" he whispered. "To find you in such a place as this."

Phil May smiled as he retorted, "Oh, but, you see, I don't eat here."

2211 *He Will Find Out*

A small boy had been told that we are here in the world to help others. "What are the others here for?" he asked.

2212 *Agreed*

Artist: "I paint a picture in three days, and think nothing of it."
Critic: "Neither do I."

2213 *Confucius No Say*

Man who leave home to set world on fire often come back for more matches.
When man works like horse, everybody ride him.
Little sugar plum today sometimes sour grapes tomorrow.
Man who beef too much find himself in stew.

2214 *Adequate*

First pelican: "Pretty good fish you have there."
Second pelican: "Well, it fills the bill."

2215 *No Progress*

Psychiatrist: "I want to congratulate you on the progress you've been making."

Patient: "Progress? Six months ago I was Napoleon. Today I'm nobody. You call that progress?"

2216    "After the Bawl Was Over" she got her new fur coat.

2217    The victor belongs to the spoils.—*F. Scott Fitzgerald*

2218    No part of the body gets harder wear than the wishbone.

2219    The person who goes around with a constant smile may just have better-looking teeth.

2220    Many a public speaker who rises to the occasion doesn't know when to sit down.

2221    Only a mediocre person is always at his best.—*Somerset Maugham*

2222    There will be fewer underpaid teachers next year because some of them will enter other occupations.

2223    Most self-made men are smart enough to employ college professors to train their sons.

2224    Most farmers who have fresh egg and vegetable roadside stands haven't any time to fool with farming.

2225    One swallow doesn't make a summer, but one lark may make a fall.

2226    All things come to him who waits, but not soon enough.

2227    No one has his ups and downs like the person in the end seat at the theater.

2228    Some people would prefer to be wrong rather than to keep quiet.

2229    Sometimes we think television is advertising with a knob to turn.

2230    When you see a man with his desk piled high with papers, you aren't sure whether he is busy or confused.

2231    When the boss has an idea, you either see the light or feel the heat.

2232    *Noah Webster:* The author who had the biggest vocabulary.

2233    An American movie actress told a reporter that she could not say for sure whether she was happily married. That sort of thing is left, of course, to one's publicity agent to decide.

2234     Many persons have more money than brains—but not for long.

2235     Sign outside a newly painted store: "Wet laqer—lacker—laquar—paint."

2236     It seems a reasonable certainty that very few big jobs are held by persons who honk and honk in a traffic jam.

2237     *Quartet:* Four men, all of whom think the other three can't sing.

2238     I think that I shall never see a billboard lovely as a tree. Indeed, unless the billboards fall, I'll never see a tree at all.

2239     If ignorance is bliss, an intelligence test is certainly a waste of time.

2240     The difference between a restaurant and a drug store is that a restaurant doesn't sell drugs.

2241     If you get up early, work late, and pay your taxes, you will get ahead —if you strike oil.

2242     This country would be completely covered with timber if the comic books had not been started.

2243     Do the underdeveloped nations count too much on being Yanked out of their economic difficulties?

2244     In a period of prosperity, it pays to remember that it is the fattest hog that goes to the butcher.

2245     A mistake is at least evidence that someone tried to do something.

2246     The person who falls down trying gets up much faster than the person who just lies down.

2247     *Prejudice:* Weighing the facts with your thumb on the scales.

2248     The person who doesn't benefit from others' mistakes must expect to live long enough to make them all himself.

2249     The fellow who doesn't let the grass grow under his feet is generally in clover.

2250     One of the biggest troubles with success these days is that its recipe is about the same as that for a nervous breakdown.

2251     Famous last words: "Well, if he won't dim his I won't dim mine!"

2252     The successful diet is based on eating more and more of less and less.

2253    We still can't understand how rumors without a leg to stand on can get around so fast.

2254    The cemeteries are filled with people who thought the world couldn't get along without them.

2255    Remember you are your own doctor when it comes to curing cold feet.

2256    An optimist is one who makes the best of it when he gets the worst of it.

2257    If you want to forget all your troubles, wear a pair of tight shoes.

2258    *Eloquence:* Saying the proper thing and stopping.—*Stanley Link*

2259    A publisher says many people think they can write novels. The delusion is especially prevalent among novelists.

2260    A scientist says the world is at least 2.8 billion years old. How could it have got itself in such a mess so soon?

2261    A raspberry will grow up, get ripe, come to town, and go to all sorts of trouble just to get a few seeds lodged in your teeth.

2262    Consider the mosquito as an example. He rarely gets a slap on the back until he goes to work.

2263    "Never again" means until the next time.

2264    It is easy to keep from being a bore. Just praise the person to whom you are talking.

2265    If biologists are right that there is not a perfect man in the world, personal opinions here and there will have to be altered.

2266    If railroads could speed up trains still faster, it would be harder for cars to hit them at grade crossings.

2267    Overproduction of butter, wheat, and beef has given us trouble. Apparently if we didn't have so many good farmers, we'd be better off.

2268    Sometimes we wish the manufacturers of power riveting machines would work on putting studs in a dress shirt.

2269    There is a difference between bettering yourself and making yourself better.

2270 A man can be high up in his own estimation and still be a long way from the top.

2271 Things are never as bad as they seem. There must be millions of Russians who don't hate anyone.

2272 If you just sit still, you never have to go out to meet trouble because it comes to you.

2273 What we used to call disgrace now brings a contract to write a book.

2274 A few years ago people thought television was impossible, and now they still do.

2275 The person who brags lacks confidence in himself.

2276 *Plagiarist:* A person who improves upon something that was poorly written.

2277 A space scientist believes that anything that works is obsolete.

2278 You are making progress if each mistake you make is a new one.

2279 Every once in a while we see a television program that makes us yearn for the good old days of static radio.

2280 Three rules for successful speakers—stand up, speak up, shut up.

2281 I raise the kind of perennials in my garden that don't come up year after year.

2282 The window washer went to the racetrack and the window cleaned him.

2283 "Heaven is not reached in a single bound," says the poet. It may be on a busy street corner.

2284 A yes man is a person who gets along well with the man nobody noes.

2285 The fellow who can look happy when he isn't is on the way to success.

2286 Nothing keeps the American people moving like the "No Parking" signs.

2287 Clothes may make the man, but we've seen some where the job still wasn't finished.

2288 It's almost impossible to succeed if you cannot do what you are told —or can do nothing else.

2289    A pessimist burns his bridges before he gets to them.

2290    *Reckless motorist:* Man of extinction.

2291    We call it "hard times" when we have to do without things our grand-parents never heard of.

2292    Worry is like a rocking chair; it gives you something to do but never gets you anywhere.

2293    There are so many TV commercials now that what used to be a simple station break now sounds like a compound fracture.

2294    The hard part of making good is that you have to do it again every day.

2295    When all is said and done at a committee meeting, you generally find more was said than done.

2296    Nothing recedes like success.—*Walter Winchell*

2297    All you need to grow fine, vigorous grass is a crack in your sidewalk.

2298    To avoid old age, keep overdrinking, overeating, and overachieving.

2299    If a man wants to succeed, he should marry early so he won't have to waste time making up his mind.

2300    The have-not nations have shoeless toes and the have nations have toeless shoes.

2301    To be successful you have to start without the advantages other people have.

2302    You never feather your nest on a wild goose chase.

2303    Getting ahead is largely a matter of putting things over and not putting them off.

2304    An honest man is one who wouldn't be crooked even if he could get away with it.

2305    Every man's got to figure to get beat sometime.—*Joe Louis*

2306    If an automobile doesn't get a pedestrian, an automobile salesman will.

2307    It's not how far you go in life but how you get there.

2308    *Pessimist:* A person who keeps an optimist from becoming satisfied with himself.

2309    If a person lives only to get a kick out of life, he may get it—but in the shins.

2310    Only the person who is going somewhere needs to watch his step.

2311    If you are big enough, your troubles will be smaller than you are.

2312    One of life's difficult decisions is picking the supermarket check-out line that will move fastest.

2313    The fellow who plays the big bass drum doesn't make good music, but he drowns out a lot of bad music.

2314    Winning is overemphasized. The only time it is really important is in surgery and war.—*Al McGuire*

2315    A go-getter is a person who can get his elbows on each arm of his theater chair.

2316    To be a leader you need a lot of people dumb enough to follow.

2317    When neither your friends nor your enemies talk about you, you're slipping.

2318    When you make a mistake and fail to correct it, you are making another mistake.

2319    It makes a great deal of difference whether a young man learns the "tricks of the trade" or the trade.

2320    The best conversationalist is the person who lets others do the talking.

2321    It's strange how we always expect to get more out of a camera than we put in.

2322    It's not too difficult to bear up under misfortune when it misses you and hits the other fellow.

2323    What is so rare in the world as a person who dries his hands on one paper towel?

2324    Some people keep you so busy listening to their troubles that you haven't time to worry about your own.

2325    The world's greatest optimist is the person who waits for his ship to come in when he didn't send one out.

2326    No one is a greater leader of men than woman.

2327     Anybody can win, unless there happens to be a second entry.—*George Ade*

2328     No one can do the things he thinks he can't do.

2329     Batting around at night doesn't help you to hit home runs in the daytime.

2330     The person who is always on the go seldom gets there.

2331     The person who never makes a mistake leads a pretty dull life.

2332     Stout people may be easygoing, but it isn't always easy to get around them.

2333     A person's reputation is a mixture of what his friends, enemies, and relatives say behind his back.

2334     You can lift your head up if you keep your nose at a lower level.

2335     If you never make a mistake, you may live and die without anyone ever noticing you.

2336     The only way to judge the future is by the past, but if some people are judged that way, they won't have any future.

2337     The question of how fast fish grow depends on who catches them.

2338     A good repairman is one who just smiles when he repairs a do-it-yourself job.

2339     In order to hit the bull's-eye, a person has to miss some other things.

2340     It is not enough simply to try your hand at different things. You have to try your head also.

2341     Success is the difference between entertaining an idea and working with it.

2342     Procrastination is putting off until tomorrow what you put off yesterday until today.

2343     A good loser is a wonderful person unless you had some bets on him.

2344     We suppose if Abraham Lincoln had been paid for not splitting rails, he might have become a rather prominent man.

2345     Many a person who burned the candle at both ends would be satisfied with even a small flame now.

2346    The world spins around so fast that no one sits on top of it for very long.

2347    Getting out of a rut is the highest mountain most of us have to climb.

2348    This country has solved about every great national problem except where to park.

2349    The person who is smart enough to keep quiet never gets picked as chairman of the committee.

2350    *Leader:* A man who has followers and therefore can't change his mind, even if he is wrong.

2351    The fellow who knows how to settle the world's problems may not know how to get along with his own mother-in-law.

2352    The fellow who can't forget business on his vacation is doomed to success.

2353    If you can keep your hands in your pockets and make a convincing talk about the fish that got away, you can be a successful salesman.

2354    If success turns your head, you'll probably end up moving in the wrong direction.

2355    If you are trying to kill time, always make sure it is your own.

2356    Almost every community has a zoo with a few social lions, some queer birds, a couple of white elephants, and a number of people who often make monkeys of themselves.

2357    A person gets into trouble if he thinks success depends on how many he can do instead of how much.

2358    All human beings are born helpless—and as time goes by, some help less than others.

2359    There is always room at the top because some people who get there go to sleep and roll off.

2360    Forget the past. No one becomes successful in the past.

2361    If you want to win friends and influence people, keep your ears open and your mouth shut most of the time.

2362    An optimist is a person who thinks that when his shoes wear out he will be back on his feet.

2363    Most persons would be satisfied if they found an oyster in the stew rather than a pearl.

2364    The chick a man marries often determines whether he winds up with a nest egg or a goose egg.

2365    Many college youngsters work their way through college by writing short stories to Father.

2366    The American people are more conservative after dinner than at any other time.

2367    After you know definitely that a thing can't be done, someone who didn't know does it.

2368    It doesn't take long for a popular melody to become a malady.

2369    To the pessimist, "0" is the last letter in "zero," but to the optimist it's the first letter in "opportunity."

2370    Man is an ambitious biped who struggles to eat, dress, and live as well as every other biped—and if possible better.

2371    *Executive:* A person who considers an idea good because he thought of it.

2372    *Has-been:* A person who thinks he has reached the top.

2373    The most frequent form of ability in the world is incapability.

2374    Whatever reputation a mule has, he gets by pulling, not by kicking.

2375    Be careful about criticizing a person when he is down, as he may get up.

2376    We appreciate the person who stands on his own feet, especially in an elevator.

2377    If a person gets what's coming to him, he is generally disappointed.

2378    The only something you get for nothing is failure.

2379    An after-dinner speaker either drives a message home to his audience or drives his audience home.

2380    The trouble with telling a good story is that it reminds the other person of a dull one.

2381    You are either smart or the boss when no one disagrees with you.

2382    You can fool all the people some of the time, but you can fool yourself all the time.

2383    The other night we heard Schubert's Unfinished Symphony finished.

2384    Remember the old days when the windshield didn't have so many stickers you couldn't look through it?

2385    Sign on the door of a bankrupt retail store: "Opened by mistake."

2386    No safety sign is as effective as the one on the side of the police car.

2387    In the old days people considered children to be necessities and automobiles luxuries, but now they're reversed.

2388    At a rock-and-roll party a waiter dropped a tray of dishes and four couples got up to dance.

2389    An argument is no stronger than its weakest think.

2390    Sweet are the uses of the other fellow's adversity.

2391    Only a know man can afford to have yes men around him.

2392    The way of the transgressor is well publicized.

2393    It's very embarrassing to be mistaken at the top of your voice.

2394    Success has always operated on the serve-yourself plan.

2395    *Experience:* Yesterday's answer to today's problems.

2396    Half a loafer is better than a whole loafer.

2397    The time to make hay is when things go haywire.

2398    You'll never get to lead the band if you can't face the music.

2399    An optimist can always see the bright side of the other fellow's misfortune.

2400    The man who is always boasting that he is self-made should be given credit for not trying to shift the blame.

2401    Whenever the going seems easy, it's well to make sure you're not going downhill.

2402    After viewing some recent films, we concluded that all the dummies in the movies don't get thrown over cliffs.

2403   It is getting to the point where a person killed in an auto accident is considered to have died a natural death.

2404   Pity the poor American Indian. The white man got his land, the coed his war paint, and the college boy his war cry.

2405   We always wondered what made Francis Scott Key famous until we remembered he knew all the verses of "The Star-Spangled Banner."

2406   Opera is when a guy gets stabbed in the back and instead of bleeding he sings.—*Ed Gardner*

2407   Leadership appears to be the art of getting others to want to do something you are convinced should be done.—*Vance Packard*

2408   Beautiful, beautiful, beautiful. A magnificent desolation.—*Edwin (Buzz) Aldrin, the second man to set foot on the moon*

2409   Banking may well be a career from which no man really recovers.—*John Kenneth Galbraith*

2410   There's no such thing as a free lunch.—*Milton Friedman*

2411   Technological progress has merely provided us with more efficient means for going backwards.—*Aldous Huxley*

2412   I rose by sheer military ability to the rank of Corporal.—*Thornton Wilder*

2413   When you're as great as I am, it's hard to be humble.—*Muhammad Ali*

2414   Motto posted on an executive's desk: "Use your head. It's the little things that count!"

2415   Remember the turtle—he never makes any progress until he sticks his neck out.

2416   The biggest problems for traffic planners: urban, suburban, and bourbon.

2417   The best way to catch a rabbit is to hide behind a tree and make a noise like a carrot.

2418   *Sophistication:* The ability to yawn without opening your mouth.

2419   *Distinction:* To have a low automobile license number.

2420    The airplane, the atomic bomb, and the zipper have cured me of any tendency to state that a thing can't be done.—*R. L. Duffus*

2421    He was an aristocratic fish—his ancestors swam under the *Mayflower.*

2422    The origin of civilization is man's determination to do nothing for himself which he can get done for him.—*H. C. Bailey*

2423    It is said that all things come to him who waits, but the fellow who goes after them gets the pick.

2424    That's one small step for man, one giant leap for mankind.—*Neil Armstrong, first man to set foot on the moon, 1969*

2425    We're Number One on the runway.—*Neil Armstrong, preparing to take off from the moon to return to earth*

2426    Gross National Product is our Holy Grail.—*Stewart Udall*

2427    I always turn to the sports page first. The sports page records people's accomplishments; the front page has nothing but man's failures.—*Earl Warren*

2428    *Sculpture:* Mud pies which endure.—*Cyril Connolly*

2429    I don't know what you could say about a day in which you have seen four beautiful sunsets.—*John Glenn, the first American to orbit the earth, 1962*

2430    Be awful nice to 'em going up, because you're gonna meet 'em all comin' down.—*Jimmy Durante*

2431    Nothing is so commonplace as to wish to be remarkable.—*Oliver Wendell Holmes*

2432    This is the only country that ever went to the poorhouse in an automobile.—*Will Rogers*

2433    Those who warn of a population explosion picture a world of too many people and not enough food—sort of like the average cocktail party.—*Bill Vaughan*

2434    Lose an hour in the morning, and you will be all day hunting for it. —*Richard Whately*

2435    Thurber did not write the way a surgeon operates; he wrote the way a child skips rope, the way a mouse waltzes.—*E. B. White*

2436    For the sake of one good action a hundred evil ones should be forgotten.—*Chinese proverb*

2437    Opportunity is that which, if you have not thought out what it means you cannot recognize when it comes.

2438    The fate of Lot's wife was all her own fault; she first turned to rubber, and then turned to salt.

2439    . . . Man is still the most extraordinary computer of all.—*President John F. Kennedy, honoring astronaut L. Gordon Cooper, Jr.*

2440    They who wish to sing always find a song.—*Swedish proverb*

2441    You may be on the right track, but if you just sit there you will be run over.

2442    Opportunity doesn't knock now, but it rings the telephone and asks you a silly question.

2443    If you don't have the advantage others have, you have a chance to be successful.

2444    An after-dinner speaker is a person who closes his mouth after the audience wishes he would.

2445    Some people have learned to drive by accident.

2446    If you flatter, your conversation is never flat.

2447    When success turns a person's head, it often wrings his neck at the same time.

2448    A comedian may be the goof that relays the olden gag.

2449    Walking in modern traffic is not only good exercise, but it also tests the wits.

2450    No one leaves a footprint on the sands of time by sitting down.

2451    You are not a dynamic person simply because you blow your top.

2452    Why not do it tomorrow? You've made enough mistakes already for one day.

2453    It takes more than a shoeshine to give a man polish.

2454    Progress might have been all right once, but it's gone on too long.— *Ogden Nash*

2455    The danger of the past was that men became slaves. The danger of the future is that men may become robots.—*Erich Fromm*

2456    I do borrow from other writers, shamelessly! I can only say in my defense, like the woman brought before the judge on a charge of kleptomania, "I do steal; but, Your Honor, only from the very best stores."—*Thornton Wilder*

2457    I am the first Eagle Scout Vice-President of the United States!—*Gerald Ford*

2458    *Pessimist:* A person who is happy when he is wrong.

2459    Many of our great men used to come from the farm. We don't have any surplus of that product now.

2460    Is it progress if a cannibal uses knife and fork?—*Stanislaw J. Lec*

2461    An efficient businessman found a machine that would do half his work at the office, so he bought two of them.

2462    The fellow who never makes a mistake takes his orders from one who does.—*Herbert V. Prochnow*

2463    Fortunately, a popular song doesn't live too long. It's murdered on TV and radio every day.

2464    A pessimist is a person who went into a partnership with an optimist.

2465    Every hero becomes a bore at last.—*Ralph Waldo Emerson*

2466    What is the use of running when you are on the wrong road?—*Proverb*

2467    If at first you do succeed, don't take any more chances.—*Kin (Frank McKinney) Hubbard*

2468    If you drive carefully, all you need is a strong rear bumper.

2469    Early to bed and early to rise is a bad rule for anyone who wishes to become acquainted with our most prominent and influential people.—*George Ade*

2470    Those men who pass most comfortably through the world are those who possess good digestion and hard hearts.—*James Martineau*

2471    Herein the only royal road to fame and fortune lies;
Put not your trust in vinegar—molasses catches flies!
—*Eugene Field*

2472    Cain was a juvenile delinquent without being born on the wrong side of the tracks.

2473     In short, whoever you may be
       To this conclusion you'll agree,
       When everyone is somebodee,
       Then no one's anybody!
         *—W. S. Gilbert*

2474 Some movie actress is going to become famous by refusing to go out with anyone but her husband.

2475 When you have a number of disagreeable duties to perform always do the most disagreeable first.*—Josiah Quincy*

2476 Who rides a tiger cannot dismount.*—Chinese proverb*

2477 Half a calamity is better than a whole one.*—Lawrence of Arabia*

2478 How can you write if you can't cry?*—Ring Lardner*

2479 Calamities are of two kinds: misfortune to ourselves, and good fortune to others.*—Ambrose Bierce*

2480 You write a hit play the same way you write a flop.*—William Saroyan*

2481 *Traffic policeman:* A person who never loses an argument.

2482 If they keep making cars that withstand harder and harder bumps, it will soon be possible to knock down a pedestrian without jarring the driver.

2483 When a politician makes a pledge to spend more money, he always keeps it.*—Herbert V. Prochnow*

2484 It rolls off my back like a duck.*—Samuel Goldwyn*

# Happiness, Joy, and Health

### 2485 *Smart Patient*

"This is a simple test to determine ordinary response," the psychiatrist told his patient. "What would happen if I cut off your left ear?"

"I couldn't hear."

"And what would happen if I then cut off your right ear?"

"I couldn't see."

"Why do you say that?"

"Because my hat would fall over my eyes."

### 2486 *Health and Wealth*

> To get his wealth he spent his health,
> And then with might and main
> He turned around and spent his wealth
> To get his health again.

### 2487 *He Had to Hurry*

The physician turned from the telephone and said to his wife, "I must hurry to Mrs. Jones's boy—he's sick."

"Is it serious?"

"Yes. I don't know what's the matter with him, but she has a book on what to do before the doctor comes. So I must hurry. Whatever it is, she mustn't do it."

### 2488 *Good Question*

Mother: "Eat your spinach, dear. It will put color in your cheeks."

Daughter: "Who wants green cheeks?"

### 2489    *Salutes*

In the United States, the characteristic salutation is "Hello" or "How do you do?"

The Arabs say on meeting, "A fine morning to you."

The Turk says, with much gravity, "God grant you His blessing."

The Egyptian is a practical man. He has to earn his taxes by toiling under a burning sun. Accordingly he asks, "How do you perspire?"

The Chinese loves his dinner. He says, "Have you had your rice?"

The Greeks, who are keen in business, ask, "How are you getting on?"

The Spaniards say, "How are you passing it?"

The Germans, "How goes it?"

The Dutch, "How do you travel?"

The Swedes, "How can you?" meaning, "Are you in good vigor?"

The Russians, "Be well!"

The English-speaking nations, in addition to "Hello," say "How are you?" and "How do you do!"

The bow, as a mark of respect, is a customary form of greeting in nearly all nations.

### 2490    *Found*

Lost and Found advertisement: "To the party who shot the arrow into the air that fell to earth you know not where. I know where. Contact room 201, General Hospital."

### 2491    *He Was Polite*

One policeman believes that the speeding driver should be talked to politely. When it becomes necessary for him to speak of safety to a driver, he doesn't yell, "Hey, you! Pull over to the curb!" He motions to him with a smile and hands him a card. It tells the driver to "Sing While You Drive" and recommends these tunes:

At 50 miles per hour, "Highways Are Happy Ways."

At 60 miles per hour, "I'm But a Stranger Here, Heaven Is My Home."

At 70 miles, "Nearer, My God, to Thee."

At 80 miles, "When the Roll Is Called Up Yonder I'll Be There."

### 2492    *My Best Friend*

I admire you very much, you never criticize; you cover my mistakes with so many little lies. In all my thoughts we both agree. I really think you're swell, because you're me.

### 2493    *Remarkable Cure*

"Dear Sir," writes a customer, "for nine years I was totally deaf, and after using your ear salve for only ten days I heard from a long-lost brother in Nebraska."

### 2494    *Confidential*

The diner in a café said, "This soup's not fit to eat!"

"Who told you so?" replied the waiter.

"If you must know," retorted the diner meekly, "it was a little swallow."

### 2495    *A Promise*

The mother, who was a believer in strict discipline, sternly addressed her little daughter, who sat woefully shrinking in the dentist's chair as he approached with forceps in hand.

"Now, Letty," she said, "if you cry, I'll never take you to the dentist's again."

### 2496    *Got It Again*

After puzzling over a patient's rash for several minutes, the doctor asked, "Have you ever had this before?"

"Yes," the patient replied. "A couple of years ago."

"Well," the doctor said sagely, "it looks like you've got it again."

### 2497    *Refreshed*

A guest speaker was talking to a member of the audience after his rather long speech. "And how did you like my talk?" he asked.

"I found it very refreshing, really refreshing," the man replied.

"Did you really?" questioned the delighted speaker.

"Oh, absolutely," he said. "I felt like a new man when I woke up!"

### 2498    *Resistance*

Cheerful people, the doctors say, resist disease better than glum ones. In other words, the surly bird catches the germ.

### 2499    *Few Ask It*

One evening, a little girl surprised her parents when they found her kneeling in prayer. After finishing with a prayer for her family and herself, she added, "And now, what can I do for You?"

### 2500    *All Planned*

Each morning the old gentleman was seen taking a short stroll across his yard before embarking on his customary longer walk around the block. One overly curious neighbor finally questioned this practice. "Oh," said the older man, "it's the preamble to my constitutional."

### 2501    *The View*

A man who had resided all his life in the midst of the Canadian Rockies one day went to the plains of Kansas. "What a beautiful country!" he exclaimed.

"Why do you call this flat, monotonous country beautiful, when you have lived all your life in the midst of the wonderful mountains of Canada?" asked a native.

"Oh, you can see so far here. Where I came from you cannot see beyond a ten-acre patch."

## 2502  *Patriotic*

Sergeant: "Stop worrying about a little sand in your soup. Did you join the army to serve your country or to complain about the food?"

Recruit: "I joined the army to serve my country, sergeant—not to eat it."

## 2503  *What's Important*

Three men were talking one day about the frailties of people. One said, "The trouble with most people is that they eat too much." The second man objected, saying, "It isn't how much you eat, but what you eat that counts." The third, a doctor, stated, "It's neither what you eat nor how much—it's what's eating you that's important."

## 2504  *Simple Operation*

"Do you mind telling me why you ran away from the operating room?"

"Because the nurse said, 'Be brave, an appendectomy is simple.' "

"So?"

"She was talking to the doctor who was going to operate."

## 2505  *Knock, Knock!*

"Knock, Knock!"

"Who's there?"

"Dwain."

"Dwain who?"

"Dwain the bathtub, I'm dwowning!"

## 2506  *What's in a Name*

Patient: "Doctor, is there anything wrong with me? Don't frighten me half to death by giving it a long scientific name. Just tell me in plain English."

Doctor: "Well, to be perfectly frank, you are just plain lazy."

Patient: "Thank you, Doctor. Now please give me the scientific name for it so I can tell the family."

## 2507  *No Appetite*

An Indian had gone to see the doctor, who, after examining him, told him to be careful about what he ate—in fact, not to eat at all until he got an appetite. Meeting the Indian a few days later, the doctor asked how he felt.

"Oh, I feel fine now," he replied. "I wait one day, appetite no come, wait two day, appetite no come, wait three day, appetite no come, get so hungry eat anyway."

2508   *Close Guess*

"Did you go to the doctor, John?"
"Yes, I did."
"Did he find out what you had?"
"Almost."
"What do you mean 'almost'?"
"Well, I had $25.75 with me and he charged $25."

2509   *Jes' Supposin'*

Jes' supposin' you were here, or I was there with you, and we could get together as we often used to do—and sit awhile and laugh and smile without no pomp or posin' or frills or fuss, but jus' be us—on Christmas—jus' supposin'!

2510   *Mistaken*

"Doctor, I'm suffering from a pain in my right leg."
"There's no cure. It's just old age."
"You must be mistaken, Doctor. The left leg is as old as the right and it doesn't hurt me at all."

2511   *Safe Driving*

> Than drinking and driving
> There's nothing worse.
> It's putting the quart
> Before the hearse.

2512   *Good Advice*

Henry: "My doctor says to play golf for your health."
Sam: "And if you already play golf, then what?"
Henry: "He says to stop."

2513   *The Reason*

Patent medicine vendor: "And now, ladies and gentlemen, I have been selling this medicine for twenty years, and have never had a complaint. What does that prove to you?"
Voice from the crowd: "Dead men tell no tales!"

2514   *Hard to Explain*

A nationally known physician tells us that the human body is composed of various ingredients which have a material value of only about 67 cents. How does he explain a doctor's bill for $500 for repairs on a 67-cent machine?

2515   *Sympathy*

When the customer sat down to dinner, it was evident that he had a bad cold in the nose. "What's the matter, sir?" asked the waiter. "Fighting a cold?"

"Yes," said the customer morosely.

The waiter shook his head gravely. "Too bad you don't have pneumonia; they know what to do for that."

2516   *Say That Again*

"I'm gonna sneeze!"

"Who at?"

"Atchoo!"

2517   *No Lotion*

Customer: "Have you anything for gray hair?"

Druggist: "Nothing, madam, but the greatest respect."

2518   *Dangerous Then*

A veteran nurse was explaining hospital procedures and giving a tour of the facilities to a pretty young nursing student, whom she warned: "This is the ward filled with what can be considered the most dangerous patients—they're almost completely recovered."

2519   *Correct Explanation*

*Prescription:* Hieroglyphics written by a physician, to be translated by a pharmacist into dollar signs.

2520   *He Snoze*

He snoze a sneeze into the air. It fell to earth, he knew not where. But later on, as he was told, some twenty others had a cold.

2521   *Absolutely Necessary*

"Doctor, do you believe this operation is necessary?"

"Absolutely, my friend. I owe three payments on my mortgage."

2522   *Why Not?*

It was considered proper in George Washington's day to eat peas with a knife and to drink tea from a saucer.

2523   *Awful*

Does a giraffe get a sore throat by getting its feet cold and wet? Yes, but not until neck's week.

### 2524  *Fine Distinction*

When the other fellow looks that way, it's because he is dissipated. When you look that way, it's because you are run down.

### 2525  *How to Get Better*

Doctor: "Your cough is a little better today."
Student: "It ought to be. I've been practicing all night."

### 2526  *Diagnosis*

Student: "I have a splinter in my finger."
Doctor: "You must have been scratching your head."

### 2527  *Ptomaine Poisoning*

Doctor: "Why do you say you have ptomaine poisoning?"
Student: "Because it's my toe that hurts."

### 2528  *Lacks a Valet Only*

"I just love to lie in bed in the morning and ring for the valet."
"My goodness, you mean to tell me you have a valet?"
"Oh, no. But I have a bell."

### 2529  *Not Particular*

A man who was filling out an application for a job in a factory came to the question "Who is the person to notify in case of accident?" His answer was "Anybody in sight."

### 2530  *Happy Ending*

Overheard in a crowded movie theater: "That movie had a happy ending—everybody was glad when it ended."

### 2531  *It's Tough*

A New Yorker had just returned from a business trip to California. He reported that it is the only place in the United States he had ever seen where people drive ten blocks to their exercise classes.

### 2532  *No Lost Art*

A health organization reports that walking is a lost art in this country. Is that so? How do they think most of us get from where we park to where we are going?

### 2533  *Helpful*

Nurse, showing a new patient to his room: "Now, we want you to be happy and enjoy yourself while here, so if there is anything you want that we haven't got, let me know and I'll show you how to get along without it."

2534    *The Hard Way*

"Well, I did my good deed today. I made at least a hundred people happy."
"How is that?"
"I chased my hat when the wind blew it down the street."

2535    *Too Expensive*

The woman asked her dentist how long it would take to pull her tooth.
"Only two seconds," he replied.
"And how much will it cost to have this done?" she asked.
"Fifty dollars," he answered.
"For only two seconds' work?"
"Well," the dentist said coolly, "I could pull it out more slowly, if you prefer."

2536    You go to a psychiatrist when you're slightly cracked and keep going until you're completely broke.

2537    For there was never yet philosopher that could endure the toothache patiently.—*William Shakespeare*

2538    No nation likes noise and "Hooey" like we do. We are cuckoo but happy.—*Will Rogers*

2539    Fun is like life insurance; the older you get, the more it costs.—*Kin (Frank McKinney) Hubbard*

2540    Fast drivers get everywhere a little sooner—even the cemetery.

2541    This makes me so sore it gets my dandruff up.—*Samuel Goldwyn*

2542    Conscience is the thing that hurts when everything else feels good.

2543    If I had known there was no Latin word for tea, I would have let the vulgar stuff alone.—*Hilaire Belloc*

2544    Happiness is pursuing something but not catching it—except chasing a bus on a rainy night.

2545    *Laugh:* A smile that burst.—*John E. Donovan*

2546    Fat people are good-natured because it takes them so long to get mad clear through.

2547    To make a smile come, so they say, brings thirteen muscles into play, while if you want a frown to thrive, you've got to work up sixty-five.

2548    Most persons are content with what they have, but they are not content with what they don't have.

2549    The art of medicine consists of amusing the patient while nature cures the disease.—*Voltaire*

2550    A hospital should also have a recovery room adjoining the cashier's office.—*Francis O'Walsh*

2551    We suppose a doctor lists a good apple crop as an occupational hazard.

2552    People at a big reception keep you from being lonely when you wish you were.

2553    Seconds count—especially when dieting.

2554    There's one thing that will give you more for your money than it would ten years ago—the penny scale.

2555    Eat, drink, and be merry, for tomorrow ye diet.—*William Gilmore Beymer*

2556    Some folks smile and some folks frown, you never need to mind them. Just keep a quiet, contented mind, and take folks as you find them.

2557    If you are quick, you are fast. If you are tied, you are fast. If you spend too much money, you are fast. And if you quit eating, you fast.

2558    *Bachelor:* A fellow who believes he is entitled to life, liberty, and the happiness of pursuit.

2559    If you can accept every loss as a gain, you're either a philosopher or dieting.—*Ken Kraft*

2560    Television has added a new dimension to boredom—eyestrain.

2561    *Optimist:* A person who saves the seed catalogue pictures to compare with the flowers and vegetables he actually grows.

2562    Happiness is a place between too little and too much.

2563    A contented man enjoys the scenery on a detour.

2564    Woman's ambition—to be weighed and found wanting.

2565    An onion a day keeps everybody away.

2566    A good many people commit suicide with a knife and fork.

2567    A centenarian is a person who has lived to be 100 years old. He never smoked or he smoked all his life. He used whiskey for 80 years or he never used it. He was a vegetarian or he wasn't a vegetarian. Follow these rules carefully and you, too, can be a centenarian.

2568    *Hide-and-sick:* A game played on any ocean liner by a large number of the passengers.

2569    *Naïve person:* Anyone who thinks you are interested when you ask how he is.

2570    *Scissor grinding:* A business that goes ahead when things are dull.

2571    There are three stages of sickness: (1) ill, (2) pill, (3) bill. And sometimes there is another: (4) will.

2572    Some people drive as if they were anxious to have their accident quickly and get it over with.

2573    We are told that healthy babies should be a delicate pink. Most are robust yellers.

2574    It may be that fruits feel pain, as that Frenchman says, but the grapefruit is the only one that fights back.

2575    "Those who have hobbies rarely go crazy," asserts a psychiatrist. Yeah, but what about those who live with those who have hobbies?

2576    If you chance to meet a sneezer, whack him promptly on the beezer; thus you stifle his cadenza and avoid the influenza.

2577    About all a pedestrian can hope for now is to be injured only slightly.

2578    We are always happy in the spring, but still there is a feeling of sadness. It looks as if everything were coming back except us.

2579    Spring is the season of balls—golf, tennis, base, and moth.

2580    Reducing takes a weight off your mind—and your feet.

2581    Insanity is probably decreasing because so many things that were considered crazy aren't anymore.

2582    If the theory of evolution is correct, we ought to produce some tough and unbreakable pedestrians pretty soon.

2583    Most of us take more than our minimum daily requirement of vitamin I.

2584    Fools rush around on tires no good garage man would tread.

2585     Most of us will do everything to shorten our lives and then pay a doctor to tell us to stop.

2586     Happiness is often punctured by a sharp tongue.

2587     On a highway, there is no fool like an oiled fool.

2588     A pessimist forgets to laugh, but an optimist laughs to forget.

2589     *Patience:* The ability to listen silently while someone else tells all about the very operation you just underwent.

2590     *Optimist:* A person who says that if the fish don't bite the mosquitoes will.

2591     In the old days you had the itch, but nowadays you have an allergy.

2592     The fellow who tells you all his troubles saves you from telling him all your troubles.

2593     *Optimism:* A synonym for Americanism.

2594     A philosopher is a person who can explain why he is happy when he has no money.

2595     If you ate two apples a day, would you keep two doctors away?

2596     Indigestion is proof that you've had too much of a good thing.

2597     What do you do if an apple a day costs more than the doctor?

2598     Uneasy lies the head that mixed hot chili, horseradish, and ice cream at dinner.

2599     Sometimes a tooth hurts so much it drives you to extraction.

2600     If we ask someone for his honest opinion of us, and he gives it, we never like him as well again.

2601     Some people aren't satisfied with a lot even when they have a lot.

2602     The motorist who thinks all other drivers are fools has a chance to live a long time.

2603     Of all the things you wear, your smile is the most important.

2604     We find dieting a grueling task.

2605     Medicine has advanced so much in recent years that it is almost impossible now for a doctor to find anything all right about a person.

2606     Nothing lasts forever, not even a bath.

2607     The best thing a pedestrian can do is get a suit of armor, insure his life, and then stay home.

2608     Nothing makes a person more comfortable than inferiority in those around him.

2609     If you can't remember what you worried about last week, you haven't any troubles.

2610     In most diets you have to struggle between getting enough roughage in your food and enough food in your roughage.

2611     Times change. The main highway is becoming the maim highway.

2612     Optimism is pessimism on a spree.

2613     Early to bed and early to rise, if you want your head to feel its normal size.

2614     When you have that sinking feeling on a scale, it's time to start reducing.

2615     An apple a day keeps the doctor away and leaves you with a new esprit de core.

2616     *Arthritis:* Twinges in the hinges.—*G. B. Howard*

2617     The first real cure for dandruff was invented by a Frenchman. He called it the guillotine.

2618     When a dentist is down in the mouth, the other person is also sad.

2619     The disheartening thing about the average diet is it does so much for the willpower and so little for the waistline.

2620     "The doctor will see you inside," said the nurse to the patient as she helped him onto the operating table.

2621     An apple a day keeps the doctor away—unless you get the seeds in your appendix.

2622     A specialist is one who has his patients trained to become ill only during his office hours. A general practitioner is likely to be called off the golf course at any time.

2623     Don't become discouraged if you have a cold in the head. Even that's something.

2624     She had her face lifted, but it fell when she got the bill for repairs.

2625     Scientists say we are what we eat. Nuts must be a bigger part of our diet than is commonly thought.

2626     Too much of life goes to waist in middle age.

2627     A kangaroo went to his doctor and complained, "I'm not feeling jumpy."

2628     An elephant lives several hundred years, but then his trunk doesn't have to travel anywhere.

2629     Even if a pessimist turns out to be wrong, he can be happy about it.

2630     A well-balanced man is one who finds both sides of an issue laughable.

2631     *Miracle drug:* Medicine children will take without screaming.

2632     We don't mind suffering in silence if everybody knows we're doing it.

2633     If it weren't for the optimist, the pessimist wouldn't know how happy he isn't.

2634     Doctor to patient: "Congratulations. The high price of meat, butter, and eggs has cleared up your cholesterol."

2635     *Optimist:* One who counts his blessings.
          *Pessimist:* One who discounts his blessings.

2636     *Potato:* An Irish avocado.—*Fred Allen*

2637     *Prune:* The sad ending of a plum.

2638     *Passport picture:* A photo of a man that he can laugh at without realizing it looks exactly the way his friends see him.

2639     *Parsley:* A chef's idea of decoration and a means of diverting your attention from the small size of the steak.

2640     When you get all wrinkled up with care and worry, it's a good time to get your religious faith lifted.

2641    The best way to eat spinach is to fatten a chicken with it and then eat the chicken.

2642    *Pessimist:* A person who is never happy unless he is unhappy.

2643    *Pessimist:* A person who says business conditions are as bad as they can get but will get worse.—*Herbert V. Prochnow*

2644    *Optimist:* A fellow who digs dandelions out of his lawn.—*Kin (Frank McKinney) Hubbard*

2645    *Optimist:* A man who gets treed by a lion but enjoys the scenery.—*Walter Winchell*

2646    *Optimist:* Someone who tells you to cheer up when things are going his way.—*Edward R. Murrow*

2647    *Optimist:* A man who hasn't got around to reading the morning papers.—*Earl Wilson*

2648    A well-known comedian protests that he is always being told one of his own stories. A clear case of the tale dogging the wag.

2649    Taste makes waist.

2650    Most men seem to like a polka-dot tie. It isn't especially pretty, but one more spot doesn't matter.

2651    Blessed are the hard of hearing, for they miss much small talk.

2652    *Happiness:* A feeling you have when you are too busy to be miserable.

2653    *Gall:* Something you have when you have nothing else.

2654    A smile is a wrinkle that shouldn't be removed.

2655    You have reached the age of discretion when you begin to wonder if it's worth what it costs.

2656    One nice thing about a dull party is that you can get to bed at a decent time.

2657    If the world was made out of chaos, we're right back where we started.

2658    It's all right to be optimistic, but no smart cook breaks an egg directly into the pan.

2659    It makes most people happy to see how much trouble the other fellow is having.

2660    One swallow doesn't make a summer, but a half-dozen swallows may make a fall.

2661    The next time you have a sore throat be glad you are not a giraffe.

2662    A special get-well card has been designed for the do-it-yourself addicts who fix their own roofs.

2663    *Diagnosis:* A physician's forecast of disease by the patient's pulse and purse.—*Ambrose Bierce*

2664    Happiness is having a scratch for every itch.—*Ogden Nash*

2665    I'm cheerful. I'm not happy, but I'm cheerful. There's a big difference. . . . A happy woman has no cares at all; a cheerful woman has cares and learns to ignore them.—*Beverly Sills*

2666    Sweet are the uses of adversity to the party it doesn't happen to.

2667    If you ever find happiness by hunting for it, you will find it, as the old woman did her lost spectacles, safe on her own nose all the time.—*Josh Billings*

2668    *Patience:* A minor form of despair disguised as virtue.—*Ambrose Bierce*

2669    Life would be infinitely happier if we could only be born at the age of eighty and gradually approach eighteen.—*Mark Twain*

2670    I'm tired of all this nonsense about beauty being only skin-deep. That's deep enough. What do you want—an adorable pancreas?—*Jean Kerr*

2671    If I could drop dead right now, I'd be the happiest man alive!—*Samuel Goldwyn*

2672    We cannot get grace from gadgets. In the Bakelite house of the future, the dishes may not break, but the heart can. Even a man with ten shower baths may find life flat, stale, and unprofitable.—*J. B. Priestley*

2673    Happiness is the interval between periods of unhappiness.—*Don Marquis*

2674    If happiness truly consisted in physical ease and freedom from care, then the happiest individual would not be either a man or a woman; it would be, I think, an American cow.—*William Lyon Phelps*

2675    He had had much experience of physicians, and said 'the only way to keep your health is to eat what you don't want, drink what you don't like, and do what you druther not.'—*Mark Twain*

2676    The secret of being miserable is to have leisure to bother about whether you are happy or not. The cure for it is occupation.—*George Bernard Shaw*

2677    When a woman tells you her age, it's all right to look surprised, but don't scowl.—*Wilson Mizner*

2678    There's another advantage of being poor—a doctor will cure you faster. —*Kin (Frank McKinney) Hubbard*

2679    A person must try to worry about things that aren't important so he won't worry too much about things that are.—*Jack Smith*

# Work, Leisure, Sports, and Weather

### 2680　*Good Job*

Friend: "How do you like your change from salesman to policeman?"

New policeman: "Fine. The pay is regular and the hours are satisfactory. But what I like best is that the customer is always wrong."

### 2681　*Who's Crazy*

Two inmates of an asylum had been given a hammer and one nail. One of the inmates placed the nail head first against the wall, and started hammering. Seeing that he was getting no appreciable results, he said to his companion: "The bird who made this nail was crazy. He put the point on the wrong end."

The other replied: "You're the one that's crazy—this nail goes in the opposite wall."

### 2682　*Not Working*

Employer: "John, I wish you wouldn't whistle at your work."

Boy: "I wasn't working, sir; only whistling."

### 2683　*A Mistake*

Mistress: "Oh, Jane, how did you break that vase?"

Maid: "I'm sorry; I was accidentally dusting."

### 2684　*Too Cold*

An American in Iceland wrote home, "It's so cold here that the inhabitants are compelled to live somewhere else."

### 2685    *Looking Ahead*

One raw cold morning in January, a snail started to climb the trunk of a cherry tree. As he inched painfully upward, a wiseguy beetle stuck his head out of a nearby crack and called, "Hey, buddy, you're wasting your time; there ain't any cherries up there."

The snail scarcely paused as he replied, "There will be by the time I get there."

### 2686    *Good Question*

A young boy was helping his grandfather dig potatoes. After a while the child began to tire.

"Grandpa," he asked wearily, "what ever made you bury these things anyway?"

### 2687    *Clever*

A young doctor and a young dentist shared the services of a receptionist, and both became fascinated with her charms. One day the dentist was called away on business, so he sent for the receptionist and said, "I am going away for ten days. You will find a little present in your room."

When the receptionist returned to her room, she found ten apples.

### 2688    *Golf*

"Daddy," said the bright child, accompanying her father on a round of golf, "why mustn't the ball go into the little hole?"

### 2689    *Just Small Ones*

Two fishermen were trying to convince their friends of their luck. "I went fishing the other day," said one, "and caught one of those big fish—let me see, what is it you call them?" he asked, turning to his fibbing partner.

"Oh yes, you mean—whale," assisted the second fisherman.

"No, not that," protested the first. "That couldn't have been it; I was using whale for bait!"

"And the fish I caught," said the second fisherman, "was too small to bother with, so I got a couple of men to help me throw it back into the water."

### 2690    *Essential Evidence*

An angler was haled into court, charged with catching eighteen more bass than the law permitted.

"Guilty or not guilty?" demanded the judge.

"Guilty, Your Honor," declared the young man.

"Ten dollars and costs," pronounced the judge.

The defendant paid the fine, then asked cheerfully, "And now, Your Honor, may I have several typewritten copies of the court record to take back home and show to my friends?"

## 2691 *Understandable*

Three bears went walking in winter. Papa Bear sat down on the ice and told a story. Then Mamma Bear told her story. Finally Baby Bear said, "My tale is told."

## 2692 *A Statement of Costs*

The painter was required to render an itemized bill for his repairs on various pictures in the church. The statement was as follows:

| | |
|---|---:|
| Corrected and renewed the Ten Commandments | $50 |
| Embellished Pontius Pilate and put a new ribbon on his bonnet | 60 |
| Put a new tail on the rooster of St. Peter and mended his bill | 45 |
| Put a new nose on St. John the Baptist and straightened his eye | 25 |
| Replumed and gilded the left wing of the Guardian Angel | 65 |
| Washed the servant of the High Priest and put carmine on his cheeks | 25 |
| Renewed Heaven, adjusted ten stars, gilded the sun, cleaned the moon | 85 |
| Reanimated the flames of Purgatory and restored some souls | 45 |
| Revived the flames of Hell, put a new tail on the Devil, mended his left hoof, and did several odd jobs for the damned | 65 |
| Put new spatter-dashes on the son of Tobias and dressing on his sack | 30 |
| Rebordered the robe of Herod and readjusted his wig | 45 |
| Cleaned the ears of Balaam's ass, and shod him | 35 |
| Put earrings in the ears of Sarah | 70 |
| Put a new stone in David's sling, enlarged Goliath's hand, and extended his legs | 30 |
| Decorated Noah's Ark | 20 |
| Mended the shirt of the Prodigal Son, and cleaned the pigs | 15 |
| | $710 |

## 2693 *Puzzled*

A magician working a cruise ship had a pet parrot who was ruining his act. The bird would say to the audience, "He has the card in his pocket," or "The card's up his sleeve," or "It went through a hole in his top hat."

One day there was an explosion and the ship sank.

The parrot and the magician found themselves together on a piece of wreckage. The parrot stared at the magician.

Finally, the parrot said, "Okay, I give up. What did you do with the ship?"

## 2694    *Close*

The harried coach pleaded with the professor who had flunked his prize tackle to give the boy another chance. Finally the professor agreed to give his boy a special make-up exam.

The next day the coach anxiously queried the professor: "How did Jones do?"

"I'm sorry," said the professor. "It's hopeless. Look at this . . . 'Five times seven equals thirty-three.' "

"But gosh, professor," said the coach, "give him a break. He only missed it by one."

## 2695    *No Miracle*

A man bought a greyhound and taught him to chase rabbits. To his astonishment, the dog one day chased a rabbit right across a sluggish stream. Instead of swimming the stream, the dog just ran across the surface of the water.

The astonished dog owner invited a friend to observe the miracle, and was disappointed when the greyhound's accomplishment failed to elicit any comment.

"Well, what do you think of my dog?" the owner prodded.

"He can't swim," the friend answered.

## 2696    *Travel*

Mark Twain once said that "Travel has no longer any charm for me. I have seen all the foreign countries I want to see except heaven and hell, and I have only a vague curiosity as concerns one of those."

## 2697    *Rushing Business*

The little boy was quite impressed by the ticket office at the planetarium which, as a publicity stunt, took reservations for a rocket trip to the moon.

"I'd like a ticket," the boy told the clerk.

"Sorry, young man," said the clerk with a twinkle, "but all the trips have been canceled for a few days."

"Why is that?" the boy asked.

"Well, right now the moon is full," the clerk answered.

## 2698    *December*

I heard a bird sing
In the dark of December,
A magical thing
And sweet to remember:
"We are nearer to Spring

Than we were in September,"
In the dark of December.
—*Oliver Herford*

### 2699    *Now He Knows*

Jimson was relating his experiences in India. "I was taking my usual morning dip when I spotted three gladiators making for me, so I had to swim for my very life!"

"You mean navigators—something like a crocodile?" interposed Johnson.

"Well, what are gladiators?"

"Gladiators? Why, they're a sort of flower grown from bulbs."

### 2700    *On Schedule*

Tourists travel according to schedule. The following conversation was overheard in Rome between a mother and daughter:

"Is this Rome?"

"What day of the week is it, Matilda?"

"Tuesday. What of it?"

"If it's Tuesday, it must be Rome."

### 2701    *One Way to Be Helpful*

The wife of the seasick passenger was about to leave the stateroom for dinner. She inquired of her husband solicitously, "George, shall I have the steward bring some dinner to you here?"

"No, my dear," he replied between groans. "Just ask him to take it on deck and throw it over the rail for me."

### 2702    *Good Game, But*

Bill: "Wasn't that a fine football game, Tom?"

Tom: "Yeah, but I don't see why they made such a big deal over twenty-five cents."

Bill: "What do you mean?"

Tom: "Every time the play started, they yelled, 'Get the quarter back, get the quarter back!'"

### 2703    *It Looks That Way*

The sports-car owner was giving a friend his first ride in one of the low-slung models. The friend appeared to be puzzled, so the driver asked what was wrong.

"I can't figure it out. What's that long wall we're passing."

"That's no wall," snapped the driver, "it's the curb."

2704    *Just Remain Quiet*

Fish do not sleep. They rest by remaining quiet in still pools. But where can you find a still pool?

2705    *Easy*

A woman lion tamer had the cats under such control they took a lump of sugar from her lips on command. When a skeptic yelled "Anyone can do that!" the ringmaster came over and asked him, "Would you like to try it?"

"Certainly," said the man. "But first get those crazy lions out of there."

2706    *Their Hobby*

The real-estate salesman spent all day Sunday showing a couple through model homes.

"And this," he said at the tenth home he had shown, "has a hobby room. Do you folks have any hobbies?"

"Yes," replied the woman, "looking through model homes on Sundays."

2707    *We Know Him*

All through the football game, on every single play, the loyal rooter had cheered his team to victory. Hoarser and hoarser he grew, until finally he whispered to the man beside him, "What d'ya know—I've lost my voice."

"Don't worry," was the tart reply, "you'll find it in my left ear."

2708    *New System*

One university football team is going to try out the three-squad system this year. One will play offense. The second will play defense. And the third will attend class.

2709    *Exercise*

The two women were talking about their husbands. "My husband," said one, "plays tennis, swims, and goes in for physical exercise. Does your husband get much exercise?"

"Well," countered the other, "last week he was out seven nights running."

2710    *Get Some Sleep*

The draftee was awakened roughly by his platoon sergeant after the rookie's first night in the army barracks.

"It's four thirty!" roared the sergeant.

"Four thirty!" gasped the recruit. "Man you'd better get to bed. We've got a big day tomorrow."

### 2711  *No*

A city boy spent his first night on a farm. Awakened much earlier than usual by the activity around him, he remarked sleepily, "It doesn't take long to stay here all night, does it?"

### 2712  *Something Wrong*

A vacationing lady mailed postcards to her friends back home each day. To her psychiatrist, she wrote: "Having a wonderful time. Wish you were here to tell me what's wrong."

### 2713  *Scots' Wisdom*

"Why are Scotsmen so good at golf?"

"Well, they realize that the fewer times they strike the ball, the longer it will last!"

### 2714  *Fishing*

We may say of angling as Dr. Boteler said of strawberries: Doubtless God could have made a better berry, but doubtless God never did, and so (if I may be judge) God never did make a more calm, quiet, innocent recreation than angling.—*Izaak Walton*

### 2715  *Wrong Time*

Bill was limping badly. "What's up?" asked the foreman. "Hurt yourself?"

"No—got a nail in my foot," Bill replied.

"Why don't you take it out, then?" exclaimed the foreman.

"What! On my lunch hour?"

### 2716  *And Do It*

Don't worry when your work's undone; no task is finished till it's begun. You can't do it by looking blue. Complaining won't help, it's up to you—to go to work!

### 2717  *No Danger*

Bill: "On the right of me was a lion, on the left a tiger, and in front of me and in back of me were wild elephants."

Bob: "What happened?"

Bill: "The merry-go-round stopped."

### 2718  *Baseball*

Connie Mack, the great man of baseball, in writing of his sixty-sixth year in the big leagues, said if he were to write his own epitaph, it would read: "He loved his God, his home, his country, his fellow man, and baseball."

2719   *Why Not?*

A little boy who went to the ballet for the first time with his father was amazed to see all the girls dancing on their toes. Finally, he turned to his father and asked, "Why don't they just get taller girls, Dad?"

2720   *His Contribution*

"Just what good have you done for humanity?" the judge asked the repeated offender before passing sentence.

"Well, Your Honor," he replied, "I've kept four detectives working steadily for the past ten years."

2721   *Seems Reasonable*

Bill: "A tomato, some lettuce, and a pail of water had a race. How do you suppose it came out?"

Herb: "The lettuce came out a head, the water kept on running, and the tomato tried to ketchup."

2722   *Done by Pros*

Dejected wife: "But our garden doesn't look like the one in the seed catalogue."

Husband: "Of course not. Those pictures were posed for by professional vegetables."

2723   *Athlete*

A professional coach was bragging about one of his rookies. "He doesn't know the meaning of the word 'fear.' Of course, there are a lot of other words he doesn't know either."

2724   *Spell of Bad Weather*

"How do you spell weather?"

"W-e-t-t-h-e-r."

"Well, that's the worst spell of weather we've had in a long time."

2725   *Confident*

Thelma: "You say your Mike is pretty cocky and sure of himself."

Velma: "I'll say he is. He does his crossword puzzles with a ballpoint pen."

2726   *Simple*

Green paint may be removed from the seat of a pair of white duck trousers with a bottle of ordinary turpentine, a stiff brush, and a pair of scissors.

### 2727    *Hold On*

This brings to mind the apprentice who after standing a long time at the foot of a ladder, told the painter, "Take a good hold of your brush, I'm taking the ladder away."

### 2728    *They Work Together*

When we think of how no two snowflakes are alike, we find it inspiring that they work so well together on such joint projects as closing schools and making roads impassable.

### 2729    *Baseball*

> The Little Leaguer homeward plods his weary way,
> Tired and bushed he hits the hay.
> His team won twenty-one to four,
> Even his Dad couldn't ask for more.
> —*Herbert V. Prochnow*

### 2730    *A Fish Story*

Canadian: "Can you recommend a good pond where I can go fishing?"
Jack: "Go over to Rocky Pond. The fish are so big you have to hide behind a rock to bait your hook. The trout are so good they're twelve inches."
Canadian: "That's not very big."
Jack: "It is when it's between the eyes. I caught one that was so big the picture of it weighed three pounds."

### 2731    *Why?*

It's hard to understand a person who travels thousands of miles to admire scenery, and then proceeds to litter it with garbage, bottles, and beer cans.

### 2732    *An Opportunist*

A truck driver, hauling clay for a fill, backed his truck too far over the dump grade. The weight of the load being dumped lifted the front end of the truck several feet off the ground.

"Now what are you going to do?" an associate asked.

The driver eased out of the cab and said, "I think I'll grease it—I'll never get a better chance."

### 2733    *Pretty Dry*

A visitor to New Mexico was talking to a sun-browned native, and commented on the lack of rain. "Doesn't it ever rain here?" he asked.

The native thought a moment and said, "Mister, do you remember the story of Noah and the Ark, and how it rained forty days and forty nights?"

"Sure I do," said the tourist.

"Well," drawled the native, "we got a half inch that time."

### 2734    *He Had Him There*

A New Englander was enjoying the wonders of California, as pointed out by a native.

"What beautiful grapefruit!" exclaimed the easterner as they passed a citrus orchard.

"Grapefruit!" replied the native in disdain. "Why—these are just small lemons."

Gazing at some huge sunflowers, the visitor asked, "And what are those enormous blossoms in that big field?"

"Just dandelions," the native replied.

A few minutes later they came to the Los Angeles river. "Ah," said the Yankee, "I see someone's radiator is leaking."

### 2735    *No Trouble Finding It*

There's the farmer who was asked what time he went to work in the morning.

"Son," he replied to the interrogator, "I don't go to work in the morning. I'm surrounded by it when I get up!"

### 2736    *Honest*

"What is the defendant's reputation for veracity?" asked the judge.

"Your Honor," said the witness, "I have known him to admit that he had been fishing all day and hadn't got a single bite!"

### 2737    *Can't Decide*

Johnny hurried to get the evening paper. Tomorrow was picnic day, and he wanted to read the weather forecast.

"Well, Johnny, what do they predict?" his mother asked.

"They haven't decided yet," said Johnny gloomily.

"Haven't decided?"

"No," said Johnny. "It says, 'Unsettled.' "

### 2738    *But Do They?*

"Is that God?" a small boy asked his mother on hearing the weather forecast on the radio.

"Why should you think that?" said his mother.

"Well," he replied, "who else would know what the weather's going to do?"

### 2739    *In Dew Time*

Hush, little snowflake, don't you cry; you'll be a dew drop next Fourth of July!

### 2740 New Position

"I hear your son is on the football team. What position does he play?"
"I think he's one of the drawbacks."

### 2741 No One Is Safe

Not so long ago three lunatics escaped from a large asylum. Posses went out and searched the surrounding countryside for twenty-four hours, and they finally brought in five.

### 2742 It Makes a Difference

"How many words can you type a minute?" asked the interviewer.
"Big ones or little ones, sir?" the would-be employee asked.

### 2743 Golf

If you watch a game, that's fun. If you play it, that's recreation. But if you work at it, that's golf.—Bob Hope

### 2744 Modern Math

"Touchdown" Sanders, football player, was having trouble with his grades. Since he was the star of the team his services were needed. He was called into the principal's office for reexamination. The school decided to give the boy a one-question examination, and since he was from Florida, the question was "What is the capital of Florida?"

"Touchdown" sweated over this for some time and finally wrote, "Monticello." He passed. In checking the answer, the officials reasoned that 100 was perfect, and Monticello is 25 miles from Tallahassee. Twenty-five from 100 leaves 75—and 75 is passing!

### 2745 The Gardener

He calls a spade a spade and a hoe a hoe—except when he drops them on his big toe.

### 2746 Not Observant

The sweet young thing was upset when her boyfriend did not help her into his car. "Where," she asked, "is your chivalry?"

And the young man said, "Didn't you notice? I traded it in for a Buick."

### 2747 Too Efficient

An efficiency expert went in to see the manager about his vacation. He came out with a hangdog expression on his face.

Asked what was wrong, he replied: "I'm only getting one week. The boss says I'm so efficient I can have as much fun in one week as other people have in two."

2748  *Didn't Hear It Today*

A visitor to an Indian trading post asked one of the clerks about the weather prospects for the following day. The clerk was unwilling to hazard a guess. But an old Indian standing around in the store volunteered, "Going to rain—much." And it did.

During the downpour the visitor reentered the store and sought out the native prophet. This time the Indian predicted "Clear and cool." Again he was correct.

When the question was repeated on the third day, the visitor received quite a shock. "Dunno," chuckled the Indian. "Didn't hear radio today."

2749  *Another Guesser?*

"What's his position?"

"He's third assistant guesser in the Weather Bureau."

2750  *We Agree*

A tourist had just arrived by automobile in California. A native asked him about the condition of the roads.

"Well," replied the tourist, "this guy Lincoln laid out a great highway. But that Frenchman, DeTour, was no road builder at all."

2751  *It Depends*

A motorist, traveling through New England, stopped for gasoline in a tiny village. "What's this place called?" he asked the station attendant.

The native shifted from one foot to the other. "All depends," he drawled. "Do you mean by them that has to live in this dad-blamed, moth-eaten, dust-covered, one-hoss dump, or by them that's merely enjoying its quaint and picturesque rustic charms for a short spell?"

2752  *Once Is Enough*

Despite warnings from his guide, an American skiing in Switzerland fell, uninjured, into a deep crevasse. Several hours later a rescue party found the yawning pit and, to reassure the stranded skier, shouted down to him, "We're from the Red Cross!"

"Sorry," the American shouted back, "I already gave at the office."

2753  *No Change*

In prehistoric times, cavemen had a custom of beating the ground with clubs and uttering spine-chilling cries. Anthropologists call this a form of primitive self-expression. When modern men go through the same ritual, they call it golf.

2754  *That Must Stop*

Football coach: "You're out of condition, Buck. Whatta ya been doin'—studying?"

### 2755    *His Position on the Team*

The youthful fan asked the retired player, "What was your playing position on your football team?"

The veteran replied, "Kind of stooped over—like this."

### 2756    *An Addition*

We've heard it proposed that this be a new addition to marriage vows:

"Through sickness and in health, for better or for worse, through football season, baseball season, basketball season, and hockey season . . ."

### 2757    *Mistake*

The park idler assumed a startled attitude. "I could have sworn I saw one of those statues move!"

A nearby policeman eased his mind. "Those are not statues," he said, "they're city workers."

### 2758    *They Are Helpful*

A man, whose wife was a rabid television fan, was housebound with a sprained ankle, and complained at the frequency and length of the commercials on the TV shows.

"I don't see how you can stand them all morning long, day after day," he told his wife.

"Stand them?" she replied. "Heavens, if it weren't for those commercials, I'd never have a chance to get any work done!"

2759    Variety may be the spice of life, but it is good old monotony that buys the groceries.

2760    Hard work never killed anyone, but it frightens some people half to death.

2761    The person who keeps pulling on the oars doesn't have much time to rock the boat.

2762    Man has never discovered perpetual motion, but he is close to perpetual commotion.

2763    You can get awfully tired climbing mountains that are not in sight.

2764    If it took any effort to go from today to tomorrow, some people would still be in yesterday—and some are.

2765    If man was not intended to work, Providence would have given him butter instead of a cow.

2766    It's all right for our presidents to play golf and tennis and to swim, but a little knowledge of poker might also help in international affairs.

2767    The other planets may not be able to support life, but this one isn't exactly finding it easy either.

2768    Loafing gets tiresome because you can't stop and rest.

2769    If you want to be just one of the hands, keep your eye on the clock.

2770    Few people carry a heavy burden farther than golf caddies.

2771    To leave footprints in the sands of time, you have to keep on the move.

2772    The fellow who fishes in a rain barrel at least saves canoe and guide hire.

2773    Some people get very tired overcoming obstacles before they come to them.

2774    If you don't feel like getting up in the morning, just jump out of bed and the feeling will go away.

2775    If you can't get away for a vacation, just stay home and tip every other person you meet.

2776    Work is the refuge of people who have nothing better to do.—*Oscar Wilde*

2777    If you think hoe, hoe, hoe is a laughing matter, you're no gardener.

2778    It's not the hours you put in your work, but the work you put in your hours.

2779    Some people jump to conclusions, but others dig for facts.

2780    Too often the person who takes his time takes yours too.

2781    Unfortunately, most of us need someone to help us do what we could do without help.

2782    Some people do nothing and give it their personal attention.

2783    Most of us can do more than we think we can, but we actually do less than we think we do.

2784    Most of the people who do great things in life are alone, especially on a golf course.

2785      What most of us need is more horsepower and less exhaust.

2786      Some people only go to work after they have tried everything else.

2787      Like every man of sense and good feeling, I abominate work.—*Aldous Huxley*

2788      A person is not overworked simply because it takes him four hours to do a three-hour job.

2789      Hard work will not hurt you if you are wealthy enough to hire someone else to do it.

2790      *Big game hunter:* A man who can spot a leopard.

2791      When you are playing golf, nothing counts like your opponent.

2792      Two Greeks were watching their first football game. Said one to the other: "This is all American to me."

2793      The surest way of establishing your credit is to work so hard that you won't need it.

2794      Perhaps the man with no experience is justified in asking for a higher wage; the work is much harder when you don't know what you're doing.

2795      Don't just put in the day—put something into the day.

2796      With all the vacation travel on the road, it's a good idea to drive with Fender Loving Care.

2797      *Buffet dinner:* A party where the guests outnumber the chairs.

2798      Two halves make a hole, and the fullback goes through.

2799      It's all right for a girl to look for a model husband, but she should try for a working model.

2800      Relatives are people who come to visit you on their vacation when the weather is too uncomfortable to stay at home and do their own cooking.

2801      *Commuter:* A man who shaves and takes a train, and then rides back to shave again.—*E. B. White*

2802      *Commendation:* The tribute that we pay to achievements that resemble, but do not equal, our own.—*Ambrose Bierce*

2803    Any golfer can be devout on a rainy Sunday.

2804    If it keeps up, man will atrophy all his limbs but the push-button finger.
—*Frank Lloyd Wright*

2805    Basic research is what I am doing when I don't know what I am doing.
—*Wernher von Braun*

2806    It's an ill wind that blows when you leave the hairdresser.—*Phyllis Diller*

2807    Sooner or later I'm going to die, but I'm not going to retire.—*Margaret Mead*

2808    *Kangaroo:* Nature's initial effort to produce a cheerleader.

2809    The fishing was so bad on our vacation that even the liars didn't catch any.

2810    With the deliberate methods of great chess players, we hear one of them left his next move to his grandson.

2811    The dissatisfied sportsman returned his Christmas gift of golf clubs because they weren't up to par.

2812    *Sunglasses:* Optical seclusion.

2813    *Housework:* Something you do that nobody notices unless you don't do it.

2814    If you daydream on office time, you might miss the coffee break.

2815    You can get quite a lot out of vegetable gardens if you cultivate the owners.

2816    It was one of those well-kept resort places that was run strictly by the book—your checkbook.

2817    And there was the cowboy who bought only one spur. He figured if one side of the horse went, the other would too.

2818    *Lightning:* The awful autograph of God.

2819    Winter is the season when we try to keep the house as hot as it was in the summer, when we complained about the heat.

2820    Pity the poor woman who marries a baseball umpire and has to have a man around the house who is always right.

2821    I'm leaving because the weather is too good. I hate London when it's not raining.—*Groucho Marx*

2822    The tanned appearance of many Londoners is not sunburn—it's rust.

2823    The difference between learning to play golf and learning to drive a car is that in golf you never hit anything.

2824    It was so hot one summer in Texas that when a dog chased a rabbit they both walked.

2825    Notice to hunters: "If you see something that wears a hat, smokes a pipe, and stands on hind legs, don't shoot—it isn't a deer."

2826    Then there was the moron who wouldn't play croquet because he heard it was a wicket game.

2827    A vacation would be ideal if the old pocketbook could enjoy the rest, too.

2828    I worry, I putter, I push, and I shove, hunting little molehills to make mountains of.

2829    *Holiday:* A day when Father works twice as hard as he does at the office.

2830    *Golf:* A game in which a ball one and a half inches in diameter is placed on a ball 8,000 miles in diameter. The object is to hit the small ball but not the larger.—*John Cunningham*

2831    *Alumni:* A group of college graduates who attend football games on Saturday to find reasons to fire the coach on Monday.—*Jimmy Cannon*

2832    *Afternoon snack:* The pause that refleshes.—*Mary B. Michael*

2833    *Ant:* An insect that attends picnics for a living.

2834    A man's first duty is to mind his own business.

2835    "This is just the place for me," said the humorist at the shore, "for here whenever I crack a joke, the breakers simply roar!"

2836    *Moonlighter:* A person who holds day and night jobs in order to go from one to the other in a better car.

2837    One football squad lists players Napiorski, Barbatski, Lesinski, Wojciecyowics, Gangemi, Gurske, and Lanechia. It could be another invincible Irish team in the making.

2838    The Soviet government pays salaries to college students. We do not understand it, as there isn't an experienced halfback in the country.

2839    *Golf ball:* A small object that remains on the tee while a perspiring citizen fans it vigorously with a large club.

2840    We can't see why some rock musicians are paid $200 a day. Riveters, who get less, make almost as much noise and do something useful besides.

2841    Boys will be boys—but girls are giving them a hot contest for the privilege.

2842    You can't tell—maybe the fish goes home and brags about the size of the bait he stole.

2843    Man blames fate for other accidents, but feels personally responsible when he makes a hole in one.

2844    We wonder if it would be possible to get as excited over things as a radio announcer thinks he makes us.

2845    Sometimes the hero in the movie is the one who sits through it.

2846    Our ideal summer resort is one where fish bite and mosquitoes don't.

2847    What's cooler on a hot July evening than the sound of a passing ice-cream peddler with sleigh bells?

2848    A new musical instrument is said to combine a saxophone and bagpipes. That's not a musical instrument—it's a weapon.

2849    Of course insects have brains. How else could they figure out where you are going to have your picnic?

2850    Song of the spring camper: "We're tenting tonight on the old damp ground."

2851    One interesting event of the millennium will be the spectacle of the mosquito and the camper lying down together.

2852    Science tells us there are twelve varieties of snow, not including "probably."

2853    A fourteen-year-old schoolboy has been expelled because his teachers claim he is incapable of telling the truth. If this young man doesn't mend his ways, he is likely to end up in the weather bureau.

2854    What a joy it is to shovel the beautiful snow off the walk—the first time, we mean.

2855    The first real touch of winter is the coal dealer's.

2856    How long a fish grows depends on how long you listen to the fisherman.

2857    The philosopher who said that work well done never needs doing over never weeded a garden.

2858    Many fishermen catch their fish by the tale.

2859    April showers bring May doubleheaders.

2860    We find it difficult to waste much time on the man with the hoe, as he is probably digging worms for bait.

2861    For some people it is simply life, liberty, and the pursuit of a golf ball.

2862    No one writes fiction like the weather man.

2863    The average suburbanite either putters around his house or the golf course.

2864    *Tourist:* A person who changes the car oil every four days and his shirt once a week.

2865    All things are difficult before they are easy.—*Thomas Fuller*

2866    A person is lucky if he is too busy to brood in the daytime and too tired to stay awake worrying at night.

2867    No one is unemployed who minds his own business.

2868    When a person can refuse to do the things he doesn't like to do so he can work himself to death doing what he likes, he is independent.

2869    You go on a vacation to forget everything, then find when you open your bag that you have.

2870    No honest man is a successful fisherman.

2871    One for the money; two for the show; three to get ready; four to go. But when you get home, it's ten for the babysitter.

2872    When a person thinks he is too big for his job, the chances are his job is too big for him.

2873    Why is it that a day off is often followed by an off day?

2874    Modern arithmetic—if one person can do a job in one hour, why does it take two men two hours?

2875    Ambition means working yourself to death in order to live better.

2876    The bigger the summer vacation bill, the harder the fall.

2877    It's all in the day's work, as the huntsman said when the lion ate him.
—*Charles Kingsley*

2878    Many people believe that work isn't a bad thing if it doesn't interfere too much with your leisure.

2879    In baseball the best team always loses because the other team got all the breaks.

2880    Nothing saves time like putting off until tomorrow what you should do today.

2881    One way to reduce is to fill a shovel with wet snow and throw it over the shoulder 781 times in rapid succession.

2882    A loafer is a person who busies himself each day keeping other people idle.

2883    An American is a man who has two legs, four wheels, and a spare tire.

2884    There is a great difference between wanting a job and wanting work.

2885    A vacation is good for you, but it's a nice thing to find a desk to put your feet under when you get back.

2886    No one is too busy to talk about how busy he is.

2887    Nothing grows faster than a fish from the time he bites until he gets away.

2888    What we want is standard time for getting up and daylight saving time for quitting work.

2889    All play and no work makes it hard to know what to do with your leisure.

2890    A decathlon is any combination of ten athletic events such as painting the garage and falling off the ladder.

2891    Even the easiest thing is difficult when you do it with reluctance.

2892    Everything comes to him who waits—if he works while he's waiting.

2893    It's surprising how many people there are who think that the way to have a good time is to make a fool of yourself.

2894    If you can't take a vacation—open the window, take off the screens, and buy a two-weeks' supply of hamburger buns and potato chips, and you can get some of the same effects.

2895    From the number of ants that show up at picnics, some believe there must have been more than two on the Ark.

2896    There is no use in walking five miles to fish when you can depend on being just as unsuccessful near home.—*Mark Twain*

2897    A well-adjusted man is one who can play golf as if it were a game.

2898    Another thing this world needs is a grapefruit that can yell, "Fore!"

2899    *Amateur athlete:* An athlete who is paid only in cash—not by check.

2900    The trouble with vacations is that sometimes you find, when you attempt to get away from it all, the people who arrived there ahead of you brought it all with them.

2901    A naturalist says that ants move faster in summer than they do in winter. Of course. They don't have to hurry to picnics in winter.

2902    Calling it a World Series must impress the world as an example of American modesty.

2903    In golf the ball usually lies poorly, but the player well.

2904    Nature-lovers on a picnic prove that Oscar Wilde was right when he said we always kill the thing we love.

2905    What can one expect from a day that begins with getting up in the morning?

2906    Rain—something that, when you take an umbrella, it doesn't.

2907    What becomes of a baseball player when his eyes go bad? Well, you know umpires were once ball players.

2908    Some people are no good at counting calories and they have the figures to prove it.

2909    For the parent of a Little Leaguer, a baseball game is simply a nervous breakdown divided into innings.—*Earl Wilson*

2910    It's a lonesome walk to the sidelines, especially when thousands of people are cheering your replacement.—*Fran Tarkenton*

2911    We read that a form of baseball was a favorite sport among the Greeks. We do remember something about a Homer.

2912    *Garden:* A thing of beauty and a job forever.

2913    Why do they arrange the motels so you go by the best ones between 7 A.M. and noon?

2914    Sometimes a person gets so busy hunting for advantages that he forgets there is work to do.

2915    It isn't the whistle that pulls the train.

2916    In some areas the people don't lock the barn door after the horse is stolen. They open a summer theater.

2917    In a modern college 2,000 can sit in the classrooms, and 50,000 in the stadium.

2918    If you give crabgrass an inch, it will take a yard.

2919    Some say that about all that's left over after deductions is the job.

2920    How far a fisherman will stretch the truth depends on the length of his arms.

2921    Some people pick one hobby to go crazy about instead of letting the world generally drive them nuts.

2922    *Dentist:* A man who runs a filling station.

2923    It has been reported that rock music is dying. There is no other way to account for the weird noise it makes.

2924    We are informed that one rock musician who used to be a boiler-riveter has gone back to his old occupation because he couldn't stand the noise.

2925    *Leisure:* The opiate of the masses.—*Malcolm Muggeridge*

2926    You have heard that swimming develops poise and grace, but did you ever take a good look at a duck walking?

2927    There are two periods when fishing is good—before you get there and after you leave.

2928    A vacation spot is where they charge you enough to make up for the eleven months you're not there.

2929    Golf is a lot of walking, broken up by disappointment and bad arithmetic.

2930    The way to get a job done is to give it to a busy man so he can give it to his secretary to do.

2931    No man has ever caught a fish as big as the one that got away.

2932    If a person isn't being paid what he's worth, he may be lucky.

2933    Civilization has advanced to the point that if you want to relax you have to work at it.

2934    The person who thinks the world owes him a living is often too lazy to collect it.

2935    Never dodge responsibility. When a bee comes in the car window, don't wait for a telephone pole to stop the car.

2936    There are some people who try to make both weekends meet in the summer.

2937    Remember that by fifty you will have spent over sixteen years in bed and three years eating.

2938    It's queer how ants acquired such a reputation for being industrious. They are always at picnics.

2939    Hard work is respectable, but it's not easy to make it popular.

2940    The smart people are those who see a thing through or see through it.

2941    *Puck:* A hard rubber disk that hockey players strike when they can't hit one another.—*Jimmy Cannon*

2942    *Plumber:* An adventurer who traces leaky pipes to their source.— *Arthur "Bugs" Baer*

2943    *Rabid fan:* A guy who boos a television set.—*Jimmy Cannon*

2944    You will never hit your thumb with a hammer if you remember to hold the hammer in both hands.

2945    *Resort:* A place where no one knows you are important.

2946    If you are planning an automobile tour, get a large road map. It will tell you all you want to know, except how to fold it up again.

2947    It is difficult to keep quiet if you have nothing to do.—*Arthur Schopenhauer*

2948    There's nothing new about the four-day week. We know some guys who have been doing four days' work in five or six days each week, for years.

2949    *Golf:* A game in which one endeavors to control a ball with implements ill adapted for the purpose.—*Woodrow Wilson*

2950    Civilization declines as we go from heavy work and light meals to heavy meals and light work.

2951    When you stop pedaling your bicycle, you fall off.

2952    In the old days we had sensible popular songs like "Daddy Wouldn't Buy Me a Bow-wow" and "Ta Ra Ra Boom De Ay."

2953    Sometimes it's hard to tell whether you are as busy as you think, or just confused.

2954    I go on working for the same reason that a hen goes on laying eggs. —*H. L. Mencken*

2955    What we want is a book called *How to Get Out of Doing It Yourself.*

2956    Laziness may be just an overwhelming ambition to live a quiet life.

2957    Actions speak louder than words—but not so often.

2958    Walking may be good exercise, but did you ever see a mailman as husky as a truck driver?

2959    The perils of duck hunting are great, especially for the duck.—*Walter Cronkite*

2960    I don't want any yes men around me. I want everyone to tell me the truth—even though it costs him his job.—*Samuel Goldwyn*

2961    *Weather forecast:* "Snow—followed by little boys on sleds."—*Henry Morgan*

2962    A wise man will never plant more garden than his wife can take care of.

2963    He was busier than a flea working his way through a dog show.

2964    It's impossible to get any sleep around some offices after eight o'clock in the morning!

2965    Pro football is like nuclear warfare. There are no winners, only survivors.—*Frank Gifford*

2966    You don't save a pitcher for tomorrow. Tomorrow it may rain.—*Leo Durocher*

2967    There are so many labor-saving devices on the market today that a man has to work all his life to pay for them.

2968    If I were running the world I would have it rain only between 2 and 5 A.M. Anyone who was out then ought to get wet.—*William Lyon Phelps*

2969    *Golf:* A day spent in a round of strenuous idleness.—*William Wordsworth*

2970    The reason some fish get so big is because they're the ones that always get away.

2971    *Truth:* When one fisherman calls another fisherman a liar.

2972    *Bottoms up:* The toast you never make to the crew in a boat race.

2973    A person has to work hard to make an easy living.

2974    Every resort hotel has a few views of the hotel they want you to take home along with your own views of the place.

2975    When ground rules permit a golfer to improve his lie, he can either move his ball or change the story about his score.

2976    I shall continue to praise the English climate till I die, even if I die of the English climate.—*G. K. Chesterton*

2977    *Springtime:* When fishermen begin to get that faraway lake in their eyes.

2978    When someone says it pays to hustle, we remember the camel always has a hump on and is only taken for a ride.

2979    If you speed on country roads in the quiet of the night, you feel as if you had escaped into another world. And you actually may at the first curve in the road.

2980    I like long walks, especially when they are taken by people who annoy me.—*Fred Allen*

2981     My father taught me to work, but not to love it. I never did like to work, and I don't deny it. I'd rather read, tell stories, crack jokes, talk, laugh—anything but work.—*Abraham Lincoln*

2982     Working like a dog brings success and a nervous breakdown.

2983     We always bait with minnows so that anything we catch will be a size larger.

2984     Fortunately the colleges aren't so finicky yet that an amateur can't make a decent living in sport.

2985     Some persons have trouble telling the difference between being tired and being lazy.

# Friends, Critics, and Enemies

### 2986 *Good Manners*

Johnny had been to a friend's birthday party and was telling his mother all about it. "I hope," said his mother, "that you didn't ask for a second piece of cake, did you?"

"Oh, no!" he replied. "I asked Mrs. Brown for the recipe so that you could make one for me and she gave me two extra pieces without my asking at all!"

### 2987 *Good Deed*

The teacher had asked her small pupils to tell about their acts of kindness to dumb animals. After several heart-stirring stories, the teacher asked Tommy if he had anything to add. "Well," he replied rather proudly, "I kicked a boy once for kicking his dog."

### 2988 *Sweet Treat*

Sue: "Have a policeman cookie."
Mary: "A policeman cookie?"
Sue: "Yes, a copcake."

### 2989 *Curfew*

"I understand they have a curfew in this village," said the visitor to the proprietor of the general store.

"No," he answered, "they did have one, but they abandoned it."

"What was the matter?"

"Well, the bell rang at nine o'clock and almost everybody complained it woke them up."

## 2990   *Smart Professor*

A retired professor was raking his lawn. A group of neighborhood small fry stood watching. Before long, the kids had taken over the job, and the professor was merely standing by, offering an occasional suggestion. Next morning the professor's doorbell rang, and his wife answered it. There stood a five-year-old girl, one of the helpers of the previous day. She smiled shyly and asked, "Can he come out to play?"

## 2991   *Smooth*

At a dinner party a financier sat next to a lady whose name he didn't catch. During the first course he noticed at the left of the host a man who had bested him in a business transaction. "Do you see that man?" he muttered to his dinner partner. "If there's one man on earth I hate, he's it."

"Why," exclaimed the lady, "that's my husband."

"Yes, I know," said the financier glibly. "That's why I hate him."

## 2992   *Some Hero*

Reporter: "What made you risk your life to save your friend?"

Boy hero: "I had to do it. He was wearing my jacket."

## 2993   *Neighbors*

"Good morning, madam, I'm the piano tuner."

"But I didn't send for a piano tuner."

"I know. It was a committee of your neighbors who called."

## 2994   *Identify Yourself*

The young army recruit was the victim of so many practical jokes that he doubted all men and their motives. One night while he was on guard duty, the figure of one of the officers loomed up in the darkness.

"Who goes there?" the recruit challenged.

"Major Moses," was the reply.

The young recruit scented a joke. "Glad to meet you, Moses," he said cheerfully. "Advance and give the Ten Commandments."

## 2995   *Lucky*

Corporal (at a party): "Do you see that old buzzard over there? He's the meanest officer in the force!"

Girl: "Do you know who I am? I'm that officer's daughter."

Corporal: "Do you know who I am?"

Girl: "No."
Corporal: "Thank heavens!"

## 2996 *Smart Sentry*

Sentry: "Who goes there?"
Voice in the dark: "Cook, with doughnuts for breakfast."
Sentry: "Pass, cook; doughnuts, halt!"

## 2997 *Close Your Eyes*

Nervous passenger: "Don't drive so fast around the corners—it frightens me."
Driver: "Do as I do—shut your eyes when we come to one."

## 2998 *Following Instructions*

A housewife in Kansas City called up a pet store and said: "Send me one thousand cockroaches at once."

"What in the world do you want with one thousand cockroaches?" asked the astonished clerk.

"Well," replied the woman, "I am moving today and my lease says I must leave the premises here in exactly the same condition I found them."

## 2999 *As He Saw It*

Closer to the truth than he meant to be was the schoolboy who wrote on an examination paper: "The Armistice was signed on the eleventh of November in 1918, and since then once in every year there has been two minutes of peace."

## 3000 *Pardon Me*

A timid little soul tapped on the arm of the formidable gentleman who had been sitting next to him at the theater. "I don't suppose you chance to be Hector Milquetoast of Hartford, Connecticut, do you?" he asked.

"No, I don't. What's it to you?"

"Just this, sir," squeaked the little guy. "I am—and that's his umbrella you're taking."

## 3001 *A Real Saver*

One friend to another: "Say, Joe, I just deposited a little more than I can afford. How about lending me twenty dollars until Saturday."

## 3002 *A Blank Page*

A clever young lady was asked to attend a public function. She was assigned a place between a noted bishop and an equally famous rabbi. It was her chance to break into high company, and she meant to use it.

"I feel as if I were a leaf between the Old and New Testaments," she said brilliantly during a lull in the conversation.

"That page, madam," replied the rabbi, "is usually a blank."

### 3003    *Sorry*

Answering the doorbell, a man found an old friend and a large dog standing on the porch.

"Come in! Come in!" he said.

The friend and the dog came in, and the man sat down to chat. Meanwhile the dog put the man's cat to flight, knocked over a bridge lamp and several knickknacks, and finally made himself comfortable on one of the best chairs in the room.

When the guest arose to leave, the host said with a touch of sarcasm in his voice, "Aren't you forgetting your dog?"

"Dog?" exclaimed the man. "I have no dog. I thought he was yours."

### 3004    *Help!*

"Hello. Humane Society?"

"Yes."

"I called to report an insurance agent sitting in a tree in front of our house teasing my dog."

### 3005    *The Typical American*

From the dark came the voice of the sentry: "Halt! Who's there?"

"An American," was the reply.

"Is that so? Well, advance and recite the second verse of 'The Star-Spangled Banner.' "

"I don't know it."

"Proceed, American."—*American Legion Magazine*

### 3006    *His Limit*

Officer: "How do you get along without a speedometer?"

Motorist: "Well, when I git to driving fifteen miles an hour, my fenders start to rattle; at twenty-five the windows rattle; at thirty the motor starts knockin' —and that's as fast as she'll go."

### 3007    *Warning*

A gentle Quaker, hearing a strange noise in his house one night, got up and discovered a burglar, so he got his gun, came back, and stood quietly in the doorway.

"Friend," he said, "I would do thee no harm for the world, but thou standest where I am about to shoot."

### 3008 *Disturbance Continued*

During a performance of rock music a member of the audience jumped on the stage and started a disturbance. He was ejected, and the original disturbance was resumed.

### 3009 *How to Make Friends*

Two women met on the street after a long absence. Said the first, "Gracious, Dorothy, I haven't seen you for seven years. You certainly look a lot older."

"You, too, Eleanor, dear. I wouldn't have recognized you except for the dress and hat."

### 3010 *No Change*

Jones: "I made an awful fool of myself at the party last night."
Smith: "Henry, I assure you that I noticed nothing unusual."

### 3011 *Toast to a Waiter*

"Gentlemen," said Jones, raising an empty glass, "I rise to toast absent friends, among whom I include the waiter for this table."

### 3012 *Never Too Late*

Guest: "I'm sorry to be late for dinner."
Hostess: "Mr. Jones, you can never come too late."

### 3013 *Somebody Else*

"As I was going over the bridge the other day," said O'Grady, "I met O'Brien. 'O'Brien,' I says, 'how are you?'

" 'Pretty well, thank you, O'Grady,' says he.

" 'O'Grady?' says I. 'That's not my name.'

" 'Faith,' says he, 'and mine's not O'Brien!'

"With that we looked at each other, and it was neither of us!"

### 3014 *Fair Offer*

A young lady stalled her car at a traffic light one winter day. She turned on the starter, tried again, choked her engine, and fumbled hopelessly around among gadgets. Behind her an impatient citizen honked his horn steadily.

Finally the young lady got out and walked back to the other car. "I'm awfully sorry, sir," she said pleasantly, "but I don't seem to be able to start my car. If you will come and start it for me, I'll stay here and lean on your horn."

### 3015 *Why?*

Joe: "I want to change my name, Your Honor."
Judge: "What is your name?"

Joe: "Joe Smells."

Judge: "I don't blame you. What would you like to change it to?"

Joe: "Charlie."

### 3016 *Serious*

"My aunt has parrot's disease."

"Sorry to hear it. Is it very serious?"

"Sure is! She repeats everything she hears."

### 3017 *A Duet*

In reporting the proceedings of the Sunday church services, the local paper printed: "Two ladies sang a duet, 'The Lord Knows Why!' "

### 3018 *Is That Nice?*

"I'll be going now; don't trouble to see me to the door."

"It's no trouble; it's a pleasure."

### 3019 *A Different Viewpoint*

MacPherson was strolling down the street when he noticed what he thought was the familiar figure of a friend. Quickening his steps, he came up to the man and slapped him on the back. To his amazement, he then saw he had greeted an utter stranger.

"Oh, I beg your pardon," he said apologetically. "I thought you were an old friend of mine, Mackintosh by name."

The stranger recovered his wind and replied with considerable heat, "And supposing I were Mackintosh—do you have to hit me so hard?"

"What do you care," retorted MacPherson, "how hard I hit Mackintosh?"

### 3020 *Bragging*

A Floridian, visiting a Californian, picked up a large melon and said, "Is this as large as your apples grow?"

The Californian replied, "Stop fingering that grape."

### 3021 *She Meant Well*

At an evening party the hostess coaxed a protesting guest to sing. After the song, she went up to him and said with a smile: "Oh, Mr. Jenkins, you must never again tell me that you can't sing; I know now!"

And she wondered why the guest left so hurriedly.

### 3022 *Fair Exchange*

A woman who was living in a hotel in San Francisco employed a Chinese boy. "What's your name?" she asked.

"Fu Yu Tsin Mei," he replied.

"Your name is too long; I'll call you John."

The Chinese boy looked surprised. "What's your name?" he asked.

"Mrs. Elmer Edward MacDonald."

"Your name too long; I call you Charlie."

### 3023    Fair Request

The driver of a fairly new car stopped for a red light and her rear bumper was hit by the car behind her. She got out, looked for damage, glared at the man driving the other car, returned to her car, and drove off.

At the next light, the same thing happened. Finally, after the third bump, the man got out of his car and came over holding out his driver's license and other credentials.

"Never mind that," said the woman. "Just give me a five-minute head start."

### 3024    Let's Have Order

The new play was a failure. After the first act, many in the audience left the theater; at the end of the second act, most of the others started out.

As he rose from his aisle seat, a critic raised a restraining hand. "Wait!" he commanded loudly. "Women and children first!"

### 3025    Reasonable Explanation

A Hoboken resident owned a goat. His next-door neighbor was the tax assessor and did not particularly like the goat, so he taxed the animal $4.

The owner of the goat demanded to know why this family pet was assessed at that sum.

"That is strictly in accordance with the statutes of the state," replied the tax assessor.

"I demand the proof," reported the irate owner.

The assessor thereupon read to the bewildered neighbor the following statute on taxes: "All property abutting and abounding on the public street shall be taxed at the rate of two dollars per front foot."

### 3026    Frank

The curiosity of the passenger was excited by the fact that his seatmate had his right arm in a sling.

"Broke your arm?"

"Well, yes, I did."

"Had an accident, I suppose?"

"Not exactly. I did it while trying to pat myself on the back."

"My land! On the back! Whatever did you want to pat yourself on the back for?"

"Just for minding my own business."

3027 *Trying to Be Fair*

One woman to another: "I've heard so much about you! Now I'd like to hear your side of the story."

3028 *The Druggist's Turn*

The druggist danced and laughed till the bottles danced on the shelves.
"What's up?" asked the clerk. "Have you been taking something?"
"No. But do you remember when our water pipes were frozen last winter?"
"Yes, but what—"
Well, the plumber who fixed them just came in to have a prescription filled."

3029 *Be Quiet*

Boss: "What do you mean by such language? Are you the manager here or am I?"
Jones: "I know I'm not the manager."
Boss: "Very well, then, if you're not the manager, why do you talk like a blamed idiot?"

3030 *Not Safe*

An actor told his friend that he had just signed a contract to tour in Africa. Instead of congratulating him, the friend shook his head dismally.
"The ostrich," he explained, "lays an egg weighing anywhere from two to four pounds."

3031 *The Reason*

Helen: "When was your son born?"
Mary: "In March—he came the first of the month."
Helen: "Is that why you call him Bill?"

3032 *Courteous*

It was one of those exasperating sidewalk situations when a man and a woman, coming from opposite directions, jockeyed to the left and to the right several times in an awkward effort to pass each other.
When the snarl was finally unraveled, the man politely tipped his hat and said, "Well, goodbye. It's been fun knowing you."

3033 *He Helped?*

Panting and perspiring, two Irishmen on a tandem bicycle at last reached the top of a steep hill.
"That was a stiff climb, Mike," said the first, breathing heavily.
"Sure, and it was," said the other. "If I hadn't kept the brake on we should have gone backward."

### 3034   Poor Question

A wiseguy stopped a street bus the other morning and said to the driver, "Well, Noah, you got here at last. Is the Ark full?"

Replied the driver, "Not quite. We need one more monkey. Come on in."

### 3035   Just a Little Difference

Maybe the old-time Indians were not so bad after all, as one old chief put it: "Indian scalp enemies; white man skin friends."

### 3036   It Took Time

The flower show had been a great success, and a few evenings later Mr. Blank, who had performed the opening ceremony, was reading the local paper's account of it to his wife. Presently he stopped reading, his justifiable pride turning to anger.

Amazed, his wife picked up the newspaper to ascertain the reason for her spouse's fury. She read: "As Mr. Blank mounted the platform, all eyes were fixed on the large red nose he displayed. Only years of patient cultivation could have produced an object of such brilliance."

### 3037   New

Sentry: "Halt! Who goes there?"

Soldier: "Aw, you wouldn't know me. I just got here today."

### 3038   That's Different

Hobo: "Can you give a piece of cake, lady, to a poor man who hasn't had a bite to eat for two days?"

Lady: "Cake? What's the matter with bread? Isn't that good enough for you?"

Hobo: "It usually is, ma'am, but this is my birthday."

### 3039   Never Heard It

"I heard a new story the other day; I wonder if I've told it to you."

"Is it funny?"

"Yes."

"Then you haven't."

### 3040   He Knew

A general and a colonel were walking down the street. They met many privates, and each time the colonel saluted he would mutter, "The same to you."

The general's curiosity was soon aroused, and he asked, "Why do you always say that when you salute a private?"

The colonel answered, "I was once a private, and I know what they are thinking."

### 3041    *A Fast Answer*

A newspaper item read, "A man in Florida has been yawning for seven days." On which a Californian commented, "A visiting Californian, no doubt." To which a Floridian retorted, "That mouth was open from amazement, brother!"

### 3042    *Quit Bragging*

The Englishman was visiting Mt. Vernon. He looked at the hedge and remarked, "Ah, I see George got this hedge from dear old England."

"You bet your life he did," said the American. "He got this whole bloomin' country from dear old England."

### 3043    *Helpful*

Girl: "Sometimes my father takes things apart to see why they don't go."
Her date: "So what?"
Girl: "So you'd better go."

### 3044    *Please Be Seated*

Diner: "Do you serve crabs here?"
Waiter: "We serve anyone—sit down!"

### 3045    *Be Careful*

The telephone rang in the fire station office. The duty fireman picked up the receiver.

"Is this the fire station?" asked a timid voice.

"Yes, that's right," replied the fireman eagerly.

"Well," continued the voice, "I have just had a new rock garden built, and I've put in some new plants—"

"Where's the fire?" yelled the fireman.

"Some of these new plants are very expensive, and—"

"Look here," said the fireman, "you want the flower shop."

"No, I don't," said the voice. "You see, my neighbor's house is on fire, and I don't want you firemen to trample all over my rock garden when you come here."

### 3046    *What He Learned*

"Ingratitude," was the reply of an old Indian chief when asked what lesson he had learned from civilization.

### 3047    *All Even*

"I don't like to bring this up," said the doctor hesitantly, "but that check of yours came back."

"I don't like to mention this, either, doc," said the patient, "but so did my gout."

3048    *How Long Ago?*

Midge: "I hate to think of my thirtieth birthday."
Marge: "Why, Midge, what happened then?"

3049    *Another Try*

A hobo knocked on the door of an inn called George and the Dragon. The landlady opened the door, and the hobo asked for something to eat.

"No!" she growled, slamming the door in the man's face.

The hobo knocked again, and the landlady opened the door.

"May I talk to George, please?" he said.

3050    *Reservations*

Smith: "Why do the Indians on some reservations seem uneasy now?"
Jones: "They probably think the whites want to give the country back to them."

3051    Do not use a hatchet to remove a fly from your friend's forehead.—*Chinese proverb*

3052    If you can't think of a nice thing to say about any of your friends, then you have the wrong friends.

3053    A friend is a person who tells you all the nice things you always knew about yourself.

3054    A person who agrees with everything you say probably isn't worth talking to.

3055    A secret is something you tell only in the greatest confidence to all your friends.

3056    If you want to know how many friends you have, just rent a cottage on a lake.

3057    When you think of all the lonely people without relatives or neighbors, you certainly envy them.

3058    When you try to reduce, the problem isn't keeping up with the Joneses, but keeping down with them.

3059    Hospitality is that generous spirit which leads us to have someone to dinner who doesn't need it and who will be expected to invite us later.

3060    There is the sad case of the man who decided to learn three new words a day and found after a week that his friends couldn't understand him.

3061    A friend in need is a frequent occurrence.

3062    When a person really knows himself, he loses interest in reforming his neighbors.

3063    The clinging-vine type of woman is a thing of the past, because it is so hard to find anything solid to cling to anymore.

3064    Friendship is an arrangement by which we undertake to exchange small favors for big ones.—*Baron de Montesquieu*

3065    We cherish our friends not for their ability to amuse us, but for ours to amuse them.—*Evelyn Waugh*

3066    *Tactful person:* One who comes to your house and makes you feel at home.

3067    With a little honey in the front seat, a young man doesn't mind a little jam in the traffic.

3068    Don't abuse your friends and expect them to consider it criticism.— *Ed Howe*

3069    A person should speak well of his enemies because he made them.

3070    The only records we would like to break are some the neighbor plays every night.

3071    When you allow some drivers the right of way, it's either courtesy or prudence.

3072    Every time a boy shows his hands, someone suggests that he wash them.—*Ed Howe*

3073    A real diplomat is a man who sends twenty-five roses to a woman on her thirty-first birthday.

3074    Don't harp on the people who insist on singing. If they didn't sing they might be even harder to endure.

3075    An argument is where two people are trying to get the last word in first.

3076    Only rarely is it worth what it costs to tell a person what you think of him.

3077    Don't tell people about your indigestion. "How are you!" is a greeting, not a question.

3078     "That's the guy I'm laying for," said the little hen as the farmer crossed the yard.

3079     Flattery is telling the other fellow what he thinks of himself.

3080     Unless you're the elevator operator, you can't get ahead simply by running people down.

3081     Singing, says a medical man, warms the blood. We'll confirm that. We've heard some that positively makes our blood boil.

3082     One kind of motorist who never runs out of gas is the backseat driver.

3083     A chip on the shoulder is often a piece of wood that has fallen from the head.

3084     We do not quite forgive a giver. The hand that feeds us is in some danger of being bitten.—*Ralph Waldo Emerson*

3085     *Women's tea:* Giggle, gobble, gabble.—*Oliver Wendell Holmes*

3086     Some people are like steamboats: they toot loudest when they are in a fog.

3087     Bores can be divided into two classes; those who have their own particular subject, and those who do not need a subject.—*A. A. Milne*

3088     One nice thing about egotists: They don't talk about other people.—*Lucille S. Harper*

3089     You have your machinery in reverse when you try to raise yourself by lowering somebody else.

3090     Some people are easily entertained. All you have to do is sit down and listen to them.

3091     You never want to give a man a present when he's feeling good.—*Lyndon Baines Johnson*

3092     *Racehorse:* An animal that can take several thousand people for a ride at the same time.

3093     There is not much to talk about at parties until one or two couples leave.

3094     He is the only case of a bull who carries his china closet with him.—*Winston Churchill*

3095   Ireland must not be Heaven, for our traffic cops come from there.

3096   Sympathizing with a person is like patting a dog on the head—they both follow you for more.

3097   A gentleman is someone who can play the saxophone, but doesn't.

3098   Money will buy a dog, but it won't buy the wag of his tail.

3099   If your efforts are criticized, you must have done something worthwhile.

3100   It takes your enemy and your friend, working together, to hurt you to the heart: the one to slander you and the other to get the news to you.—*Mark Twain*

3101   If thine enemy wrong thee, buy each of his children a drum.—*Chinese proverb*

3102   It's what the guests say as they swing out of the driveway that counts.

3103   A neck is something if you don't stick it out you won't get in trouble up to.

3104   The more arguments you win, the fewer friends you'll have.

3105   Usually the fellow who shouts the loudest for justice is the one who wants it in his favor.

3106   There is no cure for insomnia like listening to yourself talk.

3107   When you find yourself getting angry, stand still for a moment and smile.

3108   In some countries a person can talk his head off very easily.

3109   One good thing about enemies is that they tell you more truth about yourself than your friends do.

3110   *Friendship:* A holy passion, so sweet and steady and loyal and enduring in its nature that it will last through a whole lifetime, if not asked to lend money. —*Mark Twain*

3111   It would be a sad world if the opinions we held of others were the same ones they held of us.

3112   The peak of success for some people is to be bored by those who formerly snubbed them.

3113    Well, if I called the wrong number, why did you answer the phone?— *James Thurber*

3114    *Politeness:* Not speaking evil of people with whom you have just dined until you are at least a hundred yards from their house.—*André Maurois*

3115    You can make more friends in two months by becoming interested in other people than you can in two years by trying to get other people interested in you.—*Dale Carnegie*

3116    Criticism is the disapproval of people, not for having faults, but for having faults different from ours.

3117    All the world is queer save thee and me, and even thou art a little queer. —*Robert Owen*

3118    When you are arguing with a fool, make certain that he is not similarly occupied.

3119    Always label the Christmas presents you receive. Then you won't give them back to the same people next Christmas.

3120    Said the big firecracker to the little firecracker: "My pop's bigger'n your pop."

3121    Might as well keep your mouth shut. If you talk about yourself, you're a bore; and if you talk about others, you're a gossip.

3122    Confucius say: He who carries tale makes monkey of self.

3123    Some people don't have much to say, but you have to listen a long time to find it out.

3124    The most inconsiderate person is the one who wants you to listen when you want to talk.

3125    We've noticed that nothing seems to need reforming so much as other people's faults.

3126    Sign outside a small town: "Speed limit 50 miles per hour. You can't get through here too fast for us."

3127    If you wish to be a good sport you must let people teach you a lot of things you already know.

3128    A censor is a fellow who is always sticking his no's into others' business.

3129    "I've had a wonderful evening," Groucho Marx once said after a very dull party, "but this wasn't it."

3130    Punctuality is the art of arriving for an appointment just in time to be indignant at the lateness of the other people.

3131    *Gift shop:* A place where you can see all the things you hope your friends won't send you for Christmas.—*Jack Woolsey*

3132    If I valued the honorable gentleman's opinion I might get angry.—*Winston Churchill*

3133    Do not trust to the cheering, for those very persons would shout as much if you and I were going to be hanged.—*Oliver Cromwell*

3134    People will believe anything if you whisper it.

3135    When you feel dog-tired at night, it may be because you've growled all day long.

3136    I don't know how old you are, but you don't look it.

3137    Two words that are guaranteed if you want the last word in an argument: "I agree."

3138    *Tough neighborhood:* A neighborhood so rough that any cat in it with a tail is a tourist.

3139    *Beard:* What you should wear with a gift necktie.

3140    *Social tact:* Making your guests feel at home even though you wish they were.

3141    Never miss an opportunity to make others happy—even if you have to let them alone to do it.

3142    There is no man so friendless but what he can find a friend sincere enough to tell him disagreeable truths.—*Edward Bulwer-Lytton*

3143    Strip away the phony tinsel of Hollywood and you find the real tinsel underneath.—*Oscar Levant*

3144    A fan club is a group of people who tell an actor he's not alone in the way he feels about himself.—*Jack Carson*

3145    *Gentleman:* A person who could show you his home movies but doesn't.

3146    When you know nothing but good about a person, it's more fun to talk about someone else.

3147    A person who speaks well of everyone must have poor judgment.

3148    The trouble with an inferiority complex is that the right people never have it.

3149    A sense of humor enables one to get a laugh out of the other person's troubles.

3150    A smart person is one who knows when and how to play dumb.

3151    TV and radio now have a number of young sopranos who should go far. One lives next door to us.

3152    When you're in trouble you know who your friends are and who has been waiting to catch you bent over at the right angle.

3153    No one gets paid for being disagreeable except a traffic cop, and he doesn't get many Christmas presents.

3154    The closer you are, the more distant your friends are.

3155    Every time some people let the cat out of the bag it seems to be one with a white stripe along its back.

3156    Tact is the art of making a point without making an enemy.—*Howard W. Newton*

3157    Always forgive your enemies—nothing annoys them so much.—*Oscar Wilde*

3158    Tact is the ability to describe others as they see themselves.—*Abraham Lincoln*

3159    Nothing makes you more tolerant of a neighbor's noisy party than being there.—*Franklin P. Jones*

3160    To keep your friends, always give your candied opinion.

3161    *Friend:* A person who dislikes the same people you do.

3162    *The truth:* The one thing you get from a person who doesn't like you.

3163    *Braggart:* A person who enters a conversation feat first.

# XII

# Government, Taxes, and Politics

### 3164 *Overcome*

Senator Albert Gore was making a speech in the Senate, and Senator John Sparkman wanted to get in a few words. "Will the Senator yield?" Sparkman asked, using the traditional phrase.

"I yield," Gore said, "to the distinguished, able, young junior senator from Alabama."

Senator Alexander Wiley made a further addition: "And handsome," he called out.

"And handsome," Gore agreed.

"I am completely flabbergasted by the adulatory adjectives of my colleagues," Sparkman confessed. "Now, I have completely forgotten what I wanted to say."

### 3165 *Had Him*

Two opposing political candidates were in heated debate on issues before a large crowd. "There are hundreds of ways of making money," argued one, "but only one way is honest."

"And what's that?" the other responded.

"Ah ha!" replied the first speaker. "I knew you wouldn't know!"

### 3166 *Careless*

A two-sentence message received by Vice-President Lyndon Johnson came from an American Indian on a reservation: "Be careful with your immigration laws. We were careless with ours."

3167    *Russia*

The Russian city now known as Leningrad was called St. Petersburg before World War I. During World War I it was called Petrograd.

A resident of the city was being polled by the Communists as follows:

"Where did you live before the First World War?"

"St. Petersburg."

"Where did you live during that war?"

"Petrograd."

"Where do you live now?"

"Leningrad."

"Where would you like to live?"

"St. Petersburg."

3168    *Bureaucracy*

A government report says that in one department there were twenty-four supervisors supervising the work of twenty-five people. When told about this, a bureaucrat was horrified. "Imagine such a situation!" he said. "Which supervisor was absent?"

3169    *Non-Entity Cards*

Heard in Scotland: A Scottish woman and her husband were in a queue and as they approached the counter the woman said, "Hi Willie, we've forgotten our non-entity cards."

3170    *Advice to Persons Appointed to the State Department*

You will not need to review your Latin. Ad hoc and quid pro quo are virtually the only acceptable Latin phrases in general use, and it would be best to confine yourself to them.

Long Latin derivatives are looked at askance as being pretentious and having some coloration of Harvard. Incisive expressions are preferred. A few examples may be helpful.

Do not say: Give me a résumé of the political situation in Ruritania.

Say: Give me a rundown (or wrap-up) of the political situation in Ruritania.

Do not say: Who will assist the Secretary of State at Paris?

Say: Who will back up the Secretary of State at Paris?

Do not say: You had better confirm that.

Say: You had better touch base on that.

With these guidelines, you should have relatively little difficulty with State Department language.

3171    *Playing It Safe*

Three managers of chicken farms in Russia were being questioned by the authorities. "What do you feed your chickens?" the first was asked.

"Corn."

"You're under arrest! We use corn to feed the people!"

The second was asked, "What do you feed your chickens?"

"Corn husks," he replied, trying to play it safe.

"You're under arrest! We use the husks to make cloth for the people."

Then the third man was asked the same question.

"I give my chickens the money and tell them to go and buy their own food!" he answered quickly.

### 3172 *He's Wonderful—In Verse*

The statesman throws his shoulders back and straightens out his tie, and says, "My friends, unless it rains, the weather will be dry." And when this thought into our brains has percolated through, we common people nod our heads and loudly cry, "How true!"

The statesman blows his massive nose and clears his august throat, and says, "The ship will never sink so long as it's afloat." Whereat we roll our solemn eyes, applaud with main and might, and slap each other on the back, while we say, "He's right!"

The statesman waxes stern and warm, his drone becomes a roar. He yells, "I say to you, my friends, that two and two make four." And thereupon our doubts dissolve, our fears are put to rout, and we agree that here's a man who knows what he's about!—*Source unknown*

### 3173 *Wrong Number*

The telephone rang in the White House press room. The reporter who picked up the receiver heard: "Hello—is this Doctor Adams?"

"No," answered the reporter, "this is the White House."

"Oh, the White House," said the voice hesitantly. "Excuse me, Mr. President!"

### 3174 *He Knew How*

A man heard frightened screams coming from a nearby house. He ran in to investigate and found a frantic mother whose small boy had swallowed a quarter. Seizing the child by the heels, he held him up and gave him a few shakes, and the coin dropped to the floor. The grateful mother was lost in admiration.

"You certainly knew how to get it out of him," she said. "Are you a doctor?"

"No, madam," the man replied, "I'm from the Internal Revenue Bureau."

### 3175 *Wait*

At a political convention a sign had been erected on the speaker's platform for the benefit of press photographers. It read: "Do not photograph the speakers while they are addressing the audience. Shoot them as they approach the platform."

### 3176  *Not Fair*

Uncle Joe has his doubts about equality before the law. He says no one cares if a banker writes a bad poem, but a poet who writes a bad check is sent to jail.

### 3177  *Aw Come On!*

"Did you know you can't send mail to Washington?"
"Why not?"
"Because he's dead—but you can send mail to Lincoln."
"But he's dead, too."
"I know—but he left his Gettysburg Address."

### 3178  *The Bad News*

The chief executive of the company brought all his employees together and told them, "I have both good news and bad news. The good news is we're in complete compliance with government regulations. And the bad news is that we're going bankrupt."

### 3179  *Federal Aid*

There is no such thing as Federal Aid—it really is Federal Supervision of funds that are collected from every city, town, village, and rural community in the United States. Genuine Federal Aid would be the reduction of taxes by the Federal Government so the people at the grass roots level would have funds to do their own building, to meet their respective community needs.—*George M. Pendell*

### 3180  *Spend Carefully*

I just received the following wire from my generous Daddy: "Dear Jack, Don't buy a single vote more than necessary. I'll be damned if I'm going to pay for a landslide."—*John F. Kennedy*

### 3181  *Modern Politics*

When Columbus started out, he didn't know where he was going. When he got there, he didn't know where he was. When he got back, he didn't know where he had been. And he did it all on other people's money.

What a politician Columbus would have been in present days!

### 3182  *Country Life: Russia*

It is quiet here and restful and the air is delicious. There are gardens everywhere, nightingales sing in the gardens and police spies lie in the bushes.—*Maxim Gorky*

### 3183  *Not Fair*

Two country judges were arrested for speeding. When they appeared in court, no other judge was present, so they decided to try each other. The first went up to the bench and said, "You are charged with exceeding the speed limit. How do you plead?"

"Guilty," was the answer.

"You are fined five dollars."

Then the other took the bench, and asked the same question. But when the accused judge acknowledged his guilt, the one who had already been fined five dollars exclaimed, "These cases are becoming far too common. This is the second speeding case we've had this morning. I hereby fine you ten dollars, or ten days in jail."

### 3184    *One Mistake*

A new member of a government bureau made life miserable for his associates by pretending to infallibility. One day, however, he startled his co-workers by admitting that once he had been wrong.

"You wrong?" exlaimed one of his listeners.

"Yes," replied the infallible man. "Once I thought I was wrong when I wasn't."

### 3185    *The Wit of Lloyd George*

In one of Lloyd George's early campaigns, someone threw a brick through a window and it fell on the platform at his feet. Picking it up he cried: "Behold the only argument of our opponents."

Once when he was talking on "home rule" he said, "I want home rule for England, for Scotland, for Wales, for Ireland—" At this point someone shouted, "Home rule for hell."

"That's right," he shot back, "every man for his own country."

At another gathering a man shouted, "Oh you're not so much; your dad used to peddle vegetables with a donkey and cart." "Yes," said the orator, "that is true. My father was a very poor man. The cart has long since disappeared, but I see the donkey is still here."

### 3186    *That's Different*

A candidate for the Communist party was undergoing an examination. "Comrade," he was asked, "what would you do if you were left two million rubles?"

"I would give one million to the party and keep the other million for myself," he answered.

"Very good. And if you had two houses?"

"I would give one to the party and keep the other for myself."

"Excellent. Now tell me what you would do if you had two pairs of trousers?"

There was a long pause, and then the candidate said weakly, "Comrade, I don't know."

"Why not?"

"Well, you see, I have two pairs of trousers."

### 3187    Logical Choice

There's no use in denying it, observed Farmer Filkins. "Old Tumbleton is the man to send to Congress."

"I don't know so much about that," said Farmer Fowler.

"Well, I do. Tumbleton is for the farmer every time. He says if he's elected he'll introduce a bill to stop importing french-fried potatoes."

### 3188    In the Old Days

When Abraham Lincoln was elected president, he had $601 in the bank. These days it takes more than that to become an alderman.

### 3189    Maximum Sentence

A judge, in sentencing a criminal, recently said: "I am giving you the maximum punishment—I am letting you go free to worry about taxes, inflation, and everything else, just like the rest of us."

### 3190    No Prejudice

A politician was overheard saying: "I am not prejudiced at all. I am going to this political convention with an open, unbiased mind, prepared to listen to a lot of pure tommyrot!"

### 3191    After-Dinner Speaker

All you need to do to get a speech out of Ambassador Joseph H. Choate is to open his mouth, drop in a dinner, and up comes a speech.—*Chauncey Depew*

### 3192    Clarification

A government agency announced that "a full month is a period of consecutive days constituting a month." It's a relief to have that point finally cleared up.

### 3193    Not in His District

Voter: "Why, I wouldn't vote for you if you were Saint Peter himself!"

Candidate: "If I were Saint Peter, you couldn't vote for me—you wouldn't be in my district."

### 3194    Public Speaking

James Edgar told this story after becoming Secretary of State of Illinois:

"One of the things I have been cautioned about since I have become Secretary of State is to keep my remarks brief. The other day I was talking with a person who said he thinks I'm getting better in my speeches.

"I said, 'What do you mean?'

"He said, 'Well, I heard you six months ago when you were the main speaker, and then I heard you two weeks ago, when you did a lot better job.' The first time he heard me I was a main speaker. I was told to speak for 20 minutes and I did. At the second time I was asked just to say hello. There were about ten of us. And that was the one when he thought I did a much better job."

3195 *Right*

Office boy: "I think I know what's wrong with this country."
Bank executive: "What's that, son?"
Office boy: "We are trying to run this country with only one vice-president."

3196 *No End in Sight*

The *Federal Register* of 1949 carried 7,952 pages of government rules and regulations. The *Register* in 1979—just thirty years later—carried 77,498 pages.

3197 Many of the politicians these days gas their audiences instead of electrifying them.

3198 If a Republican wants to win in the South, he should at least learn how to say "you-all."

3199 The dove of peace must be a little cuckoo nowadays.

3200 *Paradox:* The candidate for vice-president either gets the job and has nothing to do, or loses the job and goes to work.

3201 We don't bid a vice-presidential nominee good-bye until after he is elected.

3202 Is it also called red tape in Soviet Russia?

3203 Nothing maddens a politician so much as the discovery that the other side is playing politics.

3204 Too many times our lawmakers in Washington think they are instruments of destiny when actually they are only wind instruments.

3205 *Political platform:* Something upon which the candidate stands while he sees which way the people choose to go.

3206 The concert of the United Nations still doesn't sound like "Sweet Adeline."

3207 The keynote of some successful political careers is dough.

3208 George Washington may have slept many places, but the modern politician also moves from bunk to bunk.

3209    Nothing keeps faith in government more than the hope that in the next election we can turn out the crooks.

3210    An urgent national project is anything for which a group of economy-minded citizens want money from Congress.

3211    What obstructs the vision and is called "smog" in our big cities is called "defining the issues" in politics.

3212    The same person apparently invented the telephone booth, the breakfast nook, and the washroom on airplanes.

3213    Sometimes we long for the good old days when all this country had to fear was an attack from the Indians.

3214    The cheapest way to have your family tree traced is to run for office.

3215    Russia is for peace, if it's a big piece of some country.

3216    As a last desperate effort to balance the budget, we might try the radical idea of spending less.

3217    Sometimes we think the less a government costs the more it's worth.

3218    Every time an Italian prime minister goes out, he meets himself coming back in.

3219    Politics is perhaps the only profession for which no preparation is thought necessary.—*Robert Louis Stevenson*

3220    A politician is continually busy running for office or for cover.

3221    He knows nothing; he thinks he knows everything—that clearly points to a political career.—*George Bernard Shaw*

3222    One way for a nation to go broke is to keep on buying wars on the deferred-payment plan.

3223    When a politician talks about efficiency in government, the accent is generally on the "fish."

3224    A minor government official has a sign on his desk reading: "This job is so secret I don't know what I'm doing."

3225    A statistician claims that the handshaking in an election would milk all the cows in the United States for four months.

3226    Some diplomats are lieabilities for their countries.

3227    When nations talk of reducing arms, every nation wants the last sword.

3228    An optimist is a person who writes a politician hoping to learn about both sides to a question.

3229    What the world needs is fewer countries casting their bullets for a new leader.

3230    In the United States a boy can grow up and hope to be president, but in some countries he only hopes to grow up.

3231    To some politicians a government payroll is only a matter of relative importance.

3232    The biggest windstorms come in the United States in election years.

3233    We don't suppose all the people of the satellite nations are Red. Some of them must be pretty blue.

3234    Nothing is impossible. Now we have peace on a war basis.

3235    Sometimes a political joke gets elected to office and then it's no joke.

3236    Parties sometimes split, and it's a wonder candidates don't split also, the way they straddle issues.

3237    An election never proves anything except that different parts of the country are mad about different things.

3238    The problem of governments in South America is to keep an ambitious sergeant from starting a revolution in order to become a general.

3239    When a political party is split by arguments, it goes several ways, none of which leads to Washington.

3240    The one thing the Communists believe in is freedom of the suppress.

3241    All Communist countries have a two-party system: the dictators and the spectators.

3242    A highly commendable government expenditure is any spending that helps my community.

3243    With an election coming, a good many courageous candidates will come out boldly for good weather, eight hours of sleep, and fresh eggs.

3244    Guidelines for bureaucrats: (1) When in charge, ponder. (2) When in trouble, delegate. (3) When in doubt, mumble.—*James H. Boren*

3245    A successful politician is one who plays both ends against the taxpayer.

3246    An honest politician is one who, when he is bought, will stay bought.
—*Simon Cameron*

3247    Sometimes we think Congress spends a lot of time playing with its blocs.

3248    Next to "the," the most common word in all nations today is "deficit."

3249    In connection with the pound, the British Conservatives like to speak of themselves as persons of sterling character.

3250    From the size of the government debt they are going to pass on, this can be called the passing generation.

3251    This country has come to feel the same when Congress is in session as when the baby gets hold of a hammer.—*Will Rogers*

3252    Perhaps the most important state right at present is the right to federal aid.

3253    When you look at defense costs over the world, you realize that they who take the sword may perish by the tax.

3254    Most politicians finally attain the pique of their popularity.

3255    All is fair in love and war, and if you win at either the expense doesn't end.

3256    In municipal politics, cash and carry in the wards go hand in hand.

3257    The speeches of some politicians are interesting because they give so many facts you can't find elsewhere.

3258    The fellow who says there is nothing new under the sun never read a government tax bill.

3259    An Italian prime minister should not think of getting married until he gets a steady job.

3260    Perhaps the Russian newspaper that says we are a warlike nation has been reading what the Democrats and Republicans say about each other in an election year.

3261    In some countries a government leader can't be sure whether the people are following him or chasing him.

3262　The world is in such confusion that sometimes you don't care what happens just so it happens soon.

3263　Modern motto: "Gimme liberty or gimme death or gimme some government money."

3264　The person today who says the government owes him a living includes an automobile, a radio, TV, and a split-level bungalow in his living requirements.

3265　It is getting so automatic equipment can do everything except fill out government questionnaires.

3266　If you look at what happened to the American Indian, it's hard to believe the government can bring you prosperity and happiness.

3267　Under capitalism man exploits man; under socialism the reverse is true.
—*Polish proverb*

3268　Communist governments have their purges now, but wait until they have one automobile for every two pedestrians.

3269　It's just as well that the meek inherit the earth. Nobody else would stand for the inheritance tax.

3270　The great misfortune of mankind is that only those out of office know how to solve great problems.

3271　You can say one thing for a monarchy: it doesn't inspire an epidemic of platitudinous speeches every four years.

3272　When a Congressman is trying to sleep, he counts his sheep in billions.

3273　*Diplomat:* A person whose job is patching up the troubles caused by other diplomats.

3274　Some people who laugh at hair restorers believe a politician who tells them they can get something for nothing from the government.

3275　A politician who does nothing but keep his ear to the ground doesn't have much vision.

3276　A nation gets into trouble when people expect government to give them more than they deserve.

3277　No matter how much the political pot boils, it still smells like applesauce.

3278　Money puts the prop in propaganda.

3279     A liberal calls it share-the-wealth; a conservative calls it soak-the-rich.

3280     A politician has a hard lot. It is easy to pick the right side, but difficult to pick the side that will hold the most votes.

3281     It might add to the Olympic Games if they included a contest to see which nation could run longest with an unbalanced budget.

3282     *Federal aid:* A system of making money taken from the people look like a gift when handed back.—*Carl Workman*

3283     Some foreigners think America can always stand a loan, and some Americans think we can stand alone.

3284     It might be a good idea to have the U.S. Marine Band play some thrilling, patriotic airs when the taxpayers line up.

3285     Only unread citizens are really afraid of the power of Red ideas.

3286     The way for nations to do away with war may be to pray more and prey less.

3287     When two diplomats shake hands, nobody can be sure whether it's friendship or time for the fight to start.

3288     Diplomats believe many powwows keep the world from going to the bowwows.

3289     In an election year it isn't necessary to fool all the people all the time —only in the period just before the election.

3290     When a traffic officer stops you, he either gives you a ticket or sells you one.

3291     In international affairs, a conference is a meeting lasting several weeks to prepare for another meeting lasting several weeks.

3292     The answer to "What is the world coming to?" is "America."

3293     As we understand it, the world will be wrecked if any nation fails to get from us what she wants.

3294     It's almost impossible for a public official to do his duty without being accused of seeking publicity.

3295     *Diplomat:* A wealthy person assigned to meddle in other people's business.

3296    You must give the Russians credit—they haven't claimed yet that they invented baseball.

3297    Apparently Russia's chief complaint is that we won't let them wrest peacefully.

3298    The ship of state is one vessel that often moves in a fog.

3299    To a foreign diplomat visiting Washington, sound ideals are vital, but sound vitals are also ideal.

3300    The Reds make their greatest progress in countries with the economic blues.

3301    *Washington, D.C.:* City bureauful.

3302    If all the people who understand Russian foreign policy were laid end to end, he would feel terribly conspicuous.

3303    Can you remember way back when governments got along without something if it cost too much?

3304    Government is an institution through which sound travels faster than light.

3305    The choice that has faced Uncle Sam abroad is whether to be busted as a Shylock or busted as a Santa Claus.

3306    As we understand it, the Administration policy is to change from the mite of a dollar to the might of a dollar.

3307    *Diplomacy:* Thinking twice before saying nothing.

3308    We need a law that will permit a voter to sue a candidate for breach of promise.

3309    One of the great blessings about living in a democracy is that we have complete control over how we pay our taxes—cash, check, or money order.

3310    According to Bob Hope, "The ten most beautiful words in the English language are: "Dear Sir: Enclosed find your income tax refund for 19—.' "

3311    To ensure permanent peace perhaps the leaders of all nations could agree not to have another war until the last one is paid for.

3312    For the next generation of Americans, life begins at over $1 trillion.

3313     A government big enough to give us everything we want would be big enough to take from us everything we have.—*Gerald Ford*

3314     In Russia when you answer questions, you may come to an unfortunate conclusion.—*Aleksandr Solzhenitsyn*

3315     Propaganda is the art of persuading others of what one does not believe oneself.—*Abba Eban*

3316     The only summit meeting that can succeed is one that does not take place.—*Barry Goldwater*

3317     If our democracy is to flourish, it must have criticism; if our government is to function, it must have dissent.—*Henry Steele Commager*

3318     How can anyone govern a nation that has 246 different kinds of cheese? —*Charles de Gaulle*

3319     I've never thought my speeches were too long: I've enjoyed them.— *Hubert Humphrey*

3320     In Maine we have a saying that there's no point in speaking unless you can improve on silence.—*Edmund Muskie*

3321     Don't be humble; you're not that great.—*Golda Meir*

3322     Nations die on the soft bed of luxury.

3323     If you destroy a free market you create a black market. If you have ten thousand regulations you destroy all respect for the law.—*Winston Churchill*

3324     *Diplomacy:* The art of saying things in such a way that nobody knows exactly what you mean.

3325     *Appeal:* In law, to put the dice into the box for another throw.— *Ambrose Bierce*

3326     *Refugees:* People who vote with their feet.

3327     *Post office:* The old stamping grounds.—*Fibber McGee*

3328     *Life as a diplomat:* Protocol, Geritol and alcohol.—*Winston Churchill*

3329     He has the greatest opportunity for public service. He can resign today. —*Winston Churchill*

3330     Govern a great nation as you would cook a small fish. (Don't overdo it.)—*Lao-Tze*

3331    Diplomacy is letting someone else have your way.

3332    *Implement* (bureaucratese): What you do to carry out a decision, policy, or program when you are doing nothing.—*Russell Baker*

3333    I am informed from many quarters that a rumor has been put about that I died this morning. This is quite untrue.—*Winston Churchill, 1951*

3334    There are two periods when Congress does no business: one is before the holidays, and the other is after.—*G. D. Prentice*

3335    Since a politician never believes what he says, he is always astonished when others do.—*Charles de Gaulle*

3336    It would be comforting to learn that this nation's fiscal policy was being planned by somebody who had to earn his own living.

3337    Communists are people who fancied that they had an unhappy childhood.—*Gertrude Stein*

3338        What is a Communist? One who has yearnings
            For equal division of unequal earnings.
                            —*Ebenezer Elliott*

3339    Look at the Swiss! They have enjoyed peace for centuries, and what have they produced? The cuckoo clock!—*Winston Churchill*

3340    Some countries not only have no unemployment but almost no wages.

3341    As a general rule, I abstain from reading the reports of attacks upon myself, wishing not to be provoked by that to which I cannot properly offer an answer.—*Abraham Lincoln*

3342    By "radical" I understand one who goes too far; by "conservative" one who does not go far enough; by "reactionary" one who won't go at all.—*Woodrow Wilson*

3343    Conservatism is the policy of "make no change and consult your grandmother when in doubt."—*Woodrow Wilson*

3344    We've debated this bill now for nine days. I heard the world was created in seven.—*Robert C. Byrd*

3345    There cannot be a crisis next week. My schedule is already full.—*Henry Kissinger*

3346    An expert gives an objective view. He gives his own view.—*Morarji Desai*

3347    Vote for the man who promises least; he'll be the least disappointing.
—*Bernard Baruch*

3348    "What you don't know doesn't hurt you" doesn't apply to the hidden taxes in the things you buy.

3349    An American is a person who yells about the government spending too much and then asks for a handout for his community.

3350    A few hair shirts are part of the mental wardrobe of every man. The President differs from other men only in that he has a more extensive wardrobe.
—*Herbert Hoover*

3351    Treaties are like roses and young girls. They last while they last.—
*Charles de Gaulle*

3352    *Dinners:* Occupational hazards for political candidates.

3353    After listening to a lot of political speakers, we have decided that we don't know much about politics either.

3354    My opponent wraps himself up in the flimsy garment of his own righteousness and then complains of the cold.—*Winston Churchill*

3355    A government bureau is the nearest thing to eternal life that we'll ever see on this earth.—*Ronald Reagan*

3356    We didn't mind so much that our local postmaster read all our mail, but when he started answering it, we thought he went too far.—*Herb Shriner*

3357    What are desirable qualifications for any young man who wishes to become a politician? It is the ability to foretell what is going to happen tomorrow, next week, next month, and next year. (Long pause) And to have the ability afterwards to explain why it didn't happen.—*Winston Churchill*

3358    Good government always pays. Of course, the other kind does too, but not the same people.

3359    It takes a lot of horse sense to maintain a stable government.

3360    "Is our government sound?" asks a contemporary. Yes, mostly, we should say.

3361    Immigration is the sincerest form of flattery.

3362    Any month that doesn't have a Q in its spelling is free from income-tax worries.

3363    The trouble with the concert of nations is the disproportion of wind instruments.

3364    A politician's life is no bed of roses. By the time he finds out what the people want, they want something else.

3365    Having state legislatures we have one form of air mastery.

3366    It is often asked, "What does this nation stand for?" The answer is easy —too much.

3367    The government is the only known vessel that leaks from the top.— *James Reston*

3368    Under some governments, the people receive free teeth but no meat to chew.

3369    We can think of several openings in government departments for good citizens looking for trouble.

3370    One lesson you'd better learn if you want to be in politics is that you never go out on a golf course and beat the President.—*Lyndon Baines Johnson*

3371    Bing doesn't pay an income tax anymore. He just asks the government what they need.—*Bob Hope*

3372    The hardest thing in the world to understand is the income tax.—*Albert Einstein*

3373    They say women talk too much. If you have worked in Congress you know that the filibuster was invented by men.—*Clare Boothe Luce*

3374    The government solution to a problem is usually as bad as the problem. —*Milton Friedman*

3375    The best minds are not in government. If any were, business would hire them away.—*Ronald Reagan*

3376    Isn't it a blessing that we're not getting all the government we're paying for?

3377    A politician is a person who approaches every subject with an open mouth.

3378    The great difficulty about reducing the expenses of government is that almost all the expenses can vote.

3379    *Imagination:* The thing that makes a politician think he is a statesman.

3380    The government seems to believe there is a taxpayer born every minute.

3381    The cynic's question: "Have we been a succor to some nations long enough?"

3382    Public life is the paradise of voluble windbags.—*George Bernard Shaw*

3383    Like the taxpayers, Uncle Sam has trouble keeping down his waste line.

3384    What a politician stands for is rigid economy with free spending.

3385    Public opinion is a great force for good when it's on that side.

3386    Some politicians begin life at the bottom and go down.

3387    A professor once said whistling is a sign of a moron. His mistake was in telling it to a traffic cop.

3388    I do not believe in the collective wisdom of individual ignorance.—*Thomas Carlyle*

3389    Santa Claus is the only guy who knows how to solve the world's problems yet doesn't want to be president.

3390    What this country needs is a Reno that will divorce politics from crime.

3391    An infallible method of conciliating a tiger is to allow oneself to be devoured.—*Konrad Adenauer*

3392    If you think the laws of this country aren't enforced, try parking your car next to a meter without putting in a coin.

3393    There is a possibility that a peanut politician will get better if the public roasts him.

3394    Communication is so good now that a half dozen nations can insult each other on the same day.

3395    When the government talks about "raising capital" it means printing it. That's not very creative, but it's what we're going to do.—*Peter Drucker*

3396    The three parties in Washington, D.C., are Democratic, Republican, and cocktail.

3397    Some people think all nations should share the atomic bomb, and the pessimists think they will.

3398    In an election year the politicians run and the taxpayers sweat.

3399    One trouble with this country is that too many people expect the government to give them more than they deserve.

3400    If you can make a better claptrap, the voters will beat a path to your door.

3401    Every four years our people are filled with zeal to save the country from each other.

3402    A politician is a person with whose politics you don't agree; if you agree with him he is a statesman.—*David Lloyd George*

3403    Why doesn't the government send Gallup to the Middle East to see who is going to win over there?

3404    A politician's promise to punish the rascals seldom carries conviction.

3405    Norfolk, Virginia, is sometimes called the peanut capital of the United States, but we understand some other capitals disagree.

3406    The most successful politician is he who says what everybody is thinking most often and in the loudest voice.—*Theodore Roosevelt*

3407    It's strange that when a politician promises to enforce the law he is considered a person of character.

3408    Washington is the only American city where a few people are paid to keep the rest of us worried.

3409    It's a question whether some nations are interested in our role or our roll in foreign affairs.

3410    Breathes there a man with soul so dead who has not in late years said: "Can this be my own, my native land?"

3411    For a man who couldn't tell a lie, George Washington went a long way in politics.

3412    In the modern world, war doesn't pay and isn't paid for.

3413    The trouble with politics is that the people desire an outstanding man and the politicians desire an outstanding winner.

3414    *Diplomat:* A ward politician with a frock coat.—*General Smedley D. Butler*

3415    *Filing cabinet:* A place where important papers get lost alphabetically.

3416    *Democracy:* Government by popular ignorance.—*Elbert Hubbard*

3417    *Congress:* Bingo with billions.—*Red Skelton*

3418    *Army:* A body of men assembled to rectify the mistakes of the diplomats.—*Josephus Daniels*

3419    *Diplomacy:* Lying in state.—*Oliver Herford*

# Inspiration and Wisdom

# XIII

# Unusual Stories and the Wisdom of the Thoughtful

**3420**    *The Old Virtues*

The principal thing we can do, if we really want to make the world over, is to try the use of the word "old" again. It was the "old" things that made this country the great nation it is.

There are the Old Virtues of integrity and truth.

There are the Old Virtues of incorruptible service, and honor in public office.

There are the Old Virtues of economy in government, of self-reliance, thrift, and individual responsibility and liberty.

There are the Old Virtues of patriotism, real love of country, and willingness to sacrifice for it.

These "old" ideas are very inexpensive. And they would help win hot and cold wars. I realize such suggestions will raise that odious word "reactionary," but some of these "old" values are slipping away rapidly from American life. And if they slip too far, the lights will go out in America, even if we win the hot and cold wars.—*Herbert Hoover*

**3421**    *That Simple*

Disgusted at being considered a genius by every person when he at all times attempted to make himself appear perfectly normal, Rachmaninoff came up with the retort courteous when a stagestruck listener gurgled, "What ever inspired you to compose such a wonderfully marvelous piece as your C-Sharp Minor Prelude?"

The master made a deep bow and, with a perfectly composed face, replied, "Because, madam, I needed the dough."

305

### 3422 *Trust*

We scorn panaceas. We respect the fortitude, the courage, the staying power of the American people. We show that respect by always speaking the plain truth, as we know it.

And we are confident for precisely this same reason: We believe in the people. We believe in the ingenuity and the industry of the American as resources that no nation on earth can match. We believe in his capacity to work, to save, to invent, to sacrifice, to create, to dream good dreams—and to bring them to true life.

To do all these things, the people need but one thing: a government they can trust—a government worthy of that trust.—*George M. Humphrey*

### 3423 *It Takes Work*

Some young people complain as if the world owed them a living. Nobody owes anybody anything; it's up to each individual to set high standards for himself or herself, and to set about working hard and creating a solid future. I see more energy, life, and spirit in many so-called senior citizens than in numerous young people I've come in contact with.—*Katharine Hepburn*

### 3424 *Still Doing It*

A reporter once asked Sir Winston Churchill whether he agreed with the prediction that women would rule the world by the year 2000.

Mr. Churchill's reply was, "Yes, they will still be at it."

### 3425 *British, French, and American*

Benjamin Franklin was dining with a small party of distinguished gentlemen in Paris when one of them said, "Three nationalities are represented here this evening. I am French, my friend next to me is English, and Mr. Franklin is an American. Let each of us propose a toast."

It was agreed, and the Englishman, who was accorded first honors, arose, and boldly said, "Here's to Great Britain, the sun that gives light to all nations of the earth."

The Frenchman was rather taken aback, but he proposed, "Here's to France, the moon whose magic rays move the tides of the world."

Everyone thought the American had been completely subdued, but Franklin arose with an air of quaint modesty, and said, "And here's to our beloved George Washington, the Joshua of America, who commanded the sun and the moon to stand still—and they obeyed!"—*Sunshine Magazine*

### 3426 *Worth Thinking About*

We cannot bring prosperity by discouraging thrift.

We cannot help small men by tearing down big men.

We cannot help the poor by destroying the rich.

We cannot lift the wage earner by pulling down the wage payer.

We—governments or people—cannot keep out of trouble by spending more than we have.

We cannot further the brotherhood of man by inciting class hatred.

We cannot build character and courage by taking away initiative and independence.

We cannot help people permanently by doing for them what they could and should do for themselves.

## 3427    Freedom

I am convinced that human beings cannot be converted to Communism if that conversion is attempted while the country is under Communist rule. Under Communist dictatorship the majority become slaves. Men born to freedom, though they may be coerced, can never be convinced. Communism is an evil which is embraced only by fools and idealists not under the actual heel of such rule.—*Stanislaw Mikolajczyk, former premier of Poland*

## 3428    Our Basic Freedoms

Our basic freedoms have become almost the very reason we exist, so that we may enjoy them and pass them unalloyed to our grandchildren. It has been said that we uphold property rights in the free enterprise system against human rights. I say that is a false statement. The right to property is only one of the human rights, and when that falls, all else falls with it. The abolition of property rights means dictatorship.—*Dwight D. Eisenhower*

## 3429    The Levelers

Books are the true levelers. They give to all who faithfully use them the society, the spiritual presence, of the best and greatest of our race.—*Lord Chaning*

## 3430    Stradivari Violins

Antonio Stradivari was the most celebrated master violin maker of all time. He was born in 1644 and died in 1737. He lived in Cremona, Italy. He probably produced more than one thousand violins.

There were more than five hundred Stradivari violins extant in 1930, in addition to a dozen violas, and about fifty cellos. Stradivari made his first violins after he was past sixty years of age. He built the violin to such perfection that improvement upon his instrument has been impossible.

Stradivari once revealed the secret of his skill in a poem attributed to him. The classic, "If my hand slacked," is so well known that it is commonly used as an impetus to conscientious effort. But not everyone knows the more complete poem, which leads up to that famous line. It is as follows:

When a master holds
'Twixt chin and hand a violin of mine,
He will be glad that Stradivari lived,
Made violins, and made them of the best.
For while God gives them skill,
I give them instruments to play upon—
God choosing me to help him.
If my hand slacked,
I should rob God—since he is fullest good—
Leaving a blank instead of violins.
He could not make
Antonio Stradivari's violins
Without Antonio!

### 3431    Lincoln's Philosophy

I am not bound to win, but I am bound to be true. I am not bound to succeed, but I am bound to live up to what light I have. I must stand with anybody that stands right, stand with him while he is right and part with him when he goes wrong.—*Abraham Lincoln*

### 3432    No Simple Formula for Peace

There is no simple formula for peace, and no single act that will assure peace. Any who preach that are dangerously deluded. Only the combined result of many efforts at different levels, and at many places, will assure peace. In these efforts everyone has a part to play. The stakes are the greatest for which men have ever played.—*John Foster Dulles*

### 3433    Fundamental Principles

When more of the people's sustenance is exacted through the form of taxation than is necessary to meet the just obligations of Government and expenses of its economical administration, such exaction becomes ruthless extortion and a violation of the fundamental principles of a free government.—*Grover Cleveland*

### 3434    Benjamin Franklin's Philosophy

Let honesty and industry be thy constant companions, and spend one penny less than thy clear gains; then shall thy pocket begin to thrive; creditors will not insult, nor want oppress, nor hunger bite.

### 3435    Inflation

I believe that we must face another problem in which our people are vitally interested. All of us are exposed to an insidious disease that stealthily robs us of our strength. It is the evil of inflation which makes the prices of food, of clothing, of all the necessities of life climb upward in a grim spiral which again and again snatches away the benefits of progress.—*George M. Humphrey*

### 3436    *The Obvious*

People criticize me for harping on the obvious. Perhaps someday I'll write an article on the importance of the obvious. If all the folks in the United States would do the few simple things they know they ought to do, most of our problems would take care of themselves.—*Calvin Coolidge*

### 3437    *The Purpose of Government*

Why was government instituted at all? Because the passions of men will not conform to the dictates of reason and justice without restraint.—*Alexander Hamilton*

### 3438    *Television*

The instrument can teach, it can illuminate. Yes, and it can even inspire. But it can do so only to the extent that humans are determined to use it to those ends. Otherwise, it is merely lights and wires in a box.—*Edward R. Morrow*

### 3439    *The Difference*

A leading actor was honored at a banquet. In the after-dinner ceremonies the actor was asked to recite for the pleasure of his guests. He consented, and asked if there was anything special anyone in the audience would like to hear.

There was a moment's pause, and then an old clergyman spoke up. "Could you, sir," he said, "recite the Twenty-third Psalm?"

A strange look came over the actor's face, but he was speechless for only a moment. "I can, sir—and I will on one condition, and that is that after I have recited, you, my friend, will do the same."

"I?" replied the surprised clergyman. "But I am not an elocutionist. However, if you wish, I will do so."

Impressively the great actor began the psalm, holding his audience spellbound. As he finished, a burst of applause broke from the guests.

After the applause, the old clergyman arose. The audience sat in intense silence. The psalm was recited, and when it was done, there was not the slightest ripple of applause, but those in the audience whose eyes were yet dry had their heads bowed.

The great actor, with hand on the shoulder of the old clergyman, his voice trembling, exclaimed, "I reached your eyes and ears, my friends; this man reached your hearts. I know the Twenty-third Psalm; this man knows the Shepherd."

### 3440    *Telling Stories*

Note on storytelling: If the story isn't funny, you can't make it sound any funnier by adding profanity.

### 3441    The First Need

The first need of the world, more urgent even than bread, is order. And the second need is food. Hungry people abandon all restraint, and defy all order. The next imperative need is to restore economic production, for the starving cannot long be supported on charity.—*Herbert Hoover*

### 3442    Learn to Bend

A person who does not learn to bend unbroken before a wind, and to adapt himself readily to changing conditions, cannot possibly be happy in a world where disaster can fall at any time with great rapidity, and where the things we hold valuable one day entirely cease to exist the next.—*John Schindler, M.D.*

### 3443    Patience and Persistence

When nothing seems to help, I go and look at a stonecutter hammering away at his rock, perhaps a hundred times without as much as a crack showing in it. Yet, at the hundred and first blow it will split in two, and I know it was not that last blow that did it, but all that had gone before.—*Jacob A. Riis*

### 3444    Certainly Not

The beloved opera singer, Madame Schumann-Heink, was sitting at a restaurant table with an enormous steak in front of her. Enrico Caruso, the famous tenor, passed by and looked in astonishment. "Surely, you're not going to eat that alone, Madame Schumann-Heink!" he said.

"Certainly not!" she replied promptly. "With potatoes."

### 3445    Culture

The most distinctive mark of a cultured mind is the ability to take another's point of view; to put oneself in another's place, and see life and its problems from a point of view different from one's own. To be willing to test a new idea; to be able to live on the edge of difference in all matters intellectually; to examine without heat the burning questions of the day, to have imaginative sympathy, openness and flexibility of mind, steadiness and poise of feeling, cool calmness of judgment, is to have culture.—*A. H. R. Fairchild*

### 3446    Make It Simple

One day a printer brought to Edwin Booth the proof of a new poster, which introduced the actor as "the eminent tragedian, Edwin Booth."

"I wish," said Booth, "that you would leave off that 'eminent tragedian' business. I would much rather have it a simple 'Edwin Booth.' "

"Very good, sir," agreed the printer.

The following week the modest Mr. Booth went for a walk and found the town plastered with posters announcing the coming of "Simple Edwin Booth."

3447     *Depending on Government*

When too many people in a nation depend on the government for their living, democracy is assassinated, freedom is gone, and the arrival of the dictator is just around the corner.—*Henry Cabot Lodge, Jr.*

3448     *Different Skin*

I am the person who was born to live in a skin with a different color from yours.

I could not choose my parents, nor you yours.

Thus, the color pigments embedded by the unchangeable hands of nature in your skin are perchance white, while mine are black, or brown, or yellow.

But, underneath I am just like you.

My muscles ripple in the same waves of power, and thrill to the same throb of joyous action.

My mind has the same functions as yours.

I reach out, just as you do, in aspirations of the soul.

I love and hate, hope and despair, rejoice and suffer, along with you.

When my children lose their fair chances at life, and become aware of the bitter road of prejudice they must tread, then I know what my color has cost.

I offer you my hand in rebuilding an unjust world, that you and I can make better than we have found it.

I am the person in a different skin.—*Sunshine Magazine*

3449     *Lost*

"We lost our first child," said a man in the course of a conversation with a friend.

The other, shocked, cried out, "I didn't know she was dead!"

"Oh, she isn't dead," was the quick response, to which was added sadly, "I was too busy."—*Holiness Worker*

3450     *Do Your Best*

I do the best I know how, the very best I can; and I mean to keep on doing it to the end. If the end brings me out all right, what is said against me will not amount to anything. If the end brings me out all wrong, ten angels swearing I was right would make no difference.—*Abraham Lincoln*

3451     *Advice Missing*

Shortly after Grace Goodhue became the wife of Calvin Coolidge, she was high-pressured by a salesman into buying a volume entitled *Our Family Physician,* paying $10 for it—a lot of money to the struggling lawyer.

Grace decided to say nothing about the purchase. When the book arrived, she placed it on the center table without comment. Coolidge glanced at the volume, but said nothing.

One day, soon after, Mrs. Coolidge, glancing at the flyleaf, read: "Don't see any recipes here for curing suckers! Signed, Calvin Coolidge."

### 3452 *Serving His Country*

The man who can make two ears of corn, or two blades of grass grow where only one grew before, would deserve better of mankind, and render more essential service to his country than all the politicians put together.—*Jonathan Swift*

### 3453 *Values*

Sometimes one pays most for the things one gets for nothing.—*Albert Einstein*

### 3454 *The Soul of a Poem*

In a little poem John Greenleaf Whittier tells of a man who visited a village where many years before he had lived as a boy. Life had been hard for him, and as he stood in the little cemetery by a grave—it was that of a young girl—he remembered how as a boy he had failed to spell a word correctly, and the girl had been advanced to his place. When school was over that day she had waited for him, and shyly said:

> "I'm sorry that I spelt the word;
> I hate to go above you,
> Because,"—the brown eyes lower fell—
> "Because, you see, I love you!"

How few, if any, the man thought, had ever been sorry to go above him. Most of them had appeared to be glad to do it. In life's stern school he had found little kindness, but a vast amount of harsh, ruthless action.

### 3455 *Some Tests*

To be able to carry money without spending it. To be able to bear an injustice without retaliating. To be able to do one's duty even when one is not watched. To be able to keep at the job until it is finished. To be able to make use of criticism without letting it whip you.

### 3456 *Political Platform*

The real question is whether a platform represents the clicking of a ghost's typewriter, if I may put it that way, or the beating of a human heart.—*Adlai Stevenson*

### 3457 *The Federal Budget*

Budgets, of course, are only estimates. When you are working with figures as large as Government figures of income and expense, differences between estimates and actual performance can easily arise. . . .

Balancing this budget is not simply a bookkeeping exercise or a businessman's fetish. It is the very keystone of financial responsibility.—*George M. Humphrey*

### 3458    *Picasso*

Everybody wants to understand painting. Why is there no attempt to understand the song of the birds? Why does one love a night, a flower, everything that surrounds a man, without trying to understand it all?—*Pablo Picasso*

### 3459    *Famous Wrong Guesses*

A six-year-old lad came home with a note from his teacher suggesting that he be taken out of school, as he was "too stupid to learn." The boy's name was Thomas A. Edison

Alfred Tennyson's grandfather gave him ten shillings for writing an elegy on his grandmother. Handing it to the boy, the old man said: "There, that's the first money you ever earned by your poetry, and take my word for it, it will be the last."

Benjamin Franklin's mother-in-law hesitated at letting her daughter marry a printer. There were already two printing offices in the United States, and she feared that the country might not be able to support a third.—*Cora M. Campbell, Sunshine Magazine*

### 3460    *The Piano*

Years ago a Chinese traveler, returning to his country after a journey in Europe, wrote this description of a piano:

"The Europeans keep a large four-legged animal which they can make to sing at will. A man, or frequently a woman, sits down in front of the animal and steps on its tail, at the same time striking its white teeth with his or her fingers, when the creature begins to sing. The singing, though much louder than a bird's, is pleasant to listen to. The animal does not bite, nor does it move, though it is not tied."

### 3461    *Progress*

Calvin Coolidge was an ardent fisherman, and fishing in the River Brule was one of his favorite ways of relaxing from his presidential duties.

Returning to Washington from one such excursion, the president was asked if he'd had any luck.

"Well," he drawled, "I estimate that there are forty-five thousand fish in the River Brule, and although I haven't caught them all yet, I've intimidated them."

### 3462    *Graceful Tribute*

President Calvin Coolidge in the White House, always modest and unassuming, was one day visited by the veteran theatrical producer David Belasco.

The gentle, white-haired visitor timidly grasped the President's outstretched hand and whispered, "Mr. President, I am deeply honored—"

"No, Mr. Belasco," Mr. Coolidge interrupted, "I am the one that is deeply honored. There have been many Presidents of the United States, but there can be only one David Belasco."—*Adrian Anderson, Sunshine Magazine*

### 3463    *Liberty*

Liberty has never come from the government; it has always come from the subjects of it. The history of liberty is a history of limitation of governmental power, not the increase of it.—*Woodrow Wilson*

### 3464    *Young Celebrities*

Demosthenes was the greatest orator of Greece at twenty-five, and at the same age Cicero was Rome's greatest speaker.

William Gladstone was a member of the British House of Commons at twenty-four. Benjamin Franklin wrote for papers at fourteen.

At eight Beethoven created astonishment by his musical ability; at thirteen Mozart was unequaled.

Pascal discovered geometry for himself at twelve. At sixteen he wrote a treatise on conic sections, and at twenty-five he published a book on atmospheric pressure.

Agassiz began the study of science at eleven years of age, and was recognized as one of the most profound scholars of his age while yet in his twenties.

Gibbon, the great English historian, began his studies at seventeen, and at twenty-four was publishing his historical work.

Ruskin was an accomplished art critic, and had written "Modern Painters" at twenty-four.

John Wesley was a polished and forceful writer, and a skilled logician, and at twenty-four he was a professor of Greek.

Moody was preaching at eighteen, and during his twenties became one of our greatest evangelists.

William Cullen Bryant wrote "Thanatopsis" at seventeen. Tennyson's first volumes of poems appeared at twenty. Whittier was editor of the *New England Review* at twenty-three; Poe's first volume was written at twenty; and Byron's appeared at seventeen. Burns was a poetic genius at twelve, and a brilliant and gifted writer at sixteen.—*Sunshine Magazine*

### 3465    *Handicaps Build Strength*

Genius knows no handicap through physical ills. Lord Byron had a club foot, Robert Louis Stevenson and John Keats had tuberculosis. Charles Steinmetz and Alexander Pope were hunchbacks. Admiral Nelson had only one eye. Edgar Allan Poe was a psychoneurotic. Charles Darwin was an invalid. Julius Caesar was an epileptic. Thomas Edison and Ludwig von Beethoven were deaf, and Peter Stuyvesant had a wooden leg. Handicaps build strength and purpose—and accomplishment.

### 3466     *Industry and Frugality*

The way to wealth is as plain as the way to market. It depends chiefly on two things: industry and frugality; that is, waste neither time nor money, but make the best use of both. Without industry and frugality, nothing will do; with them, everything.

### 3467     *If a Thing Is Old*

If a thing is old, it is a sign that it was fit to live. Old families, old customs, old styles survive because they are fit to survive. The guarantee of continuity is quality. Old-fashioned hospitality, old-fashioned politeness, old-fashioned honor in transaction and work had qualities of survival.—*Captain Edward V. Rickenbacker*

### 3468     *How to Be Rich*

There are two ways of being rich. One is to have all you want, the other is to be satisfied with what you have.

### 3469     *The Purpose of Life*

A perceptive, philosophical man has said this well: "The purpose of life is not to be happy—but to matter, to be productive, to be useful, to have it make some difference that you lived."

### 3470     *Failure*

When Thomas Edison failed the first or second or third time in his attempts to discover something new, he did not mind it. He just kept on trying. It is said he made thousands upon thousands of trials before he got his celebrated electric light to operate. And this interesting story is told of him:

One day a workman to whom he had given a task came to him and said, "Mr. Edison, it cannot be done."

"How often have you tried?" asked Edison.

"About two thousand times," replied the man.

"Then go back and try it two thousand times more," said Edison. "You have only found out that there are two thousand ways in which it cannot be done."

### 3471     *Simple but Great*

One day while in Paris, physician René Laënnec observed children tapping signals to one another from opposite ends of a hollow log. The action gave him an idea, and before the end of 1816 he had invented the stethoscope, a wooden tube with an earpiece that transmitted sounds from the heart and chest more clearly than any means formerly used.

### 3472     *Humbug*

Two boys once tried to play a trick on Charles Darwin. They took the body of a centipede, the wings of a butterfly, the legs of a grasshopper, and the head of a beetle and glued these together to form a weird monster. With the creature in a box, they visited Darwin.

"Please, sir, will you tell us what sort of a bug this is?" one boy asked.

The naturalist gave a short glance at the exhibit and a long glance at the boys. "Did it hum?" he inquired solemnly.

The boys replied enthusiastically, in one voice: "Oh, yes, sir."

"Well, then," Darwin declared, "it is a humbug."

### 3473 *Don't Be Fooled*

We in America have had too much experience of life to fool ourselves into pretending that all men are equal in ability, in character, in intelligence, in ambition. That was part of the claptrap of the French Revolution. We have grown to understand that all we can hope to assure to the individual through government is liberty, justice, equality of opportunity, and stimulation to service. —*Herbert Hoover*

### 3474 *Life*

> A walking shadow, a poor player,
> That struts and frets his hour upon the stage,
> And then is heard no more.
> —*William Shakespeare*

### 3475 *A Strong School System*

We have to have good teachers. We have to have good parents. And we have to have strong administration if we're going to do the job. If any one of those falter, it threatens our ability to do our job. If we want excellence for students, and we all do, then we have to have excellence in teaching, and we have to have excellence in parenting as well.—*Ruth B. Love, general superintendent, Chicago Public Schools*

### 3476 *Correct English*

Noah Webster, the maker of the dictionary, carried his exact knowledge as to the meaning of words into ordinary speech. A story told of him—which is, we believe, untrue—illustrates the point.

Noah's wife entered the kitchen, to find him kissing the cook.

"Why, Noah," she exclaimed, "I am surprised!"

The lexicographer regarded his wife disapprovingly, and rebuked her: "You are astonished—I am surprised."

### 3477 *Could Use Him*

A horse-trader once said to Henry Ward Beecher: "I have a good family horse I want to sell you. He is a good carriage horse. He works double with any other horse and on either side of the tongue. In short, he is a good all around horse and a good team worker.

Mr. Beecher replied: "My friend, I can't buy your horse, but I would like to have him as a member of my church!"—*Central Baptist Church Bulletin, Hot Springs, Arkansas*

### 3478   *Research*

It is a popular conception that to make rapid progress it is only necessary to concentrate large quantities of men and money on a problem. Years ago when we were developing the first electrically operated cash register I ran into this type of thinking. My boss was going to Europe and wanted the job finished before he took off. "Give Kettering twice as many men so he can finish it up in half the time." When I objected to this idea he asked, "Why can't you? If ten men can dig ten rods of ditch in a day, then surely twenty men can dig twenty rods."

I replied, "Do you think if one hen can hatch a setting of eggs in three weeks, two hens can hatch a setting in a week and a half? This is more a job of hatching eggs than digging ditches.—*Charles F. Kettering*

### 3479   *Young Inventor*

A fifteen-year-old boy who dropped out of grammar school invented earmuffs. In 1877, at the age of nineteen, Chester Greenwood patented his "ear protectors." His invention allowed him to earn a fortune as he produced millions during World War I. Soldiers were issued earmuffs, which were clipped below their helmets.

### 3480   *Satisfaction*

There's no thrill in easy sailing when the sky is clear and blue. There's no joy in merely doing things which anyone can do. But there's great satisfaction that is mighty sweet to take, when you reach a destination that you thought you couldn't make.

### 3481   *Only His Genius*

By the time Oscar Wilde arrived from England to make his first tour in America, he had built up a reputation as an egotist.

"Have you anything to delcare?" asked a custom's official while making a routine inspection of Wilde's luggage.

"Nothing," replied Wilde. "I have nothing to declare, my good man." Here he paused for a moment, then added, "Except, of course, my genius."

### 3482   *That's Telling Him*

Former Secretary of State John Foster Dulles, whose anecdotes are almost collector's items, tells of a social climber who persuaded a friend with only a dubious perch on the social ladder to take him to the home of a socially established Washington figure.

During the visit the host took his callers into the library to show them his collection of French authors.

"Do you like Proust?" he asked the climber.

"No, I like Tokay," was the response.

At the first opportunity the more advanced climber turned to the other. "You and your big mouth!" he protested. "Proust isn't a wine; it's a kind of cheese."

### 3483    *Free and Private Enterprise*

If someone comes to me and asks, "What are you going to do for us small businessmen?" I'd say, "The only thing I'm going to do for you is to make you freer to do things for yourselves."—*Margaret Thatcher*

### 3484    *That Helped*

A French taxicab driver once had Sir Arthur Conan Doyle as a passenger. He took him from the station to a hotel, and when he received his fare, he said, "Merci, Monsieur Conan Doyle."

"Why, how do you know my name?" asked Sir Arthur.

"Well, sir," replied the taxi man, "I have seen in the papers that you were coming from the south of France to Paris. Your general appearance told me that you were English. Your hair had been clearly last cut by a barber in the south of France. I put these indications together and guessed at once that it was you."

"That is very remarkable," replied Sir Arthur. "You have no other evidence to go upon?"

"Well," hesitated the man, "there was also the fact that your name was on your luggage."

### 3485    *Ambition*

One of the reasons for the restraints on power is to control ambition. The democratic system recognizes that ambition always has been and always will be a vital force in human affairs. It seeks to harness this force to the best interests of the people. Similarly, the private enterprise economy, with its rewards for performance and risk-taking, pools the efforts generated by personal ambition into a general effort to produce an endowment in which everyone shares.—*The Royal Bank of Canada*

### 3486    *Saving*

Confidence in the value of money is one of the greatest spurs to economic progress, because it is an incentive to save, and it is our people's savings over the years—large and small savings alike—which have built up our country.—*George M. Humphrey*

### 3487    *Hard to Believe*

Here is a Ford story that Mr. Ford told on himself:

Before the war he was in the habit of using a Model T driving back and forth between his factory in Detroit and his home in Dearborn. One evening, on his way home, he came across a man who could not get his Ford started. Henry stopped, got out, and tinkered with the balky motor. In a few minutes he had it running again.

The man, very much pleased, offered $5 for his trouble, but the money was politely declined. The man insisted, remarking that it would have cost him $10 to have the car towed back to the city.

Ford said, "Keep your money, my friend. I really have more now than I can possibly spend."

The man looked astonished, and exclaimed, "What? You have that much money and ride around in one of these blankety-blank puddle jumpers?"—*Capper's Weekly*

### 3488    *Decadence*

Alcoholism and race consciousness are two conspicuous sources of danger to Western civilization. A mixture of atheism, materialism, socialism and alcoholism have been the cause of the decline and decay of nineteen out of twenty-one civilizations.—*Arnold Toynbee*

### 3489    *The Trivial*

It is not merely the trivial which clutters our lives but the important as well.
—*Anne Morrow Lindbergh*

### 3490    *Work*

If we are to survive as a great nation, a land of opportunity and a place where our children and grandchildren can grow and prosper, we must get back to some of the old-fashioned American virtues. One such value is that able-bodied people ought to work for a living.—*Senator Herman E. Talmadge*

### 3491    *Property*

Property is the fruit of labor; property is desirable. It is a positive good in the world. That some should be rich shows that others may become rich, and hence is just encouragement to industry and enterprise. Let not him who is houseless pull down the house of another, but let him work diligently and build one for himself, thus by example assuring that his own shall be safe from violence when built.—*Abraham Lincoln*

### 3492    *All the Riches*

What have I learned in these fifty years? What have I worked for? Is it money? No, it's not money. I'll tell you what has given me happiness and peace of soul. It's the satisfaction of living a life that will make you stand well in the opinion of your fellow citizens; of having their good wishes, and their love, and their respect. That's all there is in life, and with that you've all the riches in the world.
—*Charles M. Schwab*

### 3493    *Unusual*

Nearly all people like talking; the more refined ones can also force themselves to listen.—*Stanley Stefan*

### 3494    *It Took Work*

Katherine Anne Porter spent twenty years writing *Ship of Fools.*

Isaac Asimov: "I can spend 300 hours on a science-fiction novel. A mystery takes 200 hours. But I can write a normal-length nonfiction book in 70 hours."

Sinclair Lewis labored for seventeen years on *Main Street,* taking the manuscript through three complete rewrites.

Margaret Mitchell rewrote the first chapter of *Gone With the Wind* 70 times.

Ernest Hemingway rewrote the last page of *A Farewell to Arms* 39 times.

Mickey Spillane: "My speed depends on the state of my bank account. When it's necessary I can write 5,000 words a day."

Plato redrafted the opening sentence of *The Republic* 50 times.—*Writer's Digest*

### 3495    *The Educated Man*

How is the educated man to show the fruits of his education in times like these? He must keep his head, and use it. He must never push other people around, not aquiesce when he sees it done. He must decline to be carried away by waves of hysteria. He must be prepared to pay the penalty of unpopularity. . . . He must insist that freedom is the chief glory of mankind and that to repress it is in effect to repress the human spirit.—*Robert Maynard Hutchins*

### 3496    *A Mother's Son*

During World War II, Brigadier General Theodore Roosevelt, Jr., was waiting at an airport for a plane. A sailor stepped to a ticket window and asked for a seat on the same plane, explaining, "I want to see my mother; I haven't much time."

The indifferent person at the ticket window was not impressed. "There's a war on, you know," she replied.

At this point General Roosevelt, who had overheard the conversation, stepped to the window and told her to give the sailor his seat. A friend said, "Teddy, aren't you in a hurry, too?"

"It's a matter of rank," came the reply. "I'm only a general; he's a son!"

### 3497    *Somebody Was Wrong*

F. W. Woolworth, founder of the five-and-dime chain, was once hired as a janitor for 50 cents a day by a retail-store owner who didn't think Woolworth had enough business sense to wait on customers.

When Zane Grey was an unknown trying to sell his book manuscripts, a publisher told him he had no ability for writing fiction; and Louisa May Alcott, author of *Little Women,* was a tomboy marked by her fellow townspeople as a girl who would never amount to much. A publisher once told her to give up the idea of writing.

The first time George Gershwin ever played the piano on the stage, he was laughed out of the theater by both the audience and his fellow performers.

### 3498    *Don't Forget Me*

The members of a crew on a submarine were about to take battle stations, and the ship's captain was worried about a young seaman second class whose job it was to close the watertight doors between certain compartments. The boy didn't seem to realize his responsibility, and the captain undertook to impress him. He told him that if he failed in his job the ship might be lost. Some of the men aboard were specialists, and it had cost Uncle Sam thousands to train each of them; they might be drowned.

"So you see how important it is that you do your job."

"Yes, sir, and then there's me, too," replied the lad.

The captain stopped worrying.

### 3499    *My Days*

My heart leaps up when I behold
    A rainbow in the sky:
So was it when my life began,
So is it now I am a man,
So be it when I shall grow old
    Or let me die!
The Child is father of the Man:
And I could wish my days to be
Bound each to each by natural piety.
        —*William Wordsworth*

### 3500    *Life*

Fear not that thy life shall come to an end, but rather fear that it shall never have a beginning.—*Cardinal Newman*

### 3501    *Small Beginnings*

Sometimes the struggle seems hardly worthwhile. Yet history tells us that out of persistence in times of discouragement comes success. A few cases are given below to illustrate:

J. L. Kraft was a grocery clerk who started with a capital of $65 to peddle cheese from a one-horse wagon.

In 1869 H. J. Heinz planted a small plot of horseradish; he and two women and a boy grated and bottled the root.

Coca-Cola was first made in the kitchen of an old home adjoining Mr. Pemberton's Drug Store.

E. A. Stuart, president of Carnation Milk Products Company, drove a team of mules in a construction gang on the Santa Fe. Later, he ran a grocery store, and in 1899 bought a bankrupt condensery situated in Kent, Washington.

### 3502    *That Should Help*

George Bernard Shaw was having lunch in a London restaurant one day when an orchestra struck up a particularly noisy tune. Without any intermission, the musicians followed it with another. Shaw called the head waiter and asked, "Does the orchestra play requests?"

"Yes, sir," the man replied. "Is there something you would like them to play?"

"There is," replied Shaw. "Ask them to play dominoes until I have finished eating."

### 3503    *His Day Came*

I will study and prepare myself, and someday my chance will come.—*Abraham Lincoln*

### 3504    *Capital*

In this country and in the whole world, we are short of capital—which means savings.—*George M. Humphrey*

### 3505    *The Most Dreaded Evil*

Of all the evils to public liberty, war is perhaps the most to be dreaded, because it comprises and develops every other. War is the parent of armies; from these proceed debts and taxes. And armies and debts and taxes are the known instruments for bringing the many under the dominion of the few. In war, too, the discretionary power of the executive is extended; its influence in dealing out offices, honors, and emoluments is multiplied; and all the means of seducing the minds are added to those of subduing the force of the people! No nation could preserve its freedom in the midst of continual warfare.—*James Madison*

### 3506    *A Happy Marriage*

I am convinced that in normal people the requirements for a happy marriage —understanding, tolerance, kindness, unselfishness—almost always exist in adequate quantities. When these qualities become stifled or blocked by lack of maturity, lack of self-discipline, lack of control, trouble begins.—*Norman Vincent Peale*

### 3507    *Tax*

When you tax something, you get less of it. When you reward something, you get more of it. In America today, we tax work, thrift, investment, employment, production, incentives, and success, while we reward non-work, unemployment, welfare, spending, consumption, leisure, idleness, and mediocrity.—*Jack Kemp*

### 3508    *The Unique Ben Franklin*

If you ask the next person you see who is generally known as the father of his country, the answer will undoubtedly be "George Washington." But that distinction could be given to Benjamin Franklin.

No figure in American history compares with Franklin, whose brilliant character marked the early days of the nation. His patriotic, scientific, and literary achievements have made him the "patron saint" of many American industries.

It is interesting to list some of the groups that claim Franklin as their own: printers, the labor movement, heating and ventilating engineers, optometrists (for his bifocal lenses), librarians, cartoonists, spelling reformers, daylight savers, and humorists.

Ben Franklin is the father of much of what our country is today.

### 3509    *It Still Is!*

In 1858 you could, for the first time, send a letter by overland coach to the Pacific Coast. The specified running time for the 2,800 miles from Tipton, Missouri, to San Francisco, California, was twenty-five days. And that was a mighty fast schedule in those times!

### 3510    *Defense*

The problem in defense is how far you can go without destroying from within what you are trying to defend from without.—*Dwight D. Eisenhower*

### 3511    *He Rose Again*

A man was going down a street in Chicago when in a store window he saw a very beautiful picture of the crucifixion. As he gazed spellbound at the vividly pictured story, he suddenly became conscious that at his side stood a young boy. The boy, too, was gazing at the picture, and his tense expression made the man know that "The Crucifixion" had really gripped the eager little soul.

Touching the boy on the shoulder, the man said, "Sonny, what does it mean?"

"Doncha know?" he answered, his face full of the marvel of the man's ignorance. "That there man is Jesus, an' them others is Roman soldiers, an' the woman what's cryin' is His mother, an'—" he added, "they killed 'im!"

The man was loath to leave the window, but he could not tarry always at such a tragic scene, so he turned away and walked down the street. In a few moments he heard footsteps, and there came rushing up the boy.

"Say, mister," he exlaimed breathlessly, "I forget to tell you, but He rose again!"—*Selection from "Inspiration, Vista, California," Sunshine Magazine*

### 3512    *The Merit of Experience*

The merit of the following (experiences) are: at a wedding to cause merriment; among mourners, to keep silent; at a lecture, to listen; at a session, to arrive early; at teaching, to concentrate; in time of fasting, to give charity.—*Talmud*

### 3513    *The Humanitarian*

It was sleeting, and slushy underfoot. Pedestrians were hurrying along Forty-second Street in New York with their coat collars up about their ears, scarcely glancing at passers-by. A young black man, carrying a heavy valise in one hand and a huge suitcase in the other, was hurrying toward Grand Central Station, slipping and skidding as he went. Suddenly a hand reached out and took the valise, and at the same time a pleasant but positive voice said, "Let me take one, brother! Bad weather to have to carry things." The black man was reluctant, but the young white man insisted, with the remark, "I'm going your way." All the way to the station the two chatted like two old friends.

Years later, Booker T. Washington, who told the story, said, "That was my introduction to Theodore Roosevelt."—*Maeanna Chesterton-Mongle in "The Chaplain," Sunshine Magazine*

### 3514    *Money*

Money may be the husk of many things, but not the kernel. It brings you food, but not appetite; medicine, but not health; acquaintances, but not friends; servants, but not loyalty; days of joy, but not peace or happiness.—*Henrik Ibsen*

### 3515    *Preparing for Government*

No man undertakes a trade he has not learned, even the meanest; yet everyone thinks himself sufficiently qualified for the hardest of all trades—that of government.—*Socrates*

### 3516    *Exchanged Speeches*

Chauncey Depew always took great delight in telling this story on himself:

Mark Twain and Mr. Depew once went abroad on the same ship. When the boat was a few days out, they were both invited to a dinner, and when speech-making time came, Mark Twain was the first on the program. He spoke twenty minutes, and was a great hit. Then Mr. Depew was announced. He stood up and said:

"Mr. Toastmaster and ladies and gentlemen: Before this dinner Mr. Clemens and I made an agreement to exchange speeches. He has just delivered my speech, and I thank you for the pleasant manner in which you received it. I regret to say, with apologies to Mr. Clemens, that I have lost the notes on his speech, and cannot remember anything he was to say." Then he sat down amid great laughter.

The next day an Englishman who had been one of the party at the dinner approached Mark Twain, and said, "Mr. Clemens, I consider you were much imposed upon last night. I have always heard Mr. Depew was a clever man, but really that speech of his you gave last night struck me as being the most consummate rot."

### 3517  *Ordinary People*

People who change the world are not usually the self-styled leaders of men, nor yet the willing martyrs who go singing to the stake. They are the very ordinary people who, in diffidence and apprehension, pursue the course they have set themselves and who have no other reason for doing so than that they would despise themselves if they gave up.—*Peter Quince*

### 3518  *Fathers*

What shall you give to one small boy? A glamorous game, a tinseled toy, a Barlow knife, a puzzle pack, a train that runs on a curving track? A picture book, a real live pet . . . no, there's plenty of time for such things yet. Give him a day for his very own—just one small boy and his dad alone. A walk in the woods, a romp in the park, a fishing trip from dawn to dark; give the gift that only you can—the companionship of his old man! Games are outgrown, and toys decay—but he'll never forget if you give him a day.

### 3519  *Excellence*

I don't think it makes sense to strive for perfection. Perfection is not attainable. I believe totally in striving for excellence, and I think there is a great deal of difference between the two. And although we're striving for excellence, we're sensible about our goals as well as ambitions because one of the most frustrating things in the world is to set your goals so high that you have no chance of reaching them.—*Bart Starr*

### 3520  *No More*

It is time for the American people to look their government straight in the eye and say, "No more! We will make the decisions about our lives. You protect us from foreign aggressors and domestic criminals, give us a stable currency and court of law, and we'll do the rest."—*Gerald Ford*

### 3521  *Impossible*

A college professor worked for many years on an invention and at last perfected it. He tramped across New England, trying to interest capitalists and political figures in this device of his for making the human voice travel miles along a wire. He was Alexander Graham Bell, and he called his invention the telephone.

Bell knew his invention could work. Scientists had admitted it was feasible. He was sorely in need of money to float his invention. But most of the neighbors laughed at him. It was, of course, idiotic to suppose the human voice could be carried along a wire and be heard for many miles, or even for a single mile.

### 3522 *Piety in the Kitchen*

The late Archbishop Temple, when he was primate of England, related this story. One morning, in a house where he was a guest, he heard from the kitchen a voice singing lustily, "Nearer, My God to Thee." He reflected on the piety of the woman who went about her morning tasks to the strains of the noble hymn, and so spoke of it to his host.

"Oh, yes," replied the host. "That's the hymn she boils the eggs to—three verses for soft boil and five for hard."

### 3523 *Federal Aid*

Federal aid is just like a man getting a blood transfusion by taking the blood out of his right arm, putting it in his left, and spilling about half of it on the way over.—*A. Sydney Herlong, Jr.*

### 3524 *The Price of a Laugh*

A Genoese mariner, Christopher Columbus, worked out a plan whereby he might "reach the East by sailing west." He carried his project to the Portuguese royal court. Portugal, just then, was Spain's rival for the colonial supremacy of the known earth.

King John of Portugal saw that the success of the scheme might make Portugal the greatest of all nations. Tentatively he agreed to send Columbus on the expedition. But his councilors showed King John that he would be laughed at from one end of Europe to the other if he financed such a crazy enterprise. So Columbus was sent away.

The mariner went next to Portugal's rival nation, Spain. There, too, the wise men laughed loudly at his idea. But Queen Isabella was not afraid of being laughed at. She declared she would pawn her jewels, if necessary, to back the expedition.

As a result of her contempt for laughter, America was discovered.

### 3525 *Young Acquaintances*

"Sir," said Dr. Johnson, "I love the acquaintance of young people; because, in the first place, I don't like to think myself growing old. In the next place, young acquaintances must last the longest, if they do last."—*James Boswell*

3526    *Little Opportunities*

Doing the best you can with the little opportunities that come along, will get you further than idly wishing for the big chance that may never arrive.

3527    *No Mystery*

Saving money and thereby creating capital is no mystery. It simply means that someone must deny himself the pleasure of spending some part of his paycheck and so save it.—*George M. Humphrey*

3528    *A Man for the Ages*

A dying mother touched with loving fingers the tear-stained face of her boy and whispered, "Be somebody, Abe."

A lanky, homely lad stretched out on the bare floor before the open fire, reading, thinking, far into the night.

A splitter of rails, a champion wrestler, a farmer, a storekeeper, a teller of funny stories who could "make a cat laught."

A young lover turning away from the grave of his sweetheart with the face of a man grown old.

A candidate for office whose first speech was "as short and sweet as the old woman's dance."

An awkward orator with coat sleeves and trousers too short, but with a spiritual light in his eyes.

A man who rode in the day coaches while his opponent traveled in a special train.

A man who was found down on his knees playing marbles with a group of boys when news came that he had been elected president of the United States.

A gaunt, tired man on the rear platform of his train in a drizzling rain, bidding good-bye to the neighbors he loved. A sincere man with one desperate idea—to save his country.

A writer of tender letters to widowed mothers who gave their sons for the cause. A pardoner of boys who could not be blamed if their legs were weak. A man with infinite patience, "who held on through blame and faltered not at praise."

A man so humble he said he would hold a general's horse if that general would win victories. A man who loved all men, and lived and preached "charity for all and malice toward none."

A man whose death set free for all mankind a great soul that shall bless and benefit, inspire and encourage, until time shall be no more.

Abraham Lincoln!—*Sunshine Magazine*

### 3529    Government Policy

There is—in world affairs—a steady course to be followed between an assertion of strength that is truculent and a confession of helplessness that is cowardly.
There is—in our affairs at home—a middle way between untrammeled freedom
of the individual and the demands for the welfare of the whole nation.—*Dwight
D. Eisenhower*

### 3530    Leisure

To some people "leisure" is time when they can't think of anything to do; to
others, their work is such fun that it is leisure. We all like to spend some time
for which we don't have to account, but to get the most out of life, we need to
keep these unaccounted hours at a minimum. As the Roman proverb says, "It
is difficult to rest if you are doing nothing."—*Royal Bank of Canada Monthly
Letter*

### 3531    Progress

Thanks to our industrial ingenuity and know-how, we live longer, better, and
more enjoyably these days. Science, electronics, and such, march on—but still
nobody has been able to figure out a way for a fireman to get downstairs faster
than by sliding down the brass pole. And that began in 1889.

### 3532    The Real Master

Leonardo da Vinci displayed great artistic talent at a very tender age. Perceiv-
ing the boy's unusual gift, his parents put him under the tutelage of an accomplished painter.

One day, while the old teacher was working on a painting called "The Baptism
of Christ," he asked his pupil to paint an angel in the picture. When it was
completed, Leonardo called his instructor to examine it. The teacher stood
dumfounded at the child's skill for many minutes. Then he laid down his brush
and vowed never to paint again.

When the work of a pupil was superior to that of his teacher, he thought, pride
itself demanded that the lesser of the two should stop!

### 3533    Complaining

What is wealth? Money—or what's worth money? Would you take a million
dollars for your health, or your eyesight, or your wife and children? Certainly
not! Well, then, what do you mean by complaining of having too little? Good
heavens, man, you're a millionaire!—*Channing Pollock*

### 3534    Prophecy?

Lenin, who was nobody's fool, once said, "Germany will arm herself out of
existence, the British Empire will expand itself out of existence, and the United
States will loan itself out of existence.—*Louis Bromfield*

### 3535     Contempt

John Marshall, pleading a case before the bar, was once fined $30 for contempt of court because of a slighting remark he made about the presiding judge.

With a profuse apology and a low bow Marshall said: "Your Honor, I have the greatest respect for this court and the judge who presides over it. I intend to carry out every wish of this court, sir, and I will therefore pay this fine immediately.

"As it happens, I have not the full amount of thirty dollars with me at the moment and since no one in this courtroom knows me better than yourself, Your Honor, I must ask you to lend me that amount so that I may pay off this assessment at once."

The judge cleared his throat and then recovered his wit. Turning to the clerk he said in his sternest voice: "Clerk, remit that fine. The United States government can better afford to lose thirty dollars than I!"

### 3536     That's the Reason

The road is strewn with motorcars, and folks would like to know why dangers stare us in the face where'er we chance to go. Investigations come galore, committees probe the cause; men check the car, its bolts and brakes, and scan the motor laws. They search the reasons, buried deep, but in the end reveal that accidents are mostly caused by the nut that holds the wheel.

### 3537     Never Return

Four things come not back: the spoken word, the sped arrow, the past, the neglected opportunity.

### 3538     The Philosophy of Confucius

The men of old, when they wished their virtues to shine throughout the land, first had to govern their states well. To govern their states well, they first had to establish harmony in their families. To establish harmony in their families, they first had to discipline themselves. To discipline themselves, they first had to set their minds in order. To set their minds in order, they first had to make their purpose clear and sincere.

To make their purpose sincere, they first had to extend their knowledge to the utmost. Such knowledge is acquired through a careful investigation of things. For with things investigated, knowledge becomes complete. With knowledge complete, the purpose becomes sincere. With the purpose sincere, the mind is set in order. With the mind set in order, there is real self-discipline. With real self-discipline, the family achieves harmony. With harmony in the family, the state becomes well governed. With the state well governed, there is peace throughout the land.—*Magazine Corporation*

### 3539    *Government*

The Federal government can give to people only what it has previously taken from them, minus the cost of administration.—*Allan B. Kline*

### 3540    *They Hear Nothing*

The talkative listen to no one, for they are ever speaking. And the first evil that attends those who know not how to be silent is that they hear nothing.—*Plutarch*

### 3541    *Youth and Age*

I know of no fallacy greater, or more widely believed, than the statement that youth is the happiest time of life. As we advance in years we really grow happier, if we live intelligently. The universe is spectacular, and it is a free show. Increase of difficulties and responsibilities strengthens and enriches the mind and adds to the variety of life. To live abundantly is like climbing a mountain or a tower. To say that youth is happier than maturity is like saying that the view from the bottom of the tower is better than the view from the top. As we ascend, the range of our view widens immensely; the horizon is pushed farther away. Finally, as we reach the summit it is as if we had the world at our feet.—*William Lyon Phelps*

### 3542    *Labor and Thought*

Men give me credit for some genius. All the genius I have lies in this: When I have a subject in hand, I study it profoundly. Day and night it is before me. My mind becomes pervaded with it. Then the effort which I have made is what people are pleased to call the "fruit of genius." It is the fruit of labor and thought. —*Alexander Hamilton*

### 3543    *Unexpected Encouragement*

I believe that any man's life will be filled with constant and unexpected encouragement if he makes up his mind to do his level best each day, and as nearly as possible reaches the high water mark of pure and useful living.—*Booker T. Washington*

### 3544    *Plodding Mediocrity*

The late Justice Cardozo once said that he was an example of "plodding mediocrity." He meant he was an ordinary person, and such progress as he had made was the result of being on the job every day.

This accounts for nearly all success. The best jobs and the largest fortunes are often the possession of ordinary people.

3545    *Eternal Power*

Let me tell you that if the people remain right, your public men can never betray you. If, in the brief term of office I shall be wicked or foolish, if you remain right and true and honest, you cannot be betrayed. My power is temporary and fleeting; yours as eternal as the principles of liberty.—*Abraham Lincoln*

3546    *Time Rushes On*

"It seems but yesterday," he would say, "that I was as young as you are. We imagine that we can turn the pages slowly, one by one, pausing at each paragraph. But it is not like that, believe me. The pages are caught by a gust of wind, a hurricane, and they flutter and rush through our fingers."—*Sir Harold Nicolson*

3547    *Who Is Answered First?*

Whoever prays on behalf of a fellowman, while himself being in need of the same thing, will be answered first.—*Talmud*

3548    *About Face*

The late President Wilson was very fond of homespun limericks and compiled quite a collection of them. The following was one of his favorites:

"For beauty, I'm not a great star. There are others more handsome by far. But my face, I don't mind it, for I am behind it; it's those in front get the jar!"

3549    *Serious*

It is not so important to be serious as it is to be serious about some important things. The monkey has a look of seriousness which would do credit to a college student, but the monkey is serious because he itches.—*Robert Maynard Hutchins*

3550    *The Power of Ideals*

The power of ideals is incalculable. We see no power in a drop of water. But let it get into a crack in the rock and be turned to ice, and it splits the rock; turned into steam, it drives the pistons of the most powerful engines. Something has happened to it which makes active and effective the power that is latent in it.—*Albert Schweitzer*

3551    *More Important*

Married people will appreciate the story of how Mrs. Albert Einstein replied to someone who asked her if she understood her husband's theory of relativity.

"No," she said, "I do not understand it. But what is more important to me, I understand Dr. Einstein."—*Answers*

3552    *Harmony*

The complexity of modern civilization is a daily lesson in the necessity of not pressing any claim too far, of understanding opposing points of view, of seeking to reconcile them, of conducting matters so that there is some kind of harmony in a plural society.—*Walter Lippmann*

3553    *What Is a Man?*

A man is the sum of his actions, of what he has done, of what he can do. Nothing else.—*André Malraux*

3554    *Beauty and Wonder*

The longer I live the more my mind dwells upon the beauty and the wonder of the world. I hardly know which feeling leads, wonderment or admiration.— *John Burroughs*

3555    *Most Important*

Andrew Carnegie was once asked by a reporter what he considered most important in industry: labor, capital, or brains. With a laugh Carnegie replied: "Which is the most important leg of a three-legged stool?"

3556    *What Is Right?*

It is not who is right that is of the greatest importance, but what is right.

3557    *Time and Patience*

> Never a tear bedims the eye
> That time and patience will not dry.
> —*Bret Harte*

3558    *The Facts of Life*

We need a campaign of education so that the public will better understand the facts of life about federal spending. We all must realize that there is no bottomless well of unlimited money in Washington. The only government money that any person can get—whether from Washington, from the city or county treasurer, or from the town selectman—must first come from the taxes he pays out of his own pocket.—*George M. Humphrey*

3559    *No Quarrel*

On his deathbed, Thoreau was asked by a pious aunt, "Henry, have you made your peace with God?"
Henry replied tranquilly, "I didn't know we'd quarreled."

### 3560    *The Soil of Ignorance*

It is in the soil of ignorance that poverty is planted. It is in the soil of ignorance that disease flourishes. It is in the soil of ignorance that racial and religious strife take root. It is in the soil of ignorance that Communism brings forth the bitter fruit of tyranny.—*Lyndon Johnson*

### 3561    *Like Tourists*

Crowds today are breathlessly snatching at pleasure. We go through life as some tourists go through Europe—so anxious to see the next sight, the next picture, the next mountain peak, that they never stop to fill their senses with the beauty of the present one.—*Courtney Savage*

### 3562    *Knowledge*

When you know a thing, to hold that you know it, and when you do not know a thing, to allow that you do not know it, this is knowledge.—*Confucius*

### 3563    *Power*

The power of the state is measured by the power that men surrender to it.—*Felix Morley*

### 3564    *Try Again*

Let the man who has to make his fortune in life remember this maxim: Attacking is the only secret. Dare, and the world always yields. If it beats you sometimes, dare it again and again and it will succumb.—*William Makepeace Thackeray*

### 3565    *The Superior Man*

The superior man will watch over himself when he is alone. He examines his heart that there may be nothing wrong there; and that he may have no cause for dissatisfaction with himself.—*Confucius*

### 3566    *Where to Begin*

There's only one corner of the universe you can be certain of improving, and that's your own self. So you have to begin there, not outside, not on other people. That comes afterwards, when you have worked on your own corner.—*Aldous Huxley*

### 3567    *Time Heals*

Time heals griefs and quarrels, for we change and are no longer the same persons. Neither the offender nor the offended are any more themselves. It is like a nation which we have provoked, but meet again after two generations.—*Blaise Pascal*

3568    *Optimist*

There is something good in all weathers. If it doesn't happen to be good for my work today, it's good for some other man's today, and will come around for me tomorrow.—*Charles Dickens*

3569    From the errors of others a wise man corrects his own.—*Publilius Syrus*

3570    After you travel through some parts of the world, you realize how lucky you are to live in this terrible country of ours.

3571    Some people believe in law and order if they can lay down the law and give the orders.

3572    After you save to pay your income tax, all you need to do is borrow enough to live on.

3573    With taxes as high as they are, you don't have to pass a civil service examination to work for the government.

3574    To have average intelligence is to be less stupid than half the people and more stupid than the other half.

3575    Nothing makes an argument more interesting than ignorance.

3576    If a person keeps his mouth shut, he can fool a lot of people.

3577    A man should be educated enough to know that education alone is not enough.

3578    We keep on making history because we don't learn from it.

3579    Most of us don't want what we can afford and can't afford what we want.

3580    It's strange how a person is smart enough to make money and not smart enough to hang on to it.

3581    A man ought to be at least as considerate of his family as he is of strangers in his office.

3582    Grief is a form of unhappiness that comforts.

3583    A young man's attitude toward life helps to determine his altitude.

3584    Good times are when you can get enough credit to live beyond your means.

3585    If you help someone in trouble, he will remember you—the next time he is in trouble.

3586    Do something for somebody every day for which you do not get paid. —*Albert Schweitzer*

3587    To be content with little is difficult; to be content with much, impossible.

3588    He who would improve mankind must start with himself.

3589    Most of us can stand a lot of trouble when it happens to someone else.

3590    The secret of being a bore is to tell everything you know—and that may take less time than you think.

3591    Your reputation depends on the company you keep and on the company you don't keep.

3592    Most of those who would like to move mountains don't like to practice on the little hills.

3593    When opportunity knocks, some people are in the backyard looking for four-leaf clovers.

3594    A person may be worth a million dollars and still be worthless.

3595    One good thing about an enemy is that he never asks for a loan or your endorsement on his note.

3596    What many people would like is an economic system that gives them more than they deserve.

3597    One fascinating thing about a luxury is that it always suggests another to keep you broke.

3598    *Modern war:* Destroy a country; restore a country.

3599    A man may know his own mind and still know next to nothing.

3600    A philosopher is a person who can make ignorance sound profound.

3601    You can be positive about anything of which others are as ignorant as you are.

3602    To some people truth is not only stranger than fiction but it's a total stranger.

3603    In life you are more apt to get what you expect than what you want.

3604    There are few things as rare as a well-spent life.

3605    Hard work is respectable but not popular.

3606    Never worry about a competitor who imitates you, because he can't pass you while following in your tracks.

3607    Laziness is an overwhelming desire for physical repose and mental serenity.

3608    If you want to relax, you have to work at it.

3609    There are many ways to be happy, but if you stay out of debt you won't need to know the others.

3610    One may live as a conqueror, a king, or a magistrate, but one must die as a man.

3611    The State cannot get a cent for any man without taking it from some other man. . . . The latter is the Forgotten Man.—*William Graham Sumner*

3612    We learn nothing from history except that we learn nothing from history.—*Heinrich Heine*

3613    No one has so big a house that he does not need a good neighbor.

3614    The family, as far as I'm concerned, is the whole bag. I've never lost my own sense of family. It's all I've ever really cared about.—*Howard Cosell*

3615    Wisdom enables one to be thrifty without being stingy, and generous without being wasteful.

3616    There is a time when we must firmly choose the course we will follow, or the relentless drift of events will make the decision.—*Herbert V. Prochnow*

3617    The surest way to destroy your enemies is to make them your friends.

3618    Joseph Mainer, a French gardener, is credited with inventing steel-reinforced cement after observing that a five-foot stem of wheat was able to hold heavy grain upright in high winds.

3619    For, lo, the winter is past, the rain is over and gone; the flowers appear on the earth; the time of the singing of birds is come.—*Song of Solomon*

3620    I've taught our children that having money is no excuse for not doing a fair share of work. All the children had regular chores around the house and they were expected to do them without question.—*Lawrence Welk*

3621    If you just make something to sell, you would be better employed doing something else. But if you make something that will do a specific thing, and do it well, then you are helping people.

3622    You can't help a person uphill without getting closer to the top yourself.

3623    Faults are the easiest things to find in others.

3624    Look not sorrowfully into the past; it comes not back again. Wisely improve the present; it is thine. Go forth to meet the shadowy future without fear, and with a manly heart.—*Henry W. Longfellow*

3625    To build an estate, you must learn to spend less than you earn.

3626    Happiness adds and multiplies as you share it with others.

3627    Don't part with your illusions. When they have gone, you may still exist, but you have ceased to live.—*Mark Twain*

3628    I never did anything worth doing by accident, nor did any of my inventions come by accident; they came by plain work.—*Thomas Edison*

3629    An old minister once said that if your troubles aren't big enough to pray about, then they certainly aren't big enough to worry and fret about.

3630    Lukewarm water won't take a locomotive anywhere nor will lukewarm purpose lift a person to any noticeable height of achievement.

3631    The formula for failure—try to please everyone.

3632    You are on the pathway to a successful life when you do more for the community than the community does for you.

3633    Temptation usually comes in through a door that has deliberately been left open.

3634    You can easily judge the character of a man by how he treats those who can do nothing for him or to him.

3635    Some folks with a sympathetic disposition often waste a lot of it on themselves.

3636    The energy and ingenuity of its people are a nation's most important resource.—*David Rockefeller*

3637    It is one of the most beautiful compensations of life that no man can sincerely try to help another without helping himself.—*William Shakespeare*

3638    To forget wrong is the best revenge.

3639    The only people to get even with are those who have helped you.

3640    Anyone who stops learning is old, whether this happens at twenty or at eighty.

3641    Winning isn't everything, but wanting to win is.—*Arnold Palmer*

3642    Morale is when your hands and feet keep on working when your head says it can't be done.

3643    A man must be worse than an infidel who does not see the goodness of God, nor has gratitude enough to acknowledge it.—*George Washington*

3644    We have tended to forget that this country was built up by immigrants who, in the vast majority of cases, came here to escape poverty, oppression, and lack of opportunity at home.—*Alfred E. Smith*

3645    Never accuse others to excuse yourself.

3646    Thoughts are things. Throw stones at people and you get one result. Give them flowers and you get another. Yours is the choice.—*Thomas Dreier*

3647    He who buys what he doesn't need steals from himself.

3648    Tolerance is sometimes the uncomfortable feeling that the other fellow may be right, after all.

3649    There is no tranquilizer in the world more effective than a few kind words.—*Pearl Bailey*

3650    It is hard to resist temptations that we go out of our way looking for.

3651    One of the fallacies of the twentieth century is that the moral character of a nation as a whole can be better than that of its citizens as individuals.

3652    Strange that some of us are satisfied with so little in ourselves but demand so much from others.

3653    Whatever we possess becomes of double value when we share it with others.

3654    No grief is so acute but time ameliorates it.—*Cicero*

3655             To live in hearts we leave behind
Is not to die.
                 —*Thomas Campbell*

3656    All sunshine makes the desert.—*Arabian proverb*

3657    In the evening of my memory I come back to West Point. Always there echoes and re-echoes: duty, honor, country.—*Douglas MacArthur*

3658    The flames kindled on the Fourth of July, 1776, have spread over too much of the globe to be extinguished by the feeble engines of despotism; on the contrary, they will consume these engines and all who work them.—*Thomas Jefferson*

3659    Time is but the stream I go a-fishing in.—*Henry David Thoreau*

3660    I have only one life and it's short enough; why waste it on things I don't want most?—*Louis D. Brandeis*

3661    The great use of life is to spend it for something that will outlast it.—*William James*

3662    There is more to life than increasing its speed.—*Mahatma Gandhi*

3663    The highest wisdom is kindness.—*Talmud*

3664    A man possesses only what he gives away.—*Elie Wiesel*

3665    Man can be as big as he wants. No problem of human destiny is beyond human beings.—*John F. Kennedy*

3666    [We] confused the free with the free and easy.—*Adlai Stevenson*

3667    Never go out to meet trouble. If you will just sit still, nine times out of ten someone will intercept it before it reaches you.

3668    We do not stop playing because we are old; we grow old because we stop playing.

3669    The measure of a man's real character is what he would do if he knew he would never be found out.—*Thomas Babington Macaulay*

3670    When you feel grateful for something others have done for you, why not tell them about it?

3671    Although the world is very full of suffering, it is also full of the overcoming of it.—*Helen Keller*

3672    Death is, after all, the only universal experience except birth.—*Stewart Alsop*

3673    The way to love anything is to realize it might be lost.—*G. K. Chesterton*

3674    Marriage is an indissoluble contract in which one party obtains from the other party more than either ever may hope to repay.—*O. A. Battista, Everybody's Weekly*

3675    Nothing is more simple than greatness; indeed, to be simple is to be great.—*Ralph Waldo Emerson*

3676    A gem cannot be polished without friction, nor a man perfected without adversity.—*Chinese proverb*

3677    The great act of faith is when a man decides that he is not God.—*Justice Oliver Wendell Holmes*

3678    'Tis not what man does which exalts him, but what man would do!—*Robert Browning*

3679    It is well, when one is judging a friend, to remember that he is judging you with the same godlike and superior impartiality.—*Arnold Bennett*

3680    We have to continue to search for knowledge, but we see now that knowledge without wisdom has brought us to the edge of destruction and may at any time push us over the brink.—*Robert Maynard Hutchins*

3681    Man is a little soul carrying around a corpse.—*Epictetus*

3682    We deem those happy who, from the experience of life, have learned to bear its ills without being overcome by them.—*Juvenal*

3683    Hope is itself a species of happiness, and perhaps the chief happiness which this world affords.—*Samuel Johnson*

3684    Man is but a reed, the weakest in nature, but he is a thinking reed.—*Pascal*

3685    It is not marriage that fails; it is people that fail. All that marriage does is show people up.—*Harry Emerson Fosdick*

3686    My reading of history convinces me that most bad government results from too much government.—*Thomas Jefferson*

3687    *Life:* A diary in which every man means to write one story, and writes another.—*Sir James M. Barrie*

3688    But when we play the fool, how wide the theater expands.—*Walter Savage Landor*

3689    *Life:* A vapor that appeareth for a little time then vanisheth away.—
*Bible*

3690    The test of a truly educated man is what he is, and what he thinks, and what his mind absorbs, or dreams, or creates, when he is alone.

3691    Marriage resembles a pair of shears, so joined that they cannot be separated; often moving in opposite directions, yet always punishing anyone who comes between them.—*Sidney Smith*

3692    If we can prevent the government from wasting the labors of the people under the pretense of caring for them, they will be happy.—*Thomas Jefferson*

3693    The richer I get and the more famous I become, the more ordinary I realize I am, and that my only real talent is luck.—*John Travolta*

3694    They said it couldn't be done, but sometimes it doesn't work out that way.—*Casey Stengel*

3695    If your foot slips, you may recover your balance, but if your tongue slips, you cannot recall your words.

3696    Often it pays to make sure you are right, and then keep still.

3697    Words without actions are the assassins of idealism.—*Herbert Hoover*

3698    Happiness is the art of never holding in your mind the memory of any unpleasant thing that has passed.

3699    By necessity, by proclivity—and by delight—we all quote.—*Ralph Waldo Emerson*

3700    He that would live in peace and at ease, must not speak all he knows, nor judge all he sees.—*Benjamin Franklin*

3701    Never answer an angry word in kind. It's the second word that makes the quarrel.

3702    Neglect a personal grievance for forty-eight hours and it will die of starvation.

3703    You cannot repent too soon, because you do not know how soon it may be too late.—*Thomas Fuller*

3704    In war: resolution. In defeat: defiance. In victory: magnanimity. In peace: goodwill.—*Sir Winston Churchill*

3705     Have I not reason to lament what man has made of man?—*William Wordsworth*

3706     The first requisite of a good citizen of this republic of ours is that he shall be ready and willing to pull his own weight.—*Theodore Roosevelt*

3707     No really great man ever thought of himself.—*William Hazlitt*

3708     There is nothing so easy but that it becomes difficult when you do it with reluctance.

3709     What I aspired to be, and was not, comforts me.—*Robert Browning*

3710     Though old the thought and oft exprest, 'tis his at last who says it best. —*James Russell Lowell*

3711     Happiness is inward and not outward; and so it does not depend on what we have, but on what we are.—*Henry van Dyke*

3712     Ambition has but one reward for all: a little power, a little transient fame, a grave to rest in, and a fading name!—*William Winter*

3713     Everybody is his own best physician when it comes to behavior.—*Hans Selye*

3714     American journalists today . . . have been forced and lured out of their normal and proper role in our society. They are becoming not just the critics in the aisle but actors in the play.—*Eric Sevareid*

3715     The world is divided into people who do things and people who get the credit. Try, if you can, to belong to the first group. There's less competition.— *Dwight W. Morrow*

3716     No wise man ever wished to be younger.—*Dean Swift*

3717     Temper gets you into trouble; pride keeps you there.

3718     In three words I can sum up everything I've learned about life. It goes on.—*Robert Frost*

3719     The conservative who resists change is as valuable as the radical who proposes it.—*Will and Ariel Durant*

3720     The difference between the men and the boys in politics is, and always has been, that the boys want to be something, while the men want to do something.—*Eric Sevareid*

3721    There have been many great men that have flattered the people, who ne'er loved them.—*William Shakespeare*

3722    The artist doesn't see things as they are, he sees them as he is.—*Robert Beverly Hale*

3723    America is the greatest force that God has ever allowed to exist on His footstool.—*Dwight D. Eisenhower*

3724    If you think education is expensive, try ignorance.—*Ruth B. Love*

3725    We make a living by what we get, but we make a life by what we give.

3726    Many men owe the grandeur of their lives to their tremendous difficulties.

3727    War would end if the dead could return.—*Stanley Baldwin*

3728    Remember that what you possess in the world will be found at the day of your death to belong to another, but what you are will be yours forever.—*Henry van Dyke*

3729    A man who has taken your time recognizes no debt, yet it is the only debt he can never repay.

3730    The Wright brothers flew right through the smoke screen of impossibility.—*Charles F. Kettering*

3731    There is an old Roman proverb that says, "A learned man has always wealth within himself."

3732    The education of a man is never completed until he dies.—*Robert E. Lee*

3733    Every man of us has all the centuries in him.—*John Morey*

3734    When the people applauded him wildly, he [Phocion] turned to one of his friends and said, "Have I said something foolish?"—*Diogenes Laertius*

3735    An idealist is a person who helps other people to be prosperous.—*Henry Ford*

3736    No man will ever bring out of the Presidency the reputation which carries him into it.—*Thomas Jefferson*

3737    Wit is the rarest quality to be met with among people of education.—*William Hazlitt*

3738  Too many people are thinking of security instead of opportunity. They seem more afraid of life than death.—*James F. Byrnes*

3739  Wise men learn by other men's mistakes, fools by their own.—*H. G. Bohn*

3740  The lust for comfort, that stealthy thing that enters the house as a guest and then becomes a host and then a master.—*Joseph Conrad*

3741  Each morning puts a man on trial and each evening passes judgment. —*Roy L. Smith*

3742  Colors fade, temples crumble, empires fall, but wise words endure.— *Edward Thorndike.*

3743  In time of war the first casualty is truth.—*Boake Carter*

3744
> We are such stuff
> As dreams are made on, and our little life
> Is rounded with a sleep.
> —*William Shakespeare, The Tempest*

3745  Few things are harder to put up with than the annoyance of a good example.—*Mark Twain*

3746  The defect of equality is that we only desire it with our superiors.— *Henry Becque*

3747  A good scare is worth more to a man than good advice.—*E. W. Howe*

3748  A man has made at least a start on discovering the meaning of human life when he plants shade trees under which he knows full well he will never sit. —*D. Elton Trueblood*

3749  The punishment which the wise suffer who refuse to take part in the government, is to live under the government of worse men.—*Plato*

3750  The difficulty is to know conscience from self-interest.—*William Dean Howells*

3751  The first destroyer of the liberties of a people is he who first gave them bounties and largesses.—*Plutarch*

3752
> In sorrow he learned this truth—
> One may return to the place of his birth,
> He cannot go back to his youth.
> —*John Burroughs*

3753    Don't meddle in useless matters; the sun is setting in the West.—*Chinese proverb*

3754    To talk good is not to be good; to do good, that is being good.—*Chinese proverb*

3755    We love flattery, even when we see through it, and are not deceived by it, for it shows that we are important enough to be courted.—*Ralph Waldo Emerson*

# XIV

# Inspiring Quotations and Meditations

### 3756    *There Is an American Idea*

As the world hums with the rising clamor of confusing opinions and propaganda, it is imperative that you and I understand clearly the significance of our citizenship and the American idea upon which it is firmly based.

It came with the Pilgrim fathers who found homes here.

It took as its emblem the freedom of the eagle and the independence of the pioneer.

It made men cry: "Give me liberty or give me death."

It dedicated itself to the care of the needy and sick in this land and in all others.

It brought forth a beneficent downpouring of free thought, free speech, a free press, and a free pulpit.

It proclaimed the dignity of labor and the right to the profits of personal effort.

It created a nation of men with free bodies, free minds, free opinions, and free souls.

It brought forth in only 200 years the greatest wealth and the highest standard of living any people in history have ever known.

That is the American idea.—*Herbert V. Prochnow*

### 3757    *Kindness*

Kindness is the inability to remain at ease in the presence of another person who is ill at ease, the inability to remain comfortable in the presence of another who is uncomfortable, the inability to have peace of mind when one's neighbor is troubled.—*Rabbi Samuel H. Holdenson*

3758    *The Right Choice*

The well-known author James A. Michener, who had been invited to the White House, wrote this elegant regret to Dwight D. Eisenhower: "Dear Mr. President, I received your invitation three days after I had agreed to speak a few words at a dinner honoring the wonderful high school teacher who taught me to write. I know you will not miss me at your dinner, but she might at hers."

The president's gracious reply: "In a lifetime a man can live under 15 or 16 presidents, but a really fine teacher comes into his life but rarely."

3759    *Victory in Defeat*

> Defeat may serve as well as victory
> To shake the soul and let the glory out.
> When the great oak is straining in the wind,
> The boughs drink in new beauty and the trunk
> Sends down a deeper root on the windward side.
> Only the soul that knows the mighty grief
> Can know the mighty rapture. Sorrows come
> To stretch out spaces in the heart for joy.
> —*Edwin Markham*

3760    *MacArthur's Prayer*

Build me a son, O Lord, who will be strong enough to know when he is weak, and brave enough to face himself when he is afraid, one who will be proud and unbending in honest defeat, and humble and gentle in victory.—*Douglas MacArthur*

3761    *The First Thing*

The first thing they did when they got off the ship was to kneel down under the open sky and thank God. That was why they had come here—to meet God in the way they thought right. It was a simple, manly way they had with Him. Each man seeking His presence, reading His Word, listening to His voice, trying to understand His way and to live it. Each man a free man, responsible to God.

It was not only on Sundays, or in church alone, that they thought of Him, but always and everywhere. They felt that the world was God's house, and they walked reverently in it, and they tried to remember to live by His ways.

So it was that when they wrote a Declaration of Independence, in that fateful moment of making themselves a nation, they called upon Him to behold the justice of what they were about to do. And when they met to draw up a Constitution, governing how Americans should behave toward each other, they sank to their knees and prayed for guidance from the Highest Lawgiver of all.

And from that day to this, when we come together to make a solemn public decision, we take a moment to ask God to make our minds wise, and our hearts good, and our motives pure.

Surely there never was a better country to find God in. Out on the open coast, where the ocean stirs forever and ever, always changing and always the same; on the prairies where the grass blows, and ripens, and dies, and is born again; in the wild, high mountains, and in the silent desert—everywhere under this wide sky the feeling comes: Some one has been here. Some one has made this beautiful for me. Some one expects me to be worthy of this!

Some one expects me to be worthy! Through most of our history we have lived with that faith. And only as long as we believe it, and go on living it, will we be secure.—*From an advertisement of the John Hancock Mutual Life Insurance Company of Boston*

3762    *Sorrow*

> I walked a mile with Pleasure
> She chattered all the way
> But left me none the wiser
> For all she had to say.
>
> I walked a mile with Sorrow
> And ne'er a word said she
> But oh the things I learned from her
> When Sorrow walked with me.
>                 —*Robert Browning Hamilton*

3763    *Exciting Drama*

We are constantly assured that preachers insist too much upon doctrine— "dull dogma," as people call it. The fact is the precise opposite. It is the neglect of dogma that makes for dullness. The Christian faith is the most exciting drama that has ever staggered the imagination of man—and the dogma is the drama. —*Dorothy L. Sayers*

3764    *The Darkest Day*

> Beware of desperate steps; the darkest day,
> Lived till tomorrow, will have passed away.
>                 —*William Cowper*

3765    *Life's Lesson*

> I learn, as the years roll onward
> And I leave the past behind,
> That much I had counted sorrow
> But proved that God is kind;

That many a flower I'd longed for
Had hidden a thorn of pain
And many a rugged bypath
Led to the fields of ripened grain.
The clouds that cover the sunshine;
They cannot banish the sun,
And the earth shines out the brighter
When the weary rain is done.
We must stand in the deepest shadow
To see the clearest light;
And often through wrong's own darkness
Comes the welcome strength of Right.

—*Anonymous*

### 3766 *A Day of Tribute*

Memorial Day was first observed, by general order of Commander-in-Chief John A. Logan of the Grand Army of the Republic, on May 30, 1868. While there had been other Memorial Day observances in both the North and South prior to 1868, this was the first fixed holiday. The original purpose of Memorial Day was to honor soldiers killed in the American Civil War, but the annual observance has come to be a day of tribute for all those brave individuals who fought for freedom throughout our nation's history.

### 3767 *Famous Cripples*

Talleyrand, the statesman, was to have a military career, but an accident in early youth rendered him a cripple for life.

Alexander Pope, the poet, is said to have inherited nothing from his father save his physical deformity, and nothing from his mother but her violent headaches. He was little more than four feet in height, and his bodily infirmities rendered his life one long disease. Yet he labored incessantly and triumphantly.

Elizabeth Browning, the poet, was of a delicate constitution and never enjoyed health. Her sufferings were due to an accident that had happened in her sixteenth year. She was trying to saddle her pony when she fell with the saddle upon her, injuring to her spine. For years she was compelled to lie on her back.

Both Lord Byron and Sir Walter Scott were lame. Josiah Wedgewood, the famous potter and scientist, suffered from a disease of the knee that necessitated the amputation of his leg.

### 3768 *Concentrate*

Most people don't realize that to perform well in whatever you do, especially in an athletic contest which is extremely emotional, concentration is the key. If you can keep your concentration, then you have a tremendous opportunity to perform at maximum efficiency. When you break your concentration, then you start to let other thoughts enter. So I'm constantly thinking about what's coming. —*Tom Landry*

### 3769    *John Wesley*

John Wesley's death inspired one of the most eloquent obituaries of all time: "When at length he came to die he left only a knife, a fork, two spoons and the Methodist Church."

But the long life of John Wesley, too, was an inspiration, motivated by his own Rule of Conduct:

> Do all the good you can,
> By all the means you can,
> In all the ways you can,
> In all the places you can,
> At all the times you can,
> To all the people you can,
> As long as ever you can.

### 3770    *George Washington's Wisdom*

Washington's wisdom has been an inspiration for large numbers of our leading men and women in every decade since his time. He had the uncanny foresight of seeking to build a nation upon the bedrock of strong patriotism, unquestioned integrity, opportunities for all, high ideals, and love of God. May our great land, conceived in prayer for peace, bring new concepts of living to all the peoples of the world.—*James Francis Cooke, The Etude.*

### 3771    *Heartache*

> As a child misses the unsaid Good-night,
> And falls asleep with heartache.
> —*Robert Frost*

### 3772    *Worthy of Our Heritage*

The *Chicago Daily News* asked presidential nominees to tell of their "most moving religious experience." The following was related by General Dwight D. Eisenhower.

"On a rainy night in the spring of 1943, I visited an infantry company preparing for action in the Tunisian hills of North Africa. I listened to the captain in command address his men. There was no outward stamp of piety on this officer, but his words moved me as deeply as any I have ever heard. Here, in essence, is what he said:

" 'Almighty God, as we prepare to move forward into an action from which some of us may not return, we humbly place our faith and trust in Thee.

" 'We do not pray for victory, nor even for our individual safety. But we pray for help that none of us may let a comrade down—that each of us may do his duty to himself, his comrades and his country, and so be worthy of our American heritage.'

"I walked away with tears in my eyes.

"Here in a few words, and in simple language, from a real leader, was expressed the very heart of the religious ideal—men, banded together under God, acting nobly, patriotically and unselfishly in a just cause."

### 3773    Segregated

On the bulletin board of a church in Ohio there was this announcement: "This is a segregated church—for sinners only. All welcome."

### 3774    Why We Have Freedom

We are a mighty nation. As we run our memories back over the pages of history, we find a race of men whom we claim as our fathers. They were iron men, and it is because of what they did that we have our freedom and prosperity. The sentiment of the Declaration of Independence gave liberty to the people of this country, and hope to the world. Let us re-adopt the Declaration of Independence, and the practices and policies that harmonize with it.—*Abraham Lincoln*

### 3775    A Child's Training

Rushed for time one morning, Celeste Sibley, one-time columnist on the *Atlanta Constitution,* took her three children to a restaurant for breakfast so that they would not be late for school and she for work. The restaurant was crowded, and they had to take separate seats at the counter. When eight-year-old Mary, seated far down at an end of the line, was served she paused and called down to her mother in a clear, loud voice: "Mother, don't people ask the blessing in this place?" Mrs. Sibley was embarrassed in the silence that followed, but before she could "shush" the child the counterman replied, "Yes we do, sister. You say it." So Mary bowed her head and began: "God is great, God is good, let us thank Him for our food." All the people at the counter bowed their heads.—*Mother*

### 3776    All Are Equal

When He afflicts the celebrated of the world, it is His way of saying, "None is privileged. In My eyes all are equal.—*Helen Hayes*

### 3777    A Rhyme for Remembering the Old Testament Books

> The great Jehovah speaks to us,
> In Genesis and Exodus,
> Leviticus and Numbers see,

Followed by Deuteronomy.
Joshua and Judges sway the land,
Ruth gleans a sheaf with trembling hand,
Samuel and numerous Kings appear,
Whose Chronicles we wondering hear;
Ezra and Nehemiah now,
Esther the beauteous mourner show;
Job speaks in sighs, David in Psalms,
The Proverbs teach to scatter alms.

Ecclesiastes then comes on,
And the sweet Song of Solomon,
Isaiah, Jeremiah then
With Lamentations takes his pen.
Ezekiel, Daniel, Hosea's lyres
Swell Joel, Amos, Obadiah's.
Next Jonah, Micah, Nahum come,
And lofty Habakkuk finds room,
Rapt Zephaniah, Haggai calls,
While Zechariah builds the walls;
And Malachi, with garments rent,
Concludes the ancient Testament.

### 3778    *Lincoln*

Perhaps Edward Everett talked a bit too long at Gettysburg, but he was an old man then, by the standards of his day—within a few months of his seventieth birthday. And this was the culminating glory of a long career. But Everett was among those who perceived the classic qualities of the Lincoln address. In a note to the President the following day he said: "I should be glad if I could flatter myself that I came as near to the central idea of the occasion in two hours as you did in two minutes."

With his customary graciousness President Lincoln replied: "In our respective parts yesterday, you could not have been excused to make a short address, nor I a long one."—*Quote Magazine*

### 3779    *The Medical Profession*

Charity is the eminent virtue of the medical profession. Show me the garret or the cellar which its messengers do not penetrate; tell me of the pestilence which its heroes have not braved in their errands of mercy; name me the practitioner who is not ready to be the servant of servants in the case of mankind . . . and whose footsteps you will not find in the path of every haunt of stricken humanity.—*Oliver Wendell Holmes*

3780   *Bibles*

In the front lines of Korea, I never saw a pin-up picture. But I saw hundreds of Bibles.—*Billy Graham*

3781   *It Wasn't Always a New Year on January 1*

The new year has in the past begun at many different times. The ancient Egyptians began the year on September 21; the ancient Greeks, on December 21; and March 25 was the usual New Year's Day among Christians during the medieval days.

The Gregorian calendar, which was introduced in 1582, put January 1 in the position of New Year's Day, and it was immediately accepted by Germany and Denmark, by Sweden about 1700, and by England in 1752.

No matter when the new year began, it was a time to forget the past year and look forward to the coming year and plan for the future.—*Sunshine Magazine*

3782   *You Can Trust Him*

You can't trust a man who has no music in his soul. A banker will ask how much security a man can give before he will trust him. But here's a new test of a man's character that is very good: He may have on a greasy hat, and the seat of his trousers may be shiny, but if his children have their noses flattened against the windowpane a half hour before he is due home for supper, he can be trusted.

3783   *Humility*

Toscanini was so humble that when his orchestra burst into applause at a rehearsal because they realized the heights to which he had lifted them, he said with tears in his eyes, "It is not me. It is Beethoven."—*Jessica Somers Driver*

3784   *Blest Be the Tie*

A beautiful story recounts the origin of the well-known hymn "Blest be the tie that binds our hearts in Christian love." It was in 1772, in England, when John Fawcett, a brilliant young minister and pastor of a small congregation in Yorkshire, was called to London to succeed the famous Dr. Gill. The call was so attractive that the Reverend Fawcett felt he could not afford to reject it.

His farewell sermon had been preached, and the wagons stood loaded with his furniture and books. People were heartbroken. Men, women, and children gathered around him and his family with tearful faces. Finally, overwhelmed with the sorrow of those they were leaving, Fawcett and his wife sat down on one of the packing cases and gave way to grief.

"Oh, John!" cried the wife, "I cannot bear this!"

"Nor I, either!" replied the husband, "and we will not go! The wagons shall be unloaded."

The people were filled with joy. Fawcett at once sent a message to London explaining the situation, and returned to his work with his beloved Yorkshire church at a mere pittance of pay.

John Fawcett wrote the hymn in commemoration of the event. It is one of the hymns immortal.

### 3785  *Freedom's Price*

Let every nation know, whether it wishes us well or ill, that we shall pay any price, bear any burden, meet any hardship, support any friend, oppose any foe in order to assure the survival and success of liberty.—*John F. Kennedy*

### 3786  *The Shopping List*

Few people ever put Christ on their "shopping list." In all the vast crowds, not one in ten thousand is looking for a present to give to the Christ child. His name never appears on these long secret lists along with Aunt Sarah and Cousin Joe. . . . Possibly this is because a few realize that no gift on sale at any store would be suitable. Tragically, the far greater truth is that most of us never think of making a Christmas gift to Christ.—*Halford E. Luccock and Robert E. Luccock, Pulpit Digest*

### 3787  *A Mother's Creed*

I believe in God.

I believe in the Word of God.

I believe in the family altar.

I believe in the sanctity of motherhood.

I believe the home to be the sphere of the mother's greatest influence.

I believe in a deep concern for the spiritual welfare of my children.

I believe in making the home the most attractive spot so that my children will not be forced to seek enjoyment elsewhere.

I believe in an intimate companionship between myself and my children.

I believe in pointing out the moral dangers to which my children are exposed, and not hiding behind a false modesty.

I believe it is my privilege and duty to know the companions of my children and to be familiar with their forms of amusement.—*Arthur C. James, Young Calvinist magazine*

### 3788  *The American Flag*

In the British colonies of North America before the Revolution, each of the thirteen colonies had its own flag. On January 2, 1776, the first flag of the United States was raised at Cambridge, Massachusetts, by George Washington. This was the Grand Union flag, thirteen alternate red and white stripes with a blue canton bearing the red cross of St. George and the white cross of St. Andrew. On June

14, 1777, Congress decreed that there should be a star and stripe for each state with the resolution "that the Flag of the United States be thirteen stars white in a blue field representing a new constellation."

The flag, first flown August 3, 1777, on the present site of Rome, New York, was under fire three days later. In 1818 Congress enacted that the thirteen stripes should represent the original thirteen states, and a star be added for each new state. In 1895, June 14 was officially designated as Flag Day, marking the anniversary of the formal adoption of the Stars and Stripes by the Continental Congress. The American flag is the third oldest of the national standards of the world—older than the Union Jack of Great Britain or the Tricolor of France. As we salute our flag, with right hands over our hearts, we remember that our Nation's flag represents our struggles and sacrifices, as well as our success and our freedom.

### 3789    *The Struggle in Life*

Everything in creation has its appointed painter or poet, and remains in bondage like the princess in the fairy tale 'til its appropriate liberator comes to set it free. The story of the Sleeping Beauty is more than a fairy tale; it is an allegory of the life of every human being who fights his way through life.—*Ralph Waldo Emerson*

### 3790    *March 1841*

The United States had three presidents, all in one month. Martin Van Buren finished his term of office in March 1841; and William Henry Harrison was sworn into office, died, and was succeeded by his vice-president, John Tyler.

### 3791    *Two Great Principles and Man's Ultimate Purpose*

In these confusing and difficult times, perhaps we need to reaffirm our stand on two great principles that have strongly motivated the conduct of our people throughout our history. The first principle is our recognition of the sovereignty of God. We need to reemphasize that man is not the center of the universe. Pleasure is not the goal of the people. Power is not the goal of the government. Expediency is not the guiding principle of conduct. It is Providence that is sovereign and gives the ultimate objectives and goals to mankind. It is the City of God, as St. Augustine said, that man is to build on earth. In a nation where faith in Providence dies, literature loses its inspiration, art its beauty, government its consecration, business its ideals, and labor its dignity.

The second great principle we need to reemphasize is the divine worth of man. We believe in the independence and dignity of every man, for he was made in the image of God and is overshadowed only by Him.

The ultimate purpose of man is not merely to fly from Chicago to London in only hours—eating a ten-course dinner en route. The great goal of free men is not simply to create a sleek and self-satisfied culture of comfort, leisure, and fun. The lasting achievement of mankind is not even the size of its gross national product or the destructiveness of its bombs.

The final measure of greatness is whether you and I, by our individual lives, have increased the freedom of man, enhanced his dignity, and brought him nearer to the nobility of the divine image in which he was created.—*Herbert V. Prochnow*

### 3792    *Our Prayer*

Before all else, we seek, upon our common labor as a nation, the favor of Almighty God. And the hopes in our hearts fashion the deepest prayers of our people.

May we pursue the right—without self-righteousness.

May we know unity—without conformity.

May we grow in strength—without pride of self.

May we, in our dealings with all people of the earth, ever speak the truth and serve justice.

May the light of freedom, coming to all darkened lands, flame brightly—until at last the darkness is no more.

May the turbulence of our age yield to a true time of peace, when men and nations shall share a life that honors the dignity of earth, the brotherhood of all. —*Dwight D. Eisenhower*

### 3793    *Faith Is the Power*

It is hard to see how a great man can be an atheist. Doubters do not believe. Skeptics do not contribute. Cynics do not create. Faith is the great motive power, and no man realizes his full possibilities unless he has the deep conviction that life is eternally important, and that his work, well done, is part of an unending plan.

### 3794    *Liberty*

Liberty is a thing of the spirit—to be free to worship, to think, to hold opinions, and to speak without fear—free to challenge wrong and oppression with surety of justice.—*Herbert Hoover*

### 3795    *When God Builds*

For centuries men have been trying to build abiding structures of international law and order—and peace. But all of these efforts of the past stand in broken fragments to remind us of man's inadequacy.

But look at what God has built! Two thousand years ago He lifted the Church upon the foundations of ancient truth, made complete and understandable by the revelations of Holy Writ. Through the centuries the divine structure has stood. Nations and empires have risen and fallen; all things have passed away; but the

Church stands undiminished and solid. It is the voice of God, telling man that he cannot build peace, law, or order, except as he builds with God.—*Adapted from Charles A. Wells, Watchman-Examiner and Sunshine Magazine*

### 3796    A Gentleman

It is almost a definition of a gentleman to say he is one who never inflicts a pain. He makes light of favors while he does them, and seems to be receiving when he is conferring. He observes the maxim of the ancient sage, that we should ever conduct ourselves toward an enemy as if he were one day to be our friend. —*John Henry Newman*

### 3797    Ultimate Good

Our ultimate good is a world without war, a world made safe for diversity, in which all men, goods, and ideas can freely move across every border and every boundary.—*Lyndon Johnson*

### 3798    Independence Day

Courageous men came long ago to this virgin land, and it blossomed under their hands. They contended with the greatest tasks of human society and government, and a great republic was reared. They cherished noble ideals, and their commonwealth reached out to lead and influence the world.

. . . They beheld enemies without fear, opposition without despair, problems without evasion, and sacrifices without cowardice.

We celebrate the ideals of our great republic—ideals of freedom and justice, and equality of opportunity, to which the founders dedicated our nation. These are the thoughts which should come to our minds on Independence Day.— *Sunshine Magazine*

### 3799    The White House

James Hoban designed the White House and also supervised its construction —all for a fee of only $500.

### 3800    Strangers and Friends

We ought to be as courteous to the members of our immediate family as we would be to strangers. Virtually all the harsh, insulting things that are said, are said to loved ones—wives, husbands, children—who will forgive even when treated meanly. Give a smile instead of a snarl, appreciation instead of criticism. Let's treat our loved ones as if they were strangers—better yet, treat them as if they were friends.—*Sunshine Magazine*

### 3801    The Lesson of the Tree

We ask the leaf, "Are you complete in yourself?" And the leaf answers, "No, my life is in the branches." We ask the branch and the branch answers, "No my life is in the trunk." We ask the trunk and it answers, "No my life is in the roots and the branches and the leaves." So it is with our lives. Nothing is completely and merely individual.—*Harry Emerson Fosdick*

### 3802    *He Could Judge*

The late Ambassador Walter Hines Page was formerly editor of the *World's Work* and, like all editors, was obliged to refuse a great many stories. A lady once wrote him: "Sir: you sent back a story of mine. I know that you did not read the story, for as a test I had pasted together pages 18, 19, and 20, and the story came back with those pages still pasted; and so I know you are a fraud and reject stories before reading them."

Mr. Page wrote back: "Madame: At breakfast when I open an egg I don't have to eat the whole egg to discover it is bad."

### 3803    *How to Live*

An old Chinese philosopher, when asked what he had found to be the greatest joy in life, said, "A child going down the road singing after asking of me the way."

### 3804    *The Modesty of George Washington*

The following quotation is from George Washington, at the time of his appointment as Commander-in-Chief of the United States:

"Tho' I am truly sensible of the high honor done me in this appointment yet I feel great distress from a consciousness that my abilities and military experience may not be equal to the extensive and important trust. However, as the Congress desire it, I will enter upon the momentous duty, and exert every power I possess in their service and for the support of the glorious cause. I beg they will accept my most cordial thanks for this distinguished testimony of their approbation.

"But lest some unlucky event should happen unfavorable to my reputation, I beg it may be remembered by every gentleman in the room that I this day declare, with the utmost sincerity, I do not think myself equal to the command I am honored with.

"As to pay, sir, I beg leave to assure the Congress that as no pecuniary consideration could have tempted me to accept this arduous employment at the expense of my domestic ease and happiness, I do not wish to make any profit from it. I will keep an exact account of my expenses. Those, I doubt not, they will discharge and that is all I desire."

### 3805    *A Father's Advice*

"My boy," a father advised his son, "treat everybody with politeness, even those who are rude to you. For remember that you show courtesy to others not because they are gentlemen, but because you are one."

### 3806    *Faith*

In my escape from the Boers in 1899, I realized with awful force that no exercise of my own feeble wit and strength could save me from my enemies, and that without the assistance of that High Power, I could never succeed. I prayed long and earnestly. My prayer, as it seems to me, was swiftly and wonderfully answered.—*Winston Churchill*

### 3807 *What Is the Happiest Season of Life?*

A wise old man, who had lived buoyantly through four score years, was asked, "Which is the happiest season of life?" He replied thoughtfully, "When spring comes, and in the soft air the buds are breaking on the trees, and they are covered with blossoms, I think, how beautiful is Spring! And when the summer comes, and covers the trees and bushes with heavy foliage, and singing birds mingle with the branches, I think, how beautiful is Summer! When autumn loads them with golden fruit, and their leaves bear the gorgeous tint of frost, I think, how beautiful is Autumn! And when it is sore winter, and there is neither foliage nor fruit, then when I look up through the leafless branches and see, as I can see in no other season, the shining stars of heaven, I think, how beautiful is the Winter of life!"

### 3808 *Perfection*

There have been a few moments when I have known complete satisfaction, but only a few. I have rarely been free from the disturbing realization that my playing might have been better.—*Ignace Jan Paderewski*

### 3809 *Failure and Success*

*Lust for Life,* by Irving Stone, was turned down by 17 publishers.

*The Ginger Man,* by J. P. Donleavy, was refused by 36 American and 10 British houses.

*Auntie Mame,* by Patrick Dennis, circulated "for five years through the halls of 15 publishers and finally ended up with Vanguard Press, which, as you can see, is rather deep into the alphabet."

*The Doctor's Quick Weight Loss Diet,* by Dr. Stillman, was rejected 16 times; it became the best selling diet book of all time.

*The Good Earth,* by Pearl Buck, was declined by more than a dozen publishers; British publisher Geoffrey Faber passed it up twice.

British novelist John Creasey collected 774 rejection slips before making his first sale. Subsequently he published 564 books under his own name and 13 aliases.—*Writer's Digest*

### 3810 *Presidential Polish*

During the Civil War days a foreign minister to the United States was shocked when, on a call to the White House, he found President Lincoln shining his own shoes. He told the President that in his country it was not the custom of gentlemen to polish their own shoes.

With his customary resourcefulness and nimble wit, President Lincoln replied, "Then whose shoes do they polish?"—*The Red Barrel*

### 3811 *How It Started*

Years ago two traveling men, strangers to each other, shared a room in a crowded hotel in Boscobel, Wisconsin, for a night. One asked the other if he objected to keeping the light on a little longer, while he read his Bible. The other said he would be glad if his roommate would read aloud.

Out of this meeting between J. H. Nicholson and S. E. Hill came the idea for the society of Gideons. The organization has placed copies of the Bible in hotel rooms, on school desks, beside hospital cots, and in prison cells all over the world.

### 3812 *Our Potential*

We have the capacity, the resources, the potential beyond the dreams of anyone, but we neglect our resources, the brainpower and energy of industry and our laboratories. Within industry and our scientific organizations we have (potentially) the greatest strength ever to bear on the problems of society.—*David Lilienthal*

### 3813 *America*

God built a continent with glory, and filled it with treasures untold. He bedecked it with soft, rolling prairies, and pillared it with thundering mountains. He graced it with deep-shadowed forests, and filled them with song. Myriads of people came, the bravest of the races, bearing the glow of adventure and the glory of hope in their souls. Out of them was fashioned a nation. They called it America!—*Sunshine Magazine*

### 3814 *Books Are Dangerous*

Reading books may be dangerous. From them there may escape, as Anatole France once said, "all kinds of images to trouble the souls and change the hearts of men."

Books bring stories of exciting adventure, lively humor, dangerous exploration, great love, the tragedy of treason and inspiration to new achievement. In them, also, there is hope for the discouraged, strength for the defeated, and faith for the doubting.

A teenage boy will open a book and suddenly find himself floating down the Mississippi River on a raft with Huckleberry Finn and whitewashing a fence with Tom Sawyer. Another youngster will find inspiration in the tales of a tall, gaunt rail splitter from Illinois who got an education from books he had borrowed. A little girl simply won't believe the fantastic story of the little crocodile that would cheerfully seem to grin, neatly spread his claws, and welcome little fishes into his gently smiling jaws.

A grown-up will sit down with a book and travel through twenty centuries watching man's desperate struggle for liberty. Another will sail from South

America to the South Sea Islands on a battered raft, or tramp over treacherous mountain trails to the seclusion of Tibet.

Books vastly increase one's vision. An astronomer writes for laymen so stars and suns break into voice. A scientist discloses the secret life of the creatures of forest and field. A scholarly historian reveals the making of decisions that destroy an empire. Presidents and prime ministers with their cabinets, and generals with their staffs, parade before us to justify themselves. Emerson and Lowell, Washington, Jefferson, and Lincoln become contemporaries. With books one reaps harvests in many fields.

By day one goes about business, profession, or housework. By night, with a book, one hears Dante and Milton talk of Paradise, and Plato teach his great philosophy. One finds that Homer and Shakespeare still live, Cervantes laughs, and Thomas à Kempis inspires. The oceans and the continents, the Arctic and the tropics, all the generations of men with their woes and wars, their cultures and civilizations, are at one's fireside with a book in an easy chair.

For many people, life may actually be an unlighted candle until some worthwhile book kindles its faculties so they glow. With faculties aflame, one does his best. Then imagination takes wing. Achievement seems easy. Judgment is sound. Obstacles grow small. Ideals are clear. Defeat is remote. Triumph is humble.

Remember, it may be dangerous to open that book, for it may destroy your prejudices and replace your pride with humility, and from it there may come all kinds of images to trouble your soul and change your heart.—*Herbert V. Prochnow*

### 3815    *Be Kind*

You may be sorry that you spoke, sorry you stayed or went, sorry you won or lost, perhaps, sorry so much was spent. But, as you go through life, you'll find —you're never sorry you were kind.

### 3816    *Gives Hope to All*

The prudent, penniless beginner in the world labors for wages for a while, saves a surplus with which to buy tools or land for himself, and at length hires another new beginner to help him. This is the just and generous and prosperous system which opens the way to all, gives hope to all, and consequently energy and progress and improvement of conditions.—*Abraham Lincoln*

### 3817    *Father's Day*

Since Father's Day was first observed on the third Sunday in June 1910, it has been a special day for honoring fathers. But "following in father's footsteps" is not something that happens only in modern times. History records that Alexander the Great followed in the footsteps of his father, King Philip II of Macedon, and conquered the world between 334 and 326 B.C., with the invincible armies that his father had spent his life in training. Johann Strauss, the composer, followed in the footsteps of his father, who was a symphony conductor in Vienna. In America, our sixth president, John Quincy Adams, was the son of John Adams, our second president.

### 3818    *He Did His Job Well*

If a man is called to be a streetsweeper, he should sweep streets even as Michelangelo painted, or Beethoven composed music, or Shakespeare wrote poetry. He should sweep streets so well that all the host of heaven and earth will pause to say, here lived a great streetsweeper who did his job well.—*Dr. Martin Luther King, Jr.*

### 3819    *The Purpose of Life*

How extraordinary is the situation of us mortals. Each of us is here for a brief sojourn; for what purpose he knows not though he sometimes thinks he senses it. But without going deeper than our daily life, it is plain that we exist for our fellow men—in the first place for those upon whose smiles and welfare our happiness depends, and next for all those unknown to us personally but to whose destinies we are bound by the tie of sympathy. A hundred times every day I remind myself that my inner and outer life depend on the labors of other men, living and dead, and that I must exert myself in order to give in the measure as I have received and am still receiving.—*Albert Einstein*

### 3820    *His Enemy*

Abraham Lincoln was questioned by one of his advisers as follows: "Mr. President, I cannot understand you. You treat your enemies with such kindness. It would seem to me that you should want to destroy them."

"My dear fellow," said the President, "I do destroy my enemy when I make him into a friend."—*Anonymous*

### 3821    *Every Day*

Every day is a little life, and our whole life is but a day repeated. Therefore live every day as if it would be the last. Those that dare lose a day, are dangerously prodigal; those that dare misspend it, are desperate.—*Bishop Joseph Hall*

### 3822    *Forgiveness*

> My heart was heavy, for its trust had been
> Abused, its kindness answered with foul wrong;
> So, turning gloomily from my fellowmen,
> One summer Sabbath day I strolled among

The green mounds of the village burial-place;
Where pondering how all human love and hate
Find one sad level; and how, soon or late,
Wronged and wrongdoer, each with meekened face,
And cold hands folded over a still heart,
Pass the green threshold of our common grave,
Whither all footsteps tend, whence none depart,
Awed for myself, and pitying my race,
Our common sorrow, like a mighty wave
Swept all my pride away, and trembling I forgave!
—*John Greenleaf Whittier*

### 3823   *Making Good at Home*

An American soldier in France won the Croix de Guerre but refused to wear it, and this is his explanation: "I was no good back home. I let my sister and my widowed mother support me. I was a deadbeat. And now they have given me the Croix de Guerre for something I did at the front. I am not going to put it on. I am going back home first. I am going to win out there. I am going to show my mother that I can make good at home. Then I will put on the Croix de Guerre." He is not the only one who has discovered that being heroic in a crisis is sometimes easier than being useful at home.—*Harry Emerson Fosdick*

### 3824   *Love Your Neighbor*

What you must do is love your neighbor as yourself. There is no one who knows your many faults better than you! But you love yourself notwithstanding. And so you must love your neighbor, no matter how many faults you see in him.
—*Hasidic*

### 3825   *Education*

Let us admit that our educational troubles stem from the American home just about as much as from the American school. . . . In your homes and with your children, please remember it is not anti-democratic to have standards of good taste. As our schools would benefit if their pupils had a better home environment, so our parents ought to have available better schools for their children. To have better schools, we must start from one simple proposition: The primary purpose of any school is education, not social adjustment; the student becomes educated by hard work, not by entertainment.—*Grayson Kirk*

### 3826   *Death*

Winter is on my head, but eternal spring is in my heart. The nearer I approach the end the plainer I hear around me the immortal symphonies of the worlds which invite me.—*Victor Hugo*

3827    *How You Can Help*

There is hardly a person who would not struggle to come back if he felt that someone believed in him, believed that he could do it.

3828    *Giving Yourself*

"How marvelously that pianist plays." Yes, but he spends six hours a day at the keys.

"How angelic is the voice of that singer!" Yes, but she works on scales every day of her life, and forgoes anything that might prove harmful to her health in order that her voice may retain its sweetness.

"What a splendid book that author has written!" Yes, but he toiled upon it day and night for years—studying, writing, revising.

"What a remarkable success that man has made of his business!" Yes, but what lean years he passed through, and how he planned and prayed and labored to make that business fruitful!

And so runs the gamut of human endeavor.

3829    *The Greatest Need*

Countless as are the needs of the present world, none is greater than its need of spiritual power, something to lift man above the sordidness of materialism; something to cause him to look out, not in; up, not down; to help him to turn the defeat of his selfish purposes into victorious living for others.—*John D. Rockefeller, Jr.*

3830    *The Measure of Man*

> Not—"How did he die?" But—"How did he live?"
> Not—"What did he gain?" But—"What did he give?"
> These are the units to measure the worth
> Of a man as a man, regardless of birth.
>
> —*Anonymous*

3831    *The Modest Thomas A. Edison*

The governor of North Carolina was complimenting Thomas A. Edison one day on being a great inventor.

The modest Edison looked uncomfortable. "I am not a great inventor," he said.

"But you have over a thousand patents to your credit, haven't you?"

"Yes, but about the only invention I can really claim as absolutely original is the phonograph," was the reply.

"Just what do you mean?" asked the governor.

"Well," explained Mr. Edison. "I guess I'm an awfully good sponge. I absorb ideas from every source I can, and put them to practical use. Then I improve them until they become of some value. The ideas I use are mostly the ideas of people who don't develop them."

### 3832 *My Country*

My country owes me nothing. It gave me, as it gives every boy and girl, a chance. It gave me schooling, independence of action, opportunity for service and honor. In no other land could a boy from a country village, without inheritance or influential friends, look forward with unbounded hope.—*Herbert Hoover*

### 3833 *If I Err*

If I err in my belief that the souls of men are immortal, I gladly err, nor do I wish this error, in which I find delight, to be wrested from me.—*Cicero*

### 3834 *John D. Rockefeller's Schedule*

When John D. Rockefeller made his first million, he wasn't surprised. He had simply been faithful to a thoughtful program. When he was sixty years old, he made up his mind he would live to be one hundred. So he made a set of rules and followed them with the same faith. These rules have now become the "ten commandments of health":
1. Never lose interest in life and the world.
2. Eat sparingly and at regular hours.
3. Take plenty of exercise, but not too much.
4. Get plenty of sleep.
5. Never allow yourself to become annoyed.
6. Set a daily schedule of life and keep it.
7. Get a lot of sunlight.
8. Drink as much milk as will agree with you.
9. Obey your doctor and consult him often.
10. Don't "overdo" things.—*The Printed Word*

### 3835 *Opportunity*

I shall pass through this world but once.

Any good therefore that I can do or any kindness that I can show to any human being, let me do it now.

Let me not defer or neglect it, for I shall not pass this way again.—*Anonymous*

### 3836 *Art*

Painting is not very difficult when you don't know how. But when you know, ah! then, it is a different matter.—*Degas, quoted in American Artist*

### 3837    *Lincoln's Letter to Mrs. Bixby*

Dear Madam: I have been shown in the files of the War Department a statement of the Adjutant General of Massachusetts that you are the mother of five sons who have died gloriously on the field of battle. I feel how weak and fruitless must be any words of mine which should attempt to beguile you from the grief of a loss so overwhelming, but I cannot refrain from tendering to you the consolation that may be found in the thanks of the Republic that they died to save. I pray that the Heavenly Father may assuage the anguish of your bereavement, and leave you only the cherished memory of the loved and lost, and the solemn pride that must be yours to have laid so costly a sacrifice upon the altar of freedom. Yours very sincerely and respectfully, Abraham Lincoln.

### 3838    *His Method*

A wise and philosophical man once said to me, when asked how he overcame his difficulties, "How do I get thru a trouble? Well, first I try to go around it, and if I can't go around it, I try to get under it, and if I can't get under it, I try to go over it, and if I can't get over it, then God and I plow right thru it."—*Wesleyan Methodist*

### 3839    *Immortality*

There is, I know not how, in the minds of men, a certain presage, as it were, of a future existence; and this takes the deepest root, and is most discoverable, in the greatest geniuses and most exalted souls.—*Cicero*

### 3840    *He Agreed*

Playwright George Bernard Shaw is a wit as well by word of mouth as by word of pen, as illustrated by this story that Booth Tarkington told of him in an Indianapolis newspaper:

One first night at a London theater a play of his had taken the audience by storm. After the final curtain the author was called for and stepped forward to make a speech of thanks, when a single but vehement hiss was heard from a man leaning over the gallery rail. The playwright looked up to where the man sat, and addressed him: "Yes, my friend, I'm of your way of thinking myself, but what can we two do against so many?"

### 3841    *Good Citizens*

Bad men cannot make good citizens. It is impossible that a nation of infidels or idolators should be a nation of free men. It is when people forget God, that tyrants forge their chains. A vitiated state of morals, a corrupted public conscience, is incompatible with freedom.—*Patrick Henry*

### 3842    Luxury

President William Howard Taft was the first occupant of the White House to have an automobile at his disposal. Whenever possible, he would take the family for a drive.

One day, when they were out in the car, his youngest son, Charles, asked, "May we go for a ride again next week?"

"Next week and every week," beamed Taft. "Four years from now, we may have to start walking again!"

### 3843    Immortal American Phrases

Certain great phrases have been spoken in times of crisis. We repeat them and are inspired by them, sometimes without even knowing the names of the men who first spoke them, or the circumstances that called them forth.

"Let us have faith that right makes might, and in that faith let us to the end, dare to do our duty as we understand it."—*Abraham Lincoln, in his address at Cooper Union, in New York, February 27, 1860*

"We must all hang together, or assuredly we shall all hang separately."—*Benjamin Franklin, after signing the Declaration of Independence, 1776*

"To be prepared for war is one of the most effectual means of preserving peace."—*George Washington, in his first annual address to both Houses of Congress, 1790*

"These are times that try men's souls."—*Thomas Paine, in "The American Crisis" in the Pennsylvania Magazine, 1776*

"I only regret that I have but one life to lose for my country."—*Nathan Hale, in a speech he made just before being hanged by the enemy as a spy, 1776*

"Men, you are all marksmen—don't one of you fire until you see the whites of their eyes."—*Israel Putnam at the Battle of Bunker Hill, 1775; also attributed to Colonel William Prescott*

"Now he belongs to the ages."—*Edwin M. Stanton, secretary of war, at Lincoln's deathbed, 1865*

"I would rather be right than President."—*Henry Clay when told that he was injuring his chances of becoming president by advocating certain compromise measures, 1850*

"That nation has not lived in vain which has given the world Washington and Lincoln, the best great men and the greatest good men whom history can show."—*Henry Cabot Lodge, in an address before the Massachusetts legislature, 1909*

"There is no right to strike against the public safety by anybody, anywhere, any time."—*Calvin Coolidge, in a telegram to Samuel Gompers at the time of the Boston Police strike, 1919*

### 3844 *Lincoln Lines*

I like to see a man proud of the place in which he lives; and so live that the place will be proud of him.

I can see how it might be possible for a man to look down upon the earth and be an atheist. But I cannot conceive how a man could look up into Heaven and say there is no God.—*Abraham Lincoln*

### 3845 *How to Govern*

Our rulers will best promote the improvement of the people by confining themselves to their own legitimate duties—by leaving capital to find its most lucrative course, commodities their fair price, industry and intelligence their natural reward, idleness and folly their natural punishment; by maintaining peace, by defending property, by diminishing the price of law, and by observing strict economy in every department of the state. Let the government do this—the people will assuredly do the rest.—*Thomas Babington Macaulay*

### 3846 *In Japan*

While in Tokyo we wanted to take the train out to the naval station some miles from the city. When we arrived at the central station, there were crowds rushing in all directions to catch their own special trains. A young man saw us hesitating, asked what train we wanted, and offered to buy our tickets for us. In a few moments he returned with the tickets and told us to proceed to Track 13.

We thanked him as best we could in the rush hour traffic. He responded by saying, "When I was in the States one of your people helped me in a railway station, and now it is my turn to return the kindness."

On the platform a young girl, a junior in a Japanese university, came up to us and said, "Perhaps I can help you, as I am taking the same train as you are, although I will be getting off before you do."

After she left us a man sitting opposite us heard us ask the conductor at what time we arrived at the naval station. The conductor showed us the time on his watch. However, when our fellow traveler left the train he handed us a handwritten list of the stations we would pass before we reached our destination. With this before us, we could sit back and enjoy the passing scenery of rice paddies and wheat fields ready for harvest. We parted from our newfound friends with a feeling of kindness toward our fellow men in a strange land.—*Experience of Mr. and Mrs. Herbert V. Prochnow in Japan*

### 3847 *Fame*

Fame is often fickle. Many people who have held prominent positions have faded into oblivion, and their names are no longer familiar. Here are some names of men, all of them prominent, who have something in common: George Clinton, George M. Dallas, William R. King, Daniel Tompkins, John C. Breckinridge,

Schuyler Colfax, Charles W. Fairbanks, Thomas A. Hendricks, William A. Wheeler, Garret A. Hobart, Levi P. Morton, James S. Sherman, Henry Wilson. It is likely that not too many readers will be able to identify these men, who are all former vice-presidents of the United States.

### 3848    Progress

A favorite theme of Harry Emerson Fosdick as he sought to relate Christian truth to the life of his day was the idea of progress: "Progress is by no means a beneficent necessity; things may evolve worse. You can evolve into a parasite. The human race is not on any divine escalator inevitably going up, and the thought that man is continually growing better and better and that his upward evolution is inescapable is the most fatuous of all fool's paradises."—*William H. Hudnut, Jr.*

### 3849    Charity

The day we decide that the government is our brother's keeper, that day the spirit of compassion will have been lost. If we abandon private charity, we will have lost something of America's material, moral, and spiritual welfare.—*Herbert Hoover*

### 3850    Our Constitution and Prayer

William E. Gladstone, the great English statesman, spoke of the United States Constitution as "the greatest piece of work ever struck off at a given time by the brain and purpose of man." Perhaps Mr. Gladstone did not know the real source of this great "piece of work."

By the middle of June 1787, the Constitutional Convention had almost bogged down in its deliberations. Representatives of the thirteen original states had haggled for a month. On the morning of June 16, Benjamin Franklin addressed George Washington in these words:

"Mr. President: The small progress we have made after four or five weeks' close attention and continual reasoning with each other is, methinks, a melancholy proof of the imperfections of human undertaking.

"In this situation of this assembly, as it were in the dark to find political truth . . . how has it happened, sir, that we have not hitherto thought of humbly applying to the Father of Light to illuminate our understanding?

"I have lived, sir, a long time; and the longer I live the more convincing proofs I see of the truth, that God governs in the affairs of men. And if a sparrow cannot fall to the ground without His notice, is it probable that an empire can rise without His aid? We have been assured, sir, in the Sacred Writings, that 'except the Lord build the house, they labor in vain who build it.'

"I firmly believe this; and I also believe that without His concurring aid we shall succeed in this political building no better than the builders of Babel; we shall be divided by our little, partial, local interests, or projects will be confounded and we ourselves shall become a reproach and a byword, down to future ages.

"And what is worse, mankind may hereafter from this unfortunate instance, despair of establishing government by human wisdom, and leave it to chance, war, conquest. I therefore beg leave to move: that hereafter prayers, imploring the assistance of Heaven, and its blessings on our deliberations, be held in this assembly every morning before we proceed to business."

Mr. Franklin's motion carried. The Constitutional Convention prayed, and made progress beyond one of the darkest hours in the career of human liberty.

### 3851    *The Secret*

An old man who seemed to have an unusual amount of trouble and relatively few pleasures surprised everyone with his cheerfulness. When asked the secret of his cheery disposition, he replied: "Well, you see, it's like this. The Bible says often, 'And it came to pass.' It never says, 'It came to stay.' "

### 3852    *Helping Others*

Make a rule and pray God to help you to keep it, never, if possible, to lie down at night without being able to say, "I have made one human being, at least, a little wiser, a little happier, or a little better this day." You will find it easier than you think, and pleasanter.—*Charles Kingsley*

### 3853    *Don't Snub*

Don't snub a boy because he wears shabby clothes. When Thomas Edison, the great inventor, first entered Boston, he wore a pair of thin yellow breeches, although it was the middle of winter.

Don't snub a boy because his home is plain and humble. Abraham Lincoln, the great emancipator, first lived in a log cabin.

Don't snub anyone; not alone because someday they may outstrip you in the race of life, but because it is neither kind nor right.

### 3854    *I Marvel at the Ways of God*

> I marvel at the ways of God,
>    For time and time again
> I see Him paint such lovely clouds
>    Above such awkward men.
>          *—E. B. White*

### 3855    *Pride in Country*

I am glad to see that pride in our country and its accomplishments is not a thing of the past. I still get a hard-to-define feeling when the flag goes up, and

I know you do, too. Let us hope that none of us loses that feeling. As our knowledge of the universe increases, may God grant us the wisdom and guidance to use it wisely.—*John H. Glenn*

3856    *His Ideals*

I have three personal ideals. One, to do the day's work well and not to bother about tomorrow. The second ideal has been to act the Golden Rule, as far as in my lay, toward my professional brethren and toward the patients committed to my care. And the third has been to cultivate such a measure of equanimity as would enable me to bear success with humility, the affection of my friends without pride, and to be ready when the day of sorrow and grief came to meet it with the courage befitting a man.—*Sir William Osler*

3857    *Religion*

"What is salt?" Johnnie was asked. To which he replied, "Salt is what spoils the potatoes when you leave it out."

What is religion? Religion is what spoils life if you leave it out. Religion is what spoils the home if there is not any in it. It is what destroys character if it is deleted. It is what leaves life flat and tasteless when it is omitted.—*Alfred W. Swan*

3858    *The Value of Difficulties*

For the upbuilding of character, conflict is better than peace, and work is better than ease. Many a person leaves half his soul in his easy chair. Heinrich Heine said, "Wherever a great thought is born there has been a Gethsemane." Easy effort never produces a strong mind, nor does an easy religion produce a worthy character.—*The United Presbyterian*

3859    *Inscribed in Marble*

At the foot of the Channel Gardens leading from New York's Fifth Avenue to the sunken area of Rockefeller Center is a sixteen-ton green marble slab upon which is inscribed the ten-point creed by which John D. Rockefeller, Jr., lived.

### The Creed

I believe in the supreme worth of the individual and in his right to life, liberty, and the pursuit of happiness.

I believe that every right implies a responsibility; every opportunity, an obligation; every possession, a duty.

I believe that the law was made for man, not man for the law; that government is the servant of the people, not their master.

I believe in the dignity of labor, whether with head or hand; that the world owes no man a living, but that it owes every man an opportunity to make a living.

I believe that thrift is essential to well-ordered living and that economy is a prime requisite of a sound financial structure, whether in government, business, or personal affairs.

I believe that truth and justice are fundamental to an enduring social order.

I believe in the sacredness of a promise, that a man's word should be as good as his bond; that character—not wealth or power or position—is of supreme worth.

I believe that the rendering of useful service is the common duty of mankind and that only in the purifying fire of sacrifice is the dross of selfishness consumed and the greatness of the human soul set free.

I believe in the all-wise and all-loving God, named by whatever name, and that the individual's highest fulfillment, greatest happiness, and widest usefulness are to be found in living in harmony with His will.

I believe that love is the greatest thing in the world; it alone can overcome hate; right can and will triumph over might.

3860    *God's Pledge to You*

> Not cloudless days;
> Not rose-strewn ways;
> Not care-free years,
> Devoid of sorrow's tears—
> But strength to bear
> Your load of human care,
> And grace to live aright
> And keep your raiment white,
> And love to see you through;
> That is God's pledge to you.
>                         —*Anonymous*

3861    *It Doesn't Matter*

Whistler, the artist, once invited Mark Twain to visit his studio to see a new picture he was finishing. The humorist examined the canvas for some time in silence, then said, "I'd do away with that cloud if I were you," and extended his hand carelessly toward one corner of the picture as though about to smudge out a cloud effect. Whistler cried out nervously, "Gad, sir, be careful! Don't you see the paint is still wet?"

"Oh, that doesn't matter," said Twain. "I've got my gloves on."

3862    *The Sea Has Another Shore*

Death is a great adventure, but none need go unconvinced that there is an issue to it. The man of faith may face it as Columbus faced his first voyage from the shores of Spain. What lies across the sea, he cannot tell; his special expectations all may be mistaken; but his insight into the clear meanings of present facts may persuade him beyond doubt that the sea has another shore. Such confident faith, so founded upon reasonable grounds, shall be turned to sight, when for all the dismay of the unbelieving, the hope of the seers is rewarded by the vision of a new continent.—*Harry Emerson Fosdick*

### 3863 *Purpose*

Too many lives are like the man Voltaire once described as an old-fashioned oven: always heating but never cooking anything. As Walt Whitman said, "I was simmering, simmering, simmering: Emerson brought me to a boil." Many of us succeed to where we almost reach the boiling point. It takes struggles in life to make strength. It takes singleness of purpose to reach an objective.—*Herbert V. Prochnow*

### 3864 *Thanksgiving*

Five women served the first Thanksgiving feast in 1621 at Plymouth. Of the eighteen adult women who arrived aboard the *Mayflower* the previous winter, the five were all that remained. Including themselves and thirteen young girls who perhaps helped, about fifty pilgrims and ninety native Americans attended the three-day feast.

### 3865 *Silent Night*

The most loved of all Christmas melodies is the beautiful "Silent Night, Holy Night."

It was Christmas Eve of the year 1818, at Oberndorf, a village in the Austrian mountains. At St. Nicholas' Church they had been preparing music for the Christmas services, and Josef Mohr, the assistant pastor, had been enthusiastic about the program. But the church organ had broken down. The organ could not be used for Christmas. Josef Mohr had an old guitar, and he glanced hopefully at the instrument. An inspiration came to him. He sat down to his desk and wrote. They were beautiful, heart-warming words.

In a few minutes there was a knock at the door of Franz Gruber, the church organist. He hastened to answer the call at the door. There stood Josef Mohr, a bright light in his eyes and a piece of paper in his hands.

"I have here a song that I have written," Josef Mohr explained, "a Christmas song. Could you compose a suitable air for it? If you could arrange it for two solo voices, a chorus, and a guitar accompaniment, we could use it at the church tomorrow."

Franz Gruber was catching at straws. Certainly he would try. He read the verses, and as he read, his heart swelled with joy. At once he went to his spinet and began to search for the chords he desired. After many heart-searching attempts, he completed the beautiful and immortal melody.

Franz Gruber took the written score to Josef Mohr, who played it on his guitar. Then Gruber and Mohr sang the song together. When they had finished, they simply stared at each other, unaware that the dearest song known to Christendom had just been created.

### 3866    *Education*

Education does not commence with the alphabet. It begins with a mother's look and a father's nod and a sister's gentle pressure on the hand and a brother's act of forbearance . . . with flowers and green dells and on hills, with birds' nests admired but not touched, with pleasant walks in shady lanes, with thoughts directed in sweet and kindly tones, with deeds of virtue, with benevolent thoughts to the source of all good to God Himself.—*Good Reading Magazine*

### 3867    *Too Helpful*

At the end of the service a woman thanked the pastor for his sermon. "I found it so helpful," she told him.

The minister responded, "I hope it will not prove so helpful as the last sermon you heard me preach."

The puzzled woman asked, "Why, what do you mean?"

"Well," explained the clergyman, "that sermon lasted you three months."

### 3868    *Character*

The most important quality in an employee is not skill; it is character. A man of good character can acquire skill; a man without good character rarely becomes a desirable and profitable employee in a legitimate business.—*C. E. Bernard*

### 3869    *Example*

Dealing with a very young child, emotionally, is like dealing with a sponge. Give a smile, tender look, kind word, gentle touch, words of encouragement, praise, and like a sponge, the child will absorb the goodwill of the "giants" in his or her world and come to know from their example that this is the way to treat others. Example is a good teacher.

### 3870    *A Great Nation*

Whether America today is in its morning of life or has already reached its noontide of ultimate existence, God alone knows. But looking backwards, we do know that no nation in recorded history accomplished more for mankind in two short centuries than has been won here. No other constitutional republic lasted as long and, happily, we are still a relatively free people. This is a nation which has been built by those who came to this land out of suffering, privation, persecution, and bondage and with great hopes, dreams, and aspirations. They sought religious and political freedom, the pursuit of happiness, and a decent standard of living for themselves and their children. Of course, we would be deluding ourselves by asserting that all Americans have seen their hopes and dreams fulfilled. Indeed, there is much that has gone amiss and much that troubles us. Yet one would have to be blind in reading our history to suggest that America's blessings have not been many.—*From a Bicentennial address on July 4, 1976, by Samuel W. Witwer*

### 3871 *War*

Twenty years after, on the other side of the globe, again the filth of murky foxholes, the stench of ghostly trenches, the slime of dripping dugouts, those boiling suns of the relentless heat, those torrential rains of devastating storms, the loneliness and utter desolation of jungle trails, the bitterness of long separation from those they loved and cherished, and the deadly pestilence of tropical disease, the horror of stricken areas of war.—*Douglas MacArthur*

### 3872 *Let Us Remember*

Let us remember that each one of us has lifted the heart and bowed the knee in humble adoration of the Almighty. Any nation that forgets God is on the road to ruin and destruction. And that nation which remembers that there is a Divine Providence, that has the will to follow Divine guidance, will ultimately survive, and lead the world into the dawn of a new day of peace and good will among men.—*John W. Bricker*

### 3873 *Freedom*

Freedom consists not in refusing to recognize anything above us, but in respecting something which is above us; for by respecting it, we raise ourselves to it, and, by our very acknowledgment, prove that we bear within ourselves what is higher, and are worthy to be on a level with it.—*Johann Wolfgang von Goethe*

### 3874 *Lost*

Towards the end of Christopher Frye's play, *The Lady's Not for Burning,* one finds the disturbing exchange . . .

Margaret says, "Have any of you seen that poor child Alizon? I think she must be lost. . . ."

Nicholas answers, "Who isn't? The best thing we can do is make wherever we're lost in look as much like home as we can. Now don't be worried. She can't be more lost than she was with us."

The disturbing line to me is . . . "The best thing we can do is make wherever we're lost in look as much like home as we can."

It speaks of an aloneness that we can barely articulate. It's more like something only we can feel. We're in a crowd of people, and suddenly a feeling of being alone comes over us. Most of the time, the presence of just one other person breaks the aloneness, but then there are those times when no amount of people around us can dispel it. Jesus said once, "We are in this world but we are not of it." I wonder at times if that comes as a clue to us, that our home is yet in another place. We belong to this world, but we belong to yet another kingdom, and that's why deep within us, the sense of being lost with a certain homesickness emerges within us.—*Richard H. Stearns*

### 3875    *Discipline*

The curious mother asked her daughter why she drank her milk in kindergarten and not at home. The child replied, "When the teacher says, 'Drink your milk,' she means it, and you don't."

### 3876    *Teachable Moments*

Imagine a person who has a weight problem, to which he will not face up. For sake of illustration, yet very true to life in this circumstance, let us assume that he is aware that for his height and build, he carries too many pounds. His doctor has twiddled him about it. Friends have ribbed him on the subject. His wife, at careful moments, has given him the needle. Almost daily, through newspaper and television ads, he is reminded of those painful entities called calories . . . all to no avail. . . .

One day at work, he suffers sharp, stabbing pains around the heart. He is forced to fight for his breath. He slumps across the desk, pale, afraid . . . weak. Minutes later he lies calmly on the office couch. His doctor, seated in a nearby chair, speaks directly and somberly about the need for weight control. This time our friend hears and heeds. Life has brought him to what psychologists like to call a "teachable moment."—*Richard H. Stearns*

### 3877    *The Question*

Dr. Wernher Von Braun, the army rocket expert, had an arresting article entitled, "Can We Withstand the Acid Test?" The Soviet challenge, he points out, is by no means restricted to military technology. It goes far beyond the realms of politics and armies. "What we are about to discover is whether a nation which has rated its homerun sluggers and its fullbacks above its scientists and philosophers, can meet the competition of aggressive Communism and still preserve its way of life."

### 3878    *Inscription Chiseled on Historic Plymouth Rock*

Reader! History records no nobler venture for faith and freedom than of this Pilgrim band. In weariness and painfulness, in watchings, often in hunger and cold, they laid the foundations of a state wherein every man, through countless ages, should have liberty to worship God in his own way. May their example inspire thee to do thy part in perpetuating and spreading the lofty ideals of our republic throughout the world.

### 3879 *First Honorary Degree*

John Winthrop, first governor of the Massachusetts Bay Colony, had the distinction of being the first person awarded an honorary degree by an American institution of learning. The degree (doctor of laws) was conferred on July 21, 1773, by Harvard College. A sentiment expressed at that time, and on other occasions, by Governor Winthrop is worthy of continued preservation: A man has liberty to do that only which is good, just, and honest.

### 3880 *In the 1850s and '60s*

A man named Albert Potts perfected the now-familiar postal letter box. In Camden, New Jersey, Richard Easterbrook was beginning to manufacture the first steel pens. And over in Philadelphia, a little-known minister to human frailty was making a memorable contribution. His name was Hyman L. Lipman. He invented the pencil with an eraser attached.

### 3881 *Plain John Smith*

There is no more typical American name than John Smith, but other nationalities have him, too. In Latin, for example John Smith becomes Johannes Smithus; in Italian he is known as Giovanni Smithi; in French he is Jean Smeet; the Russians call him Jonloff Smittonski; the Poles know him as Ivan Schittweiski, and the Welsh as Jihon Schmidt; the Germans call him Johann Schmidt; to the Greeks he is Ivon Smikton and to the Spaniards Juan Smithus. In Turkey he is identified as Yoe Seef.

### 3882 *Time Gilds with Gold*

> Has some misfortune fallen to your lot?
> This, too, will pass away; absorb the thought,
> And wait—your waiting will not be in vain,
> Time gilds with gold the iron links of pain.
> The dark today leads into light tomorrow;
> There is no endless joy, no endless sorrow.
> —*Ella Wheeler Wilcox*

### 3883 *Weather*

One optimistic minister had the habit in his opening prayer each Sunday of thanking God for the weather. On a particularly cold, icy, windy, slushy Sunday morning, the few people who had ventured out wondered how the minister could possibly refer to the weather in his morning prayer with any sense of gratitude. To their surprise, he said in the beginning of his prayer, "Dear God, we thank Thee that Thou dost send us so few Sundays like today."—*Sunshine Magazine*

3884    *No Unbelief*

> There is no unbelief;
> Whoever plants a seed beneath the sod,
> And waits to see it push away the clod,
> Trusts in God.
> —*Edward Bulwer-Lytton*

3885    **Bureaucracy and Freedom**

We must beware of trying to build a society in which nobody counts for anything except a politician or an official, a society where enterprise gains no reward and thrift no privilege. Of all the races in the world, our people would be the last to consent to be governed by a bureaucracy. Freedom is in their blood. —*Winston Churchill*

3886    **Kindness**

Be kind to people. The world needs kindness so much. You never know what sort of battles other people are fighting. Often just a soft word or a warm compliment can be immensely supportive. You can do a great deal of good by just being considerate, by extending a little friendship, going out of your way to do just one nice thing, or saying one good word.—*Ann Landers*

3887    **Sabbath**

By neglecting the holy day we fail to replenish from week to week our inner life and to quicken anew our faith and love and reverence. Soon character begins to deteriorate, the fires of faith grow dim or go out altogether, and another spiritual tragedy comes to pass.—*William T. McElroy, Christian Observer*

3888    *As You Go Through Life*

> This world will never adjust itself
> To suit your whims to the letter;
> Some things must go wrong your whole life long
> And the sooner you know it the better.
> It is folly to fight with the Infinite,
> And go under at last in the wrestle,
> The wiser man shapes into God's plan
> As the water shapes into a vessel.
> —*Ella Wheeler Wilcox*

3889    *Lincoln's Friend*

I desire to so conduct the affairs of this administration that if, at the end, when I come to lay down the reins of power, I have lost every other friend on earth,

I shall at least have one friend left and that friend shall be down inside of me.
—*Abraham Lincoln*

### 3890 *Consider Everything*

In the nineteenth century, a man could purchase sirloin steak at 17 cents a pound and build a new home for $550. However, his life expectancy was thirty-eight years and a good net income was considered to be $600 a year.

### 3891 *Absence*

In Thomas Wolfe's book *You Can't Go Home Again,* published after his death, he suggests that, if a boy leaves home for college and a career, he is not likely to find his former associates anxious to welcome him when he returns. His friends may have changed; he also has probably changed.

Goethe advised that it is usually a mistake to return to a place where you once were happy. Happiness is a fragile flower that rarely survives a lengthy absence.

### 3892 *To Those Disappointed*

I have not willingly planted a thorn in any man's bosom. While I am deeply sensible of the high compliment of reelection, and duly grateful as I trust to Almighty God for having directed my countrymen to a right conclusion, as I think, for their own good, it adds nothing to my satisfaction that any other man may be disappointed or pained by the result. May I ask those who have not differed from me to join with us in this same spirit toward those who have.—*Abraham Lincoln after his second election*

### 3893 *His Belief*

Believing as I do that man in the distant future will be a far more perfect creature than he now is, it is an intolerable thought that he and all other sentient beings are doomed to complete annihilation after such long-continued slow progress.—*Charles Darwin*

### 3894 *A Prayer for Those in Government*

A distinguished American once impressed upon me in language I shall never forget the great responsibility of public office.

In these critical times, perhaps I can set down words this great American might have used if he were living now and were asked to give a prayer at a session of the Congress:

Almighty God, Lord of all nations, help us to realize the eminent sanctity of government.

Help us in humility to recognize the call to political office as a divine call to join Thee in the wise guidance of the people of this nation.

We are in a period of unprecedented moral confusion and historical change.

The disorders of our time have stirred in us uncertainties about our ability to guide a nation that no longer seems so simple and manageable as it was to our forefathers.

Help us to find the meaning of life over which the great issues of our time have cast their shadows.

Help us to recover the lost sense of the spirituality of secular affairs.

Help us here at the seat of government not to forget our ideals, at the expense of principle, and engage solely in the morally shoddy business of seeking popularity among the voters.

Help us to effect an amicable collaboration of races and nations.

Help us to examine our dogmatic certainties and our blind and selfish prejudices.

Help us to give radiant hope to bleak areas of our society.

Grant that we may not be nobler in promise than in performance.

Grant that the political parties may not be held together merely by ruthless pressures for party regularity and lust for office and power, but by honest concern for the welfare of the people.

Grant us courage to resist despotic majorities and unreasonable minorities, when that which is true and right abides in neither.

Save us in the heat of debate from saying things that will appeal to the aggregate prejudices of our constituencies, in a sorry attempt to win elections, when we should be speaking the truth.

Save us from using deceptive slogans and slick demagoguery to discredit our political opponents and to capitalize on social discontent for our own selfish gains.

If our people demand that their government give them complete economic security, grant they may not forget that a nation's strength depends on each person, to the best of his ability, standing on his own feet.

We seem sometimes to be ungrateful, arrogant in our demands, and irresponsible in our conduct, despite the wealth and power with which we have been favored.

Almighty God, Lord of all nations, to whom all hearts are open, and from whom no secrets are hidden, may the words of our mouths, the meditation of our hearts, and the service we render in public office be acceptable in Thy sight.

As we build here a society that is socially just, economically strong, and spiritually dynamic, may we be worthy of the high calling of government.

Amen.—*Herbert V. Prochnow*

3895     *Prayers on Restaurant Menus*

A number of years ago it was agreed by various groups in a suburb of New York City that mealtime prayers should be placed on the menus of the restaurants.

A local clergyman obtained the following prayers from clergymen in the three denominations represented in the suburb.

Protestant: "Bless, O Lord, this food to our use, and us to Thy service, and make us ever mindful of the needs of others, in Jesus' name. Amen."

Roman Catholic: "Bless us, O Lord, and these Thy gifts, which we are about to receive from Thy bounty, through Christ our Lord. Amen."

Jewish: "Lift up your hands toward the sanctuary and bless the Lord. Blessed art Thou, O Lord our God, King of the universe, who bringeth forth bread from the earth."

### 3896 *A Father's Great Gift to His Son*

To my dear son: In the New Year, I shall give you one hour of each weekday, and two hours of my Sundays, to be yours, and to be used as you want them, without interference of any kind whatsoever.—Your Father.

### 3897 *Not Important*

Comedian Richard Pryor, critically burned in an accident, told Johnny Carson that when you're seriously ill, money isn't important. He said: "All I could think of was to call on God. I didn't call the Bank of America once."

### 3898 *Wisdom*

A college professor once said of a particularly poor student, "The trouble with him is that he does not know that he does not know." That is true ignorance. It is real wisdom to know when we do not know.—*The Reverend Peter H. Pleune*

### 3899 *A Vert*

Poet Robert Frost is not without the ability to coin a phrase. In Washington during a press-conference discussion of life, liberty, poetry, and politics, the venerable New Englander said, "I'm neither an introvert nor an extrovert. Just a vert from Vermont."

### 3900 *The Promise of America*

To every man his chance, to every man, regardless of his birth, his shining golden opportunity—to every man the right to live, to work, to be himself, and to become whatever thing his manhood and his vision can combine to make him —this, seeker, is the promise of America.—*Thomas Wolfe*

3901 I thank God for my handicaps, for, through them, I have found myself, my work, and my God.—*Helen Keller*

3902 How poor are they who have not patience! What wound did ever heal, but by degrees?—*William Shakespeare*

3903    In the cathedral of my heart, a candle was always burning for you.—
*S. N. Behrman*

3904    Courage is not the absence of fear; it is the mastery of it.

3905    The truest test of moral courage is the ability to ignore the insult.

3906    Gratitude is the memory of the heart.—*Herbert V. Prochnow*

3907    When I was young my teachers were old and they told me of the past.
Now I am old and my teachers are young and they tell me of the future.

3908    Gratitude is the most exquisite form of courtesy.

3909    You can never do a kindness too soon because you never know how
soon it may be too late.

3910    Spring is the time the earth tunes up for the annual symphony of the
year.

3911    There exist limitless opportunities in every industry. Where there is an
open mind, there will always be a frontier.—*Charles F. Kettering*

3912    Where others see but the dawn coming over the hill, I see the soul of
God shouting for joy.—*William Blake*

3913    Christianity taught men that love is worth more than intelligence.—
*Jacques Maritain*

3914    The further I advance along the path of life, the more do I find work
a necessity. In the long run it becomes the greatest pleasure.—*Voltaire*

3915    It is not the body's posture, but the heart's attitude, that counts when
we pray.—*Billy Graham*

3916    There is just one way to bring up a child in the way he should go, and
that is to travel that way yourself.—*Abraham Lincoln*

3917    The talk of a child in the street is that of his father and mother.—
*Talmud*

3918    There is nothing noble in being superior to some other person. The true
nobility is in being superior to your previous self.

3919    No man has ever risen to the real stature of spiritual manhood until
he has found that it is finer to serve somebody else than it is to serve himself.
—*Woodrow Wilson*

3920 The Christian life is not a way "out" but a way "through" life.—Billy Graham

3921 The greatest truths are the simplest; and so are the greatest men and women.—*H. W. Hare*

3922 I believe the first test of a truly great man is humility.—*John Ruskin*

3923 I have found out in later years we were very poor, but the glory of America is that we didn't know it then.—*Dwight D. Eisenhower*

3924 Trouble is a part of your life, and if you don't share it, you don't give the person who loves you a chance to love you enough.—*Dinah Shore*

3925 Take Christ out of Christmas, and December becomes the bleakest and most colorless month of the year.—*A. F. Wells, Link*

3926 If through all his days a man tells the truth as he sees it, keeps his word as he gives it, and works well at his task, he gets what is called a good reputation.

3927 No man is useless in this world who lightens the burdens of someone else.—*Charles Dickens*

3928 I believe that faith is the biggest gift any parent can give a child—and it's more valuable than anything money can buy. Build your faith together—by going to the church of your choice.—*Gene Autry*

3929 When love adorns a home, other ornaments are a secondary matter.

3930 Among the attributes of God, although they are all equal, mercy shines with even more brilliancy than justice.—*Cervantes*

3931 We hand folks over to God's mercy, and show none ourselves.—*George Eliot*

3932 A man, however fallen, who loves his home, is not wholly lost.—*Benjamin Disraeli*

3933 Happiness is being at peace; being with loved ones; being comfortable and free of pain. But most of all, it's having those loved ones.—*Johnny Cash*

3934 Wise sayings often fall on barren ground; but a kind word is never thrown away.—*Sir Arthur Helps*

3935 You don't necessarily observe the Sabbath because you have on a new suit or hat.

3936     There is a loftier ambition than merely to stand high in the world. It is to stoop down and lift mankind a little higher.—*Henry van Dyke*

3937     Pray for my soul. More things are wrought by prayer
            Than this world dreams of.
                                            —*Tennyson*

3938     In this world it is not what we take up, but what we give up, that makes us rich.—*Henry Ward Beecher*

3939     A teacher affects eternity; no one can tell where his influence stops.—*Henry Adams*

3940     And what doth the Lord require of thee, but to do justly, and to love mercy, and to walk humbly with thy God?—*Micah 6:8*

3941     Prayer is not asking. It is a longing of the soul.—*Mahatma Gandhi*

3942     I could not say I believe. I know! I have had the experience of being gripped by something that is stronger than myself, something that people call God.—*Carl Jung, when asked if he believed in God*

3943     That best portion of a good man's life,
            His little, nameless, unremembered acts
            Of kindness and of love.
                                    —*William Wordsworth*

3944     If the stars should appear one night in a thousand years, how would men believe and adore!—*Ralph Waldo Emerson*

3945     "I can forgive, but I cannot forget," is only another way of saying, "I cannot forgive."—*Henry Ward Beecher*

3946     It is the heart which experiences God, and not the reason. This, then, is faith: God felt by the heart, not by the reason.—*Blaise Pascal*

# Helpful Illustrations and Facts

### 3947    *Most Difficult*

"Of all my inventions," Thomas A. Edison reminisced, some years before his death on October 18, 1931, "the incandescent light was the most difficult."

One October evening the thirty-two-year-old inventor sat in his laboratory, weary from thirteen months of repeated failure to find a filament that would stand the stress of electric current. The scientific press, at first politely skeptical, were now openly derisive. Discouraged backers were refusing to put up further funds.

Idly Edison picked up a bit of lampblack mixed with tar, rolled it into a thread. "Thread," he mused, ". . . thread . . . thread . . . carbonized cotton thread." He had tried every known metal.

It required five hours to carbonize a length of thread. The first one broke before it could be removed from the mould; likewise a second and a third. An entire spool of thread was consumed; then a second spool. Finally, a perfect filament emerged, only to be broken in an effort to insert it into the vacuum tube. Another was destroyed when a screwdriver fell against it. After two days and two nights the filament was successfully inserted. The bulb was exhausted of air and sealed, the current turned on. "The sight we had so long desired to see met our eyes."

And then Edison, after working continuously for forty-eight hours, sat for an additional forty-five hours—until the light blinked out—gazing intently at the world's first incandescent electric lamp.—*Gospel Banner*

### 3948    *Fathers of Great Men*

The father of Shakespeare was a wool merchant.
The Emperor Diocletian was the son of a slave.

Abraham Lincoln's father was a poor farmer and laborer.
Vergil's father was a porter and for years a slave.
Demosthenes' father, a blacksmith and swordmaker.
Ben Franklin was the son of a soapboiler.
Daniel Webster was the son of a poor farmer.
Christopher Colombus was the son of a weaver.
Sophocles, the Greek poet, was the son of a blacksmith.

### 3949    *Their Occupations*

I do not forget that I am a mechanic. I am proud to own it. Neither do I forget that Adam was a tailor, sewing fig leaves together for aprons; Tubal-cain was an artificer in brass and iron; Joseph the husband of Mary was a carpenter, and our Savior probably followed the same trade; the apostle Paul was a tentmaker; Socrates was a sculptor; Archimedes was a mechanic; King Crispin was a shoemaker; and so was Roger Sherman, who helped to form the Constitution.—*Andrew Jackson*

### 3950    *What You Set Your Heart On*

Luther Burbank fell in love with plants; Edison fell in love with invention; Ford fell in love with motor cars; Kettering fell in love with research; the Wright brothers fell in love with airplanes. Someone has truly said: "Be careful what you set your heart on for it will surely come true." The men who harness their hearts to mighty tasks often see their dreams become realities.—*Silver Lining*

### 3951    *Children's Bill of Rights*

1. The right to the affection and intelligent guidance of understanding parents.
2. The right to be raised in a decent home in which he or she is adequately fed, clothed, and sheltered.
3. The right to the benefits of religious guidance and training.
4. The right to a school program, which, in addition to sound academic training, offers maximum opportunity for individual development and preparation for living.
5. The right to receive constructive discipline for the proper development of good character, conduct, and habits.
6. The right to be secure in his or her community against all influences detrimental to wholesome development.
7. The right to the individual selection of free and wholesome recreation.
8. The right to live in a community in which adults practice the belief that the welfare of their children is of primary importance.
9. The right to receive good adult example.—*New York Youth Commission*

### 3952    *Too Busy*

The late actor John Barrymore was invited by phone to attend a party to be given by a boring Hollywoodite. He politely replied: "It will be impossible for me to accept because of a previous engagement, which I shall make as soon as possible."—*Sunshine Magazine*

### 3953   *Our Presidents*

Ulysses S. Grant and John F. Kennedy were the only presidents whose parents were both living at the times of their inaugurations. The president who lived the longest was John Adams (90 years, 247 days).

Army generals or former generals to be elected to the presidency were: Washington, Jackson, William Henry Harrison, Taylor, Pierce, Grant, Hayes, Garfield, Benjamin Harrison, and Eisenhower. Four others were nominated but not elected. As of 1983, no admiral had ever been nominated for the presidency.

### 3954   *Sounds Better*

Winston Churchill was accused by a Laborite of "lying" to the House of Commons. Churchill demanded that the Laborite repeat his exact words and was mollified when the Victorian phrase "terminological inexactitude" was substituted for the word "lie."

### 3955   *It's Different Now*

The nomination of Lincoln in 1860 cost his friends less than $700. Judge David Davis, one of Lincoln's intimates, told Senator John J. Ingalls of Kansas that this covered everything, "including headquarters, telegraphing, music, fare of delegates, incidentals."

### 3956   *In the Old Days*

Benjamin Franklin was the first postmaster-general of the United States, being appointed in 1775. He received $1,000 a year.

### 3957   *A Precocious Student*

Paderewski arrived in a small Connecticut town about noon one day and decided to take a walk. While strolling along he heard a piano and, following the sound, came to a house on which a sign proclaimed: "Miss Jones. Piano lessons $2 an hour."

Pausing to listen, he heard the young woman trying to play one of Chopin's nocturnes, and not succeeding very well. Paderewski walked up to the house and knocked.

Miss Jones came to the door and recognized him at once. Delighted, she invited him in and he sat down and played the nocturne as only he could, afterward spending an hour correcting her mistakes. Miss Jones thanked him and he departed.

Some months later he returned to the town, and again he took the same walk.

He soon came to the home of Miss Jones, and, looking at the sign, he read: "Miss Jones (pupil of Paderewski). Piano lessons $10 per half hour."

3958    *Banking Magic*

Try this sometime on your banker. Put $50 in the bank, then make withdrawls as follows:

| | |
|---|---|
| Draw out $20, leaving | $30 |
| Draw out $15, leaving | $15 |
| Draw out $ 9, leaving | $ 6 |
| Draw out $ 6, leaving | $ 0 |

Total        $50 Total        $51

3959    *Let George Do It*

When George W. Goethals went down into the "death zone" of Panama, where 20,000 Frenchmen had perished with yellow fever, most Americans thought digging the canal was so impossible that they began to say, "Let George do it." Here is the origin of the phrase that has been used so many times to shift responsibility. To Goethals, the obstacle was the biggest opportunity in his life. Not only did he see a completed canal, but he saw a health zone established on each side.

3960    *A Great Discovery*

For a long time Charles Goodyear spent every hour seeking a method of preparing rubber to withstand all weather conditions. After many failures, his wife prevailed on him to quit his experiments. However, one day when alone, he could not resist the temptation to try one more rubber mixture. In the midst of kneading the solution, he heard his wife return. Hurriedly he shoved the material into the oven. Some hours later, removing the pan, he was astonished to find the mixture had changed into a tough substance that was affected by neither heat nor cold. Thus Charles Goodyear bumped into the method of vulcanizing rubber.

3961    *End of the "Me Decade"*

The "Me Decade" has ended. We've begun to reverse the direction—to be concerned about the family, society, institutions. Youths talk more openly of religious beliefs and concerns for the future.

3962    *Our Musical Presidents*

While the United States can include no Paderewski among its statesmen, as can Poland, it can boast of presidents who were good performers of music, and presidents who had a keen appreciation of it. All might be included in that category except possibly Grant, who claimed he knew only two tunes, "one is 'Yankee Doodle,' and the other isn't."

It is said Jefferson was a skilled violinist. He studied in Paris and found "his violin a never ending source of delight." Franklin was also musical, and he occasionally accompanied Jefferson on the guitar.

Woodrow Wilson won acclaim with his tenor voice. He sang second tenor in the Princeton University Glee Club while a student. Wilson never lost his interest in music, although he made few public appearances as a singer after entering public life.

Harding was an enthusiastic sponsor of music. His participation in music dated back to the Iberia, Ohio, brass band, where he "played every instrument but the slide trombone and E-flat clarinet." When he became president, Harding would occasionally drop in on rehearsals of the Marine Band, pick up an instrument, and play, "just to keep his hand in."

Throughout his life, music was a solace to Lincoln. "His musical tastes," says a biographer, "were simple and uncultivated, his choice being old airs, songs, and ballads." On one of his walks through Washington during the war, Lincoln passed a schoolhouse where children were singing. He took off his high beaver hat and heard the song through, his face brightening the while. Then he straightened up and walked off with a more elastic step.

McKinley inaugurated a Sunday evening hymn sing in the White House. Coolidge would often step up to the piano presided over by Mrs. Coolidge.

The musical inclinations of Harry S Truman, and his frequent informal recitals on the piano when he rendered his favorite, "Missouri Waltz," are well known.
—*Sunshine Magazine*

### 3963    *Mercy—Not Justice*

Mme. Schumann-Heink was a woman of rare charm and geniality. She was the first to make fun of her own shortcomings, and was often heard to comment good-naturedly on her decidedly matronly figure.

On one occasion a fashionable portrait painter asked her to sit for her portrait. The plump opera star hesitated a long time before making a decision.

"Don't be afraid, Madame," said the artist teasingly. "I'll do you justice."

"Ah," replied the prima donna, "it isn't justice I ask at your hands; it is mercy!"—*Woolverton Press*

### 3964    *The Show Is On*

When a man wakes up to the fact that "the show is on," that his span of life is shortening with every tick of the clock, and if he is going to live a useful life, he must be at it—at that moment life begins for him, no matter what his age. The tragedies of life are with those who drift, and never discover that life has begun. For them the curtain never rises.

### 3965    *I Still Learn*

Michelangelo was seventy-two years old when he was appointed chief architect of St. Peter's and commissioned to embellish this great temple with his paintings and statues. For eighteen years he continued this work, which made his fame as imperishable as the church itself. Toward the end, when his eyesight failed and he had become feeble, he had his servants carry him into the great halls and galleries and chapels, where he had labored with such vim and enthusiasm. He would run his hands over the statues and carvings, feeling out with his dextrous fingers the details that his eyes could no longer see, and he often exclaimed, "I still learn."

### 3966    *Animal Oddities*

Cats seldom lie with their feet to a fire. Usually they lie on the left side. Dogs lie with their forepaws to a fire.

Hens scratch for food with the sun behind them, the reason apparently being that the sun's rays reflect from the minute particles. A blind hen will pick grain, not missing a kernel.

A fly on a windowpane will crawl to the top, fly back to the bottom, and crawl up again. This order is seldom reversed; why, no one knows.

Goldfish usually swim around a tank, pursuing the direction to the right. They generally ignore the presence of other fish in the tank.

### 3967    *Every Day*

Every Christian occupies some kind of pulpit and preaches some kind of sermon every day.—*Methodist Story*

### 3968    *How Fast Can You Run?*

Suppose all the different animals in the world would line up for a short foot race. Which one do you think would cover the distance first? Doubtless you would not pick the tortoise even though, according to a fairy tale, it did beat the hare.

In speeds among animals, the cheetah, or hunting leopard, a member of the cat family found throughout Africa and South Asia, comes first, With a speed up to 70 miles an hour. Certain types of deer come second, with a speed around 60 miles an hour. Lions, racehorses, jackrabbits, kangaroos, and foxes follow with records from 40 to 50 miles an hour.

Size has little to do with the speed with which animals can travel. The large elephant, buffalo, and rhinoceros, and the tiny chipmunk are all faster than man.

Keep on friendly relations with those cheetahs, bears, and elephants if you don't want to be chased up a tree.—*Roy A. Brenner, in Boy's Life*

### 3969    *Not Bad*

By the end of a three-year period, an average hen has eaten 170 pounds of feed, laid 42 dozen eggs, and provided four and one half pounds of meat and half an ounce of feathers.

### 3970    *How They Wear Out*

One-dollar bills last about twenty-two months before wearing out. Five-dollar bills last nearly two years; tens, three years; and twenties, five years. A $100 bill will usually remain in circulation for about twenty-five years.

### 3971    *Forget the Speech*

Winston Churchill hailed a cab in the West End and told the cabbie to hurry to the BBC studios. The premier was scheduled to make a speech.

"Sorry, sir," said the driver, "but you will have to get yourself another cab. I can't go that far."

Mr. Churchill was surprised, and asked the driver why his operations were so limited.

"They hain't hordinarily, sir," he apologized, "but you see, sir, Mr. Churchill is to broadcast in an hour, and I want to get 'ome to 'ear 'im."

Churchill was so pleased that he handed the man a pound note. The man was so pleased that he exclaimed, "'Op in, sir! To blazes with Churchill!"—*Capper's Weekly*

### 3972    *The Contented Life*

Goethe, possessing one of the greatest minds in all time, set forth these nine essentials to a full and contented life:

Health enough to make work a pleasure.

Wealth enough to support your needs.

Strength to battle with difficulties and overcome them.

Grace enough to confess your sins and forsake them.

Patience enough to toil until some good is accomplished.

Charity enough to see some good in your neighbor.

Love enough to move you to be useful and helpful to others.

Faith enough to make real the things of God.

Hope enough to remove all anxious fears concerning the future.

### 3973    *Washington Kept His Mouth Shut*

It is said that when George Washington was chosen to a seat in the House of Burgesses in Virginia at the age of twenty-six, Captain Mercer described him to some friends this way:

"He is as straight as an arrow, measuring six feet and two inches in his stocking feet, and weighing 175 pounds. His head is well shaped, though not large, and is gracefully poised. He has a large, straight nose, blue-gray penetrating eyes, which are widely separated and overhung by heavy brows. A pleasing, though commanding countenance; dark-brown hair, features regular and placid, and a large mouth, generally firmly closed."

One thing to notice about this picture of George Washington is that his mouth, though large, was "generally firmly closed."

### 3974 *The New Model*

When people's cars get old and worn, and then begin to toddle, they go somewhere and trade them in, and get the latest model.

Now, I have very often thought that when my joints get achy, and when my hair has all turned gray, and knees are rather shaky; and when the onward march of time has left me rather feeble, how nice 'twould be to find a firm that deals in worn-out people.

How nice 'twould be, when feet give out, or one has damaged livers, if one could go and get new parts, just like we do for flivvers. And when my form is bent with age, and gets to looking shoddy, how nice 'twould be to trade it in and get a brand new body!—*The Telescope, Belleville, Kansas*

### 3975 *Capitalism*

Capitalism is what we have, and what most Americans want to keep. The farmer's land and his barn, his livestock and machines are capital. The merchant's store, the goods on his shelves, and the truck that delivers them are capital. The tools of the skilled mechanic are capital. Every life insurance policy, every bank account, is capital.

Everything that contributes to the production and distribution of goods is capital, from the biggest factory to the smallest newsstand.

Almost everybody in the United States is a capitalist. A capitalist isn't just a banker or a manufacturer. You couldn't throw a stick down any street without hitting a capitalist. We all belong.

The people who really hate capitalists are the socialists and communists. But it isn't capital itself that they hate. What they hate is the idea of letting the average man own and control his own capital. They want to do that instead.

Capitalism is the only system that lets everyone own capital, live where he pleases, and work at the job he chooses, without interference.—*Radio broadcast by International Harvester Company*

### 3976 *A Reminder*

Human vanity can best be served by a reminder that, whatever his accomplishments, his sophistication, his artistic pretension, man owes his very existence to a six-inch layer of topsoil—and the fact that it rains.

### 3977 *A Mile and a Half from Church*

We're a mile and a half from church, you know, and it rains today, so we can't go. We'd go ten miles to a party or show, though the rains should fall and the winds should blow. That's why, when it rains, we just can't go. But we always go to the things we like, and we ride if we can; if we can't, we hike.

We're a mile and a half from church, you know, and a tire is flat, so we can't go. We'd fix it twice to make a visit, and if there's a ball game we wouldn't miss it. We'd mend the tire if at all we could, and if we couldn't we'd go a foot, for hunting pleasure is all the style, so the church will have to wait awhile.

We're a mile and a half from church, you know, and our friends are coming, so we can't go. To disappoint our friends would seem unkind, but to neglect worship we don't mind, if we may please our friends on earth, and spend a day in feasting and mirth. But, sometime, when we come near the end of our days, we'll go to church and mend our ways.—*George C. Degen, compliments Y.M.-C.A., Wilkes-Barre, Pennsylvania*

### 3978    The Leader

A man in Paris during the upheaval in 1848, saw a friend marching after a crowd toward the barricades. Warning him that these could not be held against the troops, that he had better keep away, and asking why he followed those people, he received the reply, "I must follow them. I am their leader."—*A. Lawrence Lowell*

### 3979    Whims of the Great

James Fenimore Cooper could not write unless he was chewing gumdrops, of which he went through large quantities as he developed his novels.

Robert Browning was unable to sit still when writing, and holes were worn in the carpet at his desk as the result of the constant shuffling of his feet.

Edgar Allan Poe always took his cat to bed with him, and was very vain of the size and shapeliness of his feet.

It is recorded of Thackeray that every time he passed the house in which he wrote *Vanity Fair*, he lifted his hat; and Hawthorne always washed his hands before sitting down to read a letter from his wife.

A peculiarity of the younger Dumas was that every time he published a novel he went out and bought a painting to mark the occasion.

Oliver Wendell Holmes was given to carrying a potato in one pocket and a horse chestnut in the other, in the belief that these kept rheumatism away.

Peculiarities of dress in authors are remarkable. Disraeli wore corsets. Dickens had a weakness for flashy jewelry. Tolstoi was fond of French perfumes.

Francis Bacon was so fond of fine clothes that he spent his odd time in trying to design new styles and fashions. When he could not persuade anyone to wear them, he got what satisfaction he could by hiring men to don his grotesque creations and thus promenade the streets.

The ruling passion of Peter the Great was to ride about in a wheelbarrow, and many of his state visits to cities and towns over which he ruled were made in this fashion, the monarch being wheeled along in his homely conveyance pushed by a perspiring manservant.—*Sunshine Magazine*

3980    *Using Words Carefully*

If the story of the Creation can be told in 400 words, if the Ten Commandments contain only 297 words, if Lincoln's immortal Gettysburg Address was
only 266 words, if an entirely new concept of freedom was set up in the Declaration of Independence in about 1,300 words—it is up to some of us to use fewer
words, and thus save the time, energy, vitality, and nerves of those who must
read or listen.—*Jerome P. Fleishman*

3981    *Not Worthy*

The piano used by the great composer Ludwig van Beethoven (1770–1827) is
in a museum in Vienna. A young tourist walked casually toward it, and seating
herself on the stool, ran off a careless air. Then turning to the attendant, she asked
whether any great pianists had come to inspect the instrument. The attendant
informed her that a short time before, Ignace Paderewski had made a pilgrimage
to the shrine.

"Paderewski?" inquired the girl. "And surely, he played something beautiful
on this old instrument."

"On the contrary," replied the attendant, "Mr. Paderewski did not feel worthy
of touching it."

3982    *Historical Events on the Fourth of July*

The Fourth of July plays a memorable role in the drama of American tradi-
tions.

On July 4, 1776, a group of men, meeting in Philadelphia as the Continental
Congress, adopted a declaration drawn up by Thomas Jefferson, which dissolved
all ties binding the American colonies to Great Britain.

War followed the Declaration of Independence. Five years later, to the day,
General Cornwallis and his British troops evacuated Williamsburg and set their
feet on the road to defeat. Three months later Cornwallis surrendered at York-
town, and America was free.

On July 4, 1804, Nathaniel Hawthorne, author of numerous American classics, was born in Salem, Massachusetts. His books, among them *The Scarlet
Letter* and *The House of the Seven Gables,* are familiar to many Americans.

On July 4, 1826, Stephen Collins Foster, was born in Pittsburgh, Pennsylvania.
His songs, which include "My Old Kentucky Home" and "Old Folks at Home,"
endure.

Death came to John Adams and Thomas Jefferson, two of the distinguished
signers of the Declaration of Independence, while the nation was joyously cele-
brating the fiftieth anniversary of its adoption. Five years later, on July 4, 1831,
James Monroe, our fifth president and the framer of the Monroe Doctrine, died.

July 4, 1804, inaugurated the first stagecoach line running between Philadelphia and Pittsburgh. Exactly thirteen years later, work on the Erie Canal was

begun. On the same day in 1828 the first rail of the Baltimore and Ohio Railroad was laid.

The United States Patent Bureau was created by act of Congress on July 4, 1836.

The cornerstone of the towering obelisk erected in the nation's capital to the memory of George Washington was laid on July 4, 1848.

July 4, 1872, was the natal day of the first president to be born on the nation's birthday, the thirtieth president, Calvin Coolidge.

The Fourth of July is a notable day in our history. It is filled with memories, tragic and heroic.

### 3983    Santa Claus

When Saint Nicholas came to this country with the early Dutch settlers, he was a tall, thin, serious-looking old fellow. He would hardly recognize himself now. His Dutch name was Santa Nikalaus, but it got chopped down to Santa Klaus.

By the time Washington Irving and Dr. Clement Moore, the author of "'Twas the Night Before Christmas," got through with him, they had fattened him up, endowed him with a rollicking disposition, and brightened his complexion to a cheerful red. And the famous cartoonist Thomas Nast drew the portrait of Santa Claus that we know today—a composite of Father Knickerbocker and Old King Cole. It's wonderful what this country did for a middle-aged European saint!—*The Woman*

### 3984    Not Equal

If we could solve all the mysteries of the Universe, we would be co-equal with God. Every drop of ocean shares its glory but is not the ocean.—*Mahatma Gandhi*

### 3985    Statue of Liberty

The Statue of Liberty, located on Bedloe's Island, in New York, is made of bronze, but long exposure to the elements has resulted in the weathered, greenish-gray appearance it now has. The statue was finished in 1883 and on July 4, 1884, was presented as a gift to the United States from France. In June of 1885, the statue was brought to Bedloe's Island and assembled in 1886. A public unveiling of this monument to freedom was held October 28, 1886.

### 3986    His Opinion

If to be venerated for benevolence, if to be admired for talents, if to be esteemed for patriotism, if to be beloved for philanthropy, can gratify the human mind, you must have the pleasing consolation to know that you have not lived in vain. —*George Washington in a letter to Benjamin Franklin*

### 3987 *Don't Fear Criticism*

The galleries are full of critics. They play no ball. They fight no fights. They make no mistakes because they attempt nothing. Down in the arena are the doers. They make mistakes because they attempt things.

Ford forgot to put a reverse gear in his first automobile. Edison once spent $2 million on an invention that proved of little value.

The person who makes no mistakes lacks boldness and the spirit of adventure.

And yet it cannot be truly said that he makes no mistakes, because the biggest mistake he makes is the very fact that he tries nothing, does nothing except criticize those who do things.

### 3988 *Interesting Lives*

Lawrence Tibbett, internationally famous Metropolitan Opera star, first saw the inside of that building from the $2.20 standing-room space, because he couldn't afford to buy a seat.

Charles Dickens, who later became one of the most famous and highly paid authors in the history of literature, got nothing for the first nine stories he had published. And he received only $5 for his tenth effort.

Guglielmo Marconi had perfected his wireless to the stage where it was recognized as a transatlantic transmission, and was a world sensation when he was only twenty-seven years of age.

### 3989 *Careful Reporting*

Mark Twain in his reporting days was told by an editor never to state anything as a fact unless he could verify it from personal experience. Sent out to cover an important social event soon afterward, he turned in the following:

"A woman giving the name of Mrs. James Jones, who is reported to be one of the social leaders of the city, is said to have given what purported to be a party yesterday to a number of alleged ladies. The hostess claims to be the wife of a reputed attorney."

### 3990 *The Power of Words*

Soft words in a lullaby will put a babe to sleep. Excited words will stir a mob to violence. Eloquent words will send armies marching into the face of death. Encouraging words will fan to flame the genius of a Rembrandt or a Lincoln. Powerful words will mold the public mind as the sculptor molds his clay. Words are a dynamic force.

Words are the swords we use in our battle for success and happiness. How others react toward us depends, in a large measure, upon the words we speak to them. Life is a great whispering gallery that sends back echoes of the words we send out! Our words are immortal, too. They go marching through the years in the lives of all those with whom we come in contact.

When you speak, when you write, remember the creative power of words.—
*Wilferd A. Peterson*

3991    *Two Experiences*

On the top of a great hill, the Acropolis, in the center of Athens, there stand
the proud columns of the ruins of the Parthenon, one of the most magnificent
and inspiring architectural works man has ever created. With its eight great
Doric columns in the front and rear, and the seventeen along the two sides, this
masterpiece of Greek architecture was erected in the fourth century before
Christ. The famous Elgin marbles now in the British Museum were taken from
the Parthenon in 1806.

Late one afternoon, Mrs. Prochnow and I were climbing the long stone and
gravel steps that lead up to the Parthenon, in order to see the golden rays of the
setting sun fall upon those majestic ruins.

A large unit of the American fleet was in Greek and Turkish waters. Two
American marines on shore leave were walking near us. As we climbed the stairs,
one marine said to the other, "I suppose the day will come when others will walk
up the stone steps to the ruins of the White House, and they will say as they look
at the ruins, 'This was a great civilization before it fell.' "

The second experience was in Lebanon. By automobile it is only a short drive
from Beirut to the little city of Byblos. This city is one of the oldest in the world.
There the ruins of many early civilizations are now exposed by the excavations
of the archaeologists. Here one can stand and look down through seven thousand
years of history. One civilization was built on top of the ruins of the last. The
floor of a home of one civilization may be seen only a foot above the floor of a
home of a preceding civilization. There one sees the Stone Age, the civilizations
of the Egyptians, Phoenicians, Babylonians, Assyrians, Greeks, Arabs, Romans,
Crusaders, and Turks. One after another, through seven thousand years, great
empires and great nations rose and then fell from power. It is a sobering thought.

Through the centuries great empires have risen and fallen—Spain and Portugal in the Western hemisphere; the Netherlands in the Far East; France in
Indochina and the Middle East and now struggling to retain her position in
Northern Africa. In this generation we have witnessed the decline in power of
an empire upon which it was said, with understandable pride, that the sun never
set.

Now another power—the United States—is striding majestically across the
horizon of world affairs. Its armies, its planes, its ships, its money, its merchandise, and its industrial genius are moving to the remote parts of the world. In
a world where two-thirds of the people earn less than $100 a year, we are far
richer than any nation in history has ever been. The call of economic comfort
is loud. Leisure becomes more attractive than labor. Spending becomes more
alluring than saving. Lest we forget: Every great nation which has risen to power

has declined. Confronted with the determined challenge of Communism over the world, we must remain strong, and we must hold fast in our minds and hearts to those great ideals and those eternal values upon which freedom, human dignity, and our very survival may ultimately rest.—*Herbert V. Prochnow*

### 3992 *Time*

The ticking of the clock is one of the most important things in the world, for it marks the passage of time. It reminds us that another second, another hour, another day has gone. And yet, despite this constant reminder, most of us go along using time aimlessly, failing to get out of it either enjoyment of life or satisfaction of accomplishment. We know that the opportunity that today presents will never be repeated; that spring fades into summer, and presently winter comes, and we wake with a start to realize that another year has passed. Still we postpone. "There is plenty of time," we tell ourselves. That is the great fallacy. "The clock of life is wound but once."—*Anonymous*

### 3993 *The Best*

I have lived all my life with music, books, and works of art; yet, I cannot tell you what is the best picture ever painted, or what is the best music written, or the best play. I can, however, tell you what is the best prayer ever composed, the best sermon ever written, and the best poetry in the world. The Lord's Prayer is the best prayer; the best sermon is the Sermon on the Mount; and the best poetry ever written is the 23rd, the 90th, and the 113th Psalms.—*William Lyon Phelps*

### 3994 *Minutes*

Roderick, age four, was waiting for Mother to take him to town. She had promised to be ready in "about five minutes." Finally, worn with waiting, he ventured solemnly to ask, "Mother, are minutes any longer than they used to be?"—*Parents Magazine*

### 3995 *Boomeranged*

The boy left the farm and got a job in the city. Wanting to impress his brother with his new life he wrote: "Thursday we motored out to the club, where we golfed until dark. Then we motored out to the beach and week-ended."

But his brother on the farm failed to be impressed, and wrote back: "Sunday we motored to town and baseballed all afternoon. Yesterday we muled out to the cornfield till sundown. Then we suppered. After that we staircased to our room and bedsteaded till the clock fived."

### 3996 *Achievement*

Gladstone was prime minister of England at eighty-three; Benjamin Franklin helped frame the Constitution of the United States at eighty; Oliver Wendell Holmes retired from the Supreme Court bench at ninety-one; Henry Ford, when past eighty, took up the presidency of the Ford Motor Company for the second time, after his son's death; and Alonzo Stagg was named Football's Man of the Year at eighty-one.

### 3997    *Your Fellow Man*

If you have done your fellow man a little wrong, let it be a great wrong in your eyes and go and rectify it. If you have done him much good, let it be little in your eyes. If he has done you a little good, let it be great in your eyes. If he has done you a great wrong, let it be little in your eyes.—*Rabbi Nathan*

### 3998    *His Ambition*

A minister of modest means lived in a small town. When he was seen driving a Cadillac, tongues began to wag. One day the minister came upon a youngster who was admiring the car. As the boy looked up at him, the minister—already sensitive to the talk in town—interpreted the lad's glance as one of suspicion and accusation.

The minister explained, "I have a rich brother in Texas who sent it to me."

"Boy," said the youngster, "I hope some day I will be a brother like that."

### 3999    *No Complaint*

Our forefathers managed to survive without sugar until the thirteenth century. They did without coal until the fourteenth century, and buttered bread didn't come on the scene until the fifteenth century. Potatoes were not available until the sixteenth century, while coffee, soup, and tea weren't introduced until the seventeenth century. They did without pudding until the eighteenth century. Matches, electricity, and gas weren't used until the nineteenth century, and canned goods didn't come along until this century. Do we really have anything to grumble and complain about?

### 4000    *What You Take for Granted*

How can you expect to keep your powers of hearing when you never want to listen? That God should have time for you, you seem to take as much for granted as that you cannot have time for Him.—*Dag Hammarskjöld*

### 4001    *A Son Speaks*

At eleven years: "My parents are grand. They know simply everything."

At sixteen: "Really and truly, my parents are not quite so grand as I used to think. They don't know everything."

At nineteen: "Although my parents think they are always right, they really know very little compared with what I know already. . . ."

At twenty-two: "My parents do not understand young people; they have nothing in common with the young generation."

At thirty: "To tell the truth, my parents were right in many things."

At fifty: "My parents were wonderful people. They had a clear mind and

always did the necessary thing at the right moment. My beloved parents . . ."
—*Neues Wiener Tagblatt*

### 4002    *In Real Trouble*

Chief Justice Oliver Wendell Holmes was on a train and could not find his ticket. The conductor knew him and said, "Don't worry, send us a check." Holmes replied, "That doesn't really help me. If I don't find my ticket, I won't know where I am going."

### 4003    *Lost*

G. K. Chesterton was once in Market Harbor, England. He telephoned his wife and said, "I'm in Market Harbor. Where should I be?"

### 4004    *Helping an Individual*

If you want to raise a man from mud and filth, do not think it is enough to stay on top and reach a helping hand down to him. You must go all the way down yourself, down into mud and filth. Then take hold of him with strong hands and pull him and yourself out into the light.—*Hasidic*

### 4005    *Successful*

A little girl once said to her daddy, "I am having an awfully good time with myself." Well, when our inward nature is such that we can enjoy our company, find ourselves good company to be with, we are a success.—*H. Richard Rasmusson*

### 4006    *Three Who Plead*

At the time of man's departure from this world, there are three who plead for him: his family, his money, and his good deeds.

The first two are not deemed to be valid credentials of personal worth, but a man's good deeds precede him and prepare him for the road to eternity.—*Midrash*

### 4007    *The Real Question*

> The Government, it is probably true,
> Will take care of me and take care of you.
> Take care of our birth, our marriage, our death,
> Take care of our thoughts, take care of our rent,
> But who will take care of the Government?
> —*Chain-gang song*

### 4008    *It Would Have Been Better*

The mother of Karl Marx was a very wise woman, for she wrote: "If Karl had made a lot of Capital instead of writing a lot about Capital, it would have been much better."—*Nation's Business*

4009    *Government*

No government ever financed anything that it did not get control of. You cannot separate responsibility and power. If the government hands out a dollar, with it goes the implied responsibility of how it shall be spent and some influence on the life of the recipient.—*Dr. Alfred P. Haake*

4010    A railroad! It would frighten horses, put the owners of public vehicles out of business, break up inns and taverns and be a monopoly generally.—*Andrew Johnson*

4011    Since I myself stand in need of God's pity, I have granted an amnesty to all my enemies.—*Heinrich Heine*

4012    You feel you are no longer clothing yourself; you are dressing a national monument.—*Eleanor Roosevelt*

4013    Henry W. Longfellow sold his poem "The Village Blacksmith" to the *Knickerbocker Magazine* in 1840 for $15.

4014    He had a face like a benediction.—*Cervantes*

4015    It cost Columbus $7,250 to discover America—a small fraction of what it costs a congressional committee to discover a few facts.

4016    Don't tell me of facts, I never believe facts; you know Canning said nothing was so fallacious as facts, except figures.—*Sydney Smith*

4017    Benjamin Franklin was the fifteenth of seventeen children.

4018    If you are as happy, my dear sir, on entering this house as I am in leaving it and returning home, you are the happiest man in this country.—*Departing President James Buchanan to the newly elected Abraham Lincoln at the White House*

4019    A conclusion is the place where you got tired of thinking.—*Martin H. Fischer*

4020    Truth is with the victor—who, as you know, also controls the historians.—*Rolf Hochhuth*

4021    A speech is a solemn responsibility. The man who makes a bad thirty-minute speech to two hundred people wastes only a half hour of his own time. But he wastes one hundred hours of the audience's time—more than four days —which should be a hanging offense.—*Jenkin Lloyd Jones*

# Verse, Toasts, and Proverbs

# Light Verse

**4022**   *In Our Town*

They took a little gravel, and took a little tar, with various ingredients imported from afar. They hammered it and rolled it, and when they went away, they said they had a pavement to last for many a day.

They came with picks and smote it to lay a water main, and then they called the workmen to put it back again. They took it up for conduits, to run the telephone, and then they put it back again as hard as any stone.

Oh, the pavement's full of furrows, there are patches everywhere; you'd like to ride upon it, but it's seldom that you dare. It's a very handsome pavement, a credit to the town; they're always, always digging up, and always puttin' down!
—*The Window Trimmer*

**4023**   *The Perfect Reactionary*

> As I was sitting in my chair
> I knew the bottom wasn't there,
> Nor legs nor back, but I just sat,
> Ignoring little things like that.
> —*Hughes Mearns*

**4024**   *Unfortunate Coincidence*

> By the time you swear you're his,
>    Shivering and sighing,
> And he vows his passion is

Infinite, undying—
Lady, make a note of this:
One of you is lying.
—*Dorothy Parker*

4025   *Merry Old Souls*

Old Ben Franklin was a merry old soul,
He walked up Market Street munching a roll,
And a girl laughed loud, and her laughter was so ranklin'
That old Ben Franklin made her Mrs. Ben Franklin.

Old Julius Caesar was a merry old soul,
To be a Roman emperor was all his goal;
But he put away the crown; he was such an old teaser
That the mob put the finger on Gaius Julius Caesar.

Old Isaac Newton was a merry old soul,
He invented gravitation when out for a stroll,
And no one up to now has succeeded in refutin'
The good old hypothesis of old Isaac Newton.
—*Morris Bishop*

4026   *Sleepwear*

A sleeper from the Amazon
Put nighties of his gra'mazon—
The reason, that
He was too fat
To get his own pajamazon.
—*Anonymous*

4027   *Radio News*

So here's to the radio speaker,
Let him rave and rant and scoff;
If we do not like the things he says
We can always turn him off.
—*Anonymous*

4028   *Rock-a-Bye, Baby*

Rock-a-bye, baby, why do you fret? Are you aware of the national debt? Father has gone 'round the corner to vote—millions in bonds for his snookums to tote. Are you suspicious? Sleep while you can; you can squirm later, dear, when you're a man.

4029    *Autobiography*

> Oh, both my shoes are shiny new,
>     And pristine is my hat;
> My dress is 1922 . . .
>     My life is all like that.
> > —*Dorothy Parker*

4030    *Life with the Government*

Cheer up, Grandpa, don't you cry! You'll wear diamonds by and by. Uncle Sam has money mills made to grind out brand new bills. He will help you in your cause with his old-age pension laws. No more worry over bills, grocery duns, or doctors' pills. No more panic over rent, leave that all to government. Dine on squab and caviar, sport a streamlined motor car. When the blizzards bliz a bit, off to Palm Beach gaily flit. Lead a life on pleasure bent, but you must spend every cent!

Whoopee, Grandpa! Stay alive! Life begins at sixty-five.

4031    *A Geologist's Epitaph*

> For years he pried among the strata,
> Collecting various sorts of data,
> Uncovering many a fossil phiz;
> We hope nobody digs up his.
> > —*Jane W. Stedman*

4032    *An Epitaph*

> As I am now, so you must be,
> Therefore prepare to follow me.

Written under it:

> To follow you I'm not content;
> How do I know which way you went?

4033    *The Curfew*

The curfew tolls the knell of parting day; a line of cars winds slowly o'er the lea; a pedestrian plods his absentminded way, and leaves the world quite unexpectedly.

4034    *Payday*

'Tis the day before payday and all through my jeans I've hunted in vain for the ways and the means. Not a quarter is stirring, not even a bit. The greenbacks have left me, the pennies have quit.

Forward, turn forward, O time, in thy flight, and make it tomorrow just for tonight!

#### 4035 *Not a Cloud in the Sky*

The Indians chant and dance about
To break a crop-destroying drought,
But I've a simpler means by far:
I only have to wash my car.
—*Richard Armour*

#### 4036 *Epitaph on Charles II*

Here lies our Sovereign Lord the King,
    Whose word no man relies on,
Who never said a foolish thing,
    Nor ever did a wise one.
—*John Wilmot, Earl of Rochester*

#### 4037 *The Human Race*

I wish I loved the Human Race;
I wish I loved its silly face;
I wish I liked the way it walks;
I wish I liked the way it talks;
And when I'm introduced to one
I wish I thought What Jolly Fun!
—*Sir Walter Raleigh*

#### 4038 *The Firefly*

The firefly's flame
Is something for which science has no name.
I can think of nothing eerier
Than flying around with an unidentified glow on a person's posteerier.
—*Ogden Nash*

#### 4039 *To a Human Skeleton*

In the Museum of Natural History
It's hard to think,
    Albeit true,
That without flesh
    I'd be like you.

And harder still
    To think, old pal,
That one of these
    Fine days I shall.
—*Richard Armour*

4040    *Experience*

> Some men break your heart in two,
> Some men fawn and flatter,
> Some men never look at you;
> And that cleans up the matter.
> —*Dorothy Parker*

4041    *A Bore*

> I wish that my Room had a Floor;
> I don't so much care for a Door,
>> But this walking around
>> Without touching the ground
> Is getting to be quite a bore!
> —*Gelett Burgess*

4042    *Breathes There a Man*

> Breathes there a man with hide so tough
> Who says two sexes aren't enough?
> —*Samuel Hoffenstein*

4043    *His Beard*

> A beautiful lady named Psyche
> Is loved by a fellow named Yche.
>> One thing about Ych
>> The lady can't lych
> Is his beard, which is dreadfully spyche.
> —*Anonymous*

4044    *To Save Work*

> There was an old person of Leeds,
> And simple indeed were his needs.
>> Said he: "To save toil
>> Growing things in the soil,
> I'll just eat the packets of seeds!"
> —*Anonymous*

4045    *An Englishman*

> But in spite of all temptations
> To belong to other nations,
>> He remains an Englishman!
> —*Sir W. S. Gilbert*

4046　　*Life*

>Man's life's a vapor,
>And full of woes;
>He cuts a caper,
>And down he goes.

4047　　*Many Ways*

There're many ways of doing things, a casual glance discloses; some folks turn up their sleeves and work, and some turn up their noses.

4048　　*Twinkle, Twinkle, Little Bat!*

>Twinkle, twinkle, little bat!
>How I wonder what you're at!
>Up above the world you fly,
>Like a tea-tray in the sky.
>　　　　　　—*Lewis Carroll*

4049　　*Right or Wrong*

>And in his dim, uncertain sight
>Whatever wasn't must be right
>From which it follows he had strong
>Convictions that what was, was wrong.
>　　　　　—*Guy Wetmore Carryl*

4050　　*The Tides of Love*

>Flo was fond of Ebenezer—
>　"Eb," for short, she called her beau.
>Talk of Tides of Love, great Caesar!
>　You should see them—Eb and Flo.
>　　　　　　　—*T. A. Daly*

4051　　*I Took My Boy A-Fishin'*

Yes sir, I took my boy a-fishin'. Sure, his mother told me to, but besides, I kind of done it 'cause it seemed the thing to do.

It's a heap more fun a-fishin' when I'm out there with my son, 'cause we really get acquainted through a little fishin' fun.

When my creel of life is empty, and my life's line sort of worn, I shall always keep rememberin' that first early summer morn when I took my boy a-fishin', and I really learned the joy that comes to every father when he really knows his boy.—*Outdoor Nebraska*

4052　　*A Perfect Day in the Old Days*

Grandmother, on a winter's day, milked the cows and fed them hay, slopped the hogs, saddled the mule, and got the children off to school; did a washing, mopped the floors, washed the windows, and did some chores; cooked a dish of home-dried fruit, pressed her husband's Sunday suit, swept the parlor, made the bed, baked a dozen loaves of bread, split some firewood, and lugged in enough to fill the kitchen bin; cleaned the lamps and put in oil, stewed some apples she thought would spoil; churned the butter, baked a cake, then exclaimed, "For heaven's sake, the calves have got out of the pen"—went out and chased them in again; gathered the eggs and locked the stable, back to the house and set the table, cooked a supper that was delicious, and afterward washed up all the dishes; fed the cat and sprinkled the clothes, mended a basketful of hose; then opened the organ and began to play, "When you come to the end of a perfect day."—*Capper's Weekly*

### 4053    Think It Over

I am fully aware that my youth has been spent, that my get up and go has got up and went. But I really don't mind, when I think with a grin, of all the grand places my get up has been.

### 4054    Inflation

You may ask, "Why should my spending cause inflationary trending though I squander every penny I have got?"

If you're joined by many millions of civilians blowing billions, you'll discover that it matters quite a lot.

### 4055    Be of Good Cheer

All sunny skies would be too bright,
All morning hours mean too much light,
All laughing days too gay a strain;
There must be clouds, and night, and rain,
And shut-in days, to make us see
The beauty of life's tapestry!

—*Scrapbook*

### 4056    Break the Ice

Slippery ice, very thin. Pretty girl tumbled in. Saw a boy upon the bank—gave a shriek, and then she sank.

Boy on bank heard her shout, jumped right in—helped her out. Now they're lovers—very nice; but first she had to break the ice.

### 4057    Fishin'

How are the fish in these parts?" said I.

The red-faced angler looked up with a sigh. "Well," said he, "I really can't say. For a week I've dropped them a line each day, but so far I've had no reply."
—*Round Robin News*

### 4058  *Picnic*

Did you ever eat with your plate in your lap, and nice soft rocks for seats, while ants and bugs of species unknown dance fox trots over the eats?

The water is mixed with leaves and twigs, pine needles are in the food; but, somehow or other, there's never a time when everything tastes so good!

### 4059  *Just Like His Dad!*

"Well, what are you going to be, my boy, when you have reached manhood's years—a doctor, a lawyer, or actor great, moving throngs to laughter and tears?"

But he shook his head as he gave reply, in a serious way that he had: "I don't think I'd care to be any of them—I want to be just like my dad!"

He wants to be like his dad! You men, did you ever think, as you pause, that the boy who watches your every move is building a set of laws. He's molding a life you're the model for; and whether it's good or bad depends on the kind of example set to the boy who'd be like his dad.

Would you have him go everywhere you go? Have him do just the things you do? And see everything that your eyes behold, and woo all the gods you woo? When you see the worship that shines in the eyes of your lovable little lad, could you be content if he gets his wish, and grows up like his dad?

It's a job that none but yourself can fill; it's a charge you must answer for; it's a duty to show him the road to tread ere he reaches manhood's door. It's a debt you owe for the greatest joy on this old earth to be had—the pleasure of having a boy to raise, who wants to be just like his dad!—*Author unknown*

### 4060  *Starting from Scratch*

Planted my little garden, and the weeds grew like the dickens; so I didn't get many vegetables, but I fattened my neighbor's chickens.

### 4061  *Fickle?*

At first I had a blonde love, and now a sleek brunette; tomorrow'll bring a redhead—I'll date all colors yet. You may think I'm fickle, or that I can't be true; but these are all the same girl—it's just her hair that's new.

### 4062  *Weight of Words*

She looks like a million dollars, how sweet this flattering tribute to woman sounds! But clothed in British parlance, cruel epithet—when she looks like a million pounds.

### 4063  *A Fisherman's Lament*

A three-pound pull, and a five-pound bite; an eight-pound jump, and a ten-pound fight; a twelve-pound bend to your pole—but alas! When you get him aboard he's a half-pound bass!

#### 4064    *The Printer Ran Out of R's*

Woses is wed, voilets is blue, the wain on the woof weminds me of you—dwip
—dwip—dwip.

#### 4065    *A Dun*

I think that I shall never see the dollar that I loaned to thee. A dollar that
I could have spent for varied forms of merriment. The one I loaned to you so
gladly, the same which I now need so badly, for whose return I had great hope,
just like an optimistic dope. But dollars loaned to folks like thee, are not returned
to fools like me!—*Allstate Insurance Company house organ*

#### 4066    *Sold!*

He chugged up to the toll gate, as all old cars do chug; a look of baffled rage
was plain upon his weary mug.
"One dollar for the car, my man; the passengers go free." The driver, wife,
and kids stepped out. "Sold, bud! Here's the key."

#### 4067    *He Listens*

His thoughts were slow, his words were few, and never formed to glisten, but
he was joy to all his friends—you should have heard him listen!

#### 4068    *Hard to Park*

When Noah sailed the waters blue, he had his troubles same as you. For forty
days he drove the Ark before he found a place to park.

#### 4069    *House Guests*

It's true of all our house guests, I've learned it to my sorrow. Although they
may be here today, they're seldom gone tomorrow.

#### 4070    *Nutton*

She went to the butcher's for spareribs and suet, but found that some
others had beaten her tuet. She said she would settle for sausage or liver; the
butcher insisted he had none to giver. She pleaded for pork chops, for meat-
balls, for mutton; the butcher said, "Lady, I just ain't got nutton!"—*The Lookout*

#### 4071    *Ten Little Autos*

Ten little autos, road and weather fine; one hit a culvert—then there were nine.
Nine little autos, one a little late; driver struck a railroad train—then there
were eight.
Eight little autos—but one went to heaven running through a stop light—then
there were seven.

Seven little autos speeding through the sticks; one skidded off the road—then there were six.

Six little autos till one took a dive through an open drawbridge—then there were five.

Five little autos, one with rattling door; driver tried to shut it—then there were four.

Four little autos, one climbed a tree, but didn't do it very well—so that left only three.

Three little autos, one driver was a "stew"; loaded up on highballs—that left only two.

Two little autos, tried to beat the gun when the warning signal flashed—then there was one.

One little auto around the corner tore; hit a truck—that's all there is; there isn't any more!—*A. K. White, Sunshine Magazine*

### 4072    *Telephony*

Bad is he who breaks your slumber to mutter rudely, "Heck! Wrong number!" Worse is he who risks your wrath by phoning when you're in your bath. But worst of all is the pest who hisses, "Bet-you-can't-guess-who-this-is!"

### 4073    *Please Write Plainly*

My darkest wrath is kept for folks who write with scrawly random strokes; if one must mumble now and then, why must one do it with a pen?

### 4074    *Too True*

The Lord and soldier we adore in time of danger—not before. Danger past, all things righted—God forgotten, soldier slighted!—*American Commentator*

### 4075    *Common Things*

I'm not what folks of this day would call a big success. I've never had much money, and I never will, I guess. My home's just now a five-room flat, close to a corner store; my possessions they are scanty—I have no need for more.

### 4076    *The Ten Commandments*

In vain we call old notions fudge, and bend our conscience to our dealing; the Ten Commandments will not budge, and stealing will continue stealing.—*James Russell Lowell*

### 4077    *I Found All This*

> A room of quiet, a temple of peace;
> The home of faith, where doubtings cease.
> A house of comfort, where hope is given

A source of strength to make earth heaven;
A shrine of worship, a place to pray—
I found all this in my church today.
*—The Cheer-Up Sheet*

4078    *Left It*

As I was laying on the green,
A small English book I seen,
*Carlyle's Essay on Burns* was the edition,
So I left it laying in the same position.

4079    *The Honey Bee*

The honey bee is sad and cross
And wicked as a weasel
And when she perches on you boss
She leaves a little measle.
*—Don Marquis*

4080    *On the Vanity of Earthly Greatness*

The tusks that clashed in mighty brawls
Of mastodons are billiard balls.

4081    The sword of Charlemagne the Just
Is ferric oxide, known as rust.

4082    The grizzly bear whose potent hug
Was feared by all, is now a rug.

4083    Great Caesar's bust is on the shelf,
And I don't feel so well myself!
*—Arthur Guiterman*

4084    *Where to Nap*

If you sleep in a chair,
You have nothing to lose;
But a nap at the wheel
Is a permanent snooze.

4085    *Crossing Boston Common*

One nears with Harvard-man expression
Who graces, doubtless, high profession.
He looks as smug, although near-sighted,
As if God had him copyrighted.
*—Louise Dyer Harris*

4086    *Horses*

> They head the list
>   Of bad to bet on,
> But I insist
>   They're worse to get on.
> —*Richard Armour*

4087    **The Banquet**

> Now to the banquet we press;
>   Now for the eggs, the ham;
> Now for the mustard and cress,
>   Now for the strawberry jam!
> —*W. S. Gilbert*

4088    *Troubles*

I've got a heap of troubles, and I've got to work them out. But I look around and see there's troubles all about. And when I see my troubles, I just look up and grin, and count all the troubles that I ain't in.

4089    *Revised Nursery Rhyme*

Hey, diddle diddle, the cat and the fiddle; the cow jumped over the moon. So now you know why milk's scarce and high—please, Bossy, come down soon!

4090    **Transportation Problem**

> Kiddy cars of little tikes,
> Slightly older children's bikes,
> Skis and sleds for winter needs,
> Wagons, trucks, velocipedes,
> Skooters, ice (and roller) skates—
> How the stuff accumulates—
> Piles of articles vehicular,
> On the front porch in particular,
> Things your children go like heck on,
> And you fall and break your neck on.
> —*Richard Armour*

4091    *Not Easy*

There is so much good in the worst of us, and so much bad in the best of us, that it's hard to tell which one of us ought to reform the rest of us.

4092    *That's Different*

> If she is twenty you, with truth
> May compliment her on her youth;

But if she's forty, do not shy
At telling her a pleasing lie.

### 4093  *Dangerous Dan MiCrobe*

A bunch of germs were hitting it up in the bronchial saloon; two bugs in the edge of the larynx were jazzing a ragtime tune. Back in the teeth, in a solo game, sat dangerous Ack-Kerchoo; and watching his pulse was his light of love, the lady who's known as Flu.

### 4094  *Calories*

Methuselah ate what he found on his plate, and never, as people do now, did he note the amount of caloric count—he ate it because it was chow. He wasn't disturbed, as at dinner, he sat, destroying a roast or pie, to think it was lacking in granular fat, or a couple of vitamins shy. He cheerfully chewed every species of food, untroubled by worries or fears, lest his health might be hurt by some fancy dessert, and he lived over nine hundred years!

### 4095  *Not More Than Once*

It's the little things that bother, and put us on the rack; you can sit upon a mountain, but you can't sit on a tack!

### 4096  *Needs Encouragement*

Some men smile in the evening, some men smile at dawn. But the man worthwhile is the man who can smile when his two front teeth are gone.

### 4097  *Try O'Clock*

I do not tell the time of day, as some do, by the clock, nor by the distant chiming bell that's on the steeple top, but by the progress that I see in everything I do. It's either done o'clock to me, or just half-past through.—*Hardware World*

### 4098  *Exam Time*

Backward, turn backward, O' Time, in your flight,
And tell me just one thing I studied last night.
—*Hobart Brown*

### 4099  *Seven Ages of Man*

At twenty work to him was play, and he kept busy all the day.
At thirty he had found his stride, and sailed serenely with the tide.
At forty he enjoyed each day, and filled the hours the fruitful way.
At fifty life was good to him, and he looked very fit and trim.
At sixty he pressed on with zest, and still resolved to do his best.
At seventy he was going strong, and carried in his heart a song.
At eighty he spoke like a sage, and boasted loudly of his age!

4100 *That's Different*

We like to meet folks who inspire us, but how we love those who admire us!

4101 *Not in Excess*

>Be virtuous; not too much; just what's correct.
>Excess in anything is a defect.
>
>—*Jacques Monvel*

4102 *Two Tutors*

>A tooter who tooted a flute
>     Tried to tutor two tutors to toot.
>Said the two to the tutor,
>     "Is it harder to toot or
>To tutor two tutors to toot?"

4103 *Maybe Admirals Can*

You can tell an apprentice seaman by his look of great alarm. You can tell a petty officer by the chevies on his arm. You can tell a lieutenant by his manners, dress, and such. You can also tell an ensign—but you sure can't tell him much!
—*The Ashlar*

4104 *Confused?*

There was a little dachshund once, so long he had no notion how long it took to notify his tail of his emotion. And so it was that while his eyes were filled with woe and sadness, his little tail kept wagging on, because of previous gladness.

4105 *On Vacation*

I'm broke and tired, my health's a wreck; Oh, joyful recreation! In debt I'm mired, up to my neck—I've been on my vacation!

4106 *It's Stew Bad*

An oyster met an oyster, and they were oysters two. Two oysters met two oysters, and they were oysters, too. Four oysters met a pint of milk, and they were oyster stew.—*The Crown*

4107 *Good Reason*

They walked the lane together, the sky was covered with stars; they reached the gate in silence—he lifted down the bars; she neither smiled nor thanked him, because she knew not how; for he was just a farmer's boy, and she a Jersey cow.

4108    *The Difference*

> The fog comes
> On little cat feet.
> —*Carl Sandburg*

But

> The frogs come
> On little flat feet.
> —*Myron Kaufman*

4109    *Safety Poem*

At railroad crossings, here's how to figger: In case of a tie, the engine's the bigger!

4110    *In a Staffordshire Churchyard*

> Here lies father and mother and sister and I,
>     We all died within the space of one short year;
> They all be buried at Wimble, except I,
>     And I be buried here.
>
>                             —*Anonymous*

4111    *Spinach!*

Little drops of water, little grains of sand, make the mighty ocean and the ditto land. But why these drops of water and little grains of sand are always served with spinach, we do not understand.

4112    *The Modern Hiawatha*

> He killed the noble Mudjokivis,
> With the skin he made him mittens,
> Made them with the fur side inside,
> Made them with the skin side outside,
> He, to get the warm side inside,
> Put the inside skin side outside:
> He, to get the cold side outside,
> Put the warm side fur side inside:
> That's why he put the fur side inside,
> Why he put the skin side outside,
> Why he turned them inside outside.
>                     —*George A. Strong*

4113    *The Duck*

> Behold the duck.
> It does not cluck.

A cluck it lacks.
It quacks.
It is specially fond
Of a puddle or pond.
When it dines or sups,
It bottoms ups.

*—Ogden Nash*

4114 *Celery*

When forced to wait and wait for luncheon
A stalk or two will serve to munch on,
A use which would, indeed, be laudable,
If only it weren't quite so audible.

*—Richard Armour*

4115 *Radishes*

Though pretty things, they like as not
Are either pithy or too hot,
Nor do you know, till you have bitten,
If you've a tiger or a kitten.

*—Richard Armour*

4116 *The Humorist*

He must not laugh at his own wheeze:
A snuff box has no right to sneeze.

*—Keith Preston*

4117 *I Like to Quote*

I like to quote the fragrant lines of Keats,
    And often I am caught by Shelley's tone,
And yet for clever thoughts and quaint conceits
    Give me some little lyric of my own.

*—Mitchell D. Follansbee*

4118 *The Termite*

Some primal termite knocked on wood
    And tasted it, and found it good,
And that is why your Cousin May
    Fell through the parlor floor today.

*—Ogden Nash*

4119     *Apologies to Byron*

> For the sword outwears its sheath,
>     And the soul wears out the breast,
> And the coat outwears the pants
>     Till there's nothing left but the vest.
>                         —*Theodore Morrison*

4120     *Mike O'Day*

> This is the grave of Mike O'Day
> Who died maintaining his right of way.
> His right was clear, his will was strong,
> But he's just as dead as if he'd been wrong.
>                         —*Anonymous*

4121     *Easy to Move*

> A happy creature is your snail indeed!
> Just where he pleases he can live and feed.
> And if a neighbor gives him any bother,
> With house on back he moves off to another.
>                         —*Philemon*

4122     *Quarrels*

> Those who in quarrels interpose
> Must often wipe a bloody nose.
>                         —*John Gay*

4123     *Time Stays*

> Time goes, you say? Ah, no!
> Alas, Time stays, we go;
>     Or else, were this not so,
> What need to chain the hours,
> For Youth were always ours?
>     Times goes, you say—Ah, no!
>                         —*Pierre de Ronsard*

4124     *The General Rule*

> Sir, I admit your general rule,
> That every poet is a fool;
> But you yourself may serve to show it,
> That every fool is not a poet.

4125 *Modern Statesman*

Midas, they say possessed the art, of old,
Of turning whatso'er he touched to gold.
This modern statesmen can reverse with ease;
Touch them with gold, they'll turn to what you please.

4126 *Trust*

Give me good digestion, Lord,
And also something to digest;
But where and how that something comes
I leave to Thee, who knoweth best.
                                        —*Mary Webb*

4127 *The Difference*

The poet and ornithologist
Differ in ways absurd.
One writes—"The bird is on the wing;"
The other answers—"No such thing!
    The wing is on the bird."

4128 *Brains Are Needed*

He that makes money before he gets wit,
Will be but a short while the master of it.
                                        —*Thomas Fuller*

4129 *Be Merciful*

Being all fashioned of the self-same dust,
Let us be merciful as well as just.
                                        —*Henry W. Longfellow*

4130 *Correct*

For there was never yet philosopher
That could endure the toothache patiently.
                                        —*William Shakespeare*

4131 *What Cheer!*

Reader, what cheer!
Do you feel queer?
The end is here.

# Toasts and Quotations for Special Occasions

## Families and Friends

4132      A good woman inspires a man,
A brilliant woman interests him,
A beautiful woman fascinates him—
The sympathetic woman gets him.
                  *—Helen Rowland*

4133      If the heart of a man is depress'd with cares,
The mist is dispell'd when a woman appears.
          *—John Gay, The Beggar's Opera*

4134      The world well tried—the sweetest thing in life
Is the unclouded welcome of a wife.
                    *—N. P. Willis*

4135      She is a winsome wee thing,
She is a handsome wee thing,
She is a bonny wee thing,
       This sweet wee wife o' mine.
                 *—Robert Burns*

4136      Perhaps if you address the lady
       Most politely, most politely,
Flatter and impress the lady
       Most politely, most politely,

Humbly beg and humbly sue,
She may deign to look on you.
    —*W. S. Gilbert, Princess Ida*

4137    Our friends: May Fortune be as generous with them as she has been with us in giving us such friends.

4138    Honor women! They entwine and weave heavenly roses in our earthly life.—*Johann Schiller*

4139    Good family life is in the last resort the nation's most precious asset. —*Arthur Collis and Vera E. Poole, These Our Children*

4140    In pain or in trouble, we run to Mother. In distress or in anxiety; in grief or in joy—we look toward Mother first and she sees the message in our eyes and understands. Tonight, in happiness and thankfulness and true appreciation —we look toward Mother. She will understand what our hearts are saying.

4141    All the reasonings of men are not worth one sentiment of women.— *Voltaire*

4142        You can multiply all the relations of life,
            Have more than one sister or brother;
            In the course of events, have more than one wife,
            But you never can have but one Mother!

4143    All husbands are alike, but they have different faces so you can tell them apart.

4144    To our husbands: men when they are boys; boys when they are men; and lovable always.

4145        Disguise our bondage as we will,
            'Tis woman, woman rules us still.
                    —*Tom Moore*

4146        Beautiful in form and feature,
                Lovely as the day,
            Can there be so fair a creature
                Formed of common clay.
                    —*Henry W. Longfellow*

4147        Oh would I were a boy again,
                When life seemed formed of sunny years,
            And all the heart then knew of pain
                Was wept away in transient tears.
                    —*Mark Lemon*

4148    Great men hallow a whole people, and lift up all who live in their time. —*Sydney Smith*

4149    Man at his birth is content with a little milk and a piece of flannel: so we begin, that presently find kingdoms not enough for us.—*Seneca*

4150    Children have neither past nor future; and that which seldom happens to us, they rejoice in the present.—*Jean de La Bruyere*

4151    While the boy is small, you can see the man.—*Chinese proverb*

4152    When the first baby laughed for the first time, the laugh broke into a million pieces, and they all went skipping about. That was the beginning of fairies.—*Sir J. M. Barrie, Peter Pan*

4153    Children are the keys to paradise.—*R. H. Stoddard*

4154    Children are poor men's riches.—*Thomas Fuller*

4155    It seems impossible they should ever grow to be men, and drag the heavy artillery along the dusty road of life.—*Henry W. Longfellow*

4156    Of all of nature's gifts to the human race, what is sweeter to a man than his children?—*Cicero*

4157    I love these little people; and it is not a slight thing when they, who are so fresh from God, love us.—*Charles Dickens*

4158    Oh! Be thou blest with what heaven can send,
Long health, long youth, long pleasure—and a friend!
                                        —*Alexander Pope*

4159    While we've youth in our hearts, we can never grow old.—*Oliver Wendell Holmes*

4160    When a friend asks, there is no tomorrow.

4161    Here's a sigh to those who love me,
        And a smile to those who hate;
And whatever sky's above me,
        Here's a heart for every fate.
        —*Byron, "To Thomas Moore"*

4162    Here's to you, as good as you are,
And here's to me, as bad as I am;
But as good as you are, and as bad as I am,
I am as good as you are, as bad as I am.
                        —*Old Scotch toast*

4163    The world is filled with flowers,
      The flowers are filled with dew,
    The dew is filled with love
      For you, and you, and you.

4164  Our friends see the best in us, and by that very fact call forth the best in us.

4165  To the lamp of true friendship. May it burn brightest in our darkest hours and never flicker in the winds of trial.

4166  Our friends—may they never have to rely on their patience to remain our friends.

4167  Here's a toast from your good friend to my good friend.

4168  Long life and happiness—for your long life will be my happiness!

4169  May we be richer in friends than in money.

4170  To our best friends, who know the worst about us but refuse to believe it.

4171  It is great to have friends when one is young, but it is still more so when you are getting old. When we are young, friends are, like everything else, a matter of course. In the old days we know what it means to have them.—*Edvard Grieg*

4172  A friend is one who knows your faults yet loves you in spite of your virtues.

4173  According to the little boy's definition, a friend is a person who knows all about you and still likes you.—*Caroline Vining, Catholic World*

## Weddings, Anniversaries, and Birthdays

4174  Marriages are made in Heaven.—*Alfred Tennyson*

4175    Why, man, she is mine own,
    And I as rich in having such a jewel
    As twenty seas, if all their sand were pearl,
    The water nectar and the rocks pure gold.
    —*William Shakespeare, Two Gentlemen of Verona*

4176  To the newlyweds: May we all be invited to their Golden Wedding Anniversary.

4177    The honeymoon is over when he phones that he'll be late for supper—and she has already left a note that it's in the refrigerator.—
*Bill Lawrence*

4178    To the bride: Let her remember that we give her this husband on approval. He can be returned for credit or for exchange, but her love will not be refunded.

4179    To the bride: May she share everything with her husband, including the housework.

4180    To the blushing bride we pledge fifty years of cheer. At the Golden Anniversary we can renew the pledge.

4181
> But to see her was to love her,
> Love but her, and love forever.
>     —*Robert Burns*

4182
> I don't want no kind of angel with a
>     lot o' wings and things,
> And a golden harp and halo, and
>     them other signs o' wealth;
>     I jes' want the sort o' woman that
>     jes' smiles and loves and sings;
> And I've got her—may God bless her
>     Here's her everlastin' health!
>     —*Oliver Marble*

4183
> God, the best maker of all marriages,
> Combine your hearts in one.
>     —*William Shakespeare*

4184
> The groom's speech at the marriage feast
>     Should shew him blithe and gay:
> He must not hint that freedom's ceased
>     With this, his wedding day;
> Nor should complacency be smug
>     On his triumphant bride's sweet mug.

4185    To the health, wealth, and happiness of the groom. He is leaving us for a better life. But we are not leaving him!

4186    A toast to that nervous, fidgety, restless, impatient, uncomfortable but enviable fellow, the groom.

4187    To the groom: Such a wife not only multiplies his pleasures and his fortune, but also his friends.

4188    Here's to your happy launching of the *Courtship* on the Sea of Matrimony. May the "rocks" be confined to the cradle!

4189    He who lives without quarreling is a bachelor.—*St. Jerome*

4190    The critical period in matrimony is breakfast time.—*A. P. Herbert*

4191    To your health on this day. May you reach the happiness of your fiftieth celebration before the silver threads begin to mingle with the golden.

4192            Age is opportunity no less
                Than youth itself, though in another dress
                And as the evening twilight fades away
                The sky is filled with stars, invisible by day.
                        —*Henry W. Longfellow*

4193    May anniversaries come and anniversaries go—but may your happiness go on forever.

4194    A toast on your anniversary; and a toast now for every other anniversary until the Golden dream of your fiftieth has been realized.

4195    May your anniversaries continue until only the recording angel can recall when the first one was celebrated.

4196    May you live as long as you like and have all you like as long as you live.

4197    You make age jealous, time furious—and all of us envious.

4198    May your hours of reminiscence be filled with days of good cheer and weeks of pleasant memories.

4199            I wish thee health,
                I wish thee wealth,
                I wish thee gold in store,
                I wish thee Heaven upon earth—
                What could I wish thee more?

4200    Here's to you. No matter how old you are, you don't look it.

4201    A woman may race to get a man a gift but it always ends in a tie.—*Earl Wilson*

4202    May you live to be a hundred—and then decide if you want to go on.

4203       Drink not to my past, which is weak and indefensible,
Nor to my present, which is not above reproach;
But let us drink to our futures,
     which, thank God, are immaculate.
                                 *—Leone P. Forkner*

## Holidays

*New Year*

4204       The book is closed . . .
The year is done,
The pages full
Of tasks begun.
A little joy . . .
A little care
Along with dreams
Are written there.
This new day brings
Another year,
Renewing hope . . .
Dispelling care.
And may we find
Before the end,
A deep content . . .
Another friend.
      *—Arch Ward, Chicago Daily Tribune*

4205    One of my richest rituals at the closing of each old year is to count the roster of my friends in the mood of the poet: "And always as the Old Year ends, I clasp my rosary of friends, and pause to breathe a grateful prayer, for every bead of friendship there."

4206    Time has no division to mark its passage; there is never a thunderstorm or blare of trumpets to announce the beginning of a new month or year. Even when a new century begins, it is only we mortals who ring the bells and fire off the pistols.—*Thomas Mann*

4207    **Easter**

A friend stood one day where he could view the Golden Gate Bridge at San Francisco. At first it was completely shrouded in early morning fog. But as the sun rose the fog lifted between the upright piers of the bridge, leaving the land anchors still unseen. Is it not so with life? We see only what is between the great piers called birth and death. But Easter lifts the fog from both. Easter is the time when we see more completely the anchorages that sustain life.—*George Mecklenberg, Wesley News*

4208    God expects from men that their Easter devotions would in some measure come up to their Easter dress.—*Robert Smith, Indiana Teacher*

4209    One day during the French Revolution, a man remarked to Talleyrand, who was Bishop of Autun: "The Christian religion—what is it? It would be easy to start a religion like that."

"Oh, yes," replied Talleyrand. "One would only have to get crucified and rise again on the third day."—*Baptist Review*

4210    *Decoration Day*

The custom of placing flowers on the graves of the soldiers who fell in the Civil War originated in the South. Two years after the close of the war it became known that the women of Columbus, Mississippi, were showing themselves impartial in their offerings made to the memory of the dead. They gained the admiration of the North by placing flowers alike on the graves of the Confederate and the Union soldiers.

However, there was no general observance of this custom in the North until May 1868. General John A. Logan, commander-in-chief of the Grand Army of the Republic, issued an order setting apart the thirtieth day of May, "for the purpose of strewing with flowers, or otherwise decorating the graves of comrades who died in defense of their country during the late rebellion." The idea was soon taken up by the state legislatures, and the day is now celebrated throughout the North.

4211    *Independence Day and Freedom*

> Give me your tired, your poor,
> Your huddled masses, yearning to breathe free,
> The wretched refuse of your teeming shore.
> Send these, the homeless, tempest tossed, to me:
> I lift my lamp beside the golden door.
>     —*Emma Lazarus, inscription on the Statue of*
>         *Liberty, New York Harbor*

4212    Among the natural rights of the colonists are these: First a right to life, secondly to liberty, thirdly to property; together with the right to defend them in the best manner they can.—*Samuel Adams*

4213    . . . That this nation, under God, shall have a new birth of freedom. —*Abraham Lincoln, Gettysburg Address*

4214    Freedom is that faculty which enlarges the usefulness of all other faculties.—*Kant*

4215    Countries are well cultivated, not as they are fertile but as they are free. —*Montesquieu*

4216    The only freedom which deserves the name is that of pursuing our own good in our own way, so long as we do not attempt to deprive others of theirs or impede their efforts to obtain it.—*John Stuart Mill*

4217    Freedom has its life in the hearts, the actions, the spirit of men and so it must be daily earned and refreshed—else like a flower cut from its life-giving roots, it will wither and die.—*Dwight D. Eisenhower*

4218                    Hail, Columbia! happy land!
                    Hail, ye heroes! heavenborn band!
                    Who fought and bled in Freedom's cause.
                            —*Joseph Hopkinson*

4219    *Labor Day*

All the blessings we enjoy are the fruits of labor, toil, self-denial, and study. —*W. G. Sumner*

4220    It is only by the labor of workingmen that states grow rich.—*Leo XIII, May 15, 1891*

4221    What is there illustrious that is not attended by labor?—*Cicero*

4222    Take not from the mouth of labor the bread it has earned.—*Thomas Jefferson*

4223    Workingmen are at the foundation of society.—*Samuel Gompers*

4224    In all labor there is profit.—*Proverbs 14:23*

4225    I believe in the dignity of labor, whether with head or hand; that the world owes every man an opportunity to make a living.—*John D. Rockefeller, Jr.*

*Thanksgiving Day*

4226    The worship most acceptable to God comes from a thankful and cheerful heart.—*Plutarch*

4227    The private and personal blessings we enjoy, the blessings of immunity, safe-guard, liberty, and integrity, deserve the thanksgiving of a whole life.— *Bishop Jeremy Taylor*

4228    O Lord, who lends me life, lend me a heart replete with thankfulness.
—*William Shakespeare*

4229    If I only have the will to be grateful, I am so.—*Seneca*

4230    Cicero called gratitude the mother of virtues.—*Julius Bate*

4231    We Americans are, on the whole, a generous people. . . . but let us take
care that we do not fail to be as generous in thanking God as we are in sharing
with others the gifts He has shared with us. Thanksgiving Day? No, rather three
hundred and sixty-five "Thanksgiving Days" a year—every year!—*Indiana
Catholic and Record*

4232    Who gives not thanks to men, gives not thanks to God.—*John Lewis
Burckhardt*

4233    A single grateful thought towards heaven is the most perfect prayer.
—*G. E. Lessing*

4234    Thanksgiving Day is only our annual time for saying grace at the table
of eternal goodness.—*James M. Ludlow, D.D.*

### Christmas

4235        No trumpet-blast profaned
                The hour in which the Prince of Peace was born;
            No bloody streamlet stained
                Earth's silver rivers on that sacred morn.
                    —*William Cullen Bryant, Christmas 1875*

4236        Be merry all, be merry all,
            With holly dress the festive hall;
            Prepare the song, the feast, the ball,
            To welcome Merry Christmas.
                    —*W. R. Spencer*

4237        So remember while December
            Brings the only Christmas day,
            In the year let there be Christmas
            In the things you do and say;
            Wouldn't life be worth the living
            Wouldn't dreams be coming true
            If we kept the Christmas spirit
            All the whole year through?
                    —*Anonymous*

4238           Had my house been filled at Bethlehem,
           What should I have done
           With that request
           Of two for rest?
           Would I have guessed
           The Prince of Peace was come?
                —*Allison C. Wood, Christian Herald*

4239      May the forgiving spirit of Him to whom we dedicate this season prevail again on earth.

May hateful persecution and wanton aggression cease.

May man live in freedom and security, worshipping as he sees fit, loving his fellow man.

May the sanctity of the home be ever preserved.

May peace, everlasting peace, reign supreme.—*Sunshine Magazine*

## Seasons

### Spring

4240           If there comes a little thaw,
           Still the air is chill and raw,
           Here and there a patch of snow,
           Dirtier than the ground below,
           Dribbles down a marshy flood;
           Ankle-deep you stick in mud
           In the meadows while you sing,
              "This is Spring."
           —*C. P. Cranch, "A Spring Growl"*

4241           Earth's crammed with Heaven,
           And every common bush afire with God.
           —*Elizabeth Barrett Browning, "Aurora Leigh"*

4242           And see the rivers how they run
           Through woods and meads, in shade and sun,
           Sometimes swift, sometimes slow,—
           Wave succeeding wave, they go
           A various journey to the deep
           Like human life to endless sleep!
                —*John Dyer, "Grongar Hill"*

4243      Now the woods are in leaf, now the year is in its greatest beauty.—*Vergil*

4244    When Spring unlocks the flowers to paint the laughing soil.—*Bishop
Heber*

4245              It was a lover, and his lass
                    With a hey, and a ho, and a hey nonino,
                  That o'er the green cornfield did pass,
                    In spring-time, the only pretty ring time,
                  When birds do sing, hey ding a ding, ding;
                  Sweet lovers love the spring.
                        —*William Shakespeare, As You Like It*

4246              The first of April some do say,
                  Is set apart for All Fool's Day;
                  But why the people call it so,
                  Nor I, nor they themselves, do know.
                        —*Poor Robin's Almanac, 1760*

4247              You must wake and call me early,
                    call me early, mother dear,
                  Tomorrow'll be the happiest time
                    of all the glad New Year;
                  Of all the glad New Year, mother,
                    the maddest, merriest day;
                  For I'm to be Queen o' the May, mother,
                    I'm to be Queen o' the May.
                                          —*Tennyson*

4248              The year's at the spring
                  And the day's at the morn;
                  Morning's at seven;
                  The hillside's dew-pearled;
                  The lark's on the wing;
                  The snail's on the thorn:
                  God's in His Heaven—
                  All's right with the world!
                        —*Robert Browning*

          *Summer*

4249              The soft blue sky did never melt
                  Into his heart; he never felt
                  The witching of the soft blue sky!
                        —*William Wordsworth*

4250    Heat, ma'am! It was so dreadful here that I found there was nothing
left for it but to take off my flesh and sit in my bones.—*Sydney Smith*

4251    Last year we had summer, as I recall, on July 26.—*An English-man*

4252    For who lying in the sun can be bitter?—*Stuart Chase*

**Autumn**

4253    That beautiful season
    . . . the Summer of All-Saints
Filled was the air with a dreamy and
    magical light; and the landscape
Lay as if new-created in all the freshness
    of childhood.
Peace seemed to reign upon earth,
    and the restless heart of the ocean
Was for a moment consoled. All sounds
    were in harmony blended.
. . . And the great sun
Looked with the eye of love through the
    golden vapors around him;
While arrayed in its robes of russet and
    scarlet and yellow,
Bright with the sheen of the dew,
    each glittering tree of the forest
Flashed like the plane-tree the Persian
    adorned with mantles and jewels.
    —*Henry W. Longfellow, "Evangeline"*

4254    'Tis the last rose of summer,
    Left blooming alone.
        —*Thomas Moore*

4255    Behold congenial Autumn comes,
The Sabbath of the year.
—*John Logan, "The Country in Autumn"*

4256    There is a harmony
In Autumn, and a lustre in its sky,
Which thro' the summer is not heard nor seen,
As if it could not be, as if it had not been!
        —*Percy Bysshe Shelley*

4257    No shade, no shine, no butterflies, no bees,
No fruits, no flowers, no leaves, no buds.
    November!
        —*Thomas Hood*

4258 *Winter*

Winter comes, to rule the varied year.—*James Thomson, The Seasons: Winter*

4259 The English winter—ending in July
To recommence in August.
—*Byron, Don Juan*

4260 Out of the bosom of the Air,
Out of the cloud-folds of her garments shaken,
Over the woodlands brown and bare,
Over the harvest-fields forsaken,
Silent and soft and slow
Descends the snow.
—*Henry W. Longfellow*

4261 Autumn to winter, winter into spring,
Spring into summer, summer into fall,—
So rolls the changing year, and so we change;
Motion so swift, we know not that we move.
—*Dinah Mulock Craik, "Immutable"*

4262 February, the shortest month of the year, is truly a month of hope
. . . for soon we will be enjoying warmer days and green and grassy
slopes. We await with a joyful expectancy the blossom-laden boughs of trees and
bushes and the bright yellow heads of daffodils, popping out of the sun-warmed
earth.—*Sunshine Magazine*

# XVIII

# Witty and Wise Proverbs

**A proverb is the wisdom of many and the wit of one.**—*Lord John Russell*

4263    If you have trouble forecasting the future correctly, do it frequently at very short intervals.

4264    Visit, that ye be not visited.

4265    It is about as hard for a rich man to enter Heaven as it is for a poor man to remain on earth.

4266    The only wealth which you will keep forever is the wealth which you have given away.—*Martial*

4267         To him in vain the envious seasons roll,
             Who bears eternal summer in his soul.

4268    He that boasteth of his ancestors, confesseth he hath no virtue of his own.

4269    Those who admire strength in a rascal do not live in his town.

4270    Not to oversee workmen is to leave them your purse open.

4271    The willing contemplation of vice is vice.—*Arabian*

4272    For one rich man that is content there are a hundred that are not.

4273    Vulgarity is the rich man's modest contribution to democracy.

4274    Many persons might have attained to wisdom had they not assumed that they already possessed it.—*Seneca*

4275    Anger punishes itself.

4276    A handful of patience is worth more than a bushel of brains.—*Dutch*

4277    To live long, it is necessary to live slowly.—*Cicero*

4278    When I had money everyone called me brother.—*Polish*

4279    One life—a little gleam of Time between two Eternities.—*Thomas Carlyle*

4280    Misfortunes always come in by a door that has been left open for them. —*Czech*

4281    Some are atheists only in fair weather.

4282        A man of words and not of deeds
Is like a garden full of weeds.

4283    It is not the burden, but the overburden that kills the beast.

4284    Some people think they are worth a lot of money because they have it.

4285    Public opinion is the greatest force for good, when it happens to be on that side.

4286    Labor rids us of three great evils: tediousness, vice, and poverty.

4287    He who findeth fault meaneth to buy.

4288    Gold goes in at any gate except Heaven's.

4289    When money speaks, the truth is silent.—*Russian*

4290    Patience is a necessary ingredient of genius.—*Benjamin Disraeli*

4291    The only man who never makes a mistake is the man who never does anything.—*Theodore Roosevelt*

4292    Optimism is the madness of maintaining that everything is right when it is wrong.—*Voltaire*

4293    Life is a play! 'Tis not its length, but its performance that counts. —*Seneca*

4294     Life is like playing a violin solo in public and learning the instrument as one goes on.—*Edward Bulwer-Lytton*

4295     It is less painful to learn in youth than to be ignorant in age.

4296     He that imagines he hath knowledge enough hath none.

4297     What do we live for, if it is not to make life less difficult to each other? —*George Eliot*

4298     No one is useless in this world who lightens the burden of it to anyone else.—*Charles Dickens*

4299     The injuries we do and those we suffer are seldom weighed in the same scales.—*Aesop*

4300     We see more clearly what others fail to do for us than what they actually do.

4301     Enthusiasm for a cause sometimes warps judgment.—*William Howard Taft*

4302     Adversity reminds men of religion.—*Livy*

4303     Calamity is the perfect glass wherein we truly see and know ourselves. —*Sir William D'Avenant*

4304     God himself, sir, does not propose to judge man until the end of his days.—*Samuel Johnson*

4305     He who hunts two hares leaves one and loses the other.—*Japanese*

4306     It is a hard winter when one wolf eats another.—*French*

4307     Silence is a virtue of those who are not wise.

4308     A wise man reflects before he speaks; a fool speaks and then reflects on what he has uttered.—*French*

4309     Every path hath its puddle.—*English*

4310     Be silent or say something better than silence.—*Scotch*

4311     Years teach more than books.

4312     All time is lost which might better be employed.

4313     The secret of tiring people is to say all that can be said.

4314    The absent are always at fault.

4315    The weakness of the enemy makes our strength.

4316    In a free country there is much clamor but little suffering.

4317    A hare is not caught with a drum.

4318    The wearer knows best where the shoe hurts.—*Portuguese*

4319    The mother-in-law forgets that she was a daughter-in-law.

4320    The best mirror is an old friend.

4321    Have many acquaintances and few friends.—*English*

4322    Many words hurts more than swords.

4323    To the hungry no bread is bad.

4324    Wisdom consists in knowing one's follies.

4325    Adversity makes men; prosperity monsters.

4326    Money is a good servant but a bad master.

4327    The imagination gallops while judgment goes on foot.

4328    Eating little and speaking little can hurt no man.

4329    Experience and wisdom are the two best fortunetellers.

4330    Forgive every man's faults except your own.

4331    Hasty climbers have sudden falls.—*German*

4332    Have money and you will have kindred enough.

4333    He is rich who is contented.

4334    He is truly happy who can make others happy.—*English*

4335    Men with little business are great talkers.—*French*

4336    Brothers quarrel like thieves inside a house, but outside their swords leap out in each other's defense.—*Japanese*

4337    Patience is bitter but its fruit is sweet.

4338    It belongs only to great men to possess great defects.

4339    There is an eel under every rock.

4340    We learn by teaching.—*Latin*

4341    Never mind what ought to be done—what can be done?

4342    Lies have short legs but long wings.—*French*

4343    No one has ever repented of having held his tongue.

4344    No man is the worse for knowing the worst of himself.—*Spanish*

4345    Seldom seen, soon forgotten.

4346    Of saving comes having.

4347    Little said, sooner mended.

4348    Love thy neighbor, but do not pull down thy hedge.—*English*

4349    Nothing is impossible to a willing mind.

4350    Love lives in cottages as well as in castles.

4351    In all contentions put the bridle on your tongue.

4352    Skillful workmen need not travel far.

4353    The heaviest rains fall on the leaky house.

4354    It is better to give one shilling than lend twenty.—*English*

4355    In a calm sea every man is a pilot.

4356    He who would deceive the fox must rise early.

4357    Fools worship mules that carry gold.

4358    The face is the index of the mind.

4359    A scalded cat fears cold water.

4360    From the hand to the mouth the soup is often lost.

4361    Hope is the poor man's bread.

4362    All men are fools, differing only in degree.—*French*

4363    Pinch yourself and know how others feel.

4364  Every man complains of his memory but no man complains of his judgment.—*English*

4365  Every fire is the same size when it starts.

4366  Many captains and the ship goes on the rocks.

4367  More die from gluttony than hunger.

4368  Give neither counsel nor salt till you are asked for it.

4369  Apes remain apes though you clothe them in velvet.

4370  Beware of the man who does not talk and the dog that does not bark.

4371  Confession of faults makes half amends.—*English*

4372  Fair words make me look to my purse.

4373  A closed mouth catches no flies.

4374  More flies are taken with a drop of honey than a gallon of vinegar.

4375  We are all Adam's children, but silk makes the difference.

4376  Faults are thick where love is thin.

4377  If you would have your hen lay you must bear the cackling.

4378  The thief is sorry to be hanged, not to be a thief.

4379  Cheat me in the price but not in the goods.—*English*

4380  'Tis a foolish sheep that makes the wolf his confessor.

4381  The noisy drum contains nothing but air.—*English*

4382  Let no one be willing to speak ill of the absent.—*Propertius*

4383  Every heart hath its own ache.

4384  Adversity is the trial of courage.—*French*

4385  When angry, count a hundred.

4386  No answer is also an answer.—*Danish*

4387  Look to the mind, not to the outward appearance.—*Aesop*

4388  Nature is the art of God.—*Dante*

4389    Every artist was first an amateur.—*Ralph Waldo Emerson*

4390    Avarice is the root of all evil.

4391    The love of pelf increases with the pelf.—*Juvenal*

4392    Nothing so bad but it might have been worse.

4393    Better to wear out than to rust out.

4394    Each bird loves to hear himself sing.

4395    Brevity is the soul of wit.

4396    The weeping bride makes a laughing wife.—*German*

4397    Character is much easier kept than recovered.

4398    Little children are little sorrows but great joys.—*Italian*

4399    A good conscience is God's eye.—*Russian*

4400    Criticism is easy; art, difficult.—*French*

4401    Everyone in this world has his cross.—*French*

4402    Cynicism is intellectual dandyism.—*George Meredith*

4403    Never spend your money before you have it.

4404    A good man makes no noise over a good deed.—*Greek*

4405    The easiest way to dignity is humility.

4406    The best things are most difficult.—*Greek*

4407    Nothing is so good as it seems beforehand.

4408    There is no mortal whom sorrow and disease do not touch.—*Greek*

4409    In doing what we ought, we deserve no praise.—*Latin*

4410    The ear is the road to the heart.—*French*

4411    Put all your eggs in one basket—and watch the basket.—*Mark Twain*

4412    One foe is too many, and a hundred friends too few.—*German*

4413    Envy never enriched any man.

4414     The wisest of the wise may err.—*Greek*

4415     Why does one man's yawning make another yawn?

### Chinese Proverbs

4416     The friendship of officials is as thin as paper.

4417     If the family lives in harmony, all affairs will prosper.

4418     It is easy to govern a kingdom but difficult to rule one's family.

4419     If the main timbers in the house are not straight, the smaller timbers will be unsafe; and if the smaller timbers are not straight, the house will fall.

4420     The seats in the great hall all come in rotation: the daughter-in-law will some day be the mother-in-law.

4421     Make your whole year's plans in the spring, and your day's plans early in the morning.

4422     A lost inch of gold may be found; a lost inch of time, never.

4423     Customers are the precious things; goods are only grass.

4424     Without the aid of the divine, man cannot walk even an inch.

4425     If Heaven creates a man, there must be some use for him.

4426     To follow the will of Heaven is to prosper; to rebel against the will of Heaven is to be destroyed.

4427     To open a book brings profit.

4428     Yellow gold has its price; learning is priceless.

4429     Learning is a treasure that follows its owner everywhere.

4430     If you neglect study when you are young, what of your old age?

4431     Scholars are a country's treasure; the learned are the delicacies of the feast.

4432     Even if we study to old age we shall not finish learning.

4433     The man on horseback knows nothing of the toil of the traveler on foot.

4434     Though a tree be a thousand feet high, the leaves fall and return to the root.

4435    When you know a man, you know his face but not his heart.

4436    He uses a cannon to shoot a sparrow.

4437    A people without faith in themselves cannot survive.

4438    Those who are happy do not observe how time goes by.

4439    Our pleasures are shallow; our sorrows are deep.

4440    Kindle not a fire you cannot put out.

4441    Don't buy anything that's cheap.

4442    Don't laugh at him who is old; the same will assuredly happen to us.

4443    To see a man do a good deed is to forget all his faults.

4444    Blame yourself as you would blame others; excuse others as you would excuse yourself.

4445    One generation plants the trees under whose cool shade another generation takes its ease.

4446    In haste there is error.

4447    Words are the voice of the heart.

4448    When a word has once left the lips, the swiftest horse cannot overtake it.

4449    Speak softly, and be slow to begin your speech.

4450    One man tells a falsehood, a hundred repeat it as true.

4451    There is no high road to happiness or misfortune; every man brings them on himself.

4452    Men, not walls, make a city.

4453    When you sit alone, meditate on your own faults; when you converse, do not discuss the faults of others.

4454    It is easy to go from economy to extravagance; it is hard to go from extravagance to economy.

# Index